The vast steppe region of Inner Asia, although divided by political boundaries, is historically dominated by Mongol culture, Buddhist-shamanist religion, and an economy based on mobile pastoralism. Now, as its constituent states – China, Russia and Mongolia – adapt to market conditions, this long-standing cultural-economic zone arguably faces more radical change than any in its past.

The 'end of nomadism' refers not only to the possible demise of a way of life, but also to the fact that the very category of nomadism has ceased to be useful analytically. Pastoralism in Inner Asia is not timeless 'nomadism', but rather a series of local knowledges and techniques located in particular historical circumstances. Today's herders must adapt their economic cultures as best they can to rapid institutional changes and divergent state policies. In most areas, the result has been a steep decline in herd mobility, often accompanied by degradation of pasture land.

The authors argue powerfully that mobility and district-level management is still necessary if pastoralism is to be successful and sustainable in the steppe environment. In the light of ongoing programmes of sedentarisation and privatisation, their thesis implies not only new directions for research, but the desirability for the three central governments of rethinking policy on pastoralism.

The End of Nomadism? is co-published by Duke University Press as part of their Central Asia book series, and by the White Horse Press as a companion to their *Culture and Environment in Inner Asia*, a unique collaboration by scholars from all sides of Inner Asia's international boundaries, edited by the present authors, and published in two volumes, *The Pastoral Economy and the Environment*, and *Society and Culture*.

10. XII. 99

THE END OF NOMADISM?

THE END OF NOMADISM?

SOCIETY, STATE AND THE ENVIRONMENT IN INNER ASIA

Caroline Humphrey

and

David Sneath

The White Horse Press

First published in the United States in 1999 by
Duke University Press
Durham, NC 27708

and in the United Kingdom in 1999 by
The White Horse Press
10 High Street, Knapwell, Cambridge CB3 8NR

A catalogue record for this book is available from the British Library

ISBN 1-874267-35-9 (HB)
      1-874267-36-7 (PB)

Printed in England by Biddles Ltd, Guildford

CONTENTS

INTRODUCTION   **1**

Some common themes across Inner Asia 6
Divergent paths 8
Environments created by different ways of life 11
Prospects 14

1. CULTURES OF INNER ASIA   **17**

Region-wide cultural links 17
Historical background to cultural divergence 18
The dynamics of language and culture in Inner Asia 21
Kinship and 'clans' 26
Religious complexities 30

**2. CHANGING PASTORAL SOCIETIES AND THE
ENVIRONMENT IN THE 20TH CENTURY**   **35**

Looking back 35
Twentieth century changes in the pastoral sectors of Inner Asia 42
Sustainable agriculture 47
Sustainable pastoralism and livestock stocking rates in Inner Asia... 48
Pasture degradation and mobility 52
Pastoralism, privatisation and markets 54
Rural pastoral population 58
Standards of living 59
Cross-border trade 63
The environment for pastoralism 65

3. RURAL INSTITUTIONS   **68**

Introduction 68
Economic and social overview of Inner Asia 73
Rural institutions in pastoral regions of Russia (Buryatia,
    Chita Oblast and Tuva) 78
Rural institutions in pastoral regions of China (Xinjiang and
    Inner Mongolia) 90

Rural institutions in Mongolia 109
Security, integration and disintegration 115
'Civil society' 118
Institutions and indigenous culture 123
Conclusion: some implications with regard to the pastoral
    environment.. 127

4. KINSHIP, NETWORKS AND RESIDENCE   136

Background 136
Descriptive terminology 139
Social relations of obligation and rural networks 141
Patterns of kinship and residence.. 147
Pre-collective Mongolian pastoral residential patterns:
    the *hot-ail* or *hot*.. 174
Conclusion 175

5. SETTLEMENT AND URBANISM   179

Introduction 179
Some new tools of analysis.. 182
Sedentarisation 188
Urbanisation 197
Urbanisation and sedentarisation 209
The relation between settlement patterns and the environment 210
Conclusions.. 216

**6. SPATIAL MOBILITY AND INNER ASIAN
PASTORALISM   218**

Introduction 218
Management of pasture in the Manchu and pre-collective period ... 219
Models of pre-collective pastoralism 220
Dual productive modes 225
Movement systems in the collective period..................................... 233
Pastoral movement systems in the case-study sites 236
Comparing Inner Asian pastoral systems.. 265
Mobility and sustainable pastoralism 268
Non-equilibrial grazing systems and the allocation of pasture land 269
Mongolian pastoralism and the market.. 273
Conclusion 276

7. A Family and its Networks — 278

8. Conclusion — 292

Mobility and land-use 292
Institutions 293
Pastoral production, labour and mechanisation 296
Rural-urban integration, sedentarisation and living standards 300
Marginalisation and indigenous knowledge 302
Environmentalism, intellectuals and local culture 303
Concluding remarks 305

Notes — 307

Bibliography — 334

Index — 343

Caroline Humphrey is a Fellow of King's College, Cambridge and Professor in the Department of Social Anthropology, University of Cambridge.

David Sneath is a Fellow of St Cross College, Oxford and Lecturer at Queen Elizabeth House.

Both authors have carried out extensive fieldwork among the pastoralists of Inner Asia, and are co-editors of the journal *Inner Asia*.

THE END OF NOMADISM?

INTRODUCTION

This book aims to show how pastoralism in the vast grassland region of Inner Asia is no timeless 'nomadism' but is a series of local knowledges and techniques located in particular historical circumstances. The end of nomadism in our title thus refers not only to the possible demise of a way of life but also to the fact that the very category of nomadism has ceased to be useful analytically. Nomadism is a category imagined by outsiders and it brings with it many suppositions about pastoral life, such as that it is free and egalitarian (see discussion in Dahl 1979: 279; Gellner 1988) or based on segmentary lineages (Asad 1979) or uses a wandering type of movement (Lattimore 1962: 141–4). Other well-known images are of fierce, warlike tribes given to predatory expansion (Sahlins 1961) or simple folk whose highest cultural achievement is a colourful rug. Another, and influential view, is that nomads have a low technological capacity and are necessarily dependent on the 'outside' sedentary world (Khazanov 1984). We return to this last point in the conclusion.

However, despite governmental sedentarisation programmes and attacks on pastoralists as 'backward', we argue that mobility is still necessary for pastoralism to be successful and sustainable in this environment. We prefer the term mobile pastoralism to nomadism because it does not bring with it the suppositions such as those mentioned above.[1] Mobile pastoralism is compatible with many different social and economic systems, including technologically advanced and market-oriented ones. Therefore although 'nomadism' – if it ever existed – has disappeared virtually everywhere in Inner Asia, mobility, on the other hand, remains a central pastoral technique. We shall show that, contrary to received images, and even to their own propaganda, state socialist regimes in fact supported long-distance pastoral movement systems in many areas, recognising their productive value, while settling other parts of the rural population. This book will argue that, far from being a practice associated with the most backward herders, highly mobile livestock herding is often the basis for the most efficient, wide-ranging, well co-ordinated and specialised production, and that it is compatible with technologically advanced and profit-oriented economic activity. Today market-oriented policies in all three countries (Russia, Mongolia and China) are creating new and divisive historical conditions for mobile pastoralism, in many places unfortunately threatening its continued existence as a viable economic practice.

Our approach is to examine Inner Asia as a whole, comparing the paths being taken in the different countries of Russia, Mongolia and China. What is Inner Asia? We define it as a 'cultural-economic zone'[2] of long standing. Ecologically, it is the relatively uniform steppe region inhabited by indigenous pastoralist peoples. Deserts and arid mountain ranges cut it off from the approaches to the high tableland of Tibet in the south. Culturally, Inner Asia has been dominated since the 13th century by the Mongols, who differ sharply in their way of life from the Russians and Chinese, their main neighbours to the north and south. The indigenous Buddhist-shamanist historical legacy also differentiates the region from Islamic Central Asia to the west; and we have included Tuva because, although it has a Turkic language, it shares this cultural inheritance and ecology.[3] In sum, our area is constituted by the coincidence of Buddhist-shamanist culture with the steppe environment stretching between China and Siberia.

The Inner Asian steppe rolls away to the horizon: herding here means personal presence with the livestock on the pastures, and it is generally unaided by fences or sheepdogs. The climate is extreme, and in a day can range from burning sun to freezing sleet. The economic culture of Inner Asia is based on a complex type of pastoralism which employs several species of herbivorous livestock[4] and requires movement between specific seasonal pastures. Traditionally, domesticated animals which were ill-adapted to movement, such as pigs and poultry, were negatively valued. Agriculture, if practised at all, was a secondary activity.[5] Livestock was owned or used by households (individually and in small groups), while land was held in common, though its use was often controlled by 'higher' social bodies such as lords, patrons, monastic proprietors, or latterly by collectives. Practical activities involved a complex gendered division of labour. This economic culture, we think, has certain continuities which can be seen in its character-istic dynamics and forms of reproduction. Our aim has been to investigate how this economic culture takes form in specific historical situations, especially the different policy regimes being established in the region today.

The conventional Euro-American concept of 'the environment' has no direct equivalent in indigenous Inner Asian languages. The Mongolian term *baigal*, often translated as 'nature', is closely related to *baidal* ('state of being', 'the way things are'). More recent concepts of environment devel-oped in anthropology stress the idea of it as an entirety which is an interactive field, rather than a passive setting in which human beings take action. This recent view seems to correspond with a fundamental aspect of how the Mongols see things. *Baigal* includes animate beings as well as inanimate objects. Objects in *baigal* are attributed with a notion akin to 'spirit', often personified in ritual contexts as *ejin* ('master', see Humphrey 1996). *Baigal* thus includes animals, mountains, trees, grass, weather and so forth as active subjects which have their own ways of being that affect human beings, just as humans have ways of life that affect them. However, there are more recent terms for 'environment' in the sense of surroundings, which have diverged in Russian and Chinese spheres of influence. In Mongolia *baigal orchin* is used to translate the Russian concept of 'environment'. In Inner Mongolia we find the term *orchim toirol*, which translates the Chinese idea of environment or natural 'surroundings' (*huan jing*). In this book we try to use an idea of environment which does justice to the Mongols' understanding of *baigal*. For example, on the practical side, herders expect a grassland to respond to an initial grazing, say by cattle which leave certain grasses to grow again, and they will then reuse the altered pasture by putting sheep on it. In Tuva, violations of the ongoing existence of natural species in the world, such as pulling up grass by the roots, is often thought to bring about retaliatory action from the 'spirits' of the locality (Humphrey, Mongush and Telenged 1993). However, it is important to point out that these elements of an ancient cosmology have come to exist within a modern repertoire of attitudes which include instrumental and economically-driven practices. These practices can be part of a different, extractive logic and they are often no longer seen as interactive processes.

This book argues that the steppe environment in some areas is under threat and pastoralism of certain recently-developed types, such as settled immobile systems developed in both Russia and China, is unsustainable. Yet we also find that in other areas the grassland flourishes and pastoralism seems to be compatible with a modernised and even urbanised lifestyle. One of our main arguments, in simple form, is that the maintenance of herd mobility is the main key to sustainable pastoralism in the region. At the same time, we suggest that high-mobility pastoralism can benefit from modern technology, and in these cases it may support participation in urban and even global culture. On the other hand, herders isolated in remote but settled villages are often excluded from participating in active and creative cultural develop-ments. We shall also take our readers through important issues of social transformation, ideological differences, and externally-created economic conditions. Our aim, by the end of the book, is to convey our understanding of why it is that, although all areas of Inner Asia are experiencing grave economic problems, some regions, especially in Buryatia and parts of Inner Mongolia, have got caught in a systemic decline, while others, notably

Mongolia and Tuva, have at least retained an environment which may enable them to develop viable and flexible pastoralism.

The 'local cultures' of our region do not simply result from internal processes of change, but now reflect the much wider – even global – political and economic developments that have impacted on particular areas of the project in various ways.

The socialist governments of all three countries of Inner Asia (Russia, China and Mongolia) sought to integrate pastoralists within their national economies by means of state planning. This brought certain benefits, as well as a heavy cost in human suffering, especially in Russia and China. Pastoral production of meat and wool increased markedly and entered national systems of distribution. In general the standard of living of the herding population rose,[6] with the security given by regular salaries, the acquisition of manufactured goods, and services such as education and medicine. Privatisation, however, has brought new problems of economic integration. With the end (or reduction) of obligatory quotas supplied by herders to the state there has been a broadly corresponding reduction (or end) of guaranteed state wages and services to the herders. The effect has been a turn to subsistence production in many parts of Inner Asia, especially in Russia and Mongolia. In China rapid economic differentiation among herders has meant that some are able to use market opportunities to their advantage, while others are only subject to market vagaries and depend largely on subsistence production. Distance from towns, roads and railways is an important factor. So are cultural practices: trading and manufacturing for the market are not strong parts of Inner Asian native traditions, and they were further weakened during the socialist period. Today, 'wild traders' are resented in many areas. This part of our research shows that 'the market' does not simply emerge 'naturally', and that market institutions must be to some extent planned and put in place in order to reach all parts of the population in a relatively equitable way.

This book is one of the publications to arise from the work of the Environmental and Cultural Conservation in Inner Asia (ECCIA) Project, carried out between 1991 and 1995 and initiated by the authors of this volume.[7] The project was an international collaborative research effort. The majority of the participants were young scholars from Inner Asia, who were involved throughout in setting the agenda. They worked jointly to design the project, establish the detailed issues to be investigated, carry out fieldwork, co-ordinate local research teams, set up the database, and write and publish the results. Our idea was to reflect in our research not only the 'external' views to be obtained from statistics or standard fieldwork by outsiders, but also perspectives from inside the cultures of the region; and indeed several of the participants carried out case-studies in places where they grew up or had close contacts. Of course these accounts emerged in the context of highly authoritarian state discourse, especially in China. There was also the illuminating experience for all members of the project of *ongoing discussion*, that is, the revelation as the project progressed of the participants' different points of view and different values, some of them incompatible. Our initial concept of the relative homogeneity of Inner Asian pastoralist culture proved incorrect in several respects. The divergent paths now being taken by the pastoralist economies of Inner Asia is a major theme of this book. We intend to show how state-level decisions to adopt one path or another took form in specific regional contexts. Our researchers were able to appreciate the intense detail and variety of the herders' own perspectives, and this appears in the book through the statements of the individuals they met. We hope thereby to convey to readers the underlying values of local people and their uncertainties and dilemmas in implementing new policies in the face of the intractable facts of daily life.

Let us provide a little information on the Inner Asian peoples. Mongolia, dominated by the Halh Mongols, lies in the centre of the studied region, both geographically and historically. Inner Mongolia, Buryatia, south Chita and some parts of Xinjiang were, until this century, largely inhabited by other Mongolian peoples. Despite regional differences and identities these areas shared many cultural features: Mongolian languages, closely-related scripts, a largely mobile pastoralist lifestyle, patrilineal social organisation, and religious traditions based on an eclectic mixture of shamanic practice, 'nature worship', and Buddhism in various degrees. The other major group of indigenous pastoral peoples are classed as linguistically Turkic – the Buddhist-shamanist Tuvans in the North-West of the region, and the Islamic Kazakhs and Kirghiz in the West. In 1992 the population of Mongolia was 2.2 million, around 90% of whom were ethnically Mongolian (Mongolian SSO 1993: 3; MAS 1990: 96). Tuva had a population of just over 300,000, of whom roughly one third were Russian and two-thirds Tuvan (Sullivan 1992: 3). Buryatia had a population of just over a million in 1991, around 250,000 of whom were Buryat and the rest mostly Russian (Buryat SSD 1993: 49, 53). The Chinese parts of the region are much more densely populated, largely by Han Chinese, although in Xinjiang the Turkic Uighur still form the largest single ethnic group. As a primarily agricultural and urban people, however, the Islamic Uighur were not the subject of our studies.[8] In 1990 in Xinjiang there was a total population of about 15 million, of whom just over 7 million were Uighur, 5.6 million Han Chinese, 1.1 million Kazakh, 140,000 Kirghiz and about the same number Mongolian (Xinjiang LHCC 1991: 55). In Inner Mongolia in the same year there were over 17 million Han Chinese and around 3.3 million Mongolians in a total population of 21.4 million (Hurelbaatar 1995: 4).

In recent times Inner Asia as a whole has seen two major ideologies: the model of democracy (locally interpreted) and a liberal market economy in the former Soviet zones, and the 'Chinese model' of centralised socialist government and limited market development in Inner Mongolia and Xinjiang. In the early eighties the post-Maoist Chinese administration carried out a series of rural reforms that led to the decollectivisation of the agricultural and pastoral sectors throughout the country, including Chinese Inner Asia. These reforms left the political structure unchanged, and much dominated by the Communist Party, but replaced central economic planning with a semi-controlled market-oriented economy. By contrast, the Soviet reforms of the late eighties began with political rather than economic changes. Gorbachev's *glasnost* and *perestroika* campaigns eventually led to free parliamentary elections in 1989. After the failed coup of August 1991 further political reform resulted in the formal independence of the USSR's constituent republics, and under the administration headed by President Yeltsin, Russia implemented policies designed to gradually privatise the economy. Curiously, these different political cultures both increasingly employ the global idiom of Western 'business', but this management-speak masks a variety of local practices, intertwining deeply traditional elements with the new economic forms.

SOME COMMON THEMES ACROSS INNER ASIA

Despite the differences in Russian and Chinese policy, some of the effects on Inner Asia have been universal. There is sharply increasing economic differentiation among rural populations in all parts of the region, particularly those areas previously dominated by the Soviet Union. As mentioned earlier, large numbers of people have been reduced to subsistence production and standards of living lower than any in the past 50 years. Rural people far from roads and markets are increasingly disadvantaged. Without measures for social development and trade these areas may well be abandoned in future.

With the retreat of state redistributive institutions we observe atomisation of administrative structures and sharp decrease in deliveries of

FIGURE 0.1. Inside the dairy factory in Hargant *sum*, Hulun Buir,
Inner Mongolia, 1993

products to the state almost everywhere. This coincides with the emergence
of local self-protective economic enclaves in many places. At the same time,
a volatile centrifugal, cross-border trade has increased, often at odds with
central government policies. There is drastic under-investment in local
processing and manufacturing throughout the region (see figure 0.1). A
hindrance to investment is the grossly inadequate infrastructure. Furthermore, there is widespread uncertainty about the content and reliability of
property and fiscal law, given the long history of instrumental attitudes of
those in power to the legal system.

Accompanying the economic retreat in Russia and Mongolia, there
has been a globalisation of consumption cultures throughout Inner Asia
associated with new trade networks and the spread of video and satellite TV
to the cities. People now take an interest in manufactured goods from Japan,
Hong Kong, China, Malaysia, Turkey, etc., and often buy them even if they
are regarded with some ambivalence ('These Chinese Game-Boys are *hog*
[rubbish]', said one young Mongol herder, as he avidly flicked the keys). The
most immediate result has been the rapid spread of Chinese goods, which are
the cheapest and most easily available. The advance of commerce has

sometimes caused various disastrous 'get rich quick' stratagems on the part of individuals and enterprises, ranging from slaughter of valuable animals distributed under 'privatisation', to sale of forest exploitation rights.

It is not surprising that there are also potential threats to the fragile steppe (dry grassland) ecology throughout the region. Our research indicates that precipitating factors include the allocation of individuated pastures, the increase of plough agriculture, the volatile influence of market prices on decisions about what to produce and in what volume, and the breakdown of local social control (leading for example to a relaxation of forestry protection and wild animal conservation). Even though there are marked differences in the economic success of herders in the various regions (for example, those in Inner Mongolia are generally 'richer' measured in private livestock than those in Buryatia or Chita), there is a common perception throughout Inner Asia that economies are running out of control and that this is directly impacting on the environment. There is widespread social anomie. High rural and urban unemployment is associated with gangs of alienated youths at many settlements and towns. There has been a rapid rise of alcoholism, theft and brigandage.

DIVERGENT PATHS

Pastoralism remains central to the rural economies of all the societies of Inner Asia. Indeed, as most of the land throughout the region is used as pastoral rangeland, its management is also central to the condition of the environment. In turn, decreased grass cover and reduction in the variety of grass species soon has an impact on the productivity of herds. But why has this happened in some areas and not others? It seemed to us essential to study the actual situation in rural localities and to examine the nature of the institutions that have emerged (often unexpectedly) in response to central policy decisions. To carry out this research we conducted investigations in ten small case-study sites located throughout Inner Asia (see figure 0.2), as well as using provincial and national statistics and other materials for the purposes of comparison.[9]

To obtain both in-depth knowledge and a wide understanding of major processes the detailed case studies were carried out in person by each researcher in the local language, in conjunction with overviews of topics such as land-use, livestock stocking rates, institutional change, mobility, social organisation, education and settlement patterns. The fieldworkers in each location also conducted a large number of structured in-depth interviews

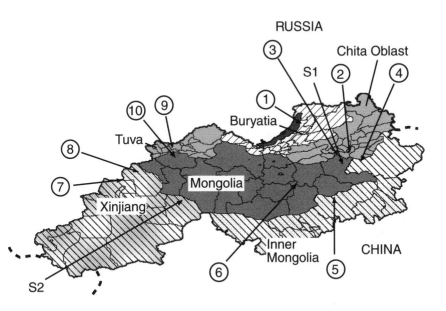

Site	Country	Location	Type	Researcher
1	Russian Republic	Argada, Barguzin, Buryatia	Temperate Steppe	Bair Gomboev
2	Russian Republic	Gigant, Chita Oblast	Temperate Steppe	Balzhan Zhimbiev
3	Mongolia	Dashbalbar *sum*, Dornod	Temperate Steppe	Batbuyan B.
4	China	Hargant *sum*, Hulun Buir	Temperate Steppe	Hurelbaatar A.
5	China	Chinggel Bulag, Shilingol	Temperate Steppe	Qi Xiao-Hong
6	Mongolia	Sumber *sum*, Dornogov'	Semi-arid Steppe	David Sneath
7	China	Hosh Tolgoi, Hoboksair	Arid Steppe	Tseren B.P.
8	China	Handagat, Altai	Mountain Steppe	Tsui Yenhu
9	Russian Republic	Solchur, Ovyur, Tuva	Mountain Steppe	Marina Mongush
10	Mongolia	Hovd *sum*, Uvs	Mountain Steppe	Telenged B.
S1*	Mongolia	Bayantümen *sum*, Dornod	Temperate Steppe	Caroline Humphrey
S2*	China	Barkol	Arid Steppe	Tsui Yenhu

FIGURE 0.2. ECCIA study sites[10]

* secondary study sites

with eighteen selected households. The same themes were covered in all ten case-study sites. The households were classified by occupation, comprising three administrators, three 'intellectuals' (teachers, doctors, etc.), three 'workers' (builders, drivers, labourers), and nine herders (grouped as 'rich', 'middling' and 'poor' by local criteria). Throughout this book we have used the comments of these local people, though personal names have been changed.

By studying comparable sites located close to one another but in different countries, we were able to hold the underlying ecology constant. We were then able to observe the *differing* effects of various administrative policies when applied in the context of the same ecology and originally similar cultural premises. For example, the case-studies in the Gigant collective-farm (Chita Oblast) and Dashbalbar *sum* (Dornod *aimag*) are located not far from one another on a relatively dry, flat, and treeless steppe and both involve largely Buryat populations; but the former has been subject to the administration of the Russian state, while the latter has experienced the different policies implemented in Mongolia.

Our project linked environment with indigenous culture because in Inner Asia the steppe grassland has been used as pasture for well over two thousand years. Therefore the grassland as we know it is not a phenomenon of 'pristine nature' but is to some extent the product of long-standing practices of nomadic pastoralism, i.e. of the *economic culture* of the people of the region. From the late 19th century onwards, however, the margins of the Inner Asian steppe have also been subject to the penetration of different types of economic culture with the advent of the Russians from the north and the Han Chinese from the south-east. Very generally we can observe that both the grassland environment and the indigenous cultures are under threat in these margins – the areas of pasture degradation broadly coincide with the regions where the culture of mobile pastoralism has been overwhelmed and native languages are weakened. At the same time these are the areas of greater economic development, associated with higher living standards for the rural population. Still, by the late 20th century the Russian and the Chinese dominated areas have come to be very different from one another and they appear to have different future trajectories. Mongolia, in the central region of the grasslands, has largely retained its culture of mobile pastoralism and has a relatively undamaged environment. Tuva is the one area of the project where native culture has strongly confronted that of the incomers (Russians) and it is significant that environmental conservation is a major issue in the confrontation.

ENVIRONMENTS CREATED BY DIFFERENT WAYS OF LIFE

The dramatic effects on the steppe environment of the different paths taken in Inner Asia can be illustrated with satellite photography. A striking Landsat image taken in 1989 shows the two case-study sites, mentioned above, one at Gigant in Chita (Russia) and the other at Dashbalbar in Mongolia (see figure 0.3). It is immediately obvious that different land-use systems are

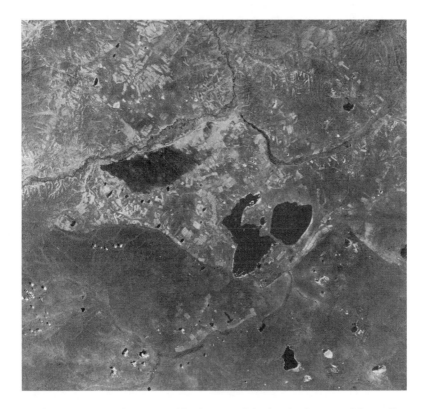

FIGURE 0.3. Landsat™ satellite image of the border between Mongolia and Chita Oblast (Russia) 19th Oct 1989.

The two Torei lakes can be seen just to the north of the border. The Gigant collective farm (case study site 2) at Novaya Zarya is located just north-west of these lakes. Dashbalbar *sum* (case study site 3) is located at the south-west of the image, with its district centre off the picture.

operative in the two regions. Although the international border itself can hardly be seen, it is clear where the border must be, because each country has developed the pastoral economy in different ways. On the Russian side the land is marked and scarred by human use, and wind erosion is clearly visible in the centre of the picture to the north of the Torei lakes. On the Mongolian side, on the other hand, apart from a few areas of strip agriculture, the visible features are natural ones. There is almost no erosion to be seen.

Let us explore these differences a little further. It is significant that, although the overall population density in the Russian areas is greater, the *rural* population density is not significantly higher than in the neighbouring Mongolian area.[11] The Russian population is concentrated in towns and cities such as Borzya and Chita. However, the livestock density on the Russian side was significantly higher than that in Mongolia in the early 1990s, and we argue that this was a direct result of differences between the two systems of land-use. These in turn are based on what we may broadly call different ways of life, especially in the management of the livestock economy.

The population on the Siberian side of the border is both Buryat and Russian. All inhabitants live in settled wooden houses and in rural areas these are heated by wood-burning stoves. Local research has shown that forest areas in the Russian border zone are both heavily exploited by the timber industry and regularly used by individuals and institutions for domestic fuel, housing and livestock sheds. This is related to the fact that livestock here consists entirely of 'improved' breeds, not the indigenous ones, and these breeds require heated sheds in winter and are unsuited for long migrations. Furthermore, they need hay and other fodder for many months of the year. Therefore extensive areas are ploughed for cultivation of fodder crops. Because the herds are relatively static they are not able to reach natural water sources at all times of year and water is often brought to the pastures on lorries; as a result a network of vehicle tracks over the pastures also causes damage to the fragile surface. The Buryat human diet has come to resemble the Russian one, with high quantities of bread, potatoes and other vegetables. The cultivation of food crops takes further land out of that available for pasture.

The population on the Mongolian side, on the other hand, uses wooden houses only in the central village of Dashbalbar, and herders use mobile dwellings (yurts, *ger*) covered with felt. Dried dung rather than wood is normally used for domestic fuel, and therefore relatively limited use is made of forest timber. The livestock breeds are local types that can use natural pasture virtually throughout the year. No fodder crops are sown. It is

FIGURE 0.4. Mongolian *ger* for a newly married couple, Hulun Buir, Inner Mongolia, 1988

true that the Mongolian human diet has long included flour products, but these were virtually all acquired by trade in former centuries. Since the 1970s Mongolia has developed arable agriculture in some northern parts of the country (as can be seen in figure 0.3), and until the late 1980s the country was self-sufficient in grain. When correctly sited in relation to the wind and carried out with fallow such agriculture need not result in erosion.[12] Fallow is also used on the Russian side of the border and the satellite picture also shows that tree strips have been planted in an attempt to stem erosion. However, the logic of the Russian system, in which until recently there was decreasing pasture for the high numbers of sheep dictated by the planners, compelled farmers to cultivate large amounts of fodder. Comparison of satellite images over the late 1980s to early 1990s shows that a three-year fallow cycle was replaced by a two-year cycle in parts of the Borzya area, thus intensifying the burden on the land.[13]

Such a comparison can be extended to the Inner Mongolian region across the border in China, this being adjacent to both Chita Oblast in Russia and Dornod *aimag* in Mongolia. These Inner Mongolian pastoral banners (counties) do not have very much greater rural population densities than the Mongolian regions across the border. Nevertheless, according to our data from case-studies they have greater problems of pasture degradation. The livestock densities tend to be higher in Inner Mongolia than in the neighbouring regions of Mongolia, especially of sheep and goats (see figures 2.7–2.9). However, in our view the most significant difference between the two countries is the allocation of pastures to households in Inner Mongolia, contrasted with a more flexible and mobile system in Mongolia. This again suggests that it is the way pasture is being used, not only numbers of people and livestock, that is the most important factor in analysing the causes of pasture degradation.

PROSPECTS

It is dismaying that Chinese policy for Inner Mongolia (see Hurelbaatar 1996; Williams 1996a) envisages measures that are similar in some respects to those which have had such disastrous results in Russia: introduction of 'improved' (more productive) breeds, use of heated winter sheds, development of fodder agriculture, and a less mobile, more static organisation of pastoralism in general. It remains to be seen what environmental effects such a policy will have (see chapter 6). However, the result is unlikely to be as disastrous as that seen in parts of Buryatia and Chita for a variety of reasons. These include the Chinese attempt to limit population, attention to stocking rates, limitations on forest logging, and the absence of Russian-type large-scale grain agriculture. Much will depend on the ability of local administrations in China to enforce these policies, a subject on which we introduce local herders' views in chapter 3.

The ECCIA project also studied the more strictly environmental aspects of contemporary pastoralism and the effects of recent changes. Much of the resulting research is found in Humphrey and Sneath 1996a. However, in *this* book we have attempted to present a more general synthetic picture. We attempt to describe for the first time the emergence of divergent economic cultures in Inner Asia, cultures which had developed their own ideals and values in the context of the 'ways of life' of a variety of forms of collectivised pastoralism. The macro-economic picture of a collapsed Russia and a rapidly growing China is well-known, but there have been virtually no comparative studies of the detailed situations in the Inner Asian provinces. Our studies show that in rural localities the contrasts found at the macro-level are by no means so clear cut. The clear contrast argued for in macro-level studies such as that of Nolan (1995) is undermined first by the heritage of common Inner Asian pastoral practices, and second by ecological problems which seem to loom over the future of Chinese pastoral areas, not just over those of Russia. Furthermore, the rapid economic development in China has hardly penetrated the distant rural localities, while the remnants of serious social investment by the Soviet government in rural communities continues to provide beneficial, if decaying, local amenities (such as schools, libraries, public baths or culture centres).

The issues described and discussed in this book (rural institutions, pastoral mobility, patterns of residence, and urbanisation) may sound familiar, but they are important issues for the late 20th century because it is through these practical arrangements that economic, legal and political processes will shape the future of pastoralism. We argue that the salient issues revolve around the changing nature of *social organisation* – what Firth long ago called the 'systematic ordering of social relations by acts of choice and decision' (1951: 40). In most of pastoral Inner Asia this 'ordering' is not principally based on clans or elaborated kinship structures, as some might suppose (although these have remained strong, or have taken on a new importance, in some regions). Nor is it yet based on class; nor even on ethnicity. Instead, the small herding group (*ail*) of one or a few families in changing combinations remains fundamental, as it has been throughout the century (see chapter 4). We have not found the *ail*s grouping themselves into strong informal neighbourhood units (see also Bruun 1996: 72). Rather, we have observed the emergence on the one hand of far-flung *networks* of families, and on the other of transformed official *institutions* (administrations, associations, companies, reconstituted collectives and so forth). Kinship plays an important role in both networks and institutions, but it does not define them. We discovered that both of these social forms strategically cross-cut ethnicity, rather than confine themselves only to uniform identities or ethnically-specific activities. In this process, the relations between the city and the countryside, the centres and the peripheries, are being rethought. The result is a sea-change in society. In putting things this way we are aware that we are going against the grain of most contemporary studies of the post-socialist countries, which tend to focus either on ethnicity and identity or on broad economic analysis. What we attempt to show is that ground-level social organisation matters. It is by means of *ail*s, networks and institutions, we argue, that policies, decisions and cultural preferences are being enacted today. Therefore their emergent forms will be quite crucial for the economic and political futures facing the peoples of the steppe.

The plan of the book is as follows. In chapter 1 we provide a brief introduction to the cultural linkages, languages, kinship and religious practices of Inner Asian peoples today. Chapter 2 goes back into the recent history of pastoralism in the socialist period, both through personal perspectives on local change and through statistically-based outlines of major trends in pastoralism, illustrated by charts. The third chapter reviews the range of institutional forms in the three countries and discusses their divergencies in the present day. Chapter 4 describes the ways in which herders constitute households and residential groups which are flexible in both time and space. Chapter 5 discussed the consequences of the processes which have settled and urbanised pastoralists in various ways, and shows that these two processes do not necessarily go hand in hand. Chapter 6 moves on to discuss the importance of the maintenance of mobility, and the forms taken by pastoral movement systems in the contexts of different institutions and economic circumstances. In chapter 7 we try to illustrate and draw together some of these themes by telling a story of a Mongolian family with its ramification of networks as it deals with the socio-economic changes described in the rest of the book. The concluding chapter makes use of the earlier analyses to pick apart some of the prevailing stereotypes about Inner Asian pastoralism. It makes the case for the continued importance of mobility for sustainable pastoralism at the end of the twentieth century. Mobility here is seen as a technique that is applicable in a range of institutions, rather than as a holistic life-style suggested by the word 'nomad'. Techniques of mobility have a long-standing and central place in the economic cultures of Inner Asia, and they are viable into the future. We argue that they are in principle quite compatible with the mechanised and culturally urbanised forms of pastoralism in which many herders in Inner Asia would like to take part.

Chapter 1

CULTURES OF INNER ASIA

REGION-WIDE CULTURAL LINKS

Earlier this century the cultures of Inner Asia could be described as having a common core, and many elements of this remain today. The Mongolian-based languages are one important strand, but one could also cite the entangled history of the region (especially in relation to the 13–14th century Mongol Empire) and more recent migrations across borders.[1] As a result of this movement, certain clans may be found in different parts of Inner Asia. It is not rare, for example, for a named clan to be represented among different 'ethnic groups', even those living far apart and in different countries. An example is the Galzuud clan which is found among the Bargas of Inner Mongolia in China and among the Buryats of Russia, and even more widespread are the Urianghai, found in Western Mongolia, Tuva, Xinjiang and in parts of Inner Mongolia. Besides this, the indigenous cultures are similar in ways which are more indefinable: we might cite a respect for age and seniority, a love of song and poetry, the cult of mythic heroes from epic narratives, an admiration for nature, and an immense generosity to guests. Religious traditions are similar throughout the region (including the Turkic-language areas of Tuva and the Altai). They comprise a mixture of folk practices, shamanism and Buddhism. The combination of mobile pastoralism with other more settled activities (agriculture, building fortresses and towns, monastic foundations, etc.) varied across Inner Asia, but some such mix was fundamental and was related to cultural features such as attitudes to landed property, leadership, warfare and trade.

However, even early this century such common cultural features did not prevent the Mongols from being socially rather divided. Lattimore has written (1943: 219):

Most Mongol tribes think and speak of most other Mongols with a mixture of dislike, suspicion and sometimes envy. At the same time all who speak the Mongol tongue, they feel, are *aha-düü*, elder and younger brothers, and ought to stand together against all who are not Mongols. [...] It is, I think, inherent in the character of the nomad life that there should be this wavering between unity and dispersal. Nomadism cannot be uniform. There are many gradations between the poorest pasture and the richest pasture, and each carries its own social character and has its own political tinge.

When Lattimore was writing it was possible to include all Mongol-speaking peoples in the category of 'the Mongols.' But by the 1990s this is no longer the case: 'the Mongols' (of Mongolia) are a different nation in the political sense from the Inner Mongols of China, for example, and the combined effects of different state policies and internal developments have separated off peoples such as the Buryats, the Daurs, or the Oirat. The groups are now not only politically distinct but increasingly culturally separate (Bulag 1998).

HISTORICAL BACKGROUND TO CULTURAL DIVERGENCE

How did this come about historically? Very briefly, the main recent historical events of the region are outlined below.

From the end of the 17th century until the 20th, all of Mongolia and what is now Xinjiang was ruled by the Manchu Qing dynasty, whose power extended north-west as far as Tuva. Buryatia, however, had become part of Russia's Siberian empire at around the same time as the Manchu expansion. The 19th century saw the decline of the Qing, in the face of the growing influence of the western powers, and in 1911, when the ailing dynasty finally collapsed, the Outer Mongolian nobility took the opportunity to declare independence. Their new head of state was the Jebtsundamba Hutagt, the head of the Buddhist church, known as the 'Holy King' – Bogd Khan. Over the next ten years, Mongolia saw incursions by Chinese and White Russian forces, and in 1921 the Communists of the Mongolian Revolutionary Party seized power with the support of Soviet troops. The final victory of the Bolsheviks in Russia led to Buryatia becoming part of the USSR. Although firmly controlled from Moscow, the new Soviet state was theoretically composed of republics based on ethno-national units.[2] The Buryats were a recognised nationality in this schema and much of their territory was included in the 'autonomous' Soviet republic of Buryatia. Tuva, although firmly within the Soviet orbit, retained a nominal independence until 1944, when its Communist leadership incorporated it into the Soviet Union.

Inner Mongolia and Xinjiang remained within the political orbit of China, although local rulers in both regions had a good deal of *de facto* autonomy during the chaotic warlord period. Despite the emergence of an Inner Mongolian independence movement led by nobles such as Prince Demchugdonggrub, in the 1930s eastern Inner Mongolia came under the growing power of the Japanese who controlled much of the region until their defeat in 1945. Four years later, when the Chinese Communists finally won the civil war and founded the People's Republic of China, Xinjiang and Inner Mongolia were both included as 'autonomous regions', province-level administrative districts which had (like the Soviet republics) no real political autonomy, but which notionally belonged to their indigenous nationalities.

The Buryats were forcibly settled in rural collective farms when the Soviet Union pushed through its harsh collectivisation programme in the late 1920s and early 1930s, causing agricultural dislocation and widespread hunger. The indigenous nobility and Buddhist church had already been persecuted and dispossessed, and although these policies provoked some Buryat resistance, this was quickly suppressed. In Mongolia the powerful church and aristocracy were also attacked and destroyed, but attempts at rural collectivisation met with such strong resistance from pastoralists in the 1930s that the regime had to shelve its plans until the 1950s, when it introduced collectives more carefully. In China the communists, having just won the civil war, quickly dismantled the 'feudal' order and removed the old elites. However, they stopped short of full collectivisation until the Great Leap Forward of 1957–9. Large collectives, called People's Communes, were rapidly established in rural districts, and the resulting disruption to agriculture was a major cause of the terrible famine that swept the country in the early 1960s.

In the USSR the collectives, even in pastoral regions, introduced large-scale farming on the agro-industrial model, with almost all rural residents settled in villages and livestock kept in fenced fields, reliant on cultivated fodder. In Mongolia and pastoral parts of Inner Mongolia and Xinjiang, the collectives and communes, although different in many respects, resembled each other in some important ways. Both forms were centred on a village in each district, which had local government, post, school and health facilities. Out on the steppe, herding households were organised into production brigades which continued to move with their livestock to seasonal pastures, supported by collective transport and deliveries of hay. In all the collective forms throughout Inner Asia, the land and livestock belonged, in effect, to the administration, and the labour of the members was commanded by officials. The workers on the farms received some form of pay, and were allowed to keep small private allotments of livestock and, in the case of settled households, usually a vegetable patch.

Buryatia, included in the Russian administrative structure since the 17th century, was to some degree protected from complete Russification by its status as an 'autonomous' Soviet republic, which entailed an official sponsorship of a Sovietised version of Buryat culture and language. However, as the administrative and higher educational systems were linguistically Russian, the new Buryat elite became largely Russian-speaking. The steady trickle of Russian settlers, which had started in the 17th century, continued in the Soviet period, and Buryats were soon outnumbered in the region by Russians. Ethnic relations remained reasonably good for much of this period, however, with rural Buryats remaining predominantly pastoral and Russians largely occupied in agricultural, industrial, forestry and mining sectors. The Tuvans, however, were never outnumbered by Russians in their region, and inter-ethnic relations were sometimes strained. Inner Mongolia had seen a series of flows of Chinese migrants into the region, as in the 1920s and 1930s warlord and republican governments sought to secure the border areas by populating them with Han Chinese settlers. Even larger influxes occurred in the fifties and late sixties, until Mongolians were vastly outnumbered by Han, who predominantly settled the urban and agricultural parts of the region. Huge numbers of Han migrants were also settled in Xinjiang, until they constituted more than a third of the population. Chinese policies towards their minority nationalities varied, from official bilingualism and a selective support for approved elements of indigenous culture, to persecution and suppression during the Great Leap and the Cultural Revolution of the late 1960s. Mongolia, however, experienced very little immigration, remaining culturally relatively homogenous and very largely Mongolian-speaking.

Today the Mongol-based languages spoken in Inner Asia are just about mutually comprehensible, but they are increasingly diverging in vocabulary and everyday expressions. The tendency to cultural fragmentation is likely to continue. Individual people of different regions may be friendly enough when they occasionally meet in business, cultural or religious contexts, but at the national level policies diverge and reflect a certain indifference to the affairs of neighbours. The Mongolian government's 1994 shelving of the policy of returning to the Mongol script (used in Inner Mongolia), the stubborn adherence to the 'Tod Bichig' by many Oirats

(Xinjiang Mongols), and the virtually total loss of the Mongol script by the Buryats, has removed one cultural feature – the native writing system – which might have provided a common medium of communication.

The divergency in language probably best expresses the underlying centrifugal dynamics of cultures in the region. Political unification is highly unlikely to occur.[3] However, it should be noted that there are some moves towards limited cultural links, such as region-wide conferences on literature, and Buddhism is also providing a framework for contacts through teaching, pilgrimages, etc. Joint environmental projects are beginning to have some impact. However, the main unifying factor, counteracting the political and cultural divergence, is business and trade. Here China is clearly dominant, as noted above.

THE DYNAMICS OF LANGUAGE AND CULTURE IN INNER ASIA

The Project did not make conventional anthropological studies of the various different ethnic groups, taking each as a separate 'culture'. Instead, our focus was on comparative exploration of factors relating to the maintenance of indigenous cultures in the region. We were especially concerned with those aspects of culture involving practices and beliefs bearing on pastoralism and the environment. This approach gives rise to two main issues: 1) Which features of the contemporary situation serve to sustain, or alternatively to subvert, indigenous cultures? and 2) What processual dynamics can we see in the operation of these features through time?

Language being one of the most central elements of culture, it is important to describe the extent to which indigenous languages are being maintained. A discussion among project members showed that the active functional use of native languages in a wide variety of social and political situations is generally felt to be extremely important. The idea that native cultures might somehow flourish through the use of another dominant language was rejected by most participants. Perhaps this view was so strongly expressed because the use of native languages, especially with a good knowledge of those languages, is in fact very variable in Inner Asia. Some official figures are given below, but this is a sensitive issue on which few accurate figures are published. It should be noted that although people may consider the native language as their 'mother tongue', this does not necessarily mean they are able to speak it well.

Region	% named population considering native language as their mother-tongue
Buryatia (Russia)	89.4% (1989)
Tuva (Russia)	99.0% (1989)
Mongolia	100% (1993)
Inner Mongolia (China)	77% (1980)

TABLE 1.1. Native languages in Inner Asia

The functional effectiveness of native languages is not uniform in either Russia or China. Thus in RUSSIA the Buryats and Tuvans have very different profiles. Many Buryats claim 'Buryat' as their mother-tongue, but a smaller number speak it well, even fewer can read it, and very few can write it correctly. The Buryat vertical script, based on the Mongolian script, is known only to scholars. The main language for public affairs in the Buryat Republic is Russian, and according to official statistics 74% of Buryats in 1989 used Russian fluently (probably an underestimate). Recently Buryat intellectuals have lamented the fact that so few young urban Buryats know their own language at all. The Buryats living outside the Buryat Republic, in areas such as Irkutsk Oblast and Chita Oblast, have a still weaker knowledge of their native language. In Tuva, on the other hand, the Tuvan language is used as a main language by virtually all of the native population. A significantly smaller number, 58.3% (1989), have fluent knowledge of Russian. With regard to the dynamics of the situation, while Russian gained at the expense of Buryat and Tuvan during the Soviet period, the process began to be reversed during the early 1990s. The trend towards 'nativisation' is, however, stronger in Tuva than in Buryatia. In Tuva, not only have many Tuvan-language medium schools been opened, but Tuvan is both the declared and the effective state language, and the proportion of Tuvan nationals in important posts is now monitored. In Buryatia some native language schools have been opened recently, but the situation is complicated by the desire not to offend the Russian majority. Even small moves towards teaching elementary Buryat via newspapers were greeted with protest from the Russian population in the early 1990s (Humphrey 1995).

In MONGOLIA native language use is unproblematic, as state schooling and all national affairs are carried out in that language. In CHINA, however, there is an interesting parallel with the situation in Russia. As in Russia, higher education and governmental affairs have been dominated by the language of the state (Chinese). The situation varies in different regions. In Inner Mongolia the predominance of Chinese is the main problem for the functional use of Mongolian. Significant numbers of Mongols (23%) do not speak Mongolian (Inner Mongolian CML 1992: 121) while another 10% use Mongolian only as a second language, and the proportion fluent in Chinese as well as Mongolian may be as high as 50% or more. Our evidence suggests that there is one major dynamic process at work in pastoral regions of Inner Mongolia. Poorer rural communities are seeing a significant drop-out rate from schools (e.g. 16% in Hargant, Hulun Buir) due to labour shortages in household economies. Although this might suggest that the use of Mongolian would be reinforced in this sector of the population, in fact it seems that a large proportion of the rural population are eager to know Chinese. Not only are there limited opportunities for young people to become herders, but many of them do not want such a life. Many tend to look for work outside the pastoral sector, and for most positions of this sort Chinese is necessary. This does not automatically mean that Mongolian is abandoned by those who leave, as it may be advantageous to retain trade links with their home community. However, among the better educated there is a reluctance to send children to Mongol-only language schools. In general, Chinese continues to dominate in administrative, business and higher educational institutions and thus the 'upwardly' and 'outwardly' mobile Mongolians are increasingly eager to master it. In Inner Mongolia there is a real threat to the use of the Mongolian language among the influential, the well-educated, as well as the urban Mongolian population. It has already become of somewhat tokenistic importance in higher education, largely confined to the study of Mongolian language and literature. However, in those rural localities with large Mongolian majorities, Mongolian often remains the dominant medium of everyday discourse, if not in administration and business.

The situation is made more complex by the fact that the Mongolian language is not only a means of communication but also a symbol of Mongol identity. On the one hand, urban Mongols from totally assimilated families and communities, are now beginning to study Mongolian (if only superficially). On the other hand, in some rural areas, as noted above, many people who speak Mongolian from childhood are sensitive to the disadvantages of only knowing this language and eagerly seek to learn Chinese. The Mongols who stay on the pastures continue to cherish their language, but there are increasing numbers for whom a Mongolian identity is not highly valued.

In Xinjiang the same processes are at work, but there is also the complicating factor of other large-scale indigenous languages which threaten

County	Total	Uighur	Han	Kazakh	Hui	Mongol
Hoboksair	**43,753**	1,081	14,850	12,015	424	15,117
Altai City	**177,564**	4,623	105,109	58,976	5,427	2,086

TABLE 1.2. Population of Hoboksair and Altai City counties in Xinjiang

Source: Xinjiang LHCC 1991: 55

Mongolian. The two case-study sites were the rural districts of Hosh Tolgoi and Handagat, located in Hoboksair and Altai City counties respectively.

The Mongolian population in the two studied counties lives alongside large numbers of Han, Uighur, Kazakh, and Hui. The Uighur, Han and Hui people are active in trade and therefore reach into Mongol communities, and it is useful for Mongols to know their languages to carry out business affairs. The Mongols and Kazakhs, with their pastoral traditions, tend to be more passive, not exporting their culture but being penetrated by those of others. However, the Kazakhs appear to have a relatively unified and coherent social organisation based on clans and centralised religion (Tsui 1996b), while the Mongols in Xinjiang are fragmented along old tribal lines across which communication is weak. Both Buddhist and 'shamanist' religious traditions continue to be important to Mongols, but neither religion has a centralised structure in Xinjiang. The Mongols are thus culturally divided and their language is further undermined by the problem of the Mongolian scripts. The majority of Xinjiang Mongols are Oirats using the 'Tod Bichig' script, which is different from the classical script used by the much larger Mongolian population of Inner Mongolia. Because the 'Tod Bichig' has restricted use, the Xinjiang government is now encouraging a move to the classical Mongol script and this is difficult and confusing for most of the Mongolian population.[4]

Our materials suggest that when a native language is seen as holding undisputed sway, as in Mongolia, no threat is perceived and attitudes with regard to foreign languages are relatively relaxed. When the native language is seen as threatened, people are insistent that it should be taught and that local government should be carried out through the native medium. However, if a native language is overwhelmed, as in Buryatia and Chita, there seems to be a cut-off point when most people feel it is no longer worth defending. In each case-study site, members of six herder households were asked if they thought a local leader of another nationality should know the native language. The answers are summarised in table 1.3.

| Region | Should a non-native leader know the local language? Household | | | | | |
	1	2	3	4	5	6
Mongolia						
Sumber	n.a.	no need	no	yes	they know it anyway	n.a.
Dashbalbar	n.a.	all speak Mongol anyway	n.a.	strange question	yes	maybe
Hovd sum	yes	yes, even if not a Mongol	yes	yes	no need to learn as everyone speaks Mongolian	yes
Russia						
Gigant (Chita)	not necessary to know	not necessary to know Buryat	we ourselves forget Buryat so probably they should	no need	yes, of course	doesn't matter
Argada (Buryatia)	should understand if not speak	yes, or life will teach them	doesn't matter	no	no need	yes
Solchur (Tuva)	obligatory	of course; must also know all customs and Tuvan culture	must know	of course	OK to have foreign leader if he speaks Tuvan	must know
China – Inner Mongolia						
Hargant	important	n.a.	yes	yes	we do not think about such things	n.a.
Chinggel Bulag	yes, for work	yes	yes	yes	yes	yes
China – Xinjiang						
Hosh Tolgoi	yes	if doesn't know should study it	yes; Mongol as well as Kazakh	should study	up to them but should learn	yes
Handagat	must know	we would not listen to them if they did not speak our language	of course	yes, even Han leaders here know Kazakh and some also know Mongol	yes	yes

TABLE 1.3. Attitudes to language spoken by local administrators

Note: n.a. = no answer

The answers from China, which virtually all strongly suggest that knowledge of the native language is important, reflect the fact that our case-study sites were in relatively remote regions, with a lower level of Chinese influence than the more urban and agricultural sectors of Xinjiang and Inner Mongolia.

Considering aspects of culture other than language, we found that indigenous ways of life (including herding techniques, housing, clothing, utensils, production of native foods, importance of religion, knowledge of oral literature and maintenance of traditional customs) are stronger in the western area of our project (Tuva, Hovd *sum* in Mongolia, and Handagat and Hosh Tolgoi in Xinjiang) than in the east. The reasons for this are not altogether clear. The situation may have to do with the mountainous terrain and difficulty of access, the retention of clans, and the relatively intense social ties within local communities in the west.

Two points may be noted here: 1) the native culture is strong in the western region in all three countries, and therefore cannot be explained by policies of the separate states; and 2) native culture is retained in this western region irrespective of the presence of a large non-native population in two of the case-study counties (in Hosh Tolgoi in Hoboksair county and in Handagat in Altai county, see table 1.2 above).

KINSHIP AND 'CLANS'

The ways in which people relate to one another as kin are central to the enactment of different ways of life (see chapters 4 and 7). Kinship can also create wide social identities, and for this reason we include here a brief discussion of clans.

Throughout the region traditional discourse on kinship proposed the symbolic complementarity of the male and female contributions to reproduction, the male symbolised as 'bone' and the female as 'flesh'. The 'bone' is visualised as a line of male ancestors going back in time from the subject, or alternatively as a series of lines descending from a single ancestor in the past. However, attention to ancestry is variable in different parts of Inner Asia. In Central Mongolia people usually 'remember' back only as far as the great-grandfather, if that, while in Buryat regions such as Barguzin there is knowledge of ancestral lines going back twenty or more generations. In Buryatia it is common to conceptualise descent 'from the beginning', that is from the first known ancestor, and the male descendants then constitute clans (*obog*) or lineages (*yasan* – 'bone' or *esege* – 'father'). In many villages there is a 'division of labour' in such knowledge, with a few elders making it their responsibility to know genealogies. Such knowledge can place hundreds of individuals in the kin network and further genealogically locate distant groups of people who are not known personally. The point to note is that the discourse of patrilinearity tends to be dominant in Inner Asia in contexts of identity, ethnicity, ritual, and life-cycle events such as birth, marriage and death. But this does not mean that the links through women are not also extremely important, and today one finds cases where people take their family identity or their ethnic identity from the mother rather than the father. It seems that bilateral kinship relations have gradually become more important since the demise of the patriarchal Manchu Qing state in 1911 and especially with the increased usefulness of networks in the informal economy. Concomitant with this is a decline in the use of the bone/flesh imagery, replaced to some extent by a discourse of 'blood' inherited from both father and mother (see Bulag 1998).

Let us now briefly discuss the distribution of 'clan consciousness' in Inner Asia. 'Clan' (*obog*, *otog*) here means an ideologically patrilineal kinship group, with its own name and identity. Such groups are normally exogamous (marriage is not permitted within them); they can be residentially scattered and members do not usually know the precise genealogical ties within them. The most renowned clan in Inner Asia is the Borjigid, descendants of the same noble lineage as Chinggis Khan. Today, the Borjigid are found throughout most of Mongolia and in parts of Inner Mongolia and Xinjiang, but they are not present in regions such as Buryatia and Manchuria which were not subject to the rule of the Chinggisids. The senior Borjigids provided ruling princes for Mongolia and Inner Mongolia until the 20th century, but paradoxically, this system of rule generally coincided with an absence of clans among the ordinary people in these areas. The Borjigid lost power when Communist administrations took control of the region. Thus today a widespread clan system is important in the regions where the Borjigid did *not* hold sway, throughout the mountainous western area, and also in Buryatia, Chita and the formerly Manchurian parts of Inner Mongolia. Table 1.4 indicates the presence of clans in the case-study sites in 1993.

Some explanations are necessary to understand the table, and this will provide an opportunity for us to describe the case-study sites briefly. In MONGOLIA, Sumber is in the central steppe zone and it is inhabited almost entirely by Halh Mongols. Here the Borjigid used to be a large presence, but aristocratic descent was of course something to be 'forgotten' in the socialist period, and now people claiming to be Borjigid are rather few, while other people have also moved into the area. In general, clans play no role in either everyday life or ritual. DASHBALBAR is located in north-east Mongolia, and is one of the regions to which Buryats fled after the Revolution. Halh Mongols and Hamnigan[5] are minorities to the Buryats here, and there are no Borjigid. Membership of clans and lineages (*echige*) is remembered by elderly Buryats and is important for exogamy and in the shamanism which is reviving here, but otherwise it is of little consequence in everyday life. As in Sumber, the mountain cults (rituals carried out at cairns called *oboo*) are conducted by Buddhist lamas and the attendance is on a territorial basis. HOVD *sum*[6], the case-study site in far western Mongolia, has a majority population of Dörvöd Mongols. Here also, there are no Borjigid and clans appear to be unimportant.

Moving to RUSSIA, we find that clans are important in most Buryat regions, especially those in the west where shamanism has remained strong. ARGADA in Barguzin has several western Buryat clans and *oboo* cults here are carried out by both shamans and lamas (see below). In CHITA (Gigant collective farm), a more Russian-dominated region to the east, clans are remembered only by the elderly, but they act as a memory reserve for everyone else. To give an example, when a young boy was killed in a riding accident in 1993 and a shaman was sought to give an explanation, the shaman insisted that he could do nothing unless the boy's clan ancestry was known, as this would define the spirits which might have caused the accident. The boy's parents did not know his clan ancestry, but they were quickly able to find it out by consulting old people and the shaman was then able to perform the ritual. In TUVA (Solchur district), in general, clanship is highly important in rural areas: everyone is mapped into a network of clans, sub-clans and lineages. It is possible that clans are rather less significant in our case-study site of SOLCHUR than elsewhere in Tuva, as this place is rather similar to Mongolia; it is a steppe region close to the border and religiously dominated by Buddhism rather than shamanism.

In CHINA, we find that clans are important in HARGANT, which is located to the north of Inner Mongolia, close to the border with Russia. Here most of the inhabitants are Bargas, some of whom have common clan names with the eastern Buryats of Russia. There have never been Borjigid in this area. Shamanism used to be strong here; both it and clanship are ideologically disapproved of by the Chinese government and now these are matters on which people prefer to remain silent. CHINGGEL BULAG is a steppe district of central Inner Mongolia where the inhabitants are almost all Abaga Mongols. This is part of the Shilingol league, earlier ruled by Borjigin princes. Far to the West in Xinjiang we turn our attention to Hosh Tolgoi, a district populated by Oirat Mongols. Hosh Tolgoi is located in Hoboksair County, which is inhabited by many Kazakh and Chinese as well as Mongols. The local Mongol clans (*arabat*) are exogamous, with a depth of around eight generations and their own seniors or heads (*ahmad*). There is an internal distinction between the princely and other clans, but as the Oirat were not part of the Chinggisid polity, they have no Borjigid. Revived after the Cultural Revolution, the largest clans today have 40-50 families and the smallest around 10. They are taking on new functions in social life (see chapter 4). Lastly, there is Handagat, a district of Mongols, Kazakhs, Uighurs and Chinese. Here clans are highly important among the Mongols and Kazakhs (Tsui 1996b). They organise aspects of practical life as well as ritual, and clan members collaborate in herding, house-building, loans, political support, etc.

Region	Presence	Clan *oboos*	Comments
Mongolia			
Sumber	No	No	Borjigid the only clan mentioned
Dashbalbar	Latent	No	Some elderly Buryats remembered clans
Hovd sum	No	No	
Russia			
Gigant	Yes	No	Only elderly people remember clans
Argada	Yes	Yes	Important in ritual and marriage; exogamy still practised
Solchur	Yes	?	Clans important in daily life
China			
Hargant	Yes	One (now defunct)	Clans formerly important
Chinggel Bulag	No	No	
Hosh Tolgoi	Yes	Yes	Aristocratic and commoner clans
Handagat	Yes	Yes	Clans especially strong among Kazakh

TABLE 1.4. The presence of clans in case-study sites

The table indicates that clans are important in a wide arc around the edge of Mongolia, but absent in the heartland. One historical explanation for this pattern is the re-organisation of Mongol society in the 13th century by

Chinggis Khan on the basis of military units rather than clans.[7] The areas peripheral to the Mongol Empire retained clans. A second historical explanation of the pattern is the Manchu attempt to formalise or re-constitute clans in the 17th century as part of their system of government of Mongol regions. In the central Halh regions clans proved to be irretrievable, but Manchu support for clans continued into the 20th century and was influential in regions like Hargant (Hulun Buir, Inner Mongolia). The general pattern was reinforced by religion: the prevalence of Buddhism, with its territorial organisation, in the central region, and the presence of shamanism, in which many shamanic spirits are conceptualised as 'ancestors', in the periphery. It is curious and interesting that clans and their sub-divisions remain so important in rural Buryatia, despite the fragility of other aspects of indigenous culture there. The recent revival of shamanism is contributing to a strengthening of clan-consciousness there.

RELIGIOUS COMPLEXITIES

It is characteristic of the whole region for people to engage in a mixture of religious activities, from folk practices to the great world religions of Buddhism and Islam. At the same time, all through Inner Asia there is the important counterweight of atheism, which was taught in schools and propaganda exercises throughout the socialist period. Buryatia and Mongolia have been exposed to the longest period of atheist education, from approximately the mid-1920s to the late 1980s. In Tuva atheist teaching was intensified after the country entered the USSR in the 1940s, while in China it really only started in the 1950s.[8] However, our studies indicate that the length of atheist teaching does *not* correlate with the strength of religion today.

In each case-study site eighteen households were asked if they had invited any religious practitioners for services during the past year. The question referred to private services, such as prayers for household members, shamanic exorcisms, or dream interpretations. The results in brief are given in table 1.5, followed by a discussion which also takes into account other information obtained during the fieldwork. This table does not indicate the number of times a religious specialist was invited (an illness or a funeral would usually involve several visits). Nor does it indicate participation by members of the household in communal religious activities, such as worship at an *oboo* (see chapter 3 for discussion of *oboo* worship).

	Lama	Shaman	Other	Combin-ation	No answer	None	Total
Buryatia and Chita							
Argada	1	0	0	17	0	0	**18**
Gigant	8	0	0	2	1	7	**10**
Mongolia							
Dashbalbar	11	0	0	1	1	5	**12**
Sumber	4	0	2	3	0	9	**9**
Hovd sum	12	0	2	4	0	2	**18**
Inner Mongolia							
Hargant	0	1	1	0	6	10	**2**
Chinggel Bulag	4	0	0	0	2	12	**4**
Xinjiang							
Hosh Tolgoi	1	0	0	15	1	1	**16**
Handagat	8	0	10	0	0	0	**18**
Tuva							
Solchur	9	2	0	1	2	4	**12**

TABLE 1.5. Private religious services in past year (18 households)

'Other' includes mullahs, bone-setters, diviners, and pronouncers of spells. 'Combination' refers to cases where households have used the services of two or more types of religious specialist. In most cases these are Buddhist lamas and shamans. 'No answer' refers to the number of households not replying to this question. 'None' refers to those households where the respondents specifically said they had invited no religious services of any kind.

Buddhism is the major religion in Inner Asia. Within the studied communities the relation between Buddhism and Islam is different from that between Buddhism and shamanism.[9] In Handagat (Xinjiang, China), the only one of the case-study sites with both Buddhism and Islam, households adhered to one or other of these religions, but never both at the same time, and the division was clearly related to ethnic differences: Mongols are Buddhists, while Kazakhs are Muslims. However, where Buddhism coexists with shamanism (notably in Argada, Gigant, Hosh Tolgoi and Solchur) households commonly participate in both kinds of religious activity. Both Buddhism and shamanism coexist with various minor religious practices, such as use of diviners to find lost animals, pronouncers of spells, and bone-setters (who use magical and quasi-religious methods). It is rare for shamans to be consulted as the only form of religious service.

Religious activity is least strong in Inner Mongolia. This is also the region which seems to be under the most comprehensive political control and has been subject to the most rigorous recent secularisation campaigns. By contrast, religious activity seems strongest in Handagat (Xinjiang, China) and in Argada (Buryatia, Russia), where all eighteen households said they had used religious services, most of them quite frequently. However, the reasons are different in the two districts. In Handagat religion is closely connected with individual life-cycle events (funerals, coming-of-age, etc.) and curing of disease (both Buddhist lamas and Islamic mullahs say prayers for the sick). It is thus part of a continuously maintained 'tradition', which we have already noted is strong in this region. Religion is also tied to ethnicity and the observance of communal festivals. Possibly the existence of two distinct ethnic groups, Mongols and Kazakhs, has strengthened the social pressures to take part in religious activities. In Argada, on the other hand, religion is now being revived after a long period of repression by the Communist authorities. Here religious activity is now flourishing despite the fact that there has been significant native language loss and most Buryat everyday traditional material culture (clothing, housing, utensils, etc.) has long since disappeared.[10] However, ethnicity remains an important source of identity in the region, and in some cases religion is used as a marker of Buryat ethnic identity.[11] The main reason given by respondents for participating in religious services was the need for psychological support in the present economic and political crisis of the country. A typical respondent said,

> I go to the shaman's *oboo* ceremony[12] and I also ask lamas to say prayers for my family well-being and the well-being of the country. In fact I am an atheist. But the political situation and the psychological climate in the country is unstable, so we have to turn to religious traditions. They help us overcome our troubles and relax from the tension. My mother said I should keep all our traditions to avoid trouble. I still have my atheist point of view, but if it is necessary to do something I do it. That is our tradition.

The wider picture that emerges is that distinctive 'traditional' Inner Asian religious practices and languages are not simply fading away in face of external cultural influences. Even this brief survey demonstrates that the dynamics of language, culture, kinship and religious activity in Inner Asia are not simple and are not changing in a unilinear direction.

1) Native language loss is severe in Buryatia (Russia) and Inner Mongolia (China); but it is probably not irreversible in either region. The counter-examples of Tuva (Russia) and Altai (Xinjiang, China) show that it is possible for small minorities in both countries to sustain native languages as active, functional means of communication in local affairs.

2) A variety of historical factors influence the strength of religious traditions, and the pattern is not clearly correlated with the preservation of other aspects of culture, such as clanship, or with the strength of native languages.

3) For a variety of historical reasons, indigenous cultural traditions in general are most strongly maintained in the 'western zone' of Inner Asia (Tuva, western Mongolia and north-western Xinjiang).

The western zone is where we find the most positive and respectful attitudes to the environment (Tsui 1996a), the most enthusiasm for native culture, as well as the continuation of a mobile life-style. We would like to point out that this does not mean the western zone is 'backward'. Though it is perhaps less economically developed than the eastern regions in terms of infrastructure and industry, its lands sustain comparable populations and herds to those in the eastern regions; this appears to have been achieved with relatively little environmental damage resulting from herding practices.

The complexities outlined in this chapter indicate that indigenous cultures of Inner Asia should not be seen as essentialised systemic wholes, now or in the past. They form a related set of contested social repertoires in the different political arenas of the nation states which now govern the region; and these political processes seem set to continue to move in different directions.

Trying to explain the centrifugal tendencies in Inner Asia, it is possible to make some even broader generalisations on the basis of our comparative field-studies. The native peoples of south-eastern Siberia inside Russia, such as various groups of Buryats, Tuvans, or Hamnigan, tend to engage with one another rather little in political and cultural terms. As debtor-regions inside Russia, they each tend to look 'vertically', as it were, towards the centre and to evaluate their success in relation to Moscow (or to Western contacts) rather than in relation to one another. From their point of view, Mongolia is regarded as undeveloped and unable to help. Meanwhile, Mongolia itself is preoccupied by its own precarious balancing act as an independent country between China and Russia. Inside China the different groups of Mongols are also divided, in what seems to be an old pattern. Since the Manchu Qing dynasty the elite of the eastern Mongols has struggled with those of the centre and west for positions of power in the regional administration. The creation of the vast Inner Mongolian Autonomous Region generated opportunities for Mongolians in senior positions, but it also created an important arena for competition over places in the administration centred on Hohhot. Perhaps less focused on the national capital Beijing than in the Russian case, these Mongol groups engage with one another 'horizontally', but often in a competitive way.

Chapter 2

CHANGING PASTORAL SOCIETIES AND THE ENVIRONMENT IN THE 20TH CENTURY

LOOKING BACK

This chapter attempts to link some local historical accounts of the recent reforms with a sketch of important macro-economic changes in the livestock economies of the region. The point we aim to make is that the commandist policies have often had unintended effects. The national policies of collectivisation, etc. are described elsewhere (Humphrey 1983; Riskin 1987; Nolan 1995) so we do not deal with them again here. But the local processes and their effects on the steppe environment are only just becoming clear. This leads us to a broadly-based argument about the key difficulties created by the socialist state policies and what these experiences reveal about certain crucial advantages of organisational forms developed historically in pastoral cultures. In this chapter we introduce these themes and provide basic background information, so as to be able to extend the analysis more fully in the rest of the book.

We start with the recent history of the region seen through the recollections of some older people. One short narrative has been chosen from each of the three countries of Russia, Mongolia and China. This will give an impression of the main events as seen by engaged participants. Far from being a time of stability, the socialist period emerges here as a period of almost ceaseless change. A common theme is collectivisation, which started in all areas of Inner Asia with small co-operatives, subsequently amalgamated into large and more rigidly organised collectives or communes. The years of 'high socialism' in the late '50s to early '80s were succeeded by a variety of forms of 'privatisation' throughout the region. Here we aim only to convey the broad outlines of the politico-organisational transformation, as it is necessary to convey a picture of this before the dramatic shifts in pastoral practice and other aspects of indigenous culture can be understood.

Russia

We begin with Garma B. Shotkhoev, aged 51 in 1993, who is the Director of the Argadinskii *sovkhoz* (state farm) in the Barguzin district (Buryatia). Shotkhoev is a Buryat and a local man. He lives with his wife, a teacher, his aged mother and his 15 year-old son in a house which the family recently built for themselves in Argada village. Their daughter is at college in the capital, Ulan-Ude. Shotkhoev's narrative expresses some regrets for the pre-modern Buryat culture, but he is a firm believer in the 'collective way' and like most of our respondents from this region he has doubts about whether privatisation will work well.

> Before collectivisation the Buryats in Kharamodun [now Argada village] had a semi-nomadic way of life. Their main activity was stock-breeding. The poor people and even rich men of the *ulus* [the Buryat local group] used a lot of natural things in their households. Toys for children, knife-handles and other things were made of bone and horn. Inner organs of animals were used as bags for keeping butter, jam, and cooked wild berries. Necessary things like tea, salt and tobacco were bought in small Chinese shops situated 20–30 km away at the *datsan* [Buddhist monastery] at Khargana. Apart from this, they used to go a Russian village, 70–90 km away, to buy bread and potatoes. They took cured skins, sheepskins and wool to exchange.
>
> There was only one Buryat school, which was in Khargana, 9–10 km to the east of Baraghan. Now nothing is left there but a few houses of herders. The local authorities of the Barguzin Buryats were at Khargana too. One or two boys from Argada studied in that school. But there were many lamas there. Almost every third family sent their second or third son to serve as a lama in the *datsan* for the rest of their lives. Everyone in the *datsan* learned the old Mongolian script. Taking this into consideration we can say that on the whole the level of literacy was high.
>
> After the October revolution and Civil war small enterprises were joined into larger ones. The first 'Bato-Baidal' co-operative community was established in 1928 on the territory of Kharamodun [Argada] *sum* (district). It took only a year to organise a sheep farm in which most of the people of Argada were members. A little bit later an agricultural farm was formed and it had several members. The first collective farm in Kharamodun sum was organised in 1930. After joining up with the 'Bato-Baidal' co-operative the two together formed the M. Sverdlov collective farm. Later on, in 1930, an agricultural collective named after M. Kalinin was moved here from Sakhuley. At the same time a similar collective called 'Munkho-Baidal' was set up in Zuun-Shartalay. It consisted of some individual farms. This economy existed for less than a year and then it joined the agricultural collective 'Ulan-Naran' formed after 'Munko-Baidal'. Several other new agricultural collectives

were organised at that period too. Gradually they all joined into one co-operative named after M. Kalinin. In 1961 the collective farm was reformed into the state farm 'Kurumkanskii', and in 1964 it was named 'Argadinskii'.

From the mid 1950s the total number of sheep increased very quickly, to reach about 25,000 by 1980. At the same time the agricultural area was expanded and reached more then 8,000 hectares. Pressure on these arable areas caused erosion and there was erosion on the pastures as well. At the maximum we had 4,500–5,000 cattle and 550–600 horses. Besides, at different times there were fox-, pig-, goat-, goose-, duck-, and chicken-farm sections too. But they were small. When the state-farm was ordered to specialise in crop production and stock-breeding (cattle and sheep) these sections were eliminated. During the last few years the livestock numbers in our *sovkhoz* [state farm] have greatly decreased : sheep to 5,500–6,000, cattle to 2,000–2,200.

Now the Argadinskii *sovkhoz* is moving towards privatisation. New peasant economies will be organised like they were sixty years ago, instead of the *sovkhoz*.

I think that the collective period was better because the people had clear prospects and everyone knew his work and place. Now we are not sure about our future. Many things are not clear nowadays. With our natural conditions and structure of production it will be very difficult to have economic success with privatisation. Our authorities and we ourselves should have thought about other forms of production. Perhaps small collectives, but with common property and labour.

Mongolia

Sodnomjav, an elderly herder, was born in 1919, in what was then Tsetsen Vangiin Borjigin *hoshuu*, and is now Sumber *sum*, Gov'sumber *aimag*.[1] As a member of the Borjigin lineage, Sodnomjav is a direct descendent of Chinggis Khan. Generally such ancestry would have conferred noble status in pre-revolutionary Mongolia. However, in practice not all the Borjigid gained noble status, and in this region there were many Borjigin families who were, like Sodnomjav's parents, common herders, in this case the ecclesiastical subjects (*shabi*) of the nearby Lamaist monstery of Zuun Choir.

When Sodnomjav was a small boy the great monastery still stood, home to more than 2,000 lamas. He particularly well remembers the grand religious meetings (*hural*) that were held twice a year, once in late winter, and once in summer, when all the lamas would meet for ceremonies and prayers. The monastery was destroyed in Choibalsan's campaign against the church in the 1930s, and nothing but ruins remain of it now. However, on one of the boulders at the foot of the sacred mountain where the monastery once stood,

FIGURE 2.1. 'Sodnomjav'

Sodnomjav would point out a holy painting of the Buddhist goddess Tara which had somehow survived. The old man, though not openly religious, still shows his respect for Buddhism; indeed with his shaved head and perpetually kindly expression, one could almost mistake him for a lama himself.

Despite the turmoil, Sodnomjav remembers the 1930s as a prosperous period. The huge herds that had belonged to the monastery had been distributed; the district was rich in livestock, and Chinese merchants still traded with herding families at this time, supplying tea, tobacco, cloth and other consumer goods. In the 1940s Sodnomjav left to serve in the Mongolian Army, and in 1945 he was a member of the Soviet-Mongolian force that entered Inner Mongolia to defeat the Japanese. His cavalry troop travelled as far south as Beijing, but Sodnomjav did not find China much to his liking, and was glad to return to Mongolia at the end of the War.

The fifties saw the collectivisation of the pastoral sector in Mongolia. In 1956 three small collectives were founded and in 1959 these were merged to form one large collective farm called 'Hödölmöriin Och' (Spark of Labour). Ten years later the old collective became Sumber State Farm, when a specialist Karakul breeding programme was moved there from another State Farm in Töv *aimag*. The Karakul sheep were an introduced breed, providing high quality lambskin for the clothing industry. Sodnomjav became something of a model herder, winning a number of awards. He recalled both the positive and negative aspects of pastoralism in the collective period:

> In the collective period the organisation of joint work, moving to other pastures, and *otor* [distant moves for fattening] was very good. The services provided to the herdsmen were also excellent. Also, the making of hay [for fodder] and the repair of *hashaa* [enclosures and sheds] was done well. People did not need to use ox or camel carts, so they became unused to this sort of work and expected to receive state motor transportation all the time. This was because the state farm concentrated all the camels in one or two *ails* [households] of specialist camel-herders. So most herders did not have camels for transportation. The specialist camel-herding households only had a few people, so they could not break-in and train the camels for transportation.
>
> The herdsmen had hay and so forth provided for them, and were instructed where and when to move, so they did not choose places to pasture the livestock themselves. They worked only at the command of, and under the direction of, their leaders, and they moved and worked as a group, together, when the leader instructed. For example, cutting and making hay, shearing sheep and taking hair from the other animals, dipping the animals, all these

things the brigade or groups (5–10 *ails*) did together. So during this period the people had no personal initiative. They ended up just following instructions and waiting to be told what to do.

Sodnomjav fell from his horse in 1986 and broke his thigh. The local doctor sent him to hospital in Ulaanbaatar, where he spent four months recovering from the operation to pin the bone. The treatment was successful, however, and although he walks with a limp and a stiff leg, Sodnomjav is sprightly and active, despite age and injury.

In 1993, Sodnomjav lived with 78 year-old Dulmaa in a small *ger* alongside a younger family with whom they had lived for a few years. Dulmaa, however, was not technically Sodnomjav's wife, as they had never formally married. Dulmaa had been married to Sodnomjav's elder brother, but when her husband had died she established a household with Sodnomjav, in accordance with a long-standing Mongolian tradition.

Although they were long past retirement age, inflation in the early 1990s had reduced the value of their pensions to next to nothing. To make ends meet, Sodnomjav and Dulmaa had come to rely upon their small number of livestock, mostly sheep and goats, which they herded with the larger herds of the friendly family. They shared the widely-held view that herdsmen have become poorer with the end of collectivisation. In the encampment, Sodnomjav was considered an authority on all things pastoral and was continually asked for advice. Each morning he would emerge from his *ger* to predict the weather for the day, and in the five months that the project researcher stayed in his encampment he was very seldom wrong.

China

Ch'edip is the Chairman of the County People's Congress in Handagat, in the far north-west corner of Xinjiang. He graduated from university in agronomy in the 1960s. Now aged 49, Ch'edip has worked in the district for thirty years, but he was born in the nearby area of Hemkhanaz. This is a region inhabited by Tuvinians (see Mongush 1996) and Ch'edip said that his own family was Tuvinian. He lives with his wife Buyan, a farmer and housewife, and their seven children.

> Before 1950, the animals were private but the pastures were the property of the *aryile* [a sub-district]. In 1952, the animals of the rich herders were bought by the state and divided between poor herdsmen. In 1955 primary co-operatives were set up, but animals were still private. However, in 1956 advanced co-operatives were set up and that was the beginning of collectivi-sation and all the herdsmen delivered their animals to the co-operatives as a

kind of 'share'. Only one horse, one cow and several sheep or goats were allowed to be kept by each household.

Then the People's Commune came and we lost all our 'shares'. We worked for *gongfen* [work-points] and generally each unit of *gongfen* was equal to a few *fen* [the smallest unit of Chinese money] and an average herdsman earned 8–10 *gongfen* a day. During the commune period there was a kind of 'responsibility system' according to which a herdsman obtained his *gongfen* according to the birth rate and survival rate of the herd he looked after, i.e., the higher the rate was, the more *gongfen* he gained. I should say that, generally, the living standard of most of the herdsmen improved during that time in comparison to before 1950, and a basic level of social service also came into being during that period. However, the system was not good as it made people lazy, and it did not work well in organising livestock production. The most disgusting thing was that in the years 1958–1963 we had to have our meals in a public dining hall run by the brigade and it was not only very inconvenient but also we often did not have enough to eat. I know that in our neighbouring areas some people died of starvation. In the collectivisation period the pastures were theoretically collective, but people in general did not have a concept of either collective or private property so they did not do much to care for pastures. The year of 1984 was a turning point. The collective system ended and animals were privatised according to a low-price buying method, i.e. each household obtained a number of animals at a low price, only 25 yuan for a sheep and 120 for a horse or head of cattle. Later the pasture was divided among herdsmen according to their herd size and family size, though it is still the property of the state. This is a kind of a very loose renting contract. As for me, I can use my pasture for 50 years.

The positive thing about the new economy is that the income of herdsmen has gone up and the increase of animal numbers has made it possible for us to develop other facilities like electricity and transport. The negative side is that you cannot live only on animals, but we have no other way. And also, with too many animals we are vulnerable to natural disasters, so our income is not stable. On the environment, you could say it is good that people notice the grassland and see it is facing a danger – it can no longer carry more animals. But what is happening? There are still more animals, the quality of grass is getting worse and the carrying capacity has become half of that we had 25 years ago.

These of course are individual perspectives, but they are characteristic of their regions in our view. Note that in Russia, where the economic situation was arguably the worst in the early 1990s, there is widespread support for continuing the collective system (Argada was almost the only collective farm in Barguzin to privatise). In Mongolia, some aspects of the collective system are criticised, although like many Mongolians Sodnomjav notes the benefits that the collectives offered and has misgivings about the privatised future. In China, which is economically the most prosperous of the three regions, strong doubts were expressed about both the past and the present courses – though in our opinion, as will be argued later, Ch'edip relies too strongly on overstocking as the main reason for the cause of pasture degradation.

Let us now illustrate certain effects of collectivisation by outlining the historical changes in pastoralism over the past seventy years or so.

TWENTIETH CENTURY CHANGES IN THE PASTORAL SECTORS OF INNER ASIA

A comparison of the dynamics of the pastoral economies of the different regions shows some interesting parallels. Statistics available for Buryatia, Mongolia and Inner Mongolia allow us to compare changes in livestock numbers from pre-collective times to the present.

Buryatia was collectivised early, relative to other parts of Inner Asia, the process being virtually complete by 1932. Total numbers of livestock show an initial drop and then a dramatic increase (figure 2.2). At first glance it appears as if the pastoral sector is larger than in the pre-collective period, and has declined only relatively recently, as the economic and environmental situation worsened. However, if livestock numbers are translated into standard stocking units[2] (SSUs, reckoned in sheep units) a very different picture emerges (figure 2.3).

These graphs indicate that the total number of animals (as measured in standard stocking units) is in fact similar today to the pre-revolutionary level; but there has been a great change in the composition of the pastoral sector. Goats have almost entirely disappeared. On the other hand, the numbers of sheep pastured in the region has risen dramatically, while the numbers of horses has declined steadily. The numbers of cattle (and indeed the overall numbers of domestic animals as measured in sheep units) declined during the civil war and the initial process of collectivisation, when some owners slaughtered their animals rather than give them up, and numbers did not recover until the sixties. Cattle, important for subsistence milk production, do not appear to have declined in the early 1990s as the sheep and goat numbers did.

In terms of the total numbers of livestock, Mongolia seems the only part of Inner Asia where the numbers of all species appear to have increased since pre-revolutionary times (figure 2.4), and this of course means that the number of standard stocking units has also risen – although estimates of the

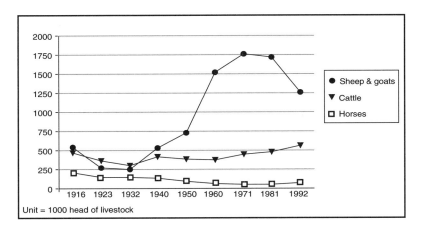

FIGURE 2.2. Buryatia – livestock numbers

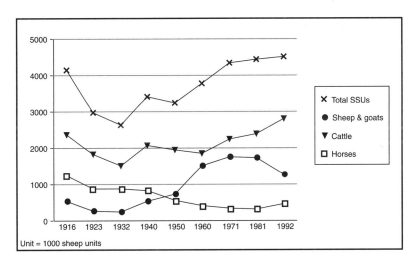

FIGURE 2.3. Buryatia – livestock in standard stocking units (SSUs)

pre-revolutionary levels vary and early attempts at collectivisation led to the loss of many animals (Telenged 1996: 169). A more detailed analysis of the changes in the Mongolian livestock sector, including the rapid increases before collectivisation in the 1950s, appears in chapter 6.

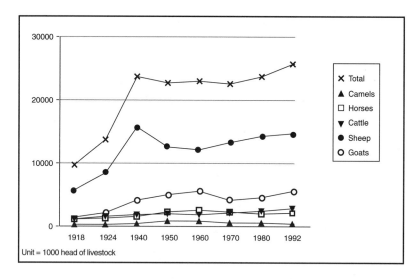

FIGURE 2.4. Mongolia - livestock numbers

At first glance Inner Mongolia seems to have had an equally marked increase in livestock numbers during the Chinese communist administration of the region (figure 2.5). If, however, one uses standard stocking units to evaluate the changes over time, the picture is once again very different (figure 2.6).[3]

As in Buryatia, it seems that relatively high numbers of livestock were supported before collectivisation. Inner Mongolia also resembles Buryatia (and Chita) in that it has also seen an important increase in the amount of land cultivated for crops (although even today the area amounts to less than 5% of the total area of the region).[4] Consequently, the amount of pasture now in use in Inner Mongolia is almost certainly less than early this century, and grazing pressure on the grassland is clearly likely to be greater as a result. However, it is still interesting to note that the pre-revolutionary economy supported approximately as many animals (measured in sheep units) as modern Inner Mongolia – around 70 million SSUs.[5]

As in Ch'edip's account of Handagat (Xinjiang), in Inner Mongolia today there is a similarly strong conviction in specialist and administrative circles that the pastures are saturated, and that overstocking is the cause of widespread grassland degradation (Yong and Cui 1988: 4).[6] Recent work by Inner Mongolian specialists suggests that as much as 35.6% of Inner

The End of Nomadism? Erratum slip (page 45)

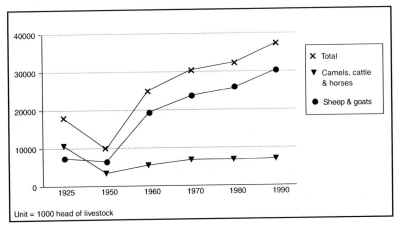

Unit = 1000 head of livestock

FIGURE 2.5. Inner Mongolia – livestock numbers

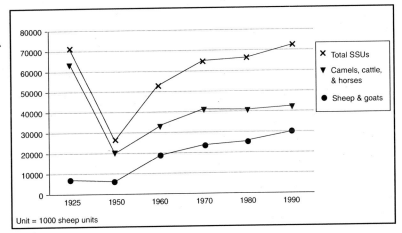

Unit = 1000 sheep units

FIGURE 2.6. Inner Mongolia – livestock in SSUs

Mongolian grassland has been degraded and they attribute this largely to overgrazing (Loucks and Jianguo 1992: 71). It is significant, then, that in terms of standard stocking units there has not been a dramatic increase over pre-revolutionary stocking levels at all. Indeed in Buryatia and Tuva, as well as Inner Mongolia, the pastoral sector supported something like the same numbers of animals (measured in standard stocking units) in pre-revolutionary times as they do today. This raises a number of important questions with regard to the perceived problem of overgrazing. If, for instance, Inner Mongolia is facing an acute and historically unparalleled problem of environmental damage in many regions, we cannot assume that this is because it now supports an unprecedentedly high number of animals.

In Buryatia and Inner Mongolia the earlier pastoral economies supported a high number of large animals, relative to sheep and goats. In the last fifty years or so, the numbers of sheep in particular have risen quickly in all the areas under study. This change in the composition of herds may be a contributory factor in the widespread degradation of the pasturelands reported in Buryatia, Chita, and Inner Mongolia. Such a view is supported by the developments in Buryatia in recent years, where collectives have faced very widespread problems of pasture degradation. The number of sheep has been drastically reduced in the last few years, partially because the pastures cannot support them, and partially because the farm management has accepted the idea that sheep have a particularly damaging effect on the grassland. A large collective farm in the Barguzin region, Bayangol, for instance, had reduced its numbers of sheep by 30% by 1993 and by 1996 was down to around 5,000 sheep from a former 120,000. Our Buryat specialist on the project, Bair Gomboev, suggests that reducing the sheep population, and keeping higher numbers of larger animals, could contribute to a more sustainable utilisation of pastureland (Gomboev et al. 1996).

Native herders' perspectives, however, are different. The case-studies found that few herders considered sheep or goats to be particularly damaging to pastures. As a cause of pasture degradation, herd composition was generally considered by informants to be relatively unimportant in comparison with the practice of keeping livestock on the same pastures all year, or the introduction of weak and slow-moving foreign breeds of livestock, both of which were blamed for the worsening condition of pastures in several study sites (see Telenged 1996: 184 and chapter 5 of this volume).

The introduction of foreign livestock breeds to the pastoral systems of Inner Asia seems to have contributed to the reduction in mobility found in most regions over the last fifty years. This has been due to the special requirements of the introduced breeds, particularly for winter shelter and relatively large amounts of fodder and hay. Government initiatives to introduce such breeds were aimed at raising absolute productivity and the quality of products of the livestock. Such schemes have been promoted by all the regional governments of Inner Asia at some time over the last 40 years or so. The results have been generally disappointing, as Telenged (1996) points out, since the new breeds have not adapted well to local conditions. In Buryatia, for example, Merino sheep had to be trucked to distant pastures rather than being driven there on foot.

It is also significant that the parts of Inner Asia that appear to have the greatest problems of pasture degradation – Inner Mongolia, Buryatia and Chita – have also experienced the greatest increase in the amount of land used for agriculture. Normally it was the best-watered land that was removed from pastoral use, and this may well have had an adverse effect by forcing hay production on to other land, and increasing the pressure on remaining pasture.

SUSTAINABLE AGRICULTURE

Inner Asia will continue to need to supply agricultural (arable farming) produce, both for fodder and for human use. Although arable farming is not the focus of this study, we note that agriculture, as it is now organised in many regions, presents a major threat to sustainable land-use. As the experience of Buryatia shows, the application of a Russian agro-industrial strategy using deep ploughing and chemical fertilisers appears to have created very serious damage to much of the thin steppe soils (Gomboev et al. 1996; Gomboev 1996). Attempts to reverse this by irrigation, planting wind-breaks, etc. have not been widely successful. In general it is doubtful if an agricultural policy based upon intensive land-use and heavy agricultural machinery is sustainable in much of this region. By contrast, Erdenebaatar (1996) describes pre-revolutionary ('traditional') agricultural practices in Uvs (Mongolia) that represent an alternative, and historically more durable, approach to crop cultivation. Land was tilled in rotation, allowing much of the agricultural land to remain fallow. The fields were worked using animal-drawn ploughs, and manured with dung from the associated herds of livestock.

Another model, specifically for intensive hay-production, was the 'traditional' Buryat *utug*, the use of riverine lands to make irrigated and manured fields producing lush fodder grasses. It may be possible in the future to develop small-scale cultivation along similar principles, with groups of households carrying out farming activities using smaller light-weight machinery, and reviving earlier techniques of irrigation. This could be carried out alongside the extensive grain-crop agriculture which is sustainable in certain parts of Buryatia, Tuva and north Mongolia (Humphrey 1984), while unproductive and damaged ploughed areas are returned to pasture.

Sustainable pastoralism and livestock stocking rates in Inner Asia

Pasture degradation in certain regions of Inner Asia is severe, and we argue that current livestock production practices are unsustainable in a few places, such as in the Barguzin valley (Buryatia). This raises the general question of 'sustainability' and how we use the term. As Arrow et al. (1995) have observed, sustainability, like 'carrying capacity', is not a fixed static or simple relation – for either animal or human populations. It is contingent on technology, preferences, and the structure of production and consumption. It is also contingent on the ever-changing state of interactions between the physical and biotic environment. Environmental sustainability is related to ecosystem resilience: economic activities are sustainable only if the ecological resource-bases on which they rely are resilient. In any one region there may be multiple locally stable equilibria, and resilience is a measure of the size of disturbances that a system can absorb before it flips over from one equilibrium to another (Arrow et al. 1995: 4). Ecological resilience is difficult to measure and varies from system to system, but there are signals that provide early warnings of essential ecological changes. We thought it would be useful to refer in our work both to local (herdsmen's) perceptions of environmental degradation and to the assessments of regional specialists. Among the former, with reference specifically to pasture conditions, we found that herders listed: marked reduction in the diversity of grass species; observed diminution in the growth of grasses over the annual cycle; increase in unpalatable grass species associated with over-used pastures; decrease in density of vegetation distribution; reduction in water levels in rivers; and expansion in sandy areas and dunes. Herders and local specialists also make assessments about the number of years required to reconstitute a flourishing pasture after it has been turned over to agricultural use, and after specific types of degradation. With regard to the assessments of regional specialists, we have taken account of professionally produced models of carrying capacity for pastures of given types (e.g. in Gomboev et al. 1996; Loucks and Jianguo 1992: 59).

These two methods of assessing sustainability each have their advantages and disadvantages. The herdsmen's judgements are specific and reliable, but they do not enable us to judge quantifiably whether a given pastoral system is sustainable or not. The professional specialists' models are based on plant productivity, mathematically abstracted over a whole region, and are subject to a variety of problems (for further discussion in relation to

Mongolia, see Sheehy 1996).[7] However, they do enable analysts to use such models to make judgements about sustainability in given sites.

Figures 2.7–2.9 show livestock densities in Inner Asia. They are based on local government statistics for each of the regions.[8] In general, livestock densities reflect the pattern of rainfall distribution shown in fig. 2.10). There are relatively high concentrations of domestic animals in much of Inner Mongolia, notably the south-eastern areas (where there are also substantial amounts of agricultural land), such as Jirim *aimag* and Chifeng prefecture. There appears to be noticeable impact upon vegetation cover in these two districts, probably linked to both agricultural and pastoral land-use.[9] These regions also have some of the highest levels of reported pasture degradation (figure 2.11). Much of the pasture land in Buryatia and Chita also has high stocking levels, and in general these regions also have both static pastoralism and the most significant problems of pasture degradation in Inner Asia. The herds tend to move only between limited summer and winter pastures, and in some areas (e.g. our Chita case-study) they remain on one site throughout the year.

Mongolia, on the whole, has lower livestock densities than other parts of the region. Interestingly, however, certain relatively well-watered regions of central Mongolia have stocking levels that are comparable with those of Inner Mongolia and the Russian districts (see figure 2.9). Such Mongolian areas have relatively high levels of annual precipitation (300–500 mm), but this is little higher than the eastern parts of Inner Mongolia. What is significant is that these densely-stocked parts of Mongolia have few if any of the problems of pasture degradation that are reported in Inner Mongolia. It is notable that the best-stocked regions of Mongolia are mountainous, particularly parts of the Hangai range. These areas are not noted for long nomadic movements, but the frequency of movements of herds is relatively high (see chapter 6). High stocking rates are also found in the mountainous west of the country, where there are some of the longest annual movements. It seems likely that the range of climatic and pasture conditions that can be found in more mountainous regions tends to allow for high numbers of livestock.

Taken together with the findings from the other case study sites discussed later, the comparison with Mongolia suggests that the severe problems of pasture degradation reported in areas of Inner Mongolia and Buryatia/Chita have at least as much to do with agriculture and the low-mobility pastoralism practised in these regions as with absolute numbers of livestock *per se*.

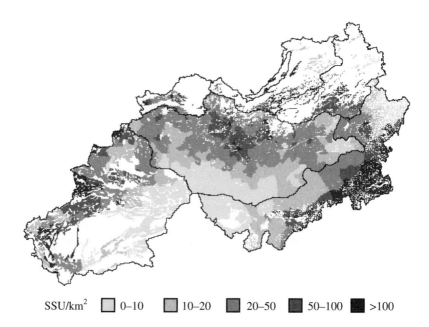

SSU/km² ☐ 0–10 ▨ 10–20 ▦ 20–50 ▦ 50–100 ■ >100

FIGURE 2.7. Camel, horse and cattle density in Inner Asia, 1992

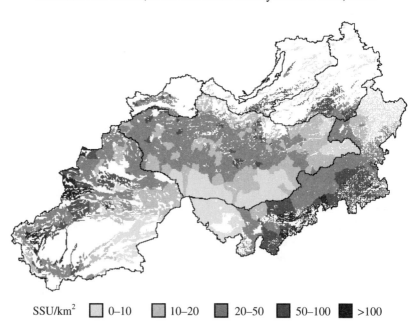

SSU/km² ☐ 0–10 ▨ 10–20 ▦ 20–50 ▦ 50–100 ■ >100

FIGURE 2.8. Sheep and goat density in Inner Asia, 1992

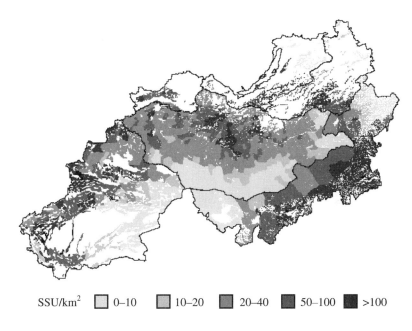

SSU/km² ▢ 0–10 ▢ 10–20 ▢ 20–40 ▢ 50–100 ■ >100

FIGURE 2.9. Total livestock density in Inner Asia, 1992

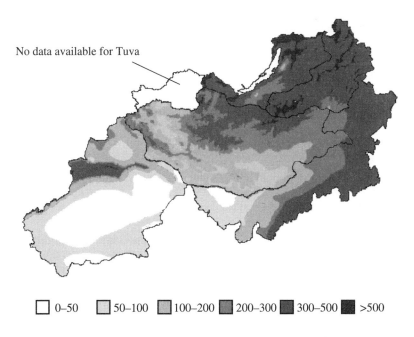

No data available for Tuva

▢ 0–50 ▢ 50–100 ▢ 100–200 ▢ 200–300 ■ 300–500 ■ >500

FIGURE 2.10. Mean annual precipitation in Inner Asia (mm)

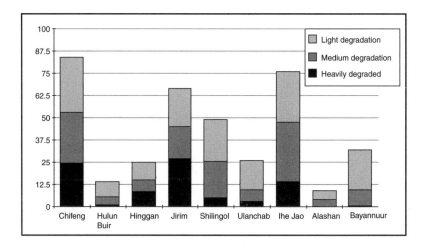

FIGURE 2.11. Percentage of pastures considered to be degraded in leagues and prefectures of Inner Mongolia

In Russia (Buryatia, Chita, and Tuva) the situation of pastoralism is not uniform. One of our most interesting findings is that while the Buryat and Chita case-study sites appear to be suffering from extremely serious problems of pasture degradation, the Tuvan site is not.[10] Tuvan stocking levels are lower, but not hugely so. This would suggest that the Tuvan pastoral strategy, being more mobile and more closely resembling that of Mongolia, is much more sustainable. Tuva has retained local breeds which do not require long periods in static winter shelters.

A particularly visible feature of figures 2.7–2.9 is the high density of sheep and goats found on the Inner Mongolian side of the Chinese-Mongolian border, most noticeably in the Gobi region. There is a less dramatic contrast in the stocking levels of large animals. This indicates that Mongolian pastoralists in the arid Gobi regions continue to keep relatively low numbers of small animals, as a proportion of the herd. Alongside low mobility, the keeping of higher numbers of small herbivores in these arid regions may be another important reason for the contrasting levels of pasture degradation reported in Inner Mongolia and Mongolia. The rise in the numbers of sheep and goats in this century, and its possible implications, are discussed below.

PASTURE DEGRADATION AND MOBILITY

If we narrow down to look at the findings of the case-studies, it appears that stocking rates alone are a poor guide to the levels of perceived pasture degradation, except at the extremely high concentrations found in the Buryatia and Chita sites. This is illustrated in figure 2.12.[11]

While in the Buryat districts of Argada and Gigant there are both high stocking rates and very severe problems of perceived pasture degradation, Ovyur, in Tuva, has a stocking rate that is higher than that of many other sites, and yet had almost no reported pasture degradation. The State Farm at Solchur in Ovyur does, however, have a relatively mobile pastoral system. Pastures are not fenced or limited by agriculture, as they are in Argada and Gigant. The comparison with Inner Mongolia is illuminating. The increasingly sedentary Hargant site in Inner Mongolia, where most pastures are allocated to individual households, actually has a comparatively low stocking rate, and yet also reported serious problems of pasture degradation.

Thus it appears that in the open steppe case-study sites the amount of livestock mobility is a better guide to the amount of reported degradation of pastures than the stocking rate. Having said this, we recognise that there are

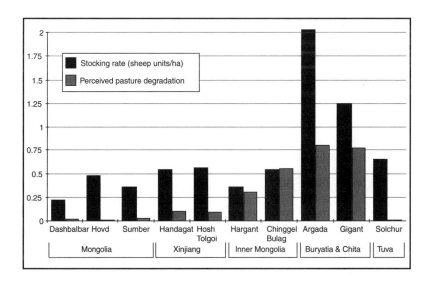

FIGURE 2.12. Comparison of stocking rates and perceived pasture degradation in case-study sites

persuasive arguments for the importance of stocking rates in arid environments (e.g. Sheehy 1996), but a wider comparison, involving whole management systems over a long period, seems to support the widespread perception among herders in our case-study sites that a low amount of livestock movement has been a major cause of pasture degradation. One of the most significant changes in the pastoral systems of Inner Asia has been a reduction in the amount of mobility of certain sectors of these pastoral economies. This topic is more fully discussed in chapter 6. Here we note only that in Mongolia and Tuva pastoralism seems to have retained mobility to a greater extent than in other parts of Inner Asia and to have less reported pasture degradation, and this suggests that mobility may have an important part to play in future sustainability.

The allocation of pasture land to individual households that is being carried out in Inner Mongolia and Xinjiang is historically unprecedented in Inner Asia. It raises the question as to what extent such allocation will continue to reduce the annual movement of livestock in the region, as this policy does seem to have reduced mobility in the case-study sites. These themes, and the implications of these developments for pastoralism, are taken up again and explored further in chapter 6.

PASTORALISM, PRIVATISATION AND MARKETS

The broad patterns outlined above developed during the collectivised period and are still evident today. However we now need to discuss how current economic organisational changes are likely to affect the situation. We move our focus from sustainable use of the steppe environment to the processes of local reform. Privatisation has developed in different ways in the region. In the Russian areas (Buryatia, Chita and Tuva) some form of collective production has been preserved in most districts and independent individual herding enterprises are few in number. This topic is discussed in detail in the next chapter, but we give a characteristic account here, from the field-notes of project member Balzhan Zhimbiev at the Gigant collective in Chita region:

> Privatisation started in May 1992, when the first private farmer Alexander Budaev separated from the collective farm with his retired father and mother and his wife. All of them took their shares of Gigant collective farm property, such as animals, vehicles and plots of land. But most of the people didn't want to separate from the collective farm, because the political and economical situation is very unstable in Russia and they are afraid of being private

farmers. When I visited Novaya Zarya settlement in October 1993 about five collective farmer households had become private. These farmers were not so successful. The farmer Budaev is an example, even though he had obtained a lot of help from the Farmer's Association in the administrative centre of the Ononsky *raion* [such associations were organised in many districts to help private farmers, but their staff mostly consists of former *raion* communist leaders because these associations have many privileges]. Budaev still has a very low interest rate for his credit in the bank. But now such arrangements are impossible. New farmers have great difficulties obtaining money, animals and vehicles. This is mostly a problem of inflation. Another trouble is that a lot of collective farm machinery, lorries and tractors are broken, and people can't divide them into shares. All this refers to the official movement of privatisation in Gigant collective farm.

But another aspect of life in the Gigant collective farm is that illegal 'privatisation' is very popular. For example, if a collective farmer drives a lorry he can use this vehicle for his own profits – he can illegally carry loads and ask for payment. The same happens with tractor drivers. And herdsmen who live on the *otara* [herdsmens' settlements] use these places as if they were their private property.

Privatisation in Mongolia has been more complete. The head of Dashbalbar *sum*, 45 year old Tsagaanhüü, explained the process in his district:

The process of privatisation started in September 1990 after the adoption of the Mongolian privatisation law. In the middle of September 1990 there was a meeting of the members of the *negdel* [collective]. Some of the members (the 'administration group') wanted to reorganise the administration but to retain the system of the *negdel*, and other members (the 'democracy movement') wanted to completely privatise the *negdel*'s property. At that time the total property of the *negdel* was valued at 34.2 million *tögrög*s and that amount should have been divided between the members of the *negdel* (and all their family members, including children). This would have meant that each person would have got 37 head of livestock (1 camel, 5 cows, 5 horses, 20 sheep, and 6 goats). After a very heated discussion only 14 families decided to leave the *negdel*.

After a few months [in February 1991] when the living standards of those 14 families had improved, there was another meeting where the members of the *negdel* decided to dissolve the *negdel* organisation completely. At that time the number of livestock per *negdel* member was 21.

Other property like houses, tractors etc. was difficult to privatise. Some of the machines became the private property of the people who had worked with this equipment, who gained them using their coupons, but most of the machines were left in the farm as the property of a company which was based on the former collective farm. Most of the herdsmen were not satisfied with this situation. After the dissolution of the *negdel* the tractors were given to the tractor-drivers as their private property. The tractors are not used very often at the moment because the drivers don't have the petrol and spare parts. This means that herdsmen now cut hay by hand or use horse-drawn hay-making machines.

In China privatisation was carried out earlier, in the early 1980s, within the parameters of the 'responsibility system' of contracts between herders and local state institutions, described in the following chapter. An administrator in the Handagat district in Xinjiang described the result as follows:

> Well, perhaps I am not a suitable person to talk about the privatised system. I think that, on the one hand, the contract system is successful as it has freed workers and managers of institutions like ours to concentrate on production. The system has brought out so much energy among the people that they can now do things which were undreamt of before, and their living standard has been raised dramatically. So the system has encouraged activity throughout the economy. But everything has its weak points. This system is no exception. In the past two years, I think the situation has been getting worse, because it is impossible to make contracts properly. For example, hospitals, banks, and other institutions important to the well-being of people, tend to be profit-orientated. I am afraid this will definitely have a negative impact on the living standard of people and they will think that the government no longer cares for them. I also think that we do not have a very effective legal system to protect the contract system and the interests of people who have made faulty contracts. So my opinion is that on the one hand, the system is working well but on the other hand, it is far from perfect and this may result in some unexpected negative effects on the stable development of our farm as well as the country.

As these comments indicate, although the picture is not black-and-white, it is clear that there is a contrast between the relative *economic* success of the Inner Asian regions inside China and those formerly under Soviet domination (Nolan 1995). Mongolia is facing particularly grave economic difficulties. Real wages halved between 1990 and 1992, and then declined by a third in 1993. More than a quarter of the population is now living below the poverty line, and that line is very low. Unemployment has shot up, and is set to increase (World Bank 1994: iii).[12] Infrastructure, local government buildings, schools, and health facilities are decaying.

The reduction in buying power of most of the population has added to the difficulties of economic disruption. The shift towards subsistence, found in the Russian and Mongolian case-studies, suggests that some of the economic measures designed to promote the circulation of goods on the market have actually subverted it. As Shombodon (n.d.) points out, privatisation led to most rural families owning livestock, and as a result the market for pastoral products has declined. This has created worse conditions for herders, and most rural households are short of consumer goods and non-locally produced foods (rice, flour products, fruit, sugar, etc.).

Sayana Shangyr, the head of the district administration of Solchur in Tuva, does not look to the market as a solution to such problems. Born in 1948, she lives with her husband and three children in the district centre, and has an intimate knowledge of local attitudes towards the pastoral economy. She explained the aims of pastoral households in her district in the following way:

> There are several ways to improve our lifestyle in the future. First of all it is necessary to increase the total number of private livestock, especially now, when there are no restrictions on the numbers, as there were in the past. This will give us a chance to supply ourselves with all kinds of necessary food-products. Surpluses could be sold.

These comments indicate that for many pastoral households the consumption and sale of private livestock is primarily aimed at meeting the household's subsistence needs. Even in Inner Mongolia, where economic reforms (including the private ownership of livestock) were introduced in the mid-1980s, the ability of many pastoralists to change their herding practice in response to market fluctuations appears to be limited, and subsistence production continues to be important.

Rural networks, often based on kinship relations, are of key importance to the pastoral societies of Inner Asia. These networks link herding and urban families, and provide channels along which many goods and services flow. One implication of the importance of this Mongolian 'indigenous service economy' for the reform process is that a fully commoditised rural economy is unlikely to develop in the near future (see chapter 4), particularly in view of the difficulties of transportation in this vast country. Networks provided a way of operating within and beyond the socialist collectives, and today in rural areas they are often the only way for herders to obtain or sell goods. Even in and near towns, where free market transactions are a possibility, individuals usually prefer to use their networks. Subsistence production, together with production for minor exchange along these networks, will probably remain the first priority for much of the pastoral population for as long as real incomes remain low relative to food prices.

A comparable situation exists in Russia, even though various forms of collective farm remain dominant. An earlier study for the ECCIA project ('The return to subsistence in Tuva', Interim Report 1993) showed that, even within collectives, subsistence production on small 'private plots' has become the priority for the members. Collective production continues to decline drastically. A cycle has developed in many places whereby low prices for meat, wool, milk, etc., late payments, and increased difficulty in obtaining credits have all resulted in the collectives being unable to make regular wage payments. Without wages the farm members are forced to turn to subsistence production as a priority. Let us take the case of buying milk in the city of Ulan-Ude. You can usually buy it in the central market, and you could even buy it far more expensively in a supermarket. But somehow one never seems to meet anyone who does not normally 'acquire' their milk from their network.

Mongolia does not have Inner Mongolia's economic advantages of inclusion in the growing Chinese economy, financial confidence, or easy access to huge markets with a wealth of consumer goods. It seems unlikely, then, that Mongolia will be very successful at promoting widespread rural market orientation in the short term, given the economic difficulties it still faces. In Inner Mongolia and Xinjiang, herders are increasingly being polarised into those with the technology to support relatively large herds and able to benefit from market conditions, and those forced to short-term (often environmentally harmful) strategies to maintain subsistence. Although the herders in the Chinese regions of the Project are generally more market-oriented than those in Mongolia, the pastoral economy as a whole in China suffers from its peripheral position in the vast national economy and from the fact that myriads of small producers are not in a position to influence market conditions.

RURAL PASTORAL POPULATION

Writers on the Soviet Union have noted that the 'period of stagnation' saw a feminisation and at the same time a tendency towards ageing of the rural population, as young people escaped from the 'dead-end' of the collective farms to the cities (Timofeev 1985). However, our studies show that, in the 1990s in Inner Asian regions, this observation is unfounded as least as far as the local statistics go. In Russia in 1992, women were under 50% of the population in Argada and Solchur, and only 51% in Gigant. Women were less than half the population in all the other sites studied (ranging between 46%

in Sumber to 48.6% in Hargant). One reason for this pattern may be higher female mortality in childbirth in rural as opposed to city locations (see Medvedeva 1996: 176-204). Although women are not subject to army call-up, they may perhaps leave rural areas more easily than men by marrying city residents; they may stay longer in higher education, and they may be more easily accepted into urban relatives' families than men. As regards the presence of aged people (60 years and over) we found no evidence of an aged population left behind in rural localities. The percentage of aged people ranged from 8.4% in Argada to around 6.5% in Dalanjargalan (near Sumber), and the highest proportion was found in districts relatively distant from cities, like Hovd *sum* and Argada, while districts close to towns, such as Solchur or Sumber, had much lower percentages (from 1.2% to 3.8% respectively in 1992). This suggests that very old people will often if possible leave the arduous life on the pastures and go to live in more comfortable urban settings.

The patterns noted above emerge from formal registration of district membership, and they may disguise temporary out-movements by young people engaged in trade, business, and 'hanging-around' in towns.

STANDARDS OF LIVING

It is notoriously difficult to compare standards of living in different countries with different political systems, currencies, and state provisions. However, one of the most important things for pastoralists is their wealth in animals. In the socialist period the majority of livestock was owned by collective or state farms, but now only in Russia are substantial numbers of livestock still owned communally. Figure 2.13 shows the proportion of private, official (e.g. state farm, army, school and other local government organisation), and friends'/relatives' livestock herded by interviewed pastoral households in each case-study site in 1993. Since then, the proportion of official livestock has decreased, and the private category, both households and friends'/relatives', has increased. Now that the incomes of pastoralists increasingly depend on their private holdings, rather than wages, the buying power of their products is a central factor in evaluating their standard of living.

The Buryat case studies show relatively low numbers of private livestock per herder household (about 17% in Gigant and 30% in Argada). At the time of the study most of the livestock in Gigant belonged to the collective, and the professional herding households were each allocated a high number of animals to raise. In other words, the number of herded animals was high (c. 620 sheep units per household), but the number

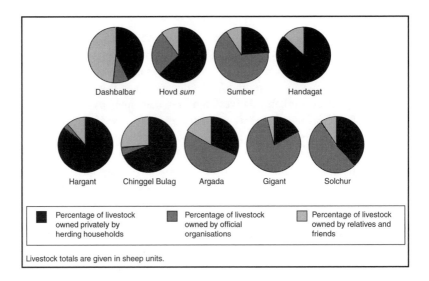

FIGURE 2.13. Comparison of ownership of livestock herded by interviewed pastoral households in case-study sites

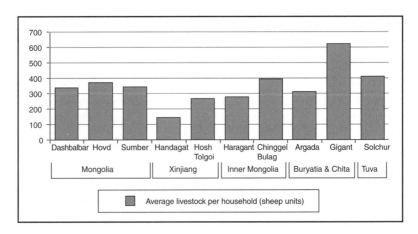

FIGURE 2.14. Comparison of average number of livestock herded per pastoral household

These are district averages calculated by dividing the total number of livestock in each district by the number of pastoral households.

privately owned was low (c. 100). In Mongolia and Inner Mongolia the number of private animals per herder household was several times higher. The improved performance of the Chinese economy is not, however, reflected in markedly higher numbers of private livestock per herder household as compared with Mongolia. Figure 2.14 shows that the Mongolian and Tuvan totals are within the same range and the Chinese figures are, if anything, slightly lower.

All through Inner Asia, it is the herder households who keep most private livestock, while officials, workers and staff such as teachers and doctors have relatively small herds.

It is often observed, both by commentators and by the people of the region, that privatisation leads to growing differences in wealth between rich and poor. We investigated the patterns among the interviewed households in the case-study sites. In the three sites in Russia the total number of livestock herded per household was not very differentiated. There was some differentiation in the holdings of private livestock (e.g. from 50 sheep units in the poorest to 500 in the richest household in Solchur), but in general these differences were less marked than elsewhere in Inner Asia. In Mongolia a growing differentiation is observable in the districts where privatisation was most advanced in 1993 (e.g. in Hovd *sum* private holdings ranged from around 50 sheep units to 800). We found the greatest differentiation in the Chinese parts of the region. In Hosh Tolgoi (Hoboksair), for example, private livestock ranged from zero in the poorest herder household to nearly 1,600 in the richest, while in Chinggel Bulag the range was from 5 to 1,800 sheep units.

Studies of Russian peasantry around the time of collectivisation suggested that, in the vast middle category of small-holders, the 'wealthy' tended to be those with the largest households and that they did not comprise a large separate class of *kulaks*. With this in mind, we investigated the relation between wealth in livestock and household size. In none of our case-study sites, however, was there a significant correlation between the two.

Even in rural areas, ownership of livestock is not the only path to wealth. In several districts we found a handful of very rich individuals, who had made money through entrepreneurial trading activities. They invested their money in trucks and other vehicles (reflecting the great economic importance of control of transport in Inner Asia) and they also invested some of their wealth in livestock, for example, establishing a herd of horses, as the Mongolian elite has done for centuries. One such rich entrepreneur in Mongolia set up a herd of horses and several flocks of sheep, treating them not as a pastime but as economic investments (see chapter 6 for discussion of this kind of strategy).

Perhaps most important for living standards is the significant difference in the buying power of key pastoral products in the different countries. Figures 2.15 and 2.16 show the much higher buying power of wool and beef in China. In order to make these comparisons we valued the pastoral products in terms of their ability to buy a basket of commonly consumed goods essential to most pastoral households (five kilos of flour, one packet of cigarettes, one kilo of beef, half a kilo of sugar, and half a litre of vodka). The graph suggests that in Mongolia pastoralists generally have worse terms of trade than in Russia and substantially worse than in China. Interestingly, there are also large differences within countries, reflecting differences in marketing opportunities and transportation costs.

The standard of living in a region is also reflected in various types of property, movable, productive, and residential property. Here we found that, contrary to the other indicators, the Russian areas did best. Pastoralists were relatively well-equipped with movable property (TVs, radios, motor-vehicles, fridges, etc.), as they were with productive property (milk separators, sewing machines, tractors, and generators) and with housing (discussed in chapter 5). In Mongolia, on the other hand, herders were generally poor in such items.

CROSS-BORDER TRADE

Since the end of the Cold War, the frontiers that have divided Inner Asia have become less impermeable, and the region has begun to regain a measure of the economic interdependence that characterised the early twentieth century.

Economic transactions across national boundaries are increasingly important. Mongolia has turned from its former almost complete dependence on Soviet and East European trade (which accounted for 97% of Mongolia's total trade in the late 1980s) to commercial links with over 20 countries.[13] Mongolian trade is, however, still dominated by the giant Erdenet company, in which Russia retains a large interest. This company, producing copper, molybdenum, coal, cement and cashmere, generates nearly 70% of Mongolia's foreign earnings and almost 60% of government income. We, however, are concerned with trade in the context of rural livestock production. As the power of the state structures has declined in Russia and Mongolia, such produce is increasingly flowing across national borders – to markets in neighbouring regions – rather than being channelled through the state administrations centred in national capitals and republic centres.

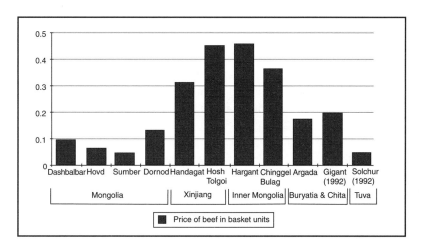

FIGURE 2.15. Buying power (1993) of 1 kilo of beef in terms of a basket of goods

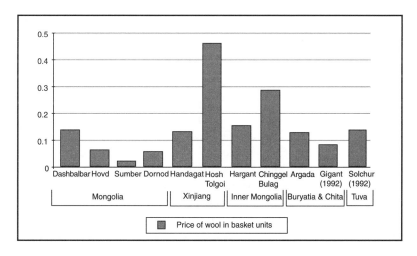

FIGURE 2.16. Buying power (1993) of 1 kilo of wool in terms of a basket of goods

Basket composed of 5kg flour, 1 packet cigarettes, 1 kg beef, 0.5 kg sugar, 0.5 litre of spirits

Such cross-border trade is carried out by means of local agreements, often by barter and often unofficially. This trade gives increased power to regional and district administrations, and even to local companies. An example is the three-cornered trade between farms in Dornod *aimag* (Mongolia), Chita Oblast (Russia) and neighbouring districts of Inner Mongolia (China). Mongolian farms trade hay to Russia and wool and milk to China, in return for which they receive petrol and spare parts from Russia and manufactured goods from China.

This is perhaps evidence that the economic dislocation experienced by Mongolia and former Soviet parts of the region is leading to Inner Asia becoming increasingly economically peripheral, supplying raw materials, including animal produce, to the more powerful industrial centres nearby – particularly in China. The marked reduction in the ability of the central Mongolian government to extract pastoral produce, and to invest in local factory production, is also contributing to the flow of materials to China, and the increasing return of Chinese consumer goods. The more 'inner' the region of Inner Asia, the more economically peripheral it seems to be becoming. Thus, although the more 'outer' regions of our Project (Buryatia, Chita and Inner Mongolia) have more dense industrial development than Mongolia, they in turn are dependent on the cities located in nationally developed zones.

The only alternative to this trend toward economic marginality is large-scale investment in processing and distribution systems. Without this, Inner Asia is bound to trade its primary produce for consumer goods manufactured in more industrial centres, which largely lie outside the region. Mongolia receives a large amount of foreign aid and soft loans – around 25% of GDP in the mid-1990s (Bruun and Odgaard 1996: 26) – but most of this goes on poverty alleviation and running costs rather than new investment (Sanders 1996: 238–45). The neighbouring pastoral districts of Chita, Buryatia and Inner Mongolia receive no foreign aid. Investing in the livestock economy is not a priority in any of these countries at present. For much of its history, the region has only experienced such investment as a result of action by the State governments of the area, and it seems unlikely that foreign companies or international organisations will readily fulfil this role in the future.

It has been argued (Campi 1996: 95–7) that 'nomadic cultural values' have disinclined the indigenous peoples of Inner Asia from entrepreneurship in general, and that modern trade with both Russia and China is usually viewed as exploitation rather than an opportunity to acquire wealth. Our studies broadly support this view, though minor trade to make ends meet is now part of many people's lives. And perhaps matters are beginning to change. In Mongolia, now that the Russians have largely left, the Mongols are now having to come to terms with trade. While it remains the case in Russia and China that industry, mining, engineering and processing tend to be dominated by Russian or Han populations, trading and retailing are activities in which native firms are starting to make an impact. In Buryatia, for example, a few such firms have become successful through links with the regional administration and through the entrepreneurial energy of the young generation.

THE ENVIRONMENT FOR PASTORALISM

It is probably true that the main threats to the relatively fragile steppe ecology come as much from factors outside pastoralism as from those internal to it. Apart from the particular dynamics of pastoralism which are the main concern of this book, the causes of environmental damage include a) industrial and military developments which destroy pasture land and cause pollution of water sources;[14] b) the break-down of social order, leading for example to relaxation of forestry protection and wild animal conservation; c) the abandonment of Soviet army bases, military airfields, and open-cast and below-ground mines without clearing-up measures; and d) new large-scale economic initiatives that, although potentially positive, require careful planning, especially the exploitation of oil deposits and construction of hydro-electric power installations. Except in Mongolia the area available for pasture has been continuously shrinking. And even in Mongolia the possible future abandonment of 'inaccessible' pasture (see chapter 3) may result in a significant decrease in productively used land. These processes must remain of the utmost political importance to the local and national governments of the region, which are increasingly being forced to adopt measures to protect the long-term productivity of the land. In the short term food security is already a problem for the poorest people in Mongolia (Griffin 1994), Buryatia, Tuva and Chita. This is largely a problem of distribution of resources.

However, in the long term, developing sustainable pastoral economies on a smaller resource base – pastoralism being the sector of the economy on which the region has always depended – may be the most difficult challenge facing regional administrations, since the population will not turn overnight to other forms of production. Furthermore, environmental proc-

FIGURE 2.17. Unloading milk at a dairy, Hargant *sum*, Inner Mongolia, 1993 (photo: Hurelbaatar)

esses cannot be divorced from the economic and political climate, or the wider cultural context in which pastoralists manage their own domestic economies.

A concrete example of the complexity of these inter-relationships is the ecologically worrying situation in Hargant (Hulun Buir, Inner Mongolia). Rising prices made it important for the poorer herders to sell milk. The allocation of specific pastures to households has not prevented many people staying all year round on their pastures closest to the district centre. One reason for this was that the only local dairy was located in the *sum* centre. It was run by a Chinese, and consisted of a large dirty shed with some ancient equipment which produced only low quality milk powder and industrial casein. Milk powder was not in great demand as cows were numerous in the district, and the quality of the product was so low that it could not be easily sold in the nearby city of Hailar. So the dairy was unable to pay the herders regularly for their milk. Nor was it able to collect milk: instead the milk was brought in by the herders. Now the pastoralists continued to deliver milk, even unpaid, because they feared that otherwise they would be left off the roster attached to the dairy. At the same time, the poorer herders tended to stay near the *sum* centre, since this made it easier to transport milk for sale. Many of them preferred a sedentary life, and had houses built for them in a radius of 1–10 km from the centre.[15] The existence of stationary dwellings fixed this pattern, with numerous small herds of cattle clustered near the village. The result was that cows churned backwards and forwards over the land each day. Hargant District in any case has hummocky, sandy and fragile land near the railway line where the village is situated. In recent years large new sand-dunes have appeared, and the sparse grass on them is damaged further by the cows. Local people told us that the dunes grew in size each year, mostly because of strong winds but also because cattle tracks destroyed the grass. Beyond the dunes, over-grazing was said to have caused the spread of non-nutritious species like *Artemesia frigida*.

The district administrators deplored this situation, but said they could do little about it. They had fenced off some small pastures, which showed a dramatic improvement in grass quality. They had also sown some fenced-off areas of the dunes with grass, but the plants looked as though they were only just managing to survive.[16] During our visit the officials were preoccupied with other matters, namely the hay harvest, from which they expected to make most of their income (see chapter 3). The overall commercial situation was advantageous to enterprising herders with good contacts and it also saved the poor households from destitution. But local milk processing did not provide a good income, either in profits to the managers or in tax to the district administration.[17] Though Hargant is not entirely typical, we can see that the local dairy there contributed to the environmental problems of the district.

Informants in some other case-study sites mentioned the problems of an institutional vacuum or lack of co-ordination: for example, in Hosh Tolgoi (Xinjiang) the County grassland authorities had established a 'suitable' stocking rate for those pastures, but local people, including officials, said, 'We have no ceiling here'.[18] Orie Loucks and Wu Jianguo (1992: 65) have written, 'The most serious problem in the grasslands of the Northeast is the absence of institutional mechanisms for translating the results of grassland research into more effective grazing systems that can be adopted on a wide scale.' Of course, there may be discussion about what constitutes an 'effective grazing system', and whose interests are advanced in its pursuit, but the point about institutions is well taken. The extent and nature of the various rural institutions of Inner Asia are the key to understanding pastoralism and how it is changing.

Chapter 3

Rural Institutions

Caroline Humphrey

Introduction

The main aim of this chapter is to compare the different institutions which support the pastoral economy in Russia, Mongolia and China. The local institutions of high socialism, People's Communes in China, and state/ collective farms in Russia and Mongolia, have been dismantled in varying degrees. The present situation is one of ongoing change toward new institutional and economic forms, particularly in Mongolia. It would be wrong to assume that there is some 'default position', some generic Inner Asian society, to which people have recently returned. What we have to analyse is a new range of institutions. These are taking form in relation to the current economic situation and yet also bear some legacy from previous eras. What follows is an attempt to analyse the role of these emergent rural institutions in the pastoral economies of Inner Asia.

The chapter first introduces the main categories of institutions and then provides an overview of economic and social developments in Inner Asia. There then follows a detailed discussion of each country, Russia, China and Mongolia. It is not possible to cover exactly the same topics in each country, as they differ from one another significantly. Mongolia is dealt with more briefly than Russia or China, as chapters 4 and 6 introduce considerable material on Mongolian institutions. This chapter then returns to a thematic discussion of security, integration, leadership and communal religious ritual over the whole region, and ends with a conclusion which suggests possible trajectories for institutional changes in the future.

Let us begin with some very general observations. If one were to go to Inner Asia today (1997) one would find in the RUSSIAN areas of Inner Asia (Tuva, Buryatia, Chita Oblast) that herders are still for the most part attached to collective institutions – the *sovkhoz* (state farm) and *kolkhoz* (collective farm). Many of these were reconstituted as 'associations', 'unions', etc. after

Moscow's agricultural reform campaign in 1991–93, but in practice they operate much like the old collectives. All of these large-scale agricultural enterprises generally have several hundred members and control most of the pastoral and crop land of the smallest district of local government, the *selsoviet*. However, since the early 1990s, the state has retreated from the running and financing of these farms. The relation of the herders to these institutions has also changed: it is now based on individual contracts, rather than the previous statutory obligation to fulfil a planned norm of production.

In MONGOLIA de-collectivisation has been pursued in many ways more radically than in Russia, though state organs retain some management functions in pastoralism. The early 1990s saw the break-up of most of the socialist institutions – *negdel* (collective farm) and *sangiin aj ahui* (state farm). They were either disbanded or divided into a number of companies (*kompan*) and at the same time a range of firms and co-operatives were set up. Recently, many of these enterprises have collapsed, so around two-thirds of the livestock in the country are kept by private family-based herding.

In CHINA (Inner Mongolia, Xinjiang) the state-managed People's Communes began to be replaced in the early 1980s. Now, the district government and other state organisations retain important managerial and service functions with respect to the pastoral economy, but the overwhelming majority of 'economic units' are more or less independent households, usually with their own allocated pastures. These have contractual relations to supply produce with the district administrations.

The 'traditional' practice in the pre-revolutionary period in the open steppes of Inner Asia was not organised solely by small-scale nomadic groups but was framed, and even arguably supported by, large organisational forms. General access to bounded pasture territories was controlled and co-ordinated by ruling officials. In Mongol-inhabited areas, along with flexibly organised small herder groups of one or more families (*ail, hot,* or *hot-ail*) the large institutions were Buddhist monasteries, banners' treasuries managed by the ruling princes,[1] and noble patrimonies. The first two of these had their own institutional property, a fund called *jas*, consisting of livestock, land and money. In Mongolia and Inner Mongolia the animals were herded by monastery serfs (*shabinar*) or banner princes' serfs (*hamjilaga*), while a further class of state subjects (*albat*) paid taxes and performed labour services.[2] The large monastic foundations with their own territories and people functioned as districts equivalent to banners, but there were also numerous smaller monasteries located inside the princely banners (see chapter 6 for further discussion).

In the forest-steppe regions of the north the Buryats and others practised a different type of pastoralism involving the use of fertilised hay-fields (*utug*) by transhumant herders living in dispersed summer and winter villages. The hay-fields were communally managed by local kin-groups which allotted inheritable shares in them to their members. The monasteries in this region were attached to parishes consisting of 'administrative clans'.[3] The economic role of monasteries was limited by regulations of the Tsarist government and they held much less land and smaller herds than in Mongolia. The large numbers of animals donated to them by the faithful were rapidly converted into other forms of wealth. However, in the easterly Aga steppe, which was open grassland, a more mobile type of pastoralism was practised, similar to that in much of Mongolia. Here certain aristocrats and lamas had vast flocks, which were herded for them by clan members and clients together with their own private animals.[4]

The property of banners and monasteries was corporate and was in principle separate from that of the high lamas and aristocrats who led them.[5] The leader's role was highly important in these institutions and, like other ideas of social status, was generally regarded as legitimate by the ordinary people: it was seen as ordained in the nature of things (by divine incarnation, by inheritance, etc.). However, small groups of revolutionary reformers appeared among both lamas and laymen in the first decades of the 20th century. As described in chapter 1, the pre-revolutionary institutions were abolished during the 1920s–30s in Mongolia and Russia and by the 1950s in China. They were replaced by socialist institutions. It is not possible here to develop any detailed comparison between the two, though similarities in the management of herd mobility are discussed in chapter 6. However, it is worth pointing out that the socialist productive institutions also operated as corporations, and that members again worked for them along with keeping their own private animals. Of course the socialist institution was vastly different from the earlier ones, notably in the fact that it did not operate through externally given social status such as 'commoner', 'nobility', etc. Instead, for the most part, by its operation, it conferred status on its members, classing them in a variety of ranks and specialist occupations ('cadre', 'technician', 'herder', etc.), which gave them both rights and duties.[6]

Very generally one might postulate that in recent years there has been a move *from status to contract* as the basis of economic relations in Inner Asia. This phrase calls up certain images: a historical shift to modernity, a move to legal as opposed to governmental sanctions, a change in the basis of property rights, or the separation of sovereignty from ownership. However, our studies show that these points are debatable as far as actual relations in rural Inner Asia are concerned. People certainly talk of and use 'contracts' (*kontrakt* in Russian, *he tong* in Chinese, *darchilig* in Inner Mongolian, *geree* in Mongolian, *keree charar* in Tuvan), but what these terms mean has to be understood within the discourse of the political economy of the various countries. Therefore, rather than searching for manifestations of some abstract notion of 'contract', it is more profitable to examine the organisational bases of the existing rural institutions in Inner Asia. This is not an easy task even for one country, let alone on a comparative basis.

In order to have some basis for comparison it is useful initially to divide rural institutions into two types: *state* (governmental) and *non-state*, and then to subdivide non-state institutions into three categories, those based on communal or corporatist principles, those based on associations, and those based on the household. Perhaps these categories require some further definition. STATE INSTITUTIONS can be very various, but their common feature is that they are part of wider hierarchically-organised structures managed and financed by the government. By CORPORATE INSTITUTIONS is meant a non-state type of organisation which is conceived as a unity, in which sub-groups or individuals are replaceable members. An ASSOCIATIVE INSTITUTION, on the other hand, is one in which the organisational form is arrived at by agreement between those who come together to set it up, and the institution's existence is dependent on continued collaboration between the participants. Finally, a HOUSEHOLD INSTITUTION is one in which the family, sometimes together with helpers or hired workers, is legally constituted as an economic actor, i.e. as a unit of decision-making and economic responsibility, and an accounting unit.[7]

On this basis, if we look in a very general way at the main institutions existing in rural Inner Asia today, we can see distinct and different distributions in the three countries.

	State	Non-state corporate	Associative	Household
Russia		*	*	
Mongolia	*	*	*	*
China	*			*

TABLE 3.1. The distribution of institutional types in rural Inner Asia

Table 3.1 is not meant to be more than an initial starting-point for discussion. It refers to the *predominant* institutional forms in each country, and only in the areas studied by the Project in 1992–3. Thus it should not be used to deduce, for example, that there are no remaining state-run economic organisations in rural Russia. The most important point is that the present situation is not immutable. Thus it will be described later how some collective institutions in Russia are changing from the corporate to the associative type, while farming for subsistence by households within collectives and associations is increasing in importance. In China there is much less strong development of associative types of institution.

This chapter focuses on rural institutions at district level. However, we can only understand local societies when we see their place in the wider structures generated by the central states and in relation to governmental policies. The state institutions at local level are like the tiny corners of giant state pyramids, constructed in each country in their own way, and made up of their own materials.

Russia	China	Mongolia
Central State	Central State	Central State
Republic/Province (*oblast*)	Province	Province (*aimag*)
County (*raion*)	Prefecture	District (*sum*)
District (*selsoviet, somon, mestnaya admin.*)	County (*hoshuu, xian*)	Sub-district (*bag*)
	District (*sum; xiang*)	
	Sub-district (*gachaa; toshun*)	

TABLE 3.2. State administrative hierarchies

In China, and to a lesser degree in Mongolia, the district governments themselves currently play important parts in economic management of the pastoral economy. This is not the case in Russia (or perhaps it would be more true to say that it is not legally the case, as will be explained shortly). In Russia the main economic agents are collective institutions recently 'freed' from state control.

The chapter now proceeds to a description of the situation in each country, using data from the case-studies carried out by the MacArthur ECCIA Project in 1992–3. The questions that form the underlying rationale for selecting the materials to follow are: What are the institutions present? What are their aims? how effective are they at achieving these aims? and, How do the institutions operate in practice in relation to the local economy?

ECONOMIC AND SOCIAL OVERVIEW OF INNER ASIA

Economically, the three regions show enormous contrasts. As noted earlier, the Buryat and Chita regions of our Project in RUSSIA have long since gone down the road of agro-pastoralism. This has involved using economies of scale, specialisation of herds, intensification (ever higher livestock density on limited pastures), mechanisation, and the introduction of new, 'more productive' breeds – all of which was done by means of the large collective farm (*sovkhoz* or *kolkhoz*). Agro-pastoralism was a central state policy in accordance with Russian ideas of progress. The more urbanised and mechanised a way of life, the more developed it was considered to be. Arable farming (bread!) was valued more highly than livestock farming, as was shown by the state prices paid for products. In a very general way, perhaps we can say that these ideas derive from the fact that the Communist revolution was inspired by the ideology of the Russian *urban* proletariat (Humphrey 1983).

The same policy was followed in Tuva, but the effects have been different from those in Buryat regions. Static dwellings and use of hay were integral to Buryat herding long before the Communist period, but Tuva had these traditions only in certain areas. Furthermore, because Tuva only entered the USSR officially in 1944, it experienced full collectivisation far later (1950s–60s) than in Buryatia. In Tuva the proportion of rural dwellers is higher than in Buryatia, the arable area is smaller in relation to available land, and the herding practices are more mobile.

State socialist policies in Russia brought by the 1970s relatively good living conditions (good infrastructure, education, medicine, veterinary support, housing, consumer goods). Unsuccessful state and collective farms were buttressed by state loans in order to even out living conditions in rural areas. But central government policy is now to make farms as independent as possible. Every one of the benefits mentioned is in decline. The personal economies of most rural people in Russian Inner Asia are now dominated by simple production for subsistence. The disastrous environmental inheritance of mass agro-pastoralism in Buryatia is documented by Tulokhonov and Manzanova (1996) and Gomboev et al. (1996). The latter authors go so far as to argue that pastoralism cannot be sustained in the Barguzin valley unless the herds are cut by two-thirds and the species composition radically changed. Hay and cultivated fodder yields are so low that in the recent past the herds in virtually all of Buryatia and Chita Oblast could only be sustained by importing hay from Mongolia. Recently this supply has stopped and livestock numbers have declined dramatically.

In CHINA the policy since the early 1980s of promoting market economics under state control has brought increased prosperity to herders. A small number of state farms are retained in most areas, but the 'household responsibility' system preponderates. This has been accompanied by divisions of most types of pasture and allocation of them to households, which has encouraged a tendency to settle or to reduce migrations. The role of the local government (state and Party) in managing the pastoral economy of districts is far less than it was during the commune period (Tsui 1996b: 218), but remains stronger than in Mongolia or Russia. Terms of trade have improved for livestock products, with the result that many herders are better off than equivalent agricultural workers. However, there are growing differences between the living conditions of richer and poorer herders.

The previous central state policies, the effects of the Great Leap Forward and the People's Communes, had already damaged large areas of pastureland in both Inner Mongolia and Xinjiang. Of course, environmental degradation varies in these vast regions, and Chinese methods of assessing over-grazing have been disputed for some areas (Goldstein, Beall and Cincotta 1990). Nevertheless, some facts appear to show that a crisis is impending. In Inner Mongolia degradation of pastures was estimated by Chinese experts at 36% of total pasture in 1988 (Longworth and Williamson 1993: 82).[8] Hay production is sought as the only way to sustain the huge herds through the winter months. But in many places the hay is insufficient. Now Chinese Inner Asia has not so far developed arable fodder cultivation to any great extent. However, the Chinese government policy is informed by an idea of progress, according to which settled and highly mechanised farming is superior in all circumstances – the upgrading of the 'peasant', as it were. Some European writers share this view. Hell and Quéré (1993: 287) conclude their study of three pastoral banners in Ujumchin (Inner Mongolia) with these words: 'The only solution to avoid a new crisis of over-grazing is to augment the fodder resources for the winter, either by sowing grasses, or by cultivation of fodder crops; in this way one would pass from a pastoral system to an agro-pastoral system.'

The agro-pastoralism envisaged here will not be the same as in the Russian case, since it is likely to be founded on household production. A great deal rests on what kind of institutions carry out agro-pastoralism, on what scale, and for whom, as well as on the technology used, the differing economic conditions and local ecologies in each region.

MONGOLIAN pastoralism has surprisingly positive features for a country that is often supposed to be developmentally 'backward'. There is virtually no serious pasture degradation in Mongolia. At the same time livestock density in standard stocking units (SSUs) in certain favourable areas of the country is comparable with that in the Russian and Chinese zones of Inner Asia. The Mongolian case studies, which were not in favourable regions, indicate that even in these places the number of SSUs per household among herders is about the same as in Russia and only slightly smaller than in China. These herds are sustained only to a small degree by hay and hardly at all by cultivated fodder. They exist on extensive grazing of natural pastures, which requires mobility, skill, flexibility of decision-making, and local co-operation on specific tasks to function at its best.

Under Russian influence Mongolia took some steps in the direction of agro-pastoralism in the socialist period: arable farming, development of new breeds, building of livestock shelters, mechanised hay cutting, etc. in state and collective farms (Humphrey 1978: 141–52). But it seems that many aspects of these developments are now being reversed, as the collectives have disbanded (Telenged 1996: 181–3). The important point is that Mongolian pastoralism was always managed in such a way that it allowed virtually the full reproduction of the grass-cover; and until recently, as noted above, the highly productive grasslands of northern Mongolia in effect subsidised the Buryat and Chita herds.

Today, to summarise, the environmental status of the pastures in the three countries contrasts with the economic prosperity (or lack of it) of herders. Economically, in China the close presence of markets and relatively high demand for pastoral products means that herders can make a good living, but in Russia and Mongolia, the distance of markets, the high cost of production inputs like fuel, and low demand, all depress the livestock economy. In Russia and Mongolia the prices for livestock products like meat, cheese, wool, etc. are very low, while food requirements like sugar, tea, flour are expensive, and manufactured goods are beyond the pocket of many people. This point is simply illustrated in table 3.3.

Let us briefly consider the pastoral district as a social community. In Russia, very small numbers of herders living in the countryside 'support' much larger numbers of village dwellers in the administrative centre – officials, pensioners, mechanics, drivers, accountants, bakers, hairdressers,

	Environment	Economy
Russia (Buryatia & Chita)	poor	decline
Russia (Tuva)	good	decline
Mongolia	good	decline
China (Xinjiang & Inner Mongolia)	problematic	growth

TABLE 3.3. Environmental conditions and economic prosperity
compared in Inner Asia

etc. (see table 3.4). In Mongolia the ratio of herders to village dwellers is variable, ranging from highly rural districts like Hovd *sum* to districts close to towns, like Sumber near Choir, where the village/countryside figures approach those in Russia. In Inner Mongolia, by contrast, the herder families are unequivocally in the large majority.[9] The number of officials is relatively small, and services employing many people tend to be located in county towns and large cities rather than rural district centres. As a result districts as communities tend to have a different social composition in the three countries. In Russia urban culture reaches into the village, which is consequently more diverse and includes more people with higher education (for further discussion see chapter 5). In China, the village is more co-extensive with the countryside and less of a centre. For example, herder households at the edge of one district are free to sell their milk to a dairy in another district rather than their own. Herdsmen may make economic links, e.g. with traders, that bypass the district-level centre altogether. In Mongolia most of the people who were previously supported by the pastoral collectives are now themselves struggling to exist with small herds.

Table 3.4, based on our field-study sites, confirms that in Russia a larger proportion of the district population lives in the village than in Mongolia and China. However, the sites were in some cases not typical: Hosh Tolgoi in China and Sumber in Mongolia have unusually large village populations because in both cases coal-mines are sited nearby and the workers live in the village; and Handagat is also untypical for China, in that a state farm is situated there.

These different patterns broadly correspond to the size and importance of the large-scale 'collective' institutions still present in Russia and, to some extent, Mongolia (in 1993 Sumber still had a state farm, which was privatised in 1994 and turned into three companies). With collective-type

	Population density person/sq.km	Livestock density SSU/sq.km	% district population in village	% of useful land cultivated	% pasture considered degraded
China					
Chinggel Bulag	0.7	54	19%	0	54.4%
Hosh Tolgoi	2.1	56	84%	0.3%	?
Handgat	3.25	54	52%	0.44%	12.0%
Hargant	1.4	36	43%	0	22.9%
Russia					
Argada	11.3	270	84%	33%	88.3%
Gigant	4.0	125	90%	18.8%	76.9%
Solchur	1.8	65	77%	0.9%	1.5%
Mongolia					
Hovd sum	0.96	48	43%	0.008%	0.07%
Dashbalbar	0.4	22	40%	0.17%	0.03%
Sumber	1.56	36	68%	1.2%	2.0%

TABLE 3.4. Population and livestock density in case-study districts ·

SSU = standard stocking unit. Sheep = 1; goat = 0.9; cattle = 5; horse = 6; camel =7.
'Useful land' is all land not specifically unusable for farming economy as a whole,
i.e. it includes arable and haymaking land. 'Pasture' is land specifically designated for
pasture.
The figures given here for Sumber do not include the administratively separate town
of Choir.
Source: local respondents at case-study sites in 1992 (Solchur) and 1993 (other sites).

institutions a relatively large percentage of the district population could stay
in the central village,[10] whereas in China most of the livestock are legally or
practically in the possession of households living in the countryside.

There are distinct differences in the socio-economic character of the
pastoral districts in Russia and China. The predominant types of institutions
are fundamental to these differences. In Russia communal (corporate)
institutions at district level are still important, even though their economic
position is dire. They include a diversity of social functions, and they support
a complex local society in which herders are in a small minority. In China and
Mongolia such communal institutions are now very few. The district administration exerts a certain control over herding, but has fewer of the other
functions found in Russia. Herders are in a majority in the district, and this

is because most non-herding activities (trade, education, construction, etc.) are performed by a number of state departments or firms based in nearby towns.

I now turn to a more detailed examination of the district-level institutions existing in the three countries, and their practical import for the pastoral economies.

RURAL INSTITUTIONS IN PASTORAL REGIONS OF RUSSIA (BURYATIA, CHITA OBLAST AND TUVA)

The state and corporate institutions

In the communist period there used to be three interlinking systems in rural areas: 1) the local government structure of Soviets, 2) the Party structure, and 3) large economic enterprises, the state (*sovkhoz*) and collective (*kolkhoz*) farms. The county (*raion*) was divided into some 5–15 districts (*selsoviet*) and each district was usually dominated by one state or collective farm (see Humphrey 1983). Close to the Chinese border there were also some military farms (*voenkhoz*) to supply army cantonments, and there were mines and industrial plants in the region, also mainly under military jurisdiction. The military complex spread into north-east Mongolia. One of our Mongolian case-study sites, Dashbalbar district, contains the 'secret' Russian town of Mardai, where there was a uranium mine with associated industries.[11] However, the Russian army withdrew from Mongolia in 1990 and also reduced its forces in Chita Oblast. Some of the military farms were returned to civil authority. In 1991 the Communist Party lost power.[12] Of the Soviet-era panoply of power, this leaves the LOCAL GOVERNMENT STRUCTURE and the DIRECTORS OF FARMS as the main players on the local scene today.

In the Soviet period the collective or state farm was something approaching a 'total social institution'. It had a corporate identity, was often given an heroic name, and farms were pitted against one another in constant competitions. The farm combined economic with numerous political, social and cultural functions. It was thus very different, and intentionally so, from the model of a western firm, which is almost entirely an economic organisation. *Kolkhoznik* (member of a collective farm) was a socio-political *status*, with its own rights and duties and political representation at higher levels. State and collective farms were large organisations with several hundred working members and up to 3,000 population. Besides the village centre there were several other smaller settlements as subordinate brigade centres and the whole had a distinct territorial boundary. A sense of community was fostered by the fact that such collectives were dominated by a single ethnic group to which the farm leaders also belonged.[13] Farms provided their members with guaranteed wages, living accommodation, pensions and social insurance, medical facilities, kindergartens and schools, shops, central heating, fuel and firewood, fodder for privately-owned livestock, transport for migrations, clubs, libraries and recreational facilities. Farms funded and organised cultural events and festivals. They also provided essential infrastructure, such as local roads, wells, and electricity. Most farms operated with substantial subsidies from the state. The economic reforms of the early 1990s, which aimed to privatise these institutions, were not thus simply economic reforms but undercut a whole way of life.

The factory-farm techniques introduced by these collectives were based on intricate bureaucratic measurements of time and labour, similar to the commoditisation of labour noted in Hungary by Lampland (1995). The resulting 'economising' attitudes towards time and labour can be contrasted with more relaxed practices still prevalent in rural Mongolia, and they seem to have unravelled after the demise of close planning and control.

As part of the reforms, according to a Presidential Decree of autumn 1992, the social functions of the enterprises were to be transferred to the local government. Meanwhile, however, local government itself was overturned. The communist-era *soviets* were closed down and replaced by Local Administrations (*mestnaya administratsiya*). The budgets for social provisions were not secure. Not surprisingly, the jurisdiction over such services has remained uncertain and now (1994) it varies in different areas of Russia. In autumn 1994 collective and state farms were still assuming responsibility for some services in parts of Russia. News of the 1992 Presidential Decree spread uncertainty. In Tuva, for example, at the end of October that year the Director of a state farm was explaining how women were the backbone of the work-force, especially in medical and education services. On hearing this, the Project researcher explained that enterprises would be freed from these responsibilities from the current year, and she notes: 'When we explained this to our respondent (the Director) he was overjoyed.' The services would be kept on, but the farm would not have to pay for them. In Buryat regions the farms moved faster. By 1993–4 in the case-study sites at Novaya Zarya and Barguzin the collective farms had handed over responsibility for paying doctors, teachers, librarians, nursery-school teachers, culture and sports workers. As a result, many of the services closed down. Though the employees continued to live 'on the farm' their wages became uncertain. The farms continued to provide fodder, transport, electricity, water, fuel and machinery for their members. Work-related pensions were also paid by the farm, though family and child-support grants were paid by the state.

In general, the communal or corporate ideas associated with these large farms are still strong. Members create histories for the farms. Even if a given farm today is a result of external decisions about boundaries, amalgamations, etc., everything is spoken of as if the history was a locally-engendered and natural process leading to the current identity. Many farms have their own museums showing their own histories. In 1990, while Moscow was in the full swing of reforms, the Karl Marx Collective Farm in Barguzin was organising an exhibit of the life of Karl Marx, illustrating his inspiration to the farmers and the visit of his grand-daughter to the farm.

Contracts within corporate institutions

In the late 1980s, under Gorbachev's *perestroika* , state and collective farms were instructed to go on to a system of CONTRACTS WITH FAMILY TEAMS, replacing the previous 'high socialist' system of production norms according to centrally allocated plans. The operation of the family team system in rural Tuva is described in Humphrey 1989. Essentially this reform made little difference to rural life, since it was adapted locally to conform to the previous system: herders continued to be paid monthly wages, though these were now termed 'advances' for the sum to be earned from handing in produce under the contract, and the level of contract work and prices were set so as to enable the continuation of the earlier planned norms. Herders had no choice about whether to take out a contract or not; they had little if any say in how many animals were to be herded, and no say whatsoever about the prices at which the farm bought them. All produce up to the level of the plan or above still had to be sold to the collective. As in the old days, there were few, if any, penalties for not fulfilling the plan. Likewise, there were no penalties if the farm did not fulfil its side of the contract either. One can only conclude that the principle of 'status' remained: herders now had the status of holders of contracts. But it was an uncertain one, sharpening their dependency on the Director. The district head of Solchur *selsoviet*, Tuva, was 44 year old Sayana Shangyr. Identifying closely with the state farm administration, she explained the way the farm was operating in 1992:

> Since we now work with the contract system we have only one approach to workers who do not fulfil the plan: dismissal and cancellation of the contract with them. If you cannot cope with the plan – go away, no further discussion. In this way the contract system wins out.

The dismissed contract-holder is no longer a member of the farm and may lose all collective benefits. There is a moral element to this: we were told that if the dismissed person is 'sorry', recognises his/her mistakes, and wishes to try again and works hard for a year, then he or she may be accepted back as a member of the farm.

Unemployment is now a recognised problem in Russian farms.[14] Women and young people are particularly badly affected (Manzanova 1995). The unemployed have no recourse but to subsist on their private plots, with help from relatives. Even the employed are not much better off, as wages often remain unpaid for months. Private plots, including vegetable and hay plots, private livestock, pigs, chickens, etc., have been much expanded. Members of farms look after these as well as carrying out their jobs for the collective. An indication of the general poverty is that 59% of the inhabitants of Buryatia were estimated to live below the poverty line established by the Trade Unions in 1992 (Budaeva et al. 1992).

Since the early 1990s prices have been freed and various edicts have been issued instructing collectives to 'privatise'. What have been the results in the Russian parts of Inner Asia? 'Privatisation' refers not to the expansion of the 'private plots' of farm members, but to 1) reconstituting collectives as private companies, and 2) the allotment of a share of the farm's assets to a household or group which then sets up as a 'private' farm.[15] The degree and nature of privatisation is variable, but the net result is that large farms basically continuing from the old Soviet type still dominate. Paradoxically, this is a result of democratisation, the right of the members to choose the form their institution will take. In Buryatia in early 1994, of the 206 former collective and state farms, 60 collective and 49 state farms (about 53%) had made no formal change to their status. Six state farms had become collective farms. The remaining 97 organisations changed their status. Sixty adopted some form of collective ownership. Twenty became limited companies, four became agricultural co-operatives, five became joint stock companies, and eight became subsidiaries of other enterprises.[16] Many of the 'companies' in fact operate like collectives, with the same internal structure. The situation in the case-study sites was:

• Solchur, Tuva: state farm with contract system (summer 1992)

• Argada, Buryatia: state farm with old socialist-era plan system (summer 1992); privatised (summer 1993) and association created 1994

• Novaya Zarya, Chita Oblast: collective farm with contract system (winter 1993).

A schematic diagram of the management structure of the state farm
Ak-Bedik at Solchur in Ovyur District in Tuva in 1992 is given in figure 3.1.

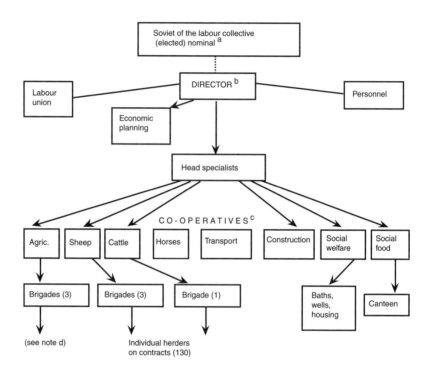

FIGURE 3.1. Organisation of a Tuvan state farm

a. The 'soviet of the labour collective' is inoperative; the fact that it was included
    on the diagram is an interesting survival from the socialist period.
b. The Director has leased land to 21 private farmers.
c. The co-operatives are sectors of the farm which now have their own financial
    balances. It is planned to turn these into joint stock companies.
d. These three brigades have collective contracts with the state farm.

Source: Director of the Sovkhoz, K.Sh. Dongak. Formerly the *sovkhoz* Ak-Bedik
(White Peak) was known as the *sovkhoz* Put' k Kommunizmu (Way to Communism).

Collective farms have a similar organisational structure. Figure 3.1 shows that the system of specialist brigades has been maintained. Sheep herding, milk and beef producing, fodder producing, arable, construction and repair sections are separate, the aim being that each works for the benefit of the whole. Since early 1994 state and collective farms have been officially renamed 'collective-share enterprises' (*kollektivno-dolevoe khozyaistvo*) but they are still called *sovkhoz* and *kolkhoz* in everyday parlance. In the rest of this chapter, I shall term this type of farm, retaining a Director, communal identity and continuity with most aspects of the Soviet period organisation, a 'collective'. This is distinguished from other types of joint farm enterprises, 'associations', which are in theory organised on the basis of groups of households (though in practice, most of them hardly differ from collectives).[17]

One reason why collective institutions have been maintained or recreated is the importance of centralised infrastructures and mechanisation. In such farms, roads, electricity, telephone exchanges, machine-maintenance, dwellings, barns and stores are all centralised and also designed for economies of scale (vast fields, massive tractors, etc.). There are many practical difficulties in constructing private household farms on this basis. Also there is the fiscal problem that counties (*raion*) still gain much of their budget from taxing enterprises under their jurisdiction. Even though most collectives are so deeply in debt that they are years behind in tax payments, retaining them is probably a better situation from the *raion*'s income point of view than creating hundreds of private herder/farmers, also unable (or unwilling) to pay. For these and other reasons, the county-level bureaucracies have not moved swiftly to grant permission to those applying to become independent farmers.

Private farmers

Though the stubborn retention of communal institutions ran counter to central government policy in the early 1990s, many farm leaders sat tight, anticipating a change of policy in Moscow. Farm managers were reluctant to hand over land and livestock to individual private farmers. They told us that each hand-over was a loss. They, and the whole corporate institution, 'lost' a worker and productive resources, and who gained? Just an individual.

Only a relatively small number of private peasant farms (*krestyanskoe khozyaistvo*) have been created. In Buryatia in February 1994 there were 2,770 such farms, with 183,000 hectares of land. While this is twice as many as existed a year earlier, it still represented only a very small part of the agricultural sector. The new farms had only 5% of the entire farmland of the republic, though a slightly higher share, 7%, of ploughing land. It is interesting that they produced only 4% of the grain, 1.3% of the potatoes, and 2.3% of the vegetables. In other words, they seem to have been less productive than the collectives (or at least would admit to producing less). This reflects the leaders' reasoning noted above: the new farmers were usually given the worst fields and pasture, and many bureaucratic hindrances were put in their way (Ovyur, Tuva; Bayangol, Barguzin).

A variant on this is the case of Gigant collective farm in Novaya Zarya, Chita Oblast. Here one or two friends of the director were pre-selected to be 'private farmers', and set up as such on central initiative early in the days of reform. Well-supplied with livestock, houses, and machinery they did not refuse. The point of this from the farm's side was pure old-style 'show' (*pokazukha*), to demonstrate that central government directives had been successfully followed.

During 1994 the rate of applications to set up private smallholdings in Buryatia decreased (Nataev 1994a). This is not surprising, given the problems the private farmers experience. Some 40% of them are economically unviable (Nataev 1994b). The legal status of private herders/farmers is still not clearly established, and the conditions of credit and insurance have become difficult. At first the new farmers were given some cash loans, but most of their means of production were allotted from the property of collective farms. The effect was both unequal and economically irrational. Ploughing land was allotted to people with no tractors.[18] One farmer might have a combine harvester, another a tractor, a third a lorry, but very few had all the machinery they needed. As a result some private farmers formed associations, both for seasonal work and for more long-term mutual help.[19] Today, some of these associations are informal, while others consist of hived-off sections of the collective.

To give some indication of the relation between collective, associative and private farms in 1993, let us give the example of the Kurumkan collective farm in Barguzin, Buryatia. The collective itself was divided into three brigades, and had 278 waged workers, six of whom were trained specialists and brigadiers. The collective used 6,324 of the total of 20,398 hectares within the farm boundary. Also within this boundary were two associations, two co-operatives, and eight single household small-holdings. The associations held 347 ha and 1795 ha respectively, the co-operatives had between 100 ha and 2,700 ha, and the private small-holdings had between 2 ha and 200 ha each (in the case of the larger groups their land included forest and other unusable land). It is interesting to consider the names given to the private farms. They had socialist-era overtones, but, unlike the Russian names of the previous collectives, were in Buryat; e.g. Darhan ('smith'), Jargal ('happiness'), Hubisgal ('revolution') or Odon ('star').[20] The household composition of associations is further discussed in the next chapter.

Private farmers/herders told our researchers that they were trying to improve their land and to re-create the traditional Buryat *utug* (fertilised and irrigated hayfields). Sometimes they had to set this land aside for one to two years to allow it to recover. However, despite these positive signs, the general economic situation of private smallholdings is extremely difficult. Even the larger associations lack credits to equip themselves. Loans are now given only to enterprises which can prove their credit-worthiness by sales. The problem is that the products of the farmers cannot easily be sold at a profit. There is a lack of trade organisations in the agricultural/pastoral sphere and the farmers themselves do not have time to engage in selling.[21] Most private farmers work primarily for their family subsistence, and sell the occasional surplus (Argada, Barguzin). There are lengthy delays in payments. For these reasons the movement towards private farming has virtually stopped. Our researchers met with several private farmers who felt that independent work was too hard and too uncertain and wished to go back to collective farming.[22] On the other hand a few (mostly younger) people prefer private farming.

Most private farms consist of a single, kin-based household. However, some are larger and comprise three to six families, with up to 40 adult members in total. In almost all cases the families are related by kinship. Patrilineal clans were still important in rural Buryat life in the 1960s–70s, and, while this form of kinship may perhaps have less force today, cognatic kin networks are used widely (see chapter 4 and Humphrey 1983). Respondents say that strong kinship ties with leaders were helpful in setting up private farms, enabling well-connected people to obtain better land and machinery. In many cases Buryat herders remember six to seven generations of ancestors who had lived on given pastures. It is also said locally that 'those with ancestral ties to the land will take better care of it'.

It is important to note that in some places, such as in Argada (Barguzin, Buryatia), privatisation has been reversed. The state farm at Argada was one of several in the Barguzin valley where land and livestock were privatised and distributed to members around 1992. But this proved unworkable, and a year or so later a collective was re-formed. In Ulyun nearby, where another privatised farm had also gone back to being a collective, 200 workers who had belonged to the earlier farm were left out of the new one.[23] These were not people who had failed to fulfil contracts, but rather they were those who did not have the skills required in the new farm, or were simply surplus to requirements. They are employed on a seasonal/ occasional basis by the new collective, and otherwise live off their private plots. The universal inclusiveness of the corporate institution is now being abandoned. The widespread impoverished rural subsistence, together with occasional destitution, recalls pre-revolutionary conditions.

Local economic solutions and household strategies

Virtually all collectives now operate on the brink of ruin, torn between the expectations of their members (which still often hark back to earlier communal models) and the absence of funds. Directors are using their own initiative to make their farms more self-sufficient. In 1992 the director of the Ak-Bedik state farm in Tuva had started that year to grow barley.

> We'll give it out to the herders. Even in this region unsuitable for agriculture it is more economical to grow grain oneself than import it from another region. We'll have to fence the land to keep out animals, and we'll have to irrigate it. But still it is better. We took this decision, because we know our own situation best. It was not dictated from above.

By June 1994 directors in some places were adopting Draconian measures in order to re-structure their farm economies. The following comments by a farm director in Tunka (Buryatia) are highly revealing, because it shows us the terms in which he understands the problems:[24]

> The more we enter market relations the more difficult our tasks become. With today's high prices, livestock production has simply become uneconomical. So we couldn't help thinking: is it worth going on trying to produce milk? It's simply laughable that we sell milk for only 200 roubles a litre, when to produce that milk we need to pay for fodder, fodder-concentrates, amortisation on our buildings, and electricity, and on top of that the wages of milkers, herders, accountants, the head of the milk production brigade, the watchman, the transport company, the milk lorry driver, the quality control inspection, and so on. The production costs in the end are ten times the price we get. (Uskeev 1994)

This indicates something of the 'top-heavy' nature of production in the Russian system. In Mongolia, all of the costs of producing milk, except perhaps the transport to the dairy, would be born by the herding household. The Director continued:

> We held a meeting and decided to turn the milk herd into a subsidiary, and to do away with mechanised milking, dung clearance, heated fodder, and even

electricity in the cow sheds. We reduced the herds and introduced horse transport. In a word, we have gone backwards, into the distant past.

Trying to solve economic problems in the conditions of this wild market is very strange to us, but we'll do all we can to make sure that redundant people are not completely without work, because the principle of collectivism is more important than anything else. So we decided to start types of production that don't cost much but require many working hands. Namely, we have decided to go into horse herding (360 head) and also Kazakh beef cattle, and for our own use to keep a small flock of sheep, a pig farm, and a fox fur farm.

In the past we used to sow hundreds of hectares of fodder. This year with the new herd structure we have not sown a single one. Instead, we've sown most of our fields with wheat. This is what we'll do with our harvest: we keep some for next year's seed, then we'll pay the working members of the farm their wages in grain, and if there is any left we'll use it to pay off our debts. The workers have already set up their own mill, so they will be able to make their own bread.

The market dictates its conditions. With our finances as they are, we decided at a general meeting not to pay the members' advances in money but in manufactured goods and food. We also decided to allot each household one hectare of land for hay for a year. This is a big gesture from the collective to the workers.

In other words, the farm is turning to an internal, largely moneyless economy, and it is now expecting the herders to make their own hay on their own plots – previously hay was cut collectively by a special brigade.

And there is one very important point. The period a hay-plot is held can only be extended beyond a year if the member works honestly throughout the year for a minimum of 240 days. If they are lazy, the plot will be taken away.

By this move the herders will be deprived of the basic winter sustenance for their private livestock unless they work 240 days for the collective.

Yes, we are all for working collectively and in a friendly way. But every family, as they say, has its runt. So it was decided at the last general meeting that anyone whose attitude to collective work is just to fold his arms will be excluded. There were 37 of them. All the same, we have temporarily given them the right to work as hired labourers for one year. If they understand their mistakes and correct them, then we'll restore them as members and they'll then receive all benefits.

Reports indicate that, in the Buryat Republic as a whole, herd numbers have been drastically reduced, grain and fodder reserves are down, and weeds had covered many ploughed fields (Nataev 1994c). By mid-1993 many collective farms were unable to pay their members money wages. In

Barguzin, for example, six months had gone by without wages in some farms, and by 1996 the situation has only become worse. The farms attempted to compensate by paying the workers in kind and in some places with internal coupons which could be used in the farm shop. The shop was supplied with whatever goods the Director could obtain by barter for products of the farm. The end result was that farm members were requested to work for the collective practically without pay, in return for services and in-kind benefits. The social rationale of retaining collectives today is the provision of services and a certain basic security to the community as a whole. They will probably remain as long as they are able to provide some services for most members.

Household strategies are directed only in a limited way to the market. More or less the only market option is fattening one or two private cattle per year for sale at a nearby town. Sheep have so little value that it is not worth the effort and transport costs. Traders in the villages are few and far between. The villagers' more energetic strategies are involved in reciprocal exchanges with networks of kin and friends, mostly through urban-rural ties. Shoes for eggs, clothes for pork, help with hay-cutting for beef to feed a town family through the winter – these are the kinds of deals being done. Poor people seek any opportunity to obtain things which might be consumed or sold: odd jobs for money, hunting for meat and furs, fishing, distilling alcohol, gathering mushrooms and berries, or taking unguarded objects from the collective. Most household income nevertheless comes from work on one's own plot, from 'wages' and allocations from the collective, and from state benefits (pensions, child benefit, etc.).

Exchange and transactions: collective institutions

Although households and production-teams engage in relatively little commercial activity, collectives were designed, as it were, as exchange organisations. In the Soviet period they were designated at Autonomous Republic (or Province) level as specialising in a certain type of production, such as wool, milk or mutton. These policies were not introduced in order to create self-sufficient units. Although a collective was (and still is) felt to be an 'organic whole', as the Director of Ak-Bedik state farm told us, even the largest farms are not autonomously self-supporting. They are parts of a system of exchange, supplying products to distant cities, while receiving manufactures and so forth in return.

During the 1930s exchange relations between city factories and distant farms were formally institutionalised by a link called 'chiefship' (*sheftsvo*), which was formerly ideological and has now become commercial. One partner in the exchange, the technologically more developed, was senior and became 'chief' over the farm. Raw material supplies were sent from the farm to the factory. It is not so clear what flowed down in the other direction: probably mostly 'technical' advice (Humphrey 1983: 144–6). Thinking this system had fallen into disuse, I was surprised to find that a long-standing relation of 'chiefship' still existed in 1993 between two of the sites studied by the MacArthur ECCIA research project. The Gigant collective farm was 'chief' over Bayantümen *sum* in Mongolia. Activating this link, Gigant was able to secure a supply of hay for its herds. In Soviet times the Mongols might have accepted their status as 'younger brothers', and made do with technical advice in return for their hay. By 1993 they were bargaining for spare parts and petrol from Gigant. This case is an example of the exchange relations which have been the very basis of the reproduction of the Russian agricultural system. *State and collective farms exist on the basis of exchange.* Gigant does not produce either petrol or spare parts. In 1993 it obtained them, partly to trade onwards to Bayantümen, from local units of the Russian army. In exchange, Gigant supplied meat to the army. The meat of course came from the very herds that were supported by the hay from Mongolia.

The herds of collective farms like Gigant still exist in order to supply livestock products to state organisations at externally set buying prices.[25] In theory the set prices aim to keep food products affordable for the city population. However, farms can receive as little as 20% of the shop price.[26] Furthermore, the dairies, meat-packing factories, etc. pay late and owe millions of roubles to the farms (Bazarzhapov 1995). Agricultural prices have risen less than those for manufactured goods. Virtually all of our respondents complained about these facts. Now if a farm supplies a respectable amount of products to the state its director is in a good position to apply for money credits, petrol allocations and so forth. However, today, the compulsory planning system has broken down and the farm management itself can decide what it will produce. Furthermore, a stable legal system to guarantee contracts between institutions is not yet in place. At the same time, private traders are buying meat directly from the herders. All this means that the state organisations, shops, etc. cannot rely on receiving what they need from the farms. Nor can the farms rely on receiving credits and inputs. In this situation, the legacy of the past, the vast flocks of sheep on the diminished, degraded pastures only create intractable problems and these herds are fast being eliminated.

Freed from Party surveillance, the previously more or less supine heads of the administration at district (*selo*) level now have greater authority, but this is counterbalanced by the social responsibilities now thrust on their shoulders. Meanwhile the position of the heads of farms has declined in relation to government officials, precisely because they are no longer masters of resources but petitioners for loans and subsidies. In fact, all local leaders are petitioners and negotiators, and their power is variable, depending on how skilful they are at such manipulations.

All leaders remain linked to centralised structures. The heads of county and district administrations are appointed directly from above. The directors of state and collective farms are sometimes elected by general meetings of their members and sometimes appointed from above. In Tuva in 1992 a state farm director told us that even though he was locally elected he still had to have his post confirmed by the President of the Republic, Sherig-ool Oorzhak. This indicates the continuing close connection between the central government and control of farms, despite democratisation. A network of relationships between farm leaders and government officials is crucial for obtaining supplies and credits. Future economic development depends very much on the interaction of these local political agents.

In short, the Russian part of Inner Asia is characterised by the dominance of large collective institutions of a corporate type occupying most of the usable land of the administrative district. Still basically agro-pastoral in tradition and orientation, they continue to be organised on specialist brigade principles whereby each given section provides services or products for the others. However, the prices and subsidies which used to enable this system to function have collapsed, and reorganisation is having the effect of creating a rump of excluded members now surviving as best they can on subsistence plots. There are relatively few 'private herders' and no new ones are starting up.

RURAL INSTITUTIONS IN PASTORAL REGIONS OF CHINA (XINJIANG AND INNER MONGOLIA)[27]

Central state policies

State institutions in China are responsible for delivering central policies to the population in a way that is no longer the case in Russia and Mongolia. Following the major reform initiated in 1978 the People's Communes were disbanded in the early 1980s. Communal property was distributed to households by contract according to the responsibility system. At the same time central state powers were significantly devolved to provincial and prefectural governments.

It is necessary first to point out some general facts about the pastoral regions.[28] Between 1959 and 1982 Xinjiang and Inner Mongolia had a far greater increase of population than elsewhere in China, and most of this was the result of Han Chinese in-migration (Yuan 1990). As compared with the agricultural regions of China the pastoral regions are disadvantaged in basic infrastructure, education, technology and economic investment (Erdenijab 1996:105). Furthermore, there has been a decline in the area of pasture available to herders. From early this century the expansion of peasant farming into the grasslands had begun to take over pastureland. During the 1950s and '60s, as in Russia, central government dictated further drastic expansion of agriculture at the expense of livestock raising. This took up much pastureland, but in areas unsuitable for crops it soon gave only low yields at best and in many areas was associated with erosion and desertification. With the end of the Great Leap Forward provincial leaders began to argue for a reduction of ploughed land and its return to grassland. The resulting areas of 'reclaimed' pastures are small and often of poor quality. At the same time, throughout this period and continuing to the present, land for industrial, mining, oil development, and military purposes could be taken from the pastures and administered under central state jurisdiction. For example, the herders at one of our sites, Hoboksair, had land removed in this way when Karamay was made a separate prefecture designated for oil development in the mid-1970s.[29] These regional factors – colossal in-migration, urbanisation, industrialisation, shrinking pastures, growing economic differentials between urban and rural areas, and between the pastoral regions and eastern China – influence the general regional conditions in which pastoralism has to survive.

'Let the peasants get rich first', was one of the leading slogans of the rural reforms of the 1980s (Yan 1992). The move towards market relations created economic conditions that allowed pastoralists to create a surge in prosperity for themselves, despite the adverse factors mentioned above. Inner Mongolian herders now have higher incomes than the agricultural peasants of the region (Hell and Quéré 1993: 284-5). Within the limits of central government instructions, households became responsible for their own production and marketing decisions. The policy was for the huge growth in livestock density to be supported by hay production, with accompanying allocation of pastures, sedentarisation, and mechanisation. Pastures were measured and classified according to quality. Stocking rates for the various pastures were estimated and controls on herd size were instituted so as to preserve the grassland. The policy is to increase the output of livestock products and to integrate their economic flow with the national economy in such a way as to produce overall development for the pastoral regions. An ever greater proportion of the pastures are allocated to specific households, and this is intended to ensure that each herder has a stake in preserving the quality of the land.

Nevertheless, the actual stocking rate may have already passed environmentally sustainable limits in some places (though in the case-study districts it is well below the Buryat rate). A seemingly irreversible differentiation of households into rich and poor has taken place (Hell and Quéré 1993: 282). It seems to many that a possible 'tragedy of the commons' is a threat in this situation. The general pressure on resources without strong social sanctions to guard against overuse of common property by those in economically advantaged positions could lead to increasing degradation. The crucial issue is how local social institutions deal with both of these things: on the one hand, the instruction to 'Get rich', and on the other the need to preserve resources so that the totality of households, including the disadvantaged, can maintain a viable pastoralism (for further discussion see chapter 6).

The social institutions of pastoral communities are not just 'structures' of abstract features; they are the locus of agency and practical action. And however much governments may plan to the contrary, they are not static but, historically speaking, transitory and diverse (Tsui 1996b). Governmental institutions in China are indubitably hierarchical, but the relations between those 'in power' and those encompassed by power is increasingly refractory, at each level. Because all institutions are engaged with a number of interconnected processes specific to their regions, the effect is one of kaleidoscopic variety. Let me list the interconnected processes which appear most important in pastoral areas: 1) population migration; 2) changes in property relations (the control of productive resources); 3) sedentarisation; 4) investment for production; 5) commercialisation; 6) provision of social services like medicine and education; and 7) initiatives in manufactures using livestock products. No two of the case-study communities is alike. Looking at how state and household institutions are taking action in respect of these general processes will allow us to see the range of variation and effectiveness.

However, some common dynamics can be observed. Li, Ma and Simpson (1993: 72) go so far as to declare that a revolutionary transformation is under way in Inner Mongolia. They lament the passing of the long era of the culture of nomadic pastoralism, but they continue:

> It is not unrealistic to expect that within a decade a substantial number of former nomadic pastoralists will have telephones, television sets and indoor plumbing. As the country mechanises, the number of draught animals will decrease. Price relationships will develop so that the grasslands will slowly but surely, be transformed from a production system in which cattle and sheep are raised to slaughter weight on grass, to one primarily orientated to a breeding system in which calves and excess lambs are shipped to farming areas for fattening. [...] The trade-off is increased income, more leisure time and greater economic security for herdsmen on China's grasslands.

Only time will tell if this vision of modernisation will be born out in practice. But the replacement of mobile pastoralism with static livestock farming may pose its own threats to sustainable development, as it has done in Buryatia and Chita.

State institutions

Since the early 1980s the local administrative structure has continued to be based on the hierarchy shown in Figure 3.2. The boundaries of the DISTRICT for the most part coincide with those of the former People's Communes. The population is usually between 1,000–4,000 people. Within the district there are some 3–6 SUB-DISTRICTS (*gachaa*). Sub-districts have a population of between 350 and 800 people. They also have definite boundaries, often based on the territories of former production brigades.

After the period of the People's Communes, major reforms from 1978–9 aimed to separate political and economic authority. Formally, four political structures now exist at district and higher levels: 1) the Party, 2) the People's Congress,[30] 3) the Local Government, and 4) the Political Consultation Committee.[31] At district level, however, the LOCAL GOVERNMENT ADMINISTRATION and the COMMUNIST PARTY combine political and economic functions and are the two major sources of power.[32] In effect they are combined, because government officials are almost all members of the Party. At the same time, there are also some large economic institutions, such as state farms, and these have their own separate jurisdiction.[33] Then there are village-based manufacturing enterprises such as dairies. These are both state- and privately-owned. Finally industrial and mining enterprises are dotted around the countryside and they are often administered directly from the state centre. The relationship between these and local institutions is often strained, and sometimes may become openly antagonistic.[34] The daily life of herders is intricately bound up with all of these institutions, or more particularly with the decisions of the officials directing them.

It is important to note that local administrations retain some rights over the land and livestock distributed to households in the economic reforms. Thus it would not be correct to see a simple division between 'state' and 'private' property (see also Bowles and Dong, 1994; Croll 1994). Rather, there is an extraordinarily complex interweaving of rights to resources, only some of which are realised. In fact, the vocabulary of 'rights' and 'claims' will give a mistaken impression of clarity, since the prevailing discourse is in terms of 'responsibilities' (this theme is further discussed below). Along with managing the productive economy, districts have obligations to provide a variety of services (roads, electricity, education, medicine, pensions, etc.).

The COUNTY (Mongolian *hoshuu*, banner) level of administration manages the complex economy of 8–24 districts (Mongolian *sum*), which even in herding areas includes agriculture, industries and trade. Counties set their own buying prices. Banner officials can even be involved in international negotiations. For example, Huuchin Barga (Inner Mongolia) officials told us that they exchanged workers with the Buryat Aga Autonomous Region in Russia: the Russians came to make roads, while the Chinese went to Russia to grow vegetables.

In many ways the DISTRICT (*sum*) level of administration is the most socially relevant for the herders and farmers. The present districts are largely based on communities which existed before the socialist period (Sneath 1991). A district has a settled village as its centre, sometimes also with outlying hamlets, and at this centre are concentrated schools, banks, shops, post office, medical and veterinary services, and small processing industries. The Party and the security services also have headquarters at the district centre. The district has economic plans (one year and 3–5 year plans). However, some districts in poorer areas do not have to supply obligatory procurements to higher-level bodies, and perhaps it is for this reason that our case-study sites varied in the seriousness with which these plans were implemented. District leaders control allocation of land to sub-districts, hay production and the distribution of subsidised fuel.

In some areas important functions continue to be delegated to the SUB-DISTRICTS (*gachaa, toshun*). These include in places a detailed production plan, tax and rent collection, and the allocation of specific pastures to herder households. A *gachaa* has a leader and sometimes other officials too. All herders belong to one or another sub-district.[35]

In-migration and districts as holders of resources

Unlike rural Siberia, where out-migration continues, in China in-migration to pastoral areas is an issue. It has an ethnic dimension, as most incomers are Han Chinese farmers. In the past in-migration was uneven, concentrating mostly on cities, pastoral districts near cities and areas suitable for agriculture. Maps of population density show that in the more remote, mono-pastoral regions close to the western borders of China it is relatively low and not in fact very different from that in the adjacent areas of Mongolia. There may well be a natural limit to the successful extension of agriculture into these areas, as there has been in the past. The integration of farmers into pastoral districts was in some places relatively harmonious (Ma 1993), but in others caused disputes between peasants and herders over water and land. In Handagat (Altai, Xinjiang), for example, such tension is evident. Disputes between sub-districts focus on the greater amount of water used in farming than in herding. However it would be a mistake to assume that such disputes always have an ethnic component, since especially in Inner Mongolia it is not the case that farmers are invariably Han while herders are always Mongols. Large numbers of Mongols are farmers, or mixed farmer-herders, particularly in Jirim and Ju Ud leagues. Whatever the ethnic composition, places subject to large in-migration and over-use of fragile natural resources are approaching ecological exhaustion, and now young people are searching for opportunities for *out-migration* (see also Ma 1993: 188). However, most of the districts studied by our Project are not in this situation. They are locally regarded as successful areas for livestock production and indigent people are still seeking to enter them.

The fact that citizens in China are 'members' of administrative units and pastoralists now have been issued with 'grassland certificates' (rights to individuated pasture) is highly important. In theory it provides a certain base-line security. This contrasts with Russia, where, as has been shown, equivalent rights in collective farms are beginning to be challenged by hard-line Directors. The question arises: how can such rights be implemented in pastoral areas of China? The issue may become urgent, as the Chinese government is attempting to reduce the vast numbers of migrant workers in cities and send them out to rural regions.[36] Although the great majority of such out-migrants are from Han agricultural areas, it is to be expected that some former herders will also be forced to return to their villages. Returnees with money may lease pasture rights from herders, employing yet others as hired workers, all of which will increase economic differentiation.

The district administration is thus the institution primarily responsible for registration of the rural population and providing its members with the means of subsistence. So although all land, and the vast majority of other natural resources, belong technically to the Chinese state as a whole, the district is the local subdivision which guards 'its' wealth.

Contracts and the household responsibility system

The older generation of herders have seen many abrupt changes in pastoral management, all of them initiated from central government. The words of one leader (Hawula, Barkol, Hami Prefecture, Xinjiang, 1993) express the uncertainty this has generated:

> Since 1952 we have undergone a kind of zigzag in ownership of animals. First distribution of livestock to poor households in the 1950s, then collectivisation of the flocks in the late 50s, then centralisation of them into huge organisation, the People's Communes, and finally, privatising them. These years I have been thinking about this problem: did we pay too heavily? And is the present form the best one or not? In my view, it is too early to come to any definite conclusion now.

The major recent economic reform, replacing centrally administered allocation of resources with increasing use of market mechanisms, started to be carried out in the study sites around 1982.[37] The policy included a two-tiered system of local economic management ('the dual responsibility system'), which combined household control of its own resources with co-operative management of larger services beyond the capacity of individual households. The idea was to combine a market orientation of households with responsibility to local and national government. The 'household responsibility' system is part of a wider scheme of responsibilities which have been implemented in a bewildering variety of ways. Figure 3.2, which is limited only to the district level, gives a schematic idea of some of the more common arrangements found in pastoral areas.

The former Commune's livestock was distributed to herding households, or more precisely, households contracted to buy livestock on credit at low prices[38] in return for which they agreed to sell a planned quota of produce to the Commune (shortly to become the District) administration.[39] The numbers of animals allocated depended on the size and labour capacity of the household. As early as the mid-1980s most districts also started to allocate pastures to herders. The period of the lease was for 15-20 years, but in 1989 it was extended to 50+ years (Handagat district, Altai, Xinjiang). Meanwhile, small and medium-sized tools were sold to the herders. Finally, larger machinery, such as hay-making equipment and tractors, was sold off. It is

---

State farms

1) State farms with waged labour
2) State farms with members holding contracts

Districts

1) Districts with livestock sold on credit to households holding contracts to sell products to the state
2) Districts with livestock sold on credit to herders, but no contracts
3) Districts with livestock distributed free to herders, without contracts but with responsibilities

Districts with 1), 2) or 3) above are combined with either of the following:

4) Districts with land allocated to herder households
5) Districts with land allocated to sub-districts and informal arrangements for households within these

---

FIGURE 3.2. Local economic management arrangements

true that in some of the case-study sites certain kinds of pasture remain communal. For example, in Hargant some winter pastures are not officially divided (though informally they may be), while in Hoboksair and Handagat summer pastures are communal and winter sites are allocated to individual households. In Chinggel Bulag all year-round pastures are allocated to each household. With all these variations, it can still be seen that the Chinese system has individualised pastoral land-use to an extent unknown in Mongolia, though the Buryat and Chita cases are not far behind.

Officials told us that they extended the livestock contracts because herdsmen could not, or would not, make the repayments in time. The herders, however, want the contracts to be longer for a different reason. Having experienced the 'zigzag' in policies mentioned above, many of them are anxious about the future. They are afraid the animals and/or pasture will be taken back. Furthermore, as Williams (1996b: 684) shows, heated arguments arise typically whenever a new fence goes up, if only because property boundaries have never clearly been identified. Fences are seen as challenges to one's own entitlement, as threats to community, as signs of government corruption, or administrative failure ('it is everyone out for themselves').

What then is the deeper social nature of the contracts? Contracts between herders and administrative institutions exist within the wider principle of 'responsibility' (*chen bao*). Responsibility at every level is usually specified according to the production plans, which serve to delimit the amounts to be transferred up the system, from households, to sub-districts, to districts, to counties, etc. Goldstein et al. (1990) are correct therefore to write of contract/quotas, and there is some similarity with the Russian system of contracts with family teams described earlier. The official line is that contracts are freely entered into. Therefore, although the prices paid by state institutions for products sold under contract/quotas are usually lower than market prices, they do move with the times, so herders are not seen to be exploited. However, there does not seem to be much choice about whether to be part of the contract/quota system. Rather, the differences observed are in the way the system is managed by districts and the kind and degree of pressure applied by officials to get households actually to abide by the agreements. The pressure is often a quid pro quo matter, arising from the fact that 'responsibility' is a two-way, two-tier system, allowing officials to withhold benefits if contract/quotas are not fulfilled.

Croll (1994) has written of the chameleon-like quality of the term 'responsibility'.[40] Though she is right to emphasise the contextuality of the idea, it is possible to give an example to show the general relation between responsibility and contract. Responsibility is always *for* an object (which could be an economic resource like livestock, or a social group like a village). So, an official A may make a contract (*le tong*) with a subordinate official, B, for B to *chen bao* (take responsibility for) a sub-district. What this indicates is a culture of hierarchy, to which 'contracts' are subordinated.

This is essentially the system operated by officials with regard to livestock and/or pastures. Thus, for example, in Chinggel Bulag sub-district officials have a certain number of households in their responsibility and these are supposed to sell products of the distributed herds to the state according to the plan-contract. Officials also claim taxes on the livestock, pastures and (since 1993) sales of these households.[41]

Nowhere do the reforms mean that land and livestock held under the responsibility system are 'private property' in the exclusive way commonly understood in western economies. Just as the members of Buryat collectives have their 'private plots' on the collective farm, herders in Inner Mongolia have their own private livestock alongside the contracted herds, and contracts of course do not exist for them. Livestock held under contract, on the other hand, are subject to residual rights of disposal (sale, slaughter) held by the district. So in practice, there is a good deal of ambiguity over 'ownership'. While officials often try to put pressure on herders, arguing that animals must be sold to the state, in practice herders sell where and to whom they like and slaughter animals on their own decision. It is not surprising that there is a difference in interpretation between officials and herders with regard to the status of the contracted livestock. Even in Chinggel Bulag, where the animals had been allocated for free over a decade earlier, officials still regard them as held in trust, and they complain, 'They (the herders) think the animals we distributed are their own.' The herders in all of our case-study districts, invariably list such animals along with their own previous herds as 'private property' making no distinction between them. However, when in the presence of the District Leader I asked a woman in Hargant who owned the sheep she was herding, she replied, 'They belong to the state.' 'And those goats?' 'Mine', she responded, with an uneasy glance at the official.

Officials are finding it harder to fulfil their responsibilities through the socialist plans. The head of Chinggel Bulag *sum*, Batbayar, lived in the centre of the district with wife, two daughters and his elderly mother. He explained the increasingly relaxed attitude of the administration towards state plans in 1993:

> In the past if herders could not fulfil the plans they would be 'educated' first, and if it was serious they would be fined. But now it is much less strict. Last year they would have been fined, but this year they will not be fined. Now herders only need to pay the taxes - on animals, on land, on sales.

Control over the flow of goods is increasingly through financial rather than authoritarian means. This is one reason why a tax on herders' outside sales was introduced in some districts recently. Other socialist-era practices are also lapsing. In Hargant (Inner Mongolia) the state grain supply system, whereby payment for produce under the plan was made partly in grain, was stopped in October 1992. Since that time, state prices paid to herders have gone up, and simultaneously grains, flour, rice, noodles, etc. sold in state shops have also risen in price.

Thus, although the responsibility system sets up the official channels through which funds, products, investment, etc. are supposed to flow, in fact they are often diverted away for financial gain. However, in some places and in some jurisdictions the official policies are more tightly adhered to than in others. This can be seen from comparing the household system described above with state farms. The comparison will enable us to see the benefits and disadvantages of greater and lesser state control in the pastoral economy.

State farms in pastoral areas

It is not always realised that state farms – i.e. large, collectively-operated enterprises approximately the size of a district – are still found in rural areas. They are corporate institutions in terms of table 3.1, but are not noted in the table because they are not numerous. However, it is useful to describe them; in many ways the Chinese state farms today are like the Russian ones in the more stable days of the Soviet system. The internal organisation is similar to that of the Tuvan state farm in figure 3.1

There are two types of state farm. The first consists of farms designated to be exemplars and show-cases, using new technology and advanced methods. The second type consists of farms previously designated for strategic and military functions. There are a string of these along the western borders of China, especially along the Xinjiang–Russian frontier and along the Hulun Buir border with Russia in Inner Mongolia.[42] Inner Asian pastoral regions appear to have few of this type, though virtually every county has at least one of the 'vanguard' type of state farm. Today, state farms exist only where there were state farms before, i.e. pre-dating the People's Communes and existing alongside them.

The 'vanguard' state farms operate like districts and are subject to the same hierarchy of senior government (counties, prefectures, provinces). The strategic state farms, on the other hand, have their own separate line of administration which by-passes local government and goes in a straight line, through a system of administrative Bureaux, up to a special Ministry of Agriculture in Beijing. The Ministry provides a separate line of funding from that of the central government. It is a huge organisation, with one central service system for all the farms. The leader of the Bureau in Hailar has the rank of Deputy-Governor of the Prefecture and holds a great deal of power.[43] Workers in this state farm system tend to be better paid than elsewhere, and have good equipment and supplies. They usually include Han Chinese brought in to the area to manage some particular type of production, as well as the native people who were originally living where the state farm was set up.[44] The Bureau provides its own schools, hospitals and pensions. This means the state farms in this system have a light burden of social expenditure, as compared with those under the ordinary administration. Districts under the ordinary administration find social provision expensive to maintain (see below). State farms under the Bureau, on the other hand, can be economically competitive, as they are able to use their profits for investment. State farms can choose whether to opt for the contract system, or the more controlled system whereby herders and workers are paid wages to fulfil plans and the products unequivocally belong to the farm.

Let us briefly review the positive and negative aspects of state farms as recounted to Tsui Yenhu in the course of research in Barkol, Hami Prefecture, Xinjiang. Here the Red Star State Farm (not in the Agricultural Bureau administration) is compared with the neighbouring district of Sarq'ok, which is completely 'privatised'. In Sarq'ok livestock numbers increased much more dramatically than in the state farm (in 1983 the Sarq'ok livestock were already five times the number held in 1953, and from 1983 to 1992 they increased from 234,008 to 298,900 head, even though the district suffered several severe droughts during these ten years). The Red Star State Farm, on the other hand, had restricted herd size.[45] There was an average 10.7 head of livestock per head of population in the state farm as compared to 78.5 per person in Sarq'ok. This does not necessarily mean that the herders of Sarq'ok were generally better off, as we shall see. Hawula, the 51 year-old leader of the state farm explained:

The main function of our farm is to serve as a model for local herdsmen in management and new technologies. In this sense I think we have achieved what we have been asked to do. We never gave up introducing new technologies and new methods of management. Even though in 1984 we were under very severe pressure to sell the animals to the households as they did next door, we tried it only for one year and then we changed the system.[46] We found that when animals were private property there was no way to use new technologies, and it was very difficult to control the herd size and composition and to ask the herders to use the pastures properly. From the production point of view, sometimes we have been successful and in some years we did not do well. The reasons are complex, and the climate in those years is responsible for a large part of our failure. We believe that state production has its shortcomings and its advantages. Since 1984 the grassland of other districts has been seriously degraded, but our situation is much better. As an economist of animal husbandry I am convinced that control of land-use to a certain degree is absolutely necessary. In the past we controlled it too tightly, which was not correct, but this does not mean that government should do nothing to control land-use at all. Otherwise there will be a big disaster for our pastures. You have been to Sarq'ok and seen the situation there. I have been working in this area for 35 years, and I have the feeling that the last 10 years have been a time of unprecedented development of livestock production, but also the time of most serious degradation of grassland and retrogression in breeding of fine animals.

In Sarq'ok the head of the district was gloomy about the future. 56 year-old Turson, who grew up in a pastoral family, explained that in his district herders had increased the number of animals so fast that overgrazing was serious. Every year since 1980 about 5% of the grassland had been degraded, and now only 75–80% of the pastures were usable at all. The height of grasses and their variety had been reduced. The life span of animals had become shorter; for example, the average age of the Barkol horse in the 1960s was 18 years, but now was only 11–14. Then he went on to make an important point. One reason for the decline in pasture quality was that individual herders, based on their own specific territories, could no longer graze different species of herds on a range of suitable pastures. When all the different types of animals graze on one pasture all the best grasses are quickly eaten up early in the year, without leaving seeds for reproduction next year. As a result, low-quality grasses and even poisonous grasses were spreading in Sarq'ok. Turson said:

> Up to now we have not found any way to solve the problem. You cannot stop people from using their pastures in the way they are doing now. And as we do not have a law strong enough to regulate this disastrous way of herding, I am afraid that more damage will be done to our pastures in future. Furthermore, as we have no more pastures to offer new households, they have to share the pastures with their kinsmen, and the pressure on the grassland can only increase.

In the Red Star collective, on the other hand, herders have charge of specialised flocks (e.g. ewes of a certain breed, lambs, or castrated sheep) and particular pastures are designated for each type of flock. Herders are obliged to use artificial insemination to maintain quality. Payment is by monthly wage, with a bonus for overfulfilment of the plan and fines for failure to reach the plan.[47] The contract includes stipulations about pasture-use to avoid degradation of grasses. Leaders claimed that the system had worked well, with 75% of herders increasing their income in a relatively egalitarian way, while the breeding and grassland protection had been effective.

Our research indicates that state farms have a certain degree of freedom in organising their economies. For example, the Yiwu State Horse Farm in Barkol fell on hard times when the Chinese Army ceased to require large supplies of horses; the farm then diversified into agriculture, forestry, and trading. It now includes four trade companies and three factories, including a beer brewery which is the only one in East Xinjiang, and its income has shot up again. Such commercial income is used by both districts and state farms to finance public services. These include not only agricultural services (farm inputs, credit, machinery, product processing, irrigation, etc.) but also the crucial social services, like primary education, pensions and health care, which are such a problem in Russia. Chinese researchers have pointed out that peasants in villages where collective institutions have a strong hold enjoy much better social services than in those villages where collective economies were completely dismantled (see references in Bowles and Dong 1994).

It is not clear to what extent this is a result of extra investment via the Bureaux, or whether state farms are more economically successful in their own right.[48] In state farms leaders are held more responsible for economic performance than in more 'privatised' districts. For example, in Red Star State Farm, leaders and brigadiers as well as herders are fined if the plan is not fulfilled, whereas in Handagat (Altai) herders are fined if they fail to fulfil the plan and leaders are not. The stricter system in state farms seems to encourage better provision of both investment and services. Most importantly, this type of institution has definite benefits for long-term reproduction of the pastoral economy, since with sensible management it enables across-the-board decisions about herding to be practically implemented.

However, an important issue in state farms is the extent to which people can exercise claims for services or have influence over wages. Although an active Trade Union exists in a few state farms, in most districts unions are more or less redundant. People have to make do with whatever is provided.

Household strategies and the market

The slogan 'breaking the great bowl' was used by one of the respondents in Handagat (Altai) to refer to the end of the Commune system, when people were 'fed' by the state. Perhaps the final remnant of the old system was the subsidy of food grains, which ended in October 1992. Now both buying and selling prices on all products have risen dramatically. In general herders have become richer. But what lies behind these statements?

It might be imagined that herders are turning unequivocally to market-oriented production. This is not the case; rather, households engage in a number of practices that react to cultural values and the economic exigencies of particular groups as well as to market incentives. The practices are varied and unexpected, and local administrators have difficulty in steering people along the tracks of government policy. To look at this in the widest perspective we can say that there is a contradiction between the aim of guiding or controlling local herding practice and the general state policy of economic liberalisation. As Madar in Handagat said (referring to his efforts to control herd sizes in his district):

> Before 1984 the leaders, including me, did have the power to take overall decisions. But now, as you know, the animals are the property of the herdsmen and they have a legal right to use their own pastures, which means that they take more decisions than we do. So now our power is limited to supervising them to ensure they keep pace with the development of the whole district, providing the services and new technology they need, and ensuring that the rural development policies of the government and party are carried out. We do make decisions about the livestock and farming economy, but whether they are carried out or not you can test for yourself.

Among the practices herders follow are keeping the 'wrong' kind of livestock, not selling livestock or products, and making the 'wrong' use of land. These will be discussed briefly in turn, together with some further observations on the growing differentiation into wealthy and poor households, as this is an important factor in herders' decisions.

Let us start with market considerations. In 1993 cashmere prices in Handagat were as follows, relative to other livestock products:

sheep wool	1.8 –2.6 yuan/kg, depending on quality
goat cashmere	58–110 yuan/kg
camel wool	1.8–3.0 yuan/kg
sheep	130–150 yuan per sheep (state price)
	135–160 yuan/sheep (private trader)
goats	120–140 yuan/goat

This shows clearly the commercial incentive to keep goats for the purpose of cashmere sales. Goats are an important source of cash income in all the studied sites. In large numbers and in certain areas goats cause environmental problems: they gnaw off the bark of trees and shrubs as well as dig up grass roots, especially in winter and spring. In some pastoral areas of China measures against the keeping of goats have been implemented depending on the severity of the problem. The paradox is that government-backed cashmere factories are also sited in the grasslands of Inner Mongolia. Goats were banned altogether in two districts of Otog Right Banner in Ordos near a large cashmere factory (U. E. Bulag, personal communication; see also Ma 1993: 182). Herders may, or may not, conform to the restrictions. Ma (1993: 182-3) recounts how one rich Mongolian goat-herder laughed at a speech made by the Party Secretary of Sanyiefu asking people to limit the number of their goats. He told his friends that he would only sell his huge (2,000 head) herd of goats when all the grass and bushes in the village were eaten up. Then he would move to the city to enjoy his money. 'What a devil', said the neighbours. 'He will leave us only desert. But what can we do about it?' Far from curbing him, in 1988 the banner (county) government even borrowed a large amount of money from him, at a high rate of interest.

Mutual cynicism is not surprising when government regulations are often wielded to benefit local administrations *as institutions*, not to benefit pastoralism. In the districts studied by the Project goats were not in fact a particular problem, nor were 'excessive' numbers kept. But in Hargant, Hulun Buir, the tax on goats was higher (1.5 yuan per year) than on sheep (1 yuan), to the benefit of the officials. In all pastoral areas there are limitations on herd size.[49] The way this is implemented is variable (for example, the law may state that tax is to be taken on land according to quality while officials actually take tax according to the number of animals). How these regulations are put into force depends on the local power and goals of the officials, and thus they operate to some extent on a different plane from the actual environmental conditions.

However, for their part herders may have less choice than one might imagine about what types and numbers of livestock they keep. This is especially the case for poor households. To maintain a culturally respectable life they must have a variety of sources of meat, milk, etc. that can be sustained and reproduced, and they must be able to cope with additional demands at festivals, weddings and so forth. Although bought goods are replacing home-produced clothing, utensils, and transport animals, we found that the species composition of household herds include a wide range of livestock.[50] Almost no private herders keep just one or two types of animal, so as to gain the maximum profit from their 'investment'. The experience and values of previous generations lie behind these preferences and also influence decisions about what to sell. Neither Urianghai nor Kazakh herders in Altai sell milk, as this is against their tradition. They also do not sell meat, but sell live animals. As Erdenijab (1996: 113) points out selling at the 'wrong' time of year, like spring, does not make best use of available grass; but poorer herders may have little choice. A higher consumption rate together with increased breeding would enhance the productive forces of the pastoral economy. However, it is a widespread attitude among herders in all the case-studies in China that it is better to have wealth on the hoof than in the bank. The result of all these habits and decisions is that, from the policy point of view, herders may have the 'wrong' livestock in the 'wrong' numbers and be 'obstinate' about change.

If rich herders sometimes get away with keeping too many animals, poor herders have recourse to another environmentally damaging practice. In Handagat officials were unable to prevent poor herders from ploughing up the grassland at the spring pastures. The herders complained that since shop prices for grains had risen they had no alternative but to grow their own grain. Grassland specialists in Xinjiang estimate that it takes 15–20 years for ploughed land to return to its previous productivity as pasture.

The differentiation in income between rich and poor herders is substantial and growing. In Handagat the average cash income per household in 1993 was 9,348 yuan per year according to local leaders.[51] The highest income reported to us was 59,050 yuan, while that of the poorest household was 4,603 yuan (both figures for 1992). In Chinggel Bulag a rich herder made 45,500 yuan in 1992. This was made up of 8,500 yuan from sale of cashmere, 2,000 from wool, 2,000 from sale of skins, 15,000 from packing grass, and 18,000 from sale of hay. By contrast, a poor herder made only 1,660 yuan, made up of 560 from sale of cashmere, 1,000 from sale of fox furs hunted by the household head, and 100 poor relief from the district. Impoverished households found it difficult to manage, and were often reduced to slaughtering livestock to make money, thus entering a downward economic spiral in which herding alone no longer made a viable income. A few households had killed or sold all their livestock.[52] Poor herders, and even people only on state salaries like teachers, searched for any opportunity to make money: repairing tools, hunting for furs and meat, selling wood cut in the forest (illegal), gathering mushrooms for sale, collecting precious stones, or raising chickens (note the similarity with strategies in Russia).[53]

The richest herders in our case-study districts were involved in business. In Handagat this took them away to Altai city and they hired two or three hands to look after the herds in their absence. Hiring of herdsmen on a monthly or daily basis was on the increase also in Hargant and Chinggel Bulag. However, the richer herdsmen said it was difficult to find reliable herders for hire. This reflects the fact that competent herders can soon acquire animals of their own and set up independently, while a sizeable proportion of young people are not interested in herding however indigent their circumstances.

Which herders had become rich? We did not hear complaints about the distribution of animals in the 1984 reforms (it was done mainly according to the availability of labour in the household), but allocation of equipment and particularly pastures were another matter. Some herders, those with good contacts among the officials, were able to acquire tractors and hay-making machinery while others were not – a similarity with the setting up of 'private farmers' in Russia in the early 1990s. As Sneath (n.d.) and Hell and Quéré (1993) point out, having mechanised technology allows a household to provide adequate fodder for the crucial winter and spring period, while non-mechanised households usually have to buy hay. Furthermore, the mechanised households make a substantial income from sales over their own needs. The income break-down for the rich man of Chinggel Bulag quoted above shows what a dramatic difference it makes to have machines for hay-cutting and packing grass. In Inner Mongolia small tractors are widely used for traction instead of horses, camels or oxen, and they enable herders to perform numerous tasks more efficiently (fetching water, taking products to sell, moving between pastures, etc.). The general increase in wealth of the last few years has enabled around seven out of ten herder households in Hargant and Chinggel Bulag to obtain small tractors. But only around half the households have hay-cutting machinery.[54] Meanwhile the richest households in Hargant have three or more hay-cutters, which they can use to make substantial profits from sales. In many cases an initial advantage in the distribution of machinery will have contributed to their prosperity.

The most friction has been caused by distribution of pastures. It was impossible to make the initial allocation fair in terms of quality and distance from the centre, even if the amount of land was determined by rules about household size and livestock holdings. The ruling in the early 1990s that households can hold their pastures for 50+ years is intended to make sure that there is an incentive to care for the land. However, as the years passed households changed in their needs for pasture. In the most crowded areas of Inner Mongolia, though not in our case-study sites, many districts re-allocate pastures every few years. This causes endless friction. A boundary is moved, and suddenly neighbours who have been good friends become enemies. In our case-study sites where pastures had been distributed to households, re-allocation is not practised. Therefore, new young herding households cannot always be accommodated.[55] As a result, either a given household is forced to expand in size or members of herding families have to make a living in some other way. Salaried jobs are rarely available. The result of all this is that people in herding districts have a great number and variety of practices that have their own momentum, irrespective of the approval or disapproval of the Party and District officials.

Commerce and trade

Both rich and poor families turn to commerce, though for different reasons. Handagat in Altai was the most remote of our case-study sites in China, but even there shops, restaurants and repair shops had increased nearly three-fold since 1984. (Contrast this with the Buryat situation, where private shops in rural areas have mostly folded through lack of custom). Almost all of these enterprises, etc. are private. Some are run by relatively prosperous village women, and some by people from herding households where there is spare labour. However, particularly in areas near railways and large towns these small businesses suffer from competition with larger outside concerns.

In pastoral regions one reason for herders selling outside the contract-quota is that firms from elsewhere seek raw materials (e.g. cashmere, wool, hides). Inner Mongolia and Xinjiang are natural resource areas for industries in the south and east of China. The huge flow of resources from the west to the east cannot be handled by the central planning system. These voracious in-coming industries are generally in conflict with the interests of local administrations, which would prefer to set up their own industries and make profits themselves by adding value to raw materials. However, they cannot afford to pay the same high prices to herders. Furthermore they have poorer technology. The finished products from local industry often end up unsold because of their low quality. A vicious circle is created (see below).

An Inner Mongolian citizen, whether Chinese or Mongol, can buy up cashmere and sell it anywhere, with the tacit agreement of the provincial government. On the other hand it would be difficult for a trader from Shensi, say, to come in and buy directly, because the roads are blocked by local police who will not let 'their' goods out. Now the police are centrally administered by the Ministry of Public Security, but their loyalty is often to local government (this is called 'local economic war-lordism' in the Chinese press). It turns out that while some sections of the local administration are eager to keep the raw materials in, others are intent on finding ways to make a profit by trading them with outside firms. A network of contacts is required in order to get these cross-province deals through. Herding districts themselves are often keen to establish long-term, large-scale and dependable trade relations outside. For example, Otog Front Banner in Ordos sought to sell its meat regularly to a big steel factory in Beijing, where there were thousands of workers who needed feeding.[56] Or, in our case-study at Hargant, the district administration had arranged to sell large quantities of hay directly to a large dairy farm near Beijing, and some said the *sum* officials had also made a deal to export hay to Japan. Low-level units like districts need contacts higher up the administrative chain, formal or informal, in order to make such distant arrangements.

Now from the herder's point of view, it is financially advantageous to sell to the highest bidder. In places closer to towns dozens of traders wander round the grasslands. The local contract/quota price is fixed and known to everyone. But herders also know what is going on in neighbouring districts and counties – salesmen tell them, and differences in prices are gleaned from newspapers, radio, and TV. Herders regularly listen. Well-off people do not rush to sell.

Astute people from poorer families often act as middlemen. For example, Buyan, the uncle of a colleague from Ordos was trying to make a living from collecting sheepskins and selling them. He had been a herder, but his children grew up and left, and then his wife died. Buyan did not know what to do. He was wandering around, mourning. Then he had the idea of using his herder's knowledge: he knew how to judge the quality of sheepskins, and he also knew a lot of herders personally, people who would trust him with the skins in advance. Furthermore, he had another crucial advantage: he had a contact in the banner (county) administration, and this man had a contact with a firm buying skins at good rates. Everything was done by verbal agreement, not by written contract. Buyan knew that to succeed he only had to pay slightly higher prices than the local ones, or guarantee actually *to pay cash*. The reason for this is that most small local industries are in such a parlous state that they cannot pay cash; they give IOUs (*da bai tiao*) instead.

To summarise: in the Chinese case-studies the district administration was the only authority to attempt to manage the practical aspects of herding in the district as a whole. Except in districts with state farms, the principle of specialised production has been abandoned. The district is also responsible for carrying out government policy and the recommendations of grassland research institutes, but its practical authority to do so has much diminished. Households now engage in heterogeneous production on their own account and their strategies often run counter to the public policy of the district authorities.

RURAL INSTITUTIONS IN MONGOLIA

Mongolia has a wider variety of local institutions than either Russian or Chinese areas of the Project and the situation is in flux.[57] This makes it impossible to provide a summary of the distribution of such institutions in the country as a whole. So in order to give an indication of the types of institution and the relations between them, I will focus on one district, Bayantümen *sum* in Dornod *aimag*. The district is in eastern Mongolia, not far from Dashbalbar to the north and Hargant (in Inner Mongolia) to the east.

The issue in Mongolia is not overburdened pastoral resources and problems stemming from that, as in China, but the integration of herders with wider economic exchange, and the problems stemming from that.

The presence of herds of approximately equivalent size in SSUs per herder in Mongolia suggests that perhaps it is Mongolia's low rural population that has held back the huge increase of livestock found in China and Russia.[58] However, since the Mongolian reforms of 1990 there has been a net flow of people from the cities to the countryside. The number of herders went up as people took advantage of the distribution of herds when the *negdel*s (collectives) were disbanded. Livestock numbers did not rise at first. In one of the case study sites, for example, Dashbalbar, Dornod *aimag*, livestock numbers fell, having totalled 111,775 in 1990 and falling to 81,800 by 1993. The reasons for this was only partly that the new herders were inexperienced. General economic conditions render *making an adequate living* by herding extremely difficult. The low prices herders can obtain for their livestock products are confronted with abruptly rising prices for food, fuel, transport and clothing. There is a lack of market institutions (banks, shops, trading companies, market-places), and those that exist often do not reach to the herders located on distant pastures. The return to an economy of subsistence alone is even more marked in Mongolia than it is in Russia, and one consequence of this may be an increasing number of livestock kept by pastoralists, who do not or cannot sell them (see chapter 6).

In many ways Mongolia's rural institutions can be seen as having characteristics of both the Russian and Chinese types. As in China in the period of the Communes, the jurisdiction of the previous Mongolian collective farm (*negdel*) coincided with the boundaries of the district and often had the same leadership.[59] Today the district authorities continue to oversee the administration of pastoralism, but their power to control herders have declined. The structure and ideology of *negdel*s and state farms followed Russian models (Humphrey 1978). All over Mongolia these have now disappeared; in many districts they have been replaced by one or more smaller institutions called companies (*kompan*) and a variety of other firms and associations. These are often based on sections of the former *negdel*, but some are quite new organisations. The leadership of all these companies and firms is now separate from that of the district administration. However, most herding households are not members of any such organisation.

The district *(*sum*) office*

One difference from Russia, and similarity with China, is that pasture use in Mongolia is supervised by the district and sub-district rather than the collectives/companies. The office of the district leaders is the place where information is held on population and livestock numbers, and where firms, companies and other groups are registered. District officials know the pastures well, and most of the herders by name. Herders are not supposed to go outside the boundaries of the sub-district, but quite often do so with the permission of the leaders. District officials consist of the elected head (*zasag darga*), a chief accountant, an official secretary and the heads of the sub-districts, who have charge of the overall organisation of the herding.[60] Among their various activities, the *sum* officials collect tax, set prices for meat by agreement with the nearby meat-factory, for example, allocate machinery, etc. to new companies, barter sheepskins and cattle hides for commodities with private traders, take care of poverty-stricken families, and make arrangements on behalf of the district with foreign organisations. In 1993 Bayantümen officials had invited some Chinese experts to teach them about vegetable growing. The *sum* officials also keep up the important relation whereby they are 'subject to the chiefship' of the Gigant collective farm in Chita Oblast, Russia. The relationship has now become one of naked self-interest: the Bayantümen people send hay to Gigant, in exchange for which they receive petrol and spare parts.

The *sum* now has much smaller central government resources than earlier. In 1993 many services, such as schools, local hospitals, artificial insemination, post, travelling shops, repair workshops, etc. were falling into disrepair or had closed altogether. Brigade centres for specialist production were abandoned and broken down. External exchange, in which district officials as well as company heads acted as 'brokers', was crucial to acquiring the income to allow the district to function at all, as we found all over rural Inner Asia.

In the past the district officials were closely linked to the Soviet-backed Mongolian People's Revolutionary Party hierarchy and were respon-sible for delivering central state policies. This is no longer the case. The three main officials in Bayantümen belonged to three different political parties. The leader told me: 'In the past there were four kinds of social status: officials, intellectuals, herders, and workers. They have all gone. Now there is only rich and poor.' The main problem now was the destitution of some families, and this was caused, as he saw it, by the lingering psychology of dependency. Young people assumed their parents or the *sum* would care for them. In 1992 each household had been given at least 50 head of livestock. But by the beginning of 1993 some of them had no animals left: they had slaughtered or sold the lot. They drifted to the *sum* or *aimag* centres where they expected to be looked after. 'We know it is their fault', the leader continued, 'but we cannot deny them. We have tried to train them in simple jobs like carpentry or knitting, but they are terribly lazy.' The officials were concerned to help alleviate the central problem of low demand and low prices for livestock products and inflationary prices for flour, sugar, tea, etc. For example, they were supporting with loans families who were willing to raise chickens and rabbits.

Companies

In Bayantümen in summer 1993 there were four companies, each located in a sub-district (*bag*).[61] The companies were based on the brigades of the *negdel* and continued to use their machinery, sheds, stores, etc. A majority of shares in the companies had been bought by the state, and so they were not private companies. However, they were expected to be financially self-supporting. Just over half the herders (210) of the district were attached to these companies, where they were paid wages as 'advances' for fulfilment of contracts for products to be sold to the company. They were allocated 'norms' of company-owned flocks, which were herded alongside their own. At the end of the year they got a bonus if the company was successful in selling the products. The company made or acquired hay, which it distributed to members according to herd size, and the cost of this was deducted from the end of year bonus. Depending on the circumstances companies might also pay pensions, give food rations, and run a shop to sell goods to members. In all the above, Mongolian companies are similar to collectives in Tuva, Chita and Buryatia, though they tend to be much smaller (in Bayantümen around 80 member households, as compared with 400–600 in Buryat collectives).

Although a company in itself does not have a defined boundary like a Russian collective, it usually operates in essentially the same way and in this case can be regarded as a 'corporate' institution. However, there are companies and companies. The Bayantümen companies, whatever the special herds held by the earlier brigades, herded all five types of livestock. Some former state farms, on the other hand, were turned into companies wholesale. They continued to specialise in a particular type of production, e.g. Karakul sheep in Sumber. In this case the company remained state-owned and large in size (over 500 adult workers) at first; however, in 1995 it was divided into smaller companies. In other places, such as Dashbalbar, companies have been quite short-lived. They ended after being voted out by their members or falling into bankruptcy. The term 'company' thus encompasses a range of actual organisations. In general, in contrast to firms and associations, the companies represent the conservative option, the continuance of the 'steady wage - communal organisation' model. But economic circumstances or bad management can make them unviable.[62]

In Bayantümen, apart from the companies there were three 'co-operatives' (*horshoo*), one for trading, one for providing services, and one for vegetable growing. Each of them used the infrastructure and the personnel of previous sections of the *negdel*.

Just under half (195) of the herders of Bayantümen lived only on their private household economies.[63] They were supposed to observe the sub-district boundaries in pasturing, but otherwise were free to move and to sell their products as and where they could. On the whole the private herders were richer in livestock than the company herders, but the general differentiation of wealth was far below that of China. The private herders formed themselves into an indefinite number of temporary associations (also called *horshoo* or *horshoolol*), for particular tasks, such as hay-making. However, some of these associations were more substantial and were intended to be long-lasting.

Associations

The 'Rich White Horshoolol' was founded in 1992 by an experienced former head of the horse brigade in the *negdel*. He had been in charge of 2,000 horses and was clearly a man held in high regard.[64] The ten families who started the association included some kin but also some unrelated people, both rich and poor. They had put their own livestock into a common fund, and these were known as *alban mal* 'official livestock', like the herds in the collectives and those held in trust for the authorities under previous regimes. The 3,000 or so head were herded on suitable pastures arranged by the head of the group with the sub-district officials. The association was run not by its founder but by a younger man, who was a driver by profession and had contributed a vehicle. The association besides had an accountant, a lorry-driver and two tractor-drivers. It aimed to be self-sufficient, and so besides herding it did its own hay-making, production of foods and alcohol, potato and maize growing. Inside the group, relations were rather egalitarian. Women, people of the poor families and young people took part on an equal basis, and there was relatively little division of labour (women herded horses on occasion; men hoed the potatoes). Children did much of the herding. The *horshoolol* had its winter base at a well which it had recently renovated, which was located by a hay-cutting area with a storage shed and livestock pens. The group was relatively market-oriented and the founder listed its sources of income in order: selling cashmere and wool; selling meat; selling potatoes; selling hay in winter; hiring out its car and lorries; selling fodder made from maize. They did not sell milk, because this was produced more cheaply by a nearby dairy. They sold meat to the *aimag* meat-factory, but insisted that they would never sell wool locally. This was where the founder came in: he had emigrated from Inner Mongolia after the war as a boy and still had relatives there. He took the wool and cashmere over the border in October, sold it and brought back goods from China: rice, noodles, sugar, thermos flasks, silk, and buttons. Although the association appeared to be successful, and cheerful families were staying at the winter-camp for the hay-cutting when I visited, no-one was predicting the future with certainty. All the members had retained some private livestock of their own, and some of the women also had other jobs in the city of Choibalsan. They said they would disband the group if it did not work well after a year. Indeed by 1996, in Mongolia as a whole, many of these *horshoolol* had gone bankrupt or become inactive.

This example suggests that Mongolia has at least experimented with economic forms with rationales that are midway between the Chinese and the Russian models: corporate like the Russian and commercial like the Chinese.

In summary, we can see an immense diversity in Mongolia. Even one small rural district, like Sumber, may have a *tögrög* multi-millionaire living alongside numerous desperately poor households. What is significant is that the very rich do not become so from pastoralism, but from business and entrepreneurial deals. Client networks with district and country officials are crucial to success (see Sneath 1993a) and sources of large income are increasingly from outside Mongolia. This is true even of a district like Bayantümen, which is not on the frontier.

There has been a significant retreat of the state from direct investment in the pastoral economy. Thus, although on the one hand we can see the present variety of institutions as a positive phenomenon, answering to the people's diverse interests, on the other hand, the wider organisational capacity of the *negdels* has been lost, together with the advantages of specialised production. The *sum* has the task of co-ordinating the activities of various groups and households, but in a market context the problem is that all produce the same products. Competition and conflict between herders is increasing.

SECURITY, INTEGRATION AND DISINTEGRATION

The issue of security in a general sense is very important in rural Inner Asia. Economic security (or insecurity) influences which kinds of institutions people will join and support, and in Russia and Mongolia it directly affects the ability of enterprises to obtain funding for investment. In all three regions of Inner Asia the difficulty rural institutions face in obtaining investment is one of the main problems facing the pastoral economy. Personal, physical security is also a crucial issue.[65] Theft, vandalism, attacks on people, and rustling of livestock have all increased in Russia and Mongolia. This can limit the possibilities for trade and deters people from setting up private herding enterprises.

It seems that the most acute problems of funding are found in RUSSIA. A high level of funding is needed to sustain the way of life established earlier in Russian regions. In Mongolia rural people are generally capable of managing a subsistence and non-mechanised life with few external inputs, even if they complain about this. But in Russia a large proportion of people have non-productive occupations (book-keepers, secretaries, nurses, teachers, etc.) or are dependent on technology (tractorists, drivers, etc.), and they live in villages which rely on electricity and central heating. They would have little idea how to set about independent mixed farming. Every fourth person in Buryatia is in receipt of one or another kind of pension, benefit or allowance (*Buryatia,* 7th Jan 1995, p. 1). Yet the disastrous economic position of collective farms, dairies, etc. has cut away an important source of tax revenues for local government. This makes it extremely difficult for them to carry out the social functions previously undertaken by the collectives.[66]

The parity of authority between collective and district and the weakness of both (see figure 3.2) causes conflict to arise between collective and the district authorities, and between collective and private farmers. Where productive institutions once held undisputed sway, now there are overlapping jurisdictions with the local administrations. For example, the director of the Tunka farm quoted earlier complained that the county administration had: 1) given 10 hectares of his potato fields to another farm; 2) allowed villagers' private cattle to wander and eat up state farm crops – this had entirely ruined the harvest of one large sector; and 3) given permission for a 24-hour commercial shop to open just beside the precious fields. This shop had brought about uncontrolled traffic, drunkenness, fights and muggings. It was hopeless, he wrote, to try to find watchmen to guard the fields – people were afraid for their lives. 'Would the district or county administration ever get round to closing this fount of moral degradation which inflames people and creates criminality?' he wrote (Uskeev 1994).

Collectives tried to avoid conflict over pastures between collective and private herders by strictly delimiting the land available to the private farmers. However, according to some respondents in Tuva and Buryatia the farm's right to make such allocations was questionable; people would ask why someone had been given 'their' customary pasture, and this caused quarrels to arise. This situation was also present, to some degree, in Mongolia, though it is less acute because there is usually adequate land for all – at least there was in the case-study sites. In Dashbalbar and Sumber herders can use some pastures in neighbouring districts according to long-standing practice and no-one thinks twice about it. In China the right of local administrations to allocate pastures is not questioned. However, disputes may arise between district jurisdictions, particularly when herders need to pass through the land of another district in order to reach given pastures.

The disorganisation and despair in Russia is not just a reaction to poverty but is becoming an active agency of economic disintegration. For example, the Chitkan state farm in Barguzin had obtained a loan from the Agricultural Bank to buy 20,000 centners of hay to feed the livestock over the winter of 1994–5. But the farm members had drunk this money away. They had cut hay, by hand, for their own private animals; they had even cut extra hay to exchange for vodka. But it was beyond anyone's power to make them cut the collective hay. The result was that the state herds had no fodder. The state farm had mortgaged all its herds, machinery, and even its own central offices to the bank. Now it faced collapse, a prospect the members seemed at first to welcome. However, the bank announced that if the farm went into liquidation and was divided up among the members, they would be held individually responsible for repayment of their share of these colossal debts. It was predicted that the members would find any way they could to avoid dissolving the collective (*Buryatia*, 15th December 1995, p. 1).

It can be seen that a disastrous cycle is created: the economy of mechanised public livestock production is unsupportable without co-ordinated work from each sector (hay, arable fodder, maintenance, etc.). The more decrepit this collective sector becomes, the more its existence is a temptation for people to use it, steal from it, sell it on the side, etc. The more this happens, the less willing are people to work to support it. Yet, as the general rural atmosphere becomes more lawless and the threat of destitution more real, people are unwilling to leave the 'safety' of the collective to set up on their own. Although this is not necessarily the authors' own view, it is important to record that local *people attribute these demoralising processes largely to the changing nature of institutions themselves.*

> A fact is a fact. After the reform of the Friendship state farm into a Union of Farmers, everything went haywire. In the state farm, as everyone remembers, the way of life was settled: everyone knew their place, or else was firmly told what it was, and no-one had any doubt about the next day. But now we have total uncertainty. Freedom, with a significant amount of universal licence, has suddenly mixed up our orientations, our rules of behaviour, our measures of value. There is not even elementary order in collective production, and thieving and drunkenness have become uncontrollable (*Buryatia*, 9th December 1994, p 4).

MONGOLIA faces similar difficulties, although perhaps not as severe as in Buryatia. Much of the privatised vehicles and machinery is underused, as owners found it difficult to find and afford spares and fuel to run them. Individual herding households are often struggling to survive amid continually rising prices for the basic goods they need, and disappointments in the prices of the animal products that they can sell. Many Mongolian pastoral families have large numbers of children, (despite recent declines in national fertility rates),[67] making food provision a particular concern. The dissolution of the collectives has also brought an end to large-scale mechanised haymaking, and most families now have to cut their own hay by hand.

Mogoltsogt was born in 1926 in Hovd *sum*, Uvs *aimag*, and has spent his entire life herding in the district. Serjid, his wife, was a year older than Mogoltsogt and both had been pensioners for several years. The old couple lived with 11 year old Batmünh, their grandson, in a *ger* alongside the family of their son and daughter-in-law, Sürenjav and Nimsüren, and their 7 other children. Sürenjav had recently bought a tractor, although he could not afford to make much use of it. The old man articulated a widely-held dissatisfaction with the way that privatisation had been implemented, recalling some of the positive aspects of the collective era:

> In the past the government's policies represented the interests of the people, but now, in this transition period towards a market economy, the government cannot present its policies to the people. Personally, I have no idea what they are, so I'm not satisfied. The policies of the government are not understood by the people and because of this the people cannot govern themselves.

'CIVIL SOCIETY'

Democratic reforms under Western influence envisaged a replacement of many state institutions with 'civil society', i.e. independent, freely-formed associations mediating between individuals and the state. The problems with applying this American-European model to the quite differently organised post-socialist societies have been analysed in Hann and Dunn 1996. A major element in the western bias is the assumption that individual agents and their interests are opposed to those of the state. Here the issue is briefly reviewed in relation to Inner Asia.

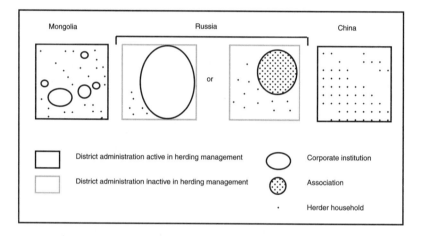

FIGURE 3.3. Schema of relations between institutions, 1993

Figure 3.3 is a formalised representation of the different patterns of organisation of pastoral activities found in the case-studies. Although very schematic, it highlights certain important differences in relations between institutions, and indicates the variable presence of 'associations' (the institutions most approximating to the notion of 'civil society').

In Mongolia, we have seen that associations like the Rich White Horshoolol have been set up, but have fared badly in market conditions. For such small independent enterprises to survive requires either outside funding (e.g. via international development agencies) or particularly favourable conditions (such as proximity to a town, providing a market for products).

Nevertheless, the fact that many such small groupings were set up at all shows that there is potential support in Mongolia for independent associations, and that kinship relations and friendship networks can serve as their socially integrative basis.

In Buryatia, on the other hand, the first 'private farmers' were mostly established on the initiative of officials. These units had no separate social rationale, but were designed either to demonstrate compliance with reform policy or to make a profit from splitting off a well-resourced bit of the collective farm (or both). Many of these farms have turned to trade and do little productive work. Some of them have formed associations, but they tend to have a strictly profit-oriented rationale and ordinary people widely assume they are corrupt fronts for illegal deals of one kind or another. Other types of independent association are not completely absent in Buryatia (e.g. Veterans' Associations), but they are rather rare. Mostly, people still look to the large collectives and the state as the arenas where they may interact as citizens and take part in social and cultural groups (Anderson 1996). The large 'associations' represented in figure 3.3 therefore tend in practice to operate not like a coming together of separate productive groups but like the old corporative, 'top-down' organisations of state and collective farms. There is little impetus to create separate associations, and considerable suspicion that were such groups to appear they would be narrowly self-interested and anti-social.

In China, the conventional opposition of state to society requires qualification at the local level. Between district administrations and households there is in a sense no gap, in that sub-district officials, grassland advisors, enumerators, etc. proliferate. As Flower and Leonard (1996: 218–9) have pointed out, this in fact constitutes a 'messy layer of interaction' which is not simply an opposition of a universalist state to individual interests. This is a crucial arena of gift-giving, which as several observers have pointed out is an important institution in China. Furthermore, as has been shown here, it is cross-cut by the various relations in which state officials themselves act as individuals. However, the existence of centrist control from Beijing, which is especially harsh in border regions such as those we have studied, has dampened the possibilities of spontaneous *associations* forming, with their own projects for their common good.

As in other areas of China, people seem to look to historical memory to create a moral order against what they see as amoral commercialisation around them. Our researchers found some evidence of the re-emergence of earlier kin-based groupings. However, their capacity for independent joint action was limited. In Chinggel Bulag the *hoton*, a group of around two to five households, had official recognition, with common allocation of pastures and a designated head-man. But one has the sense that in their current form the *hoton*s are extensions of administration and are artificially 'frozen' versions of indigenous groups which might otherwise have had their own rationale.[68] In Xinjiang there is evidence of somewhat larger and more autonomous groups, without official recognition. Unfortunately our information on them is limited. The Torgut Mongolians had a kin-based group called *ailer* (2–5 households in the north and 5–9 households in the south). A similar grouping among the Kazakhs was called *awer* (5–11 households). Tsui (1996b) has suggested that some households are now spontaneously coming together to reconstitute such 'traditional' kin groups for joint herding and that this, together with the reintroduction of religious rituals, may possibly be signs of a new re-emerging clan consciousness. However, the number of such groups is still small and their existence does not solve overall management problems. This leaves the district administration and the household as the two major institutional forms at district level in China.

Leadership

Rural leaders (*darga* in Mongolian) in Inner Asia have wide-ranging powers in their districts. This is partly because in all three countries they are brokers between the members and the outside world; and partly, maybe, because indigenous ideas of order and power conceptualise such leadership as 'necessary' and natural. Furthermore, in all three countries leaders still have some vital state resources to distribute (petrol until recently was one of the most important of these).[69] Leaders, often male, are accompanied by obsequious assistants, monopolise the best transport, commandeer products when they need them, expect to be given presents, and find lavish dinners laid on for them when they appear in some places. However, there are differences in how the various types of institution affect relations between leaders and ordinary members.

In Russia even corporate institutions like state and collective farms now elect their leaders, often for quite short periods.[70] This means that leaders have to adapt to the members' interests to some extent, but they sometimes share the general apathy and use their position to their own advantage (for example, on a farm in Chita Oblast, where the leader of the collective set up his wife in a private shop in the central office of the farm). The main task of the leader is to organise a mutually supportive relationship between the different specialised sectors of large unwieldy farms. To do this they must somehow get the workers to take part in public work. They get little support from the local district administration, which has now withdrawn from productive decision-making. We have seen that some farm directors are resorting to compulsory redundancies and other threats to make people work.

In Mongolia leaders are also elected and we found that they are often chosen from among the elite families of previous leaders. This gives a kind of stability to the scene, as for example in Bayantümen, where the district leader in 1993 was the son of the man who had founded the earlier *negdel* in the 1950s. The leader's main task was to allocate resources as privatisation continued, and they are still able to co-ordinate the activities of the companies, firms and associations. Leaders have the authority to do this, as the district is normally a much larger entity than any of the enterprises in it. The tasks are less intractable than those facing the leaders in Russia, since most of the Mongolian enterprises are multi-faceted rather than specialised and therefore do not depend on the reliability of institutions other than their own. This kind of co-ordination is well suited to the type of leader who operates through networks and strategies. There may be accusations of favouritism, but in general the leader's interests usually coincide with those of the various groups under him.

In the case-study districts in China, the situation is more complex. Leaders, though formally elected, are proposed by senior bodies, are generally members of the Communist Party, and often come from outside the region. They have the authority of the state behind them, and yet because sheer purchasing power is coming to challenge political status, their influence over households is declining (Yan 1992: 14–17). With an absence of clear legal statutes, and faced with the sea of households, leaders even now have recourse to the 'charisma politics' of earlier Maoist inspiration. The leaders must try to implement state policies. Yet they are often short of funds and may have to order the herders themselves to pay for new projects, sometimes against their wishes. Madar in Handagat described some of the difficulties he faced in 1993:

> Sometimes we have to be strong in facing a lot of harsh words about our decisions. For example, we made a decision to build a new road to the city, and we asked all households to give either labour or funds as a contribution to it. Some people said this was too heavy a burden for them. We will never give up! I believe that in the long run every household and the local livestock economy will benefit from it.

In Hosh Tolgoi in 1993 the officials' salaries, and those of other state employees like teachers, had not been paid for some months. Erdenejav, the

42 year-old deputy head of the district, said that if the banner did not pay the salaries he would raise the money directly from the herders and farmers in his district, and probably this was being done to some extent already. The herders in this area were generally coming to resent the leaders who come out to visit them. In the past they treated the officials to extravagant hospitality because the leaders might be helpful to them. Increasingly they had come to consider the leaders to be parasites, who only visit them in order to collect money, receive meat, a sheep and a drink. It is interesting that Hosh Tolgoi, where leaders are most resented, is also the only place among the case-study sites where cadres have a higher income than herders.[71]

Leaders are tempted to privatise public services to increase their (public) revenue. In Handagat in 1993 the district's doctors wanted to move from state service to a contract system and they proposed signing an agreement whereby a certain percentage of their profit would go to the administration. The leaders were on the point of signing at the time of the case-study, but the workers were against the idea. They were afraid the doctors would turn the hospital into a profit-making business, that patients would have to pay higher fees, and that the medical service would decline. The leaders were placed in a dilemma by such a strong public reaction, but workers predicted that they would go down the contract road. Namsüren, a 55 year-old driver, said sarcastically, 'If I could, I would make a contract with anyone, even devils, to sell the leaders of the farm!' Even the local cadres were pessimistic, linking the general fallibility of contracts with the tendency of everyone to make money in whatever way they could. In other words, the political function of leaders as state functionaries was compromised by the economic exigencies of rural life *in which they too had to participate*. However, it might be more correct to see these economically active leaders as characteristic of the new, post-reform Chinese state – using economic forces as best they can to benefit both the lowest rung of the state hierarchy and themselves.[72]

To summarise: we can see subtle differences in the leadership of the rural institutions at district level in the three countries. As a generalisation, one can say that the corporate leader in Russia contrasts with the 'traditional' leader in Mongolia and with the representative of the state and Party in China. However, there are probably as many similarities as differences. In all three regions, after the ending of the era of rule backed by fear, leaders also have to cope with a decline in their external economic resources from the state. Therefore they have seen the reduction of the powers of control which used to come with managing the distribution of resources. Now, in each country district leaders act as brokers and filters between the members of their communities and the outside world. Instead of channelling flows only through the hierarchical 'pyramid' of the state economy as in the past, even district leaders are making their own arrangements, sometimes very far afield.

INSTITUTIONS AND INDIGENOUS CULTURE

The present official institutions in Inner Asia virtually all originated on the basis of external models generated in the respective state capitals, or by foreign advisors. Some of them are now deeply entrenched in regional pastoral ways of life. Nevertheless they are not all that exists in social life. To assess the relation of the present official institutions to the specific cultures of the region it is useful briefly to consider some indigenous institutions of social identity. Here I look at *oboo* rituals (see chapter 1) which link communities to land. Indigenous ideas of nature (*baigal*, see introduction) were manifest in these rituals, where the humans of a locality made offerings to the 'spirits' of that same area, aiming thereby to ensure the ongoing natural processes of fertility and good fortune for humans, livestock, grass and so forth during the coming season. In general, it seems from our data that these rituals are strongest (i.e. most frequent, with largest participation) in Russia, the region with the strongest 'corporate' traditions in official institutions. They are weakest in China, where corporate institutions are fewest. However, there are some interesting qualifications to this general pattern, described briefly below.

The cult at the ritual cairn (*oboo*), usually dedicated to mountain spirits, is found in all the studied regions. More patchily there are also cults of sacred trees, lakes, irrigation channels or springs (see table 3.5). The rituals were forbidden during periods of intense socialist campaigns, but have now revived everywhere to some extent. In the pre-revolutionary period the celebrants at the *oboo* corresponded closely with the local definition of the socio-political community. All males were supposed to attend and to make some contribution to the offerings. The rituals sometimes had a patron, who donated the major part of the sacrificed livestock; otherwise they were organised by local elders or princes, often with a Buddhist lama officiating to pronounce the prayers. Strangers and women were generally excluded from the ritual itself, though they took part in the subsequent feasting.

The revived *oboo* cults have kept the idea that the ritual is for the benefit of a community. In many places women are now included. However, the *oboo* rituals are less universal than they used to be, because (depending on the place) some people do not accept their religious aspect. It is thus interesting to see who attends, who officiates, and who is the patron. In all the case-study sites the district government also sponsors summer festivals of games, dancing and feasting. Such festivals (*naadam*, in Mongolian, *nadym* in Tuvinian, *surharban* in Buryat) used to follow the *oboo* ritual on the same day. However, in socialist times the games were separated from the *oboo* and taken up as official celebrations (for example, lists of production prize winners might be announced at them). The revived *oboo* rituals are different from this; they represent a specifically *native* reworking of past traditions. It is suggested here that when a present-day official institution sponsors the *oboo* it is consciously linking itself with indigenous culture.

Table 3.5, which lists *oboo* ceremonies in the case-study sites, shows that the involvement of district governments in supporting *oboo* rituals is not a matter of official policy in the three countries. Rather, in each country we see a variety of relationships between the local governments and their communities. This shows that the official institutions have not 'taken over' *oboo* worship in a blanket sense, but intermesh with it (or not) in a variety of ways. Thus in Argada, where clans remain significant and there are several of them in each locality, the collective and district governments do not attend the *oboo* of any one clan. In Gigant, which is untypical of Buryat settlements in this respect, the *oboo* is unimportant and people attend Buddhist monasteries. In Hovd in Western Mongolia the *oboo* is located in a sub-district (*bag*) and its ritual is aimed at the success of that *bag* – there is a complete coincidence between the administrative and the social communities. Similarly, in Dashbalbar and Sumber the *oboo* today represents a geographical idea of community which corresponds with the *sum* district. In Chinggel Bulag we find a gathering centred on a patron or 'owner' of the *oboo*, and although the *oboo* is called the 'sub-district *oboo*', worship ceased when the old man died. In Solchur the *oboo*'s blessings were called on for fertility and the health of children of the whole present community. It was the state farm which supported this ritual, and interestingly gave it a socialist-era flavour by holding the rite on the day officially designated for the festival of children (in Russian *Den' Zashchita Detei*).

Perhaps most interesting of all is the case of Hosh Tolgoi in Xinjiang. Here the pre-revolutionary *sum*, a division of the banner, had its own *oboo* and one of the main tasks of the *sum* leader (*jangi*) was to organise the rites.

Site	Number and type	Sponsors	Frequency	Attendance	Officiant	Other rituals
Russia						
Argada	2 *oboos* for clans	community clans	three times in summer	'everyone'	shaman	spring; tree; attend monastery at Kurumkan
Gigant	1 *oboo*, wayside	individuals	no communal rite	when passing	none	tree 'Gants Narahan'; spring; attend monasteries at Tsugol and Aga
Solchur	1 *ovaa*, 'for blessing children'	state farm	annually on day of 'children's defence'	'everyone'	?	spring; tree and irrigation channel, all supported by state farm
Mongolia						
Dash-balbar	1 *oboo*, 'Dashbal-bar Oboo'	community	once in summer	1000 ($^1/_3$ of total population)	local elders or lama	Buddhist monastery, 20 lamas
Sumber	1 *oboo*, 'White Oboo'	community	once in summer	about $^1/_3$ of population	lamas	Buddhist mona-stery, small (about 6 lamas)
Hovd sum	1 *oboo* for *bag*	district government, community	in spring and autumn	60–70, all adult men of *bag*	elders	Buddhist monastery
China						
Hargant	1 *sum* oboo, 4 *gachaa* *oboo*s	district government, community	once in summer	few	?	none
Chinggel Bulag	1 *gachaa* oboo	local patron (deceased 1990)	discontinued as 'owner' died	? all *gachaa* members	elders or lamas	none
Hosh Tolgoi	1 *sum* oboo	district government and clans	once in summer; large ritual every 2 yrs	community of pre-rev. *sum*	elders; rite said to be 'shamanist'	fire ritual (shaman); lamaist prayers
Handagat	1 *oboo*	district government, community	in April each year	about 200	lamas	tree; Buddhist temple, small (? 1 lama)

TABLE 3.5. *Oboo* ceremonies in case-study sites, 1992–3

FIGURE 3.4. *Oboo* ritual, Hoboksair, Xinjiang, 1993 (photo: Balzhan Zhimbiev)

Today, the revived ceremony is for the members of this earlier *sum* (all Mongols), not the present-day one which includes Chinese and Kazakhs. The old man who goes round collecting donations to give the *oboo* is called *jangi*. It is perhaps not surprising that the present *sum* officials do not support this re-creation of an earlier version of the district. Attendance is not a matter of confrontation, however. One respondent, Dorj, said: 'I don't believe in religion, because I am a member of the Communist party. According to our tradition, the people know each other in clan and *sum*. For this reason, I go to *oboo* worship.'

From the table it can be seen that *oboo* rituals are carried out practically everywhere, but it seems from what people say that the reasons for performing them may differ somewhat in different regions. Therefore it is not possible to conclude either that *oboo* rituals are simple survivals of tradition or that they are new responses to environmental problems. However, what they *do* do is to make the celebrants aware both of social communities and of 'nature' (*baigal*) in a general sense, since the prayers and offerings are aimed at the successful reproduction of both.

CONCLUSION: SOME IMPLICATIONS WITH REGARD TO THE PASTORAL ENVIRONMENT

Central government policies in the recent past were probably the most important influence on pastoral management in Inner Asia, and rural institutions were the instruments for state policy. Now that decision-making has devolved to a great extent to regions and localities it is important to understand the dynamics of rural institutions and the role they are playing. Certain forces driving the pastoral economy – relative prices, transport and communications, the wider demand for livestock products, market organisation, etc. – are beyond the control of local institutions. However, it is possible to draw some conclusions concerning the local management of pastoralism and its relation with perceived environmental problems. I take each country in turn.

In RUSSIA as long as rural people feel the collectives provide security and are suited to their accustomed way of life these institutions look set to stay. The large corporate farm has as its source of income agriculture and herds supported by a range of other specialised sectors. This conglomerate is kept afloat by a particular type of organisation developed in Soviet times, which necessitates the interdependence of the different sectors and a high degree of mechanisation. In other words, the requirements of this form of organisation are that all sectors continue to operate to some degree and that the technical apparatus is kept going (electric milking, electric shearing, heated byres in winter, etc.). The structure of labour has adapted to this organisation, so if the technology fails production has to be drastically reduced when all the work is done by hand. Furthermore, there is no possibility of changing the livestock species overnight to hardier breeds. This means that, for the time being, the collectives have to keep arable land for fodder, have to use large areas of pasture for hay, and have to keep the animals penned for large parts of the year.

As we have seen many farms cannot manage to reproduce this system. They are letting the public herds decline or attempting to restructure in various ways. But in most cases this only presages a drastic fall in income, to the extent that the rationale for maintaining the collective at all is threatened. The surviving collective is still one which maintains the complex economy to some degree and manages to sell its products to state and private organisations. The relatively successful collective leader is the one who can negotiate these deals with dairies and meat-factories. All of this has environmental implications. By 1996 almost all collectives had reduced herds, especially sheep, by a huge amount (two-thirds in some places) in line with the predictions made earlier by our researcher (Gomboev et al. 1996). This may allow the exhausted pastures to revive. However, as long as the non-native livestock species remain the mechanised fodder-based technologies are also likely to remain, and pastures will therefore continue to be limited. Greater pastoral movement might improve the situation in a relatively large farm such as Gigant, as might the re-use of hayfields for grazing,[73] but greater mobility is highly unlikely to happen on a wide scale, as sedentarisation is already ingrained in Buryat ways of life.

However, Buryat mechanised agro-pastoral collectives are not the only model for collective pastoral management in Russia. We contrast them with the positive example of the state farm in Ovyur (Tuva). Here, though stocking rates are fairly high, environmental damage is minimal. There are several reasons for this: first, the Tuvans have continued to keep native breeds, and this has enabled them to use a mobile type of pastoralism. The indigenous breeds can live on the open pasture for most, if not all, of the year, and do not have to be kept in fixed and heated shelters. It follows from this that their requirement in human-produced fodder is much smaller. The Tuvan collective hardly plants fodder and uses only a relatively small amount of hay. Until recently, the farm did not sow grains for human consumption. The farm leaders are conscious of the problems of over-stocking and plan for a steady-state in livestock production, and they realise that collective/state farms provide large-scale pastoral co-ordination (on the importance of this, see chapter 6). Although the economic future of such state farms is very uncertain, especially given the low prices for agricultural products and high prices of fuel, power and manufactured goods – all of which look set to stay – we would suggest when such farms retain the above-mentioned indigenous techniques they can interact positively with the environment.

The Tuvan example, and also the case of the state farms in China, show that the large collective type of institution can operate in a way that conserves the environment. Furthermore, the Chinese case shows that, contrary to received wisdom, such collectives if given sufficient investment can be economically successful in a market environment.

It can be expected that increasing numbers of collective farms in Russia will founder and become no more than shells within which people scratch a subsistence life. Some may break apart, and perhaps turn into smaller corporations or associations. In either case, the huge arable fields may be abandoned and a great proportion of the collective herds will probably perish. It is possible that many people will leave the land and take refuge in cities. Small-holdings, many of them the successors of the 'private plots', will be increasingly important. It is unclear what the environmental effects of this will be.

A positive scenario for the future is suggested by the Buryat agricultural expert Potaev (1994). The associations of farmers are in many cases joint-stock companies. When a collective is disbanded all members can have shares in these associations, even if they themselves are not farmers. If agricultural prices are stabilised (a big 'if'), the non-farming population as well as the farmers would benefit from profits. This would prevent the rural community from falling apart. The new farm associations would leave the existing private plots to the service workers and would themselves use the previous collective land. They would gradually build new small-holdings at some distance from one another, to allow each one space for its own pasture-hayfield complex. Potaev observes that this is not some unreal projection but simply a revival of the pre-collectivisation Buryat settlement pattern which was always scattered and not village-based. He is referring here to the *utug* system of manured hayfields referred to earlier. The massive collectives discarded the *utug*s and concentrated livestock near big settlements in a way that could only be damaging to pasture (even between 1959 and 1993 the number of rural settlements in Buryatia was reduced from 2,436 to only 615). As Gomboev et al. (1996) show convincingly, environmental damage is concentrated around villages and decreases with a wider radius. It is interesting that Potaev's project does not suggest increasing mobility along Mongolian or Tuvan lines. His is a model of scattered but settled development that may well be an answer to the particular situation of Buryatia.

Potaev has another point to make: with the end of the collectives, the *contradiction* always said to have existed between them and the private plots would disappear. He argues that the plots took people's labour from collective work and have always therefore been restricted by the collectives. If the collectives disappear, in Potaev's optimistic view, this will unleash people's undivided energy. They will no longer allow other organisations to plunder their natural resources (perhaps he has forests in mind here) and they will make sure that the present paralysing vandalism is no longer possible in their neighbourhood.

As yet we have only a little evidence that such a transformation is taking place.[74] The future in Russia in the short term looks bleak. However, if small private farms and associations were to be combined with scaled-down versions of the collectives for more extensive and specialised production this could provide a more positive future. It seems likely that this would work well only if the district administrations gained more authority, in order to manage inter-institutional land-use.

In CHINA the dynamic of pastoral development over the past ten years has also created severe environmental problems. Chinese officials are interested first and foremost in keeping district revenues afloat, and in the taxes, fees and re-payments of loans they gather from the herders. They may turn a blind eye to the accumulation of herds. This, together with the allocation of fixed pastures, is potentially damaging to the environment. Pasture degradation is evident in many places, such as Hargant and Chinggel Bulag, even though the stocking-rates are not at maximal levels according to Chinese specialists. The central state policy of allocating the most scarce types of pasture to individual households is partly responsible for this. The resulting reduction in mobility has caused grazing pressure at particular places. However, it is arguable that such a policy would not have been necessary had there been a different institutional arrangement at district level. If the perception had not been that the administration task was controlling each and every household, but instead that the authorities had incorporated in their operational structure a variety of functional associations and had taken on the role of co-ordinating a mobile use of the districts as a single unit (see chapter 6), some of the advantages of the collective could be achieved in a different way.

The present situation is that the district authorities, faced with the mass of herders, are unable to enforce use of all the pasture. In Hargant, as was described, the poorer herders crowd round the central village in order to minimise transport costs, sell their milk, etc. The sandy hummock land near the village (*bolderu*) is reasonable winter pasture. Settling and building houses there, many herders no longer make the effort to travel far away to other seasonal pastures. This is increasing the area of sand dunes. It seems that as grass cover in the *bolderu* is reduced to a few tufts, the wind carries the sand to form further dunes nearby.

The declining level of officials' pay as compared with that of herders appears to have the result that they compete with the very people they are supposed to govern. This might seem to have nothing to do with environmental questions, but indirectly in some places it does. Hargant was one of the case-study sites where there was pasture to support a larger number of animals than exist at present. Yet there was significant pasture degradation there. One aspect relates to the fact that a very large area of grassland was designated as hay-land and herders were not allowed to use it for grazing. They could cut their own hay there at specific places, but most of the vast

FIGURE 3.5. Hay-cutting in Shilingol, Inner Mongolia, 1988

territory was set aside by the officials as *sum* hay-land. The district sold large proportion of the resulting hay for profit.[75] The rich herders with several hay-cutters must have negotiated with the district for hay resources. Although one cannot be certain of the details, it seems that the result for the pastoral economy of the district was as follows: lack of funds required the leaders to capitalise on the hayfields for district income; this both left the herders with smaller and less convenient areas for pasture, and also put some of them in the position of having to compete for hay resources with their own leaders. It was not that the hay-lands were themselves damaged, but that the resulting use of land elsewhere in the district was distorted (overburdened in some areas and unused in others). More generally, if rural districts become increasingly de-linked from counties and the state hierarchy, in China there are no other institutions to organise the management of overburdened pasture resources.

All Chinese pastoral districts make some efforts with pasture improvement, fencing of degraded areas, etc. These are a drop in the ocean (see Hurelbaatar 1996: 163–4). Some of the herders in our studies said that if they had the money they would like to fence their own pastures. In the long run an optimistic scenario is that this would result in such owners making improvements, limiting herds, and having a quick livestock turnover. But at present many people simply want to have more animals on the land. This herding rationality is only sustainable in Inner Asian conditions when combined with mobility suited to the region, and in any case appears to be at odds with fixed allocated pastures. The present institutional arrangements are most unlikely to enable a general increase in mobility to take place, since the settlement of herders is both a method of control as well as being regarded as a sign of progress. It is true that even if sedentarisation continues the households could establish associations for limited joint mobile herding (e.g. long-distance moves of horses or sheep pastured by rota). However, we did not hear of such ventures and in general the atomisation of rural society seems to make their emergence unlikely.

This chapter ends with the case of MONGOLIA. From the environmental point of view Mongolia has some of the best conditions of all the studied countries. It is important to point out that this is not only due to the low stocking rates and wide availability of pastures. Rural Mongols positively value an unpolluted environment. Herders have sophisticated techniques for planning migrations, inspecting the growth of different species of grass, and deducing from the behaviour of animals when it is time to move. Some districts in the north-east are relatively sedentarised (e.g. Dashbalbar); but those responsible for the herds still manage to avoid causing degradation, except very locally, around wells, animal sheds etc.

Flexibility of social groupings like *ails*, and the combination of larger and smaller units are the keys to this. It is significant that in these respects the range of institutions now found in Mongolia is comparable with that of pre-collectivisation times. Of course the present social make-up is completely different, but from the point of view of pastoralism the new groups may have some of the same advantages and disadvantages.

However, the present institutional organisation tends to be less mobile than either the pre-revolutionary set up or the *negdels* of the socialist period (see chapter 6). Among private herders the need to sell, rather than to deliver (including the requirement to bear transport costs rather than have the products collected) may influence some herders to stay near the district centre (similar to the situation in Hargant in Inner Mongolia). Another pattern is for town dwellers to acquire livestock and leave them with kinsmen in nearby districts for pasturing. The kin do not take these extra animals to far pastures but allow them to stay close to the centre, particularly cows for milking. This causes severe pasture damage in the immediate vicinity of such district centres. However, in Mongolia, at least in the studied districts, most professional herders have their movements overseen by the district and sub-district authorities. This ensures that some overall planned use of pastures is maintained.

There are important economic effects of the institutional changes. The creation of a myriad of small producers has had the result that the specialisation and economic integration of the *negdel* period has largely been lost. The state farms and *negdels* produced on a large scale for particular known state purchasers, and they also had breeding programmes for special purposes. Now, in general, the herders are all producing the same things at the same times, which causes a lowering of prices, and there are few guaranteed purchasers. In the past this situation was an important cause of the indebtedness of Mongol herders to Chinese traders. Today the likely result is that some young herders will be forced to leave the pastoral life, particularly in areas distant from roads and buyers. They may move to towns and district centres, but in many cases will still continue to own livestock which they leave with relatives in the nearby countryside. This may result in some remote areas of pasture becoming underused, while others close to towns suffer environmental damage.

In Mongolia pastoralism is far more important in the national economy than it is in either Russia or China. In the latter two countries local officials have little power to object to 'their' land being taken for industrial, mining, military or logging developments. This used to be the case in Mongolia too, with regard for example to the installations of the Red Army. But now such developments are subject to *aimag* and district agreement. These authorities appear to have the last say in the siting of potentially polluting developments. For example, in Bayantümen there was an objection to the construction of a new wool washing plant on the grounds that its chemicals would pollute local water sources (the Herlen River). What is significant about this is that such an objection was made at all, when the plant could only have been economically beneficial to the area. Though desperate problems of poverty are present in Mongolia, in some cases the local institutions seem to be sufficiently strong to ensure that development – if it takes place at all – takes place their way.

In conclusion, the form taken by local institutions is an extremely important aspect of herding practice and consequently of human-environmental relations. Local institutions have a 'middle role' between the networks of kin and household relations described in the next chapter and the broad ethnic and regional social identities described in Tsui (1996b). Chapter 4 examines the predominantly kin-based, flexible, and far-flung networks of Mongolia and Buryatia on the one hand and the emerging hierarchical 'patron-client' relations in Inner Mongolia on the other. Tsui describes how economic diversification in north Xinjiang has engendered the proliferation of new ethnic and regional loyalties, and he argues that this is likely to cause increased competition over economic interests and hence more pressure on the environment. This chapter broadly agrees with Tsui's analysis, but points out that comparison of all three countries shows that local institutions vary in whether they reinforce competition or serve to mediate it. Governmental control over local institutions is on the retreat in all three countries. However, the subsequent situation is not uniform across Inner Asia but increasingly diverse, as the people of each region establish their own new institutional forms. The analysis suggests that problems occur when there is no institution that can co-ordinate pastoralism at the district level. In Buryatia and Chita the institutions remain but are unable to support a pastoralism that had become reliant on mechanised inputs. In China the weakened local governments have largely rescinded responsibility for pastoral management to individual households, which makes it difficult to implement co-ordinated policies. While it may be possible that individual 'peasant' farms in Buryatia will become viable, our studies of the mid-1990s suggest that larger corporations (like the state farms in Tuva and Xinjiang) have the best chance of success.

However, any economic success is likely to rely on serious investment (as in the Red Star in Xinjiang) and environmental sustainability will depend on how well pastoral management is adapted to local conditions – and a good guide to this is the retention of certain indigenous methods developed over centuries (see chapter 6).

Chapter 4

KINSHIP, NETWORKS AND RESIDENCE

David Sneath

Within the official institutions that still operate in the rural regions of Inner Asia, people continue to order their own social relations in particular ways. The discernible patterns by which people work, socialise and choose to reside, can be seen as the basis of social organisation on the steppe. This chapter aims to describe the underlying principles that have generated the differing observed forms of rural residence and social organisation throughout the region, and to discuss the way in which these have recently adapted to economic and social change.

BACKGROUND

Throughout the region it appears that decollectivisation has lead to an increase in the importance of kinship and kin networks. In Buryatia, for example, as the family becomes responsible for economic activities it has had flexibly to adjust its residence so as to facilitate production and gain allocated resources. The self-help networks of kin and friends are now very important. The 'mafia' of the large cities is in some ways only an outgrowth of these networks.[1] It would be misleading to talk of there being a kinship *system* which is increasingly important in the rural economy. Kinship is one of the principles on which local social organisation is based; it is not generally elaborated into a large formal system.

While in formerly Soviet regions the increasing importance of kinship and networks can be seen as a response to shortages and economic change, in Chinese parts of the region kinship is at least as important, but for slightly different reasons. In Inner Mongolia, as mentioned earlier, the local government has strengthened and made permanent the economic importance of kinship relations by allocating pastureland to small groups of one, two or three families. As these families were generally close kin the government's allocation of resources created economic units that were almost always groups of kin. This tendency is also emerging in the former Soviet regions where in some cases property has been allocated to private family farms. People we talked to often commented that when it came to important matters, such as property, the only people they trusted were their close kin.[2]

In the former Soviet and Mongolian regions, as collective and State institutions relinquish ownership of livestock and other rural resources, the role of families in productive activity increases in importance. Rural families are property-owning corporations, and – apart from the (as yet very small) property holdings of the Buddhist Church – the other important such corporations are generally based on remnants of the formerly state structures (which often have a new status as Joint Stock Companies or other 'private' enterprises). In Tuva and Russia thereare a small number of rural associations and these are often, but not always or entirely, composed of kin. In the Chinese regions which have seen the emergence of relatively large private holdings of livestock, these are generally extensions of 'family-farming' domestic producers.

It is important to recognise, however, that rural Inner Asian families are not clearly bounded units. They are part of a network of relations of social obligation that links settlement with steppe. Such a socio-economic web[3] pre-dated collectivisation, of course, but it also adapted remarkably well to the non-commercialised economy of the Soviet period. When formerly collective assets are privatised, then, it is unsurprising that the networks continue to operate. In Mongolia, for instance, pastoral households often keep animals belonging to friends and relatives.

The most commercialised of the pastoral economies studied was that of Inner Mongolia, which reflects the relative proximity of large urban markets, an expanding Chinese economy, and the relatively good communications to be found in the region. In part this also reflects the importance of Chinese culture in this area, with its long tradition of trade. As mentioned earlier, the Chinese economy has not suffered the dislocation that has affected other parts of the region. There is confidence in the currency, and consumer goods are widely available. This has made cash important enough for it to fill a much more influential role in Inner Mongolia than in the former Soviet economic zone. Arrangements to keep livestock for relatives or friends that would generally be non-financial arrangements elsewhere in the study area, tend to be paid for with cash in the Inner Mongolian study sites. In both Hargant and Chinggel Bulag a third of the interviewed pastoral families hired labour regularly.[4] By contrast, in the other case-study sites, including those in Xinjiang, little or no regular hiring of labour was recorded. Thus, although networks of social relations of obligation remain important in Inner Mongolia, cash is playing an increasingly important role, particularly in the relations between rich and poor.

The other important general tendency throughout Inner Asia has been the ability of social organisation and residence to adapt to changes in property ownership. This can be seen in Inner Mongolia in the clusters of kin around allocated land and housing in Chinggel Bulag, for example; in Mongolia with the grouping of kin working in the Bayan Tsagaan *horshoolol* (co-operative) in Dornod *aimag*; and in the extended families of Tuva which arrange their domestic arrangements so as to occupy dwellings in both the village and the pastures in order to retain their rights to both.

In the Introduction, we mention the heritage of a common pastoral culture in Inner Asia. Although many aspects of this culture are becoming increasingly varied, household relations are relatively similar all over the region. The organisation of work within pastoral households generally follows a well-established 'traditional' form, well described elsewhere (Shombodon 1996: 222–7; Bruun 1996: 69–71; Humphrey 1983: 189, 272; Jagchid and Hyer 1979:110–12; Vainshtein 1980). Gender roles remain central elements of the conceptual scheme by which tasks are allocated in most pastoral families. The female sphere of capability and responsibility is centred on the household and includes preparing food products (such as cheeses, yoghurt and blood sausages), cooking and making tea, making and repairing clothes, washing, childcare, cleaning the dwelling, milking, and looking after animals close to the encampment. Women and children also usually collect the dried dung that is used for fuel. In fact some of these tasks may be done by men from time to time, but the responsibility for their completion is generally held to be that of the women of the household. The male sphere includes those tasks associated with herding animals (particularly at some distance from the *ail*), such as watering livestock and moving them to and from pastures, monitoring and protecting the herds, cutting and transporting grass (hay) in the summer. They also generally have responsibility for lassoing and breaking horses, making and repairing enclosures and animal sheds, the killing, skinning and castration of livestock, harnessing animals, loading heavy goods on carts or trucks for movement, repairing *ger* frames, carts, saddles and harnesses. Many herding tasks are done by both male and female pastoralists, e.g. penning and counting livestock, shearing sheep and combing goat hair. Apart from gender the other organising principle is that of age and familial status. Parents generally direct the activities of their children and other junior household members in areas appropriate to their gender. This managerial role generally passes gradually to adult children as they raise their own families, and as the original parents become less active in their old age.

Descriptive terminology

Three categories have been used in this chapter to classify residential forms:- firstly there is the HOUSEHOLD meaning a hearth group that shares one dwelling (or a self-contained home in a building), and whose members consume meals together regularly. Secondly there is the RESIDENTIAL GROUP, that is those people who live together in one house, group of dwellings or encampment. In Mongolian rural regions this is known as the *ail, hot,* or *hot-ail.* The households composing an *ail* usually herd their livestock jointly, and help each other in numerous everyday tasks. In this sense it is important economically. There is constant everyday interaction between members of the residential group, but the group itself can be temporary, and indeed in the case of mobile pastoral families it often varies from season to season. Being flexible, residential groups made up of yurts may also change to reflect changing personal relations between individuals and families.

Thirdly, there is what I have termed the 'RESIDENTIAL FAMILY GROUP' to mean immediate kin who are part of the same residential group. This group usually shares food, herds livestock jointly, and shares all major tasks. Membership usually changes gradually over time in line with the domestic cycle, but a common form was the stem family (a conjugal couple, the parent(s) of one of them, and their unmarried children).

To clarify: as one travels in the Mongolian steppe in summer one may see a group of four yurts (*ger*), for example. This cluster is the 'residential group'. Within the group there may be four separate 'households'. Some of these four may be related by close kinship and these are termed the 'residential family group'.

In fact these groupings are only the product of the underlying principles of social organisation and kinship that are described below. The most important conceptual scheme is that of general relatedness. Rather than bounded units and groupings, kith and kin (friends and relatives) form a network. Interestingly, Mongolian terms for kin groups refer to rather unbounded fields centred on the speaker, such as *xamaatan* (relatives), *ah duu* (kin and close friends) or *töröl sadan* (kindred). The other terms

commonly used refer to the more concrete forms that such kin relations take
– such as *ail ger, am örh,* and *ger bül.*[5]

Within the social network, the closest kin relations are generally
found between members of a minimal lineage of around three generations
depth (particularly if they live near each other). For convenience this can be
termed the 'RITUAL FAMILY', in that it is a category of kin that would ideally
gather for important kin rituals such as New Year. On another level we can
see that this ritual family is made up of nuclear families, some of which
usually live together (see figure 4.1). This gives rise to residential groups
which reflect the different conditions in the various parts of the region. The
ritual family, although an extremely important kin unit for most indigenous
Inner Asians, is largely 'invisible' in that it is rarely a residential unit in its
entirety. However, the members are obliged to meet, if possible, for important ritual events such as funerals, marriages, hair-cutting ceremonies,
celebrations of advanced age, and the lunar New Year.[6]

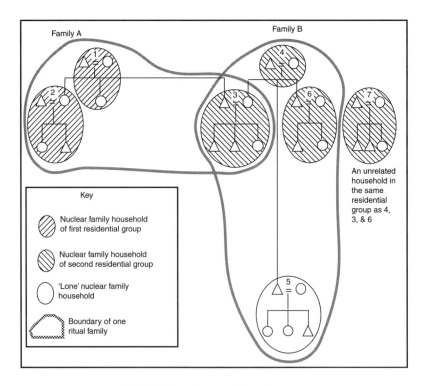

FIGURE 4.1. Types of family group

The use of the term ritual family allows us to clarify the other terms outlined above. The residential family group is the part of the ritual family that is contained within the residential group. In Inner Asia this is often the stem family, with a tendency towards virilocality so that it is frequently a married son with whom the parental couple live. The household is based on the subgroup of the residential family group that share one hearth (although it may include non-family members), and is usually centred on the nuclear family. I call this the 'component nuclear family' when it forms a component of a larger family residential group. It is the kin basis for almost all households.

All the single parent households recorded in the case-studies consisted of a mother with her children, and for this reason I term them 'LONE MOTHER HOUSEHOLDS'. Finally, in a number of case-study sites there is a household form that we have termed the 'GRANDPARENTAL HOUSEHOLD', which is composed of one or both members of an old conjugal couple and one or more grandchildren, but without the child's parents.

SOCIAL RELATIONS OF OBLIGATION AND RURAL NETWORKS

I use the term 'social relations of obligation' to describe the nature of the networks of relationships that I describe in this chapter. If we take networks to mean social relations that exist in reality,[7] then those links along which assistance can be definitely expected to flow can be distinguished from more conditional relations by using the term 'social relations of obligation'. These relations are marked by the giving of goods and services, and also by requests for the same.

The social network spreads out from each individual, but this field of social relationships is by no means even. Firstly there is the high intensity of the bonds between members of the 'ritual family'; secondly other relationships may be selectively used so that relatives (*hamaatan* or *töröl sadan* in Mongolian), friends (*naiznar*), or even acquaintances (*tanil*) who are particularly important to each other at a given time will have closer and stronger bonds. The expectations that relatives have of one another differ somewhat, depending upon their relative ages. In general, elder kin are expected to provide assistance such as advice, influence, and material goods or money; while juniors are expected to provide respect, obedience and labour. Connections with affines seem to be no less important than those to cognates. This is particularly true in respect of the son-in-law, because – as Humphrey (1983: 347–50) notes in the Buryat case – there is a tradition of sons-in-law providing labour and assistance for their wife's parents. Close friends, who are usually of the same generation, tend to have more symmetrical relations with one another, and the importance of the obligations that such relations entail is indicated by the way in which friends are often spoken of using the idiom of kinship. The Mongolian term *ah duu*, which literally means 'elder and younger siblings' is often used to describe good friends.

Although obligations apply to both the persons linked by these bonds, there is rarely any sort of tally kept as to the help provided by each side, and in this sense it is unhelpful to describe the relationship in terms of 'exchange'. Rather than classify this network of relationships by the way in which they engender the transfer of objects, I suggest characterising them by the obligations that they entail. The transfers of goods or services that might accompany these links are a product of the social obligations of the relationship.[8] This perspective is comparable to that of Alfred Gell, although arrived at independently. Gell (1992: 151) writes: 'Moral obligation dictated by role-definitions provides a basis for a political economy and social-reproductive regime, which I will name "the indigenous services economy"'.

The importance of such networks certainly pre-dated the Communist era: Jagchid and Hyer (1979: 136) note the high traditional value placed on relations between friends, Aberle (1967) mentions the importance of kinship relations in the administration in pre-communist Inner Mongolia,[9] and Gillmour's accounts indicate the significance of personal connections in 19th century Outer Mongolia.[10] In the collective era the plethora of bureaucratic procedures, and the need for authorisation for all sorts of matters, made connections of vital importance. (The drivers of collective vehicles, for example, although technically subordinate to various officials, still managed to provide transportation for family and friends.) Resources of all sorts were accessed through persons in key positions, rather than (for example) with cash; and this often made the use of one's network the best – even the only – way to get things done. In general, relations with kin still provide the most important strands in these networks in pastoral regions. Although the birth rate has declined, Mongolians still tend to have large families (Randall 1993: 220), and the kin network of most people is generally large and well-extended. Although in China birth control regulations seek to limit family size, Mongolians are allowed more children than Han Chinese and pastoral families frequently have three or more children.[11]

In the following pages I will deal mostly with the instrumental and functional aspects of these relationships, but it should be stressed that they are also largely emotional bonds, and affection, respect, and the pleasure of another's company play an important part. Nevertheless, it is interesting to note the practical use to which these relationships are put.

Networks are of importance when it comes to the ownership of livestock and pasturing arrangements. Here I shall first describe the pastoral linkages between the *sum* centre and the herders, and then go on to discuss the networks of the herders in the countryside. As noted in the previous chapter many rural families live in settlements and they own livestock that are herded for them by pastoral households. In all of the case-study sites the majority of non-pastoral family residential groups that were interviewed owned animals that were herded for them by full-time herding households. Elsewhere these have been termed 'absentee' owners (IDS 1993: 9), but here we term them 'herd-placers'[12] since these people often participate in the work and activities of the pastoral households that are keeping their livestock. As figure 4.2 demonstrates, there is a strong tendency for these animals to be herded by kin, particularly close kin. The arrangements are generally outside formal economic relations, so that if they give anything at all, the owners give some present to the herdsman from time to time, rather than paying any sort of set fee. More commonly they simply help the herding household in a variety of ways, as part of relationships of social obligation. A typical arrangement was described by Dorj, a 42 year-old male administrator in Hosh Tolgoi, Xinjiang: 'My father-in-law herds all of my animals. I do not

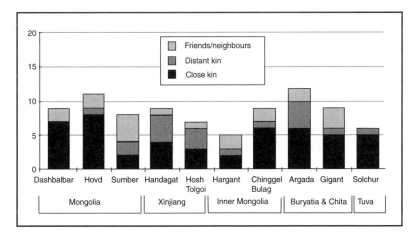

FIGURE 4.2. Categories of those who herd animals for interviewed 'herd placers'

give him anything for this, but whenever he needs to move, I help him with loading and transportation.'

As Tsagaanhüü, the 45 year-old head of Dashbalbar *sum*, noted:

> Most of the families who have their own livestock in the countryside but who have to live and work in the *sum* centre help the herdsmen in some seasonal work. For example in summer they help with repairing sheds and fences, herding livestock, and shearing; in autumn with cutting hay; in winter by cleaning snow from roofs; in spring they help with lambing and so on [...]

The term 'gift' is almost inappropriate to describe the supplies given to herders by livestock owners, because they are so expected. They may take the form of cash, but are more usually food, tobacco, alcohol or some other useful commodity. Their amount and frequency is often explicitly unspecified, and left to the owner to decide. An example of this informal arrangement is that of 40 year-old male driver Sodnomdorj, who told me: 'Sechin (my father's elder sister's husband) herds some cattle for us, a two year-old cow and a calf. We give them presents three or four times a year. For example, we give some silk material for making a *deel* [robe], a bottle of alcohol or a 25kg sack of flour.'

Of the 71 non-pastoral families interviewed in the case-study sites who had livestock herded for them by other households less than 10% paid a regular monetary fee (but the rest generally provided assistance or gifts).[13] In some cases the herding family kept animal products, such as wool, from the livestock they kept for the owners, (an arrangement that was apparently common in Mongolia before collectivisation), but these instances also made up less than 10% of our sample, see figure 4.3.

The forms of assistance most often mentioned by respondents were help with transportation, mowing hay and shearing sheep; and in general it seems to be slightly more common for close kin to help each other in this way than just giving presents. When goods are given they are generally adapted to the needs of the recipient and, of course, the resources available to the giver: tobacco for a smoker, hay to a herdsman who requires it, tea for the whole family, and so on. Although only some of the respondents described it explicitly in the interviews, the general obligation to help relations and friends find scarce resources makes this a very common way in which those in rural settlements help the pastoral members of their network.

Turning now to the pastoral households themselves figure 4.4 shows a classification by male and female interviewees of those individuals outside their household on whom they most relied for help. It is interesting to note

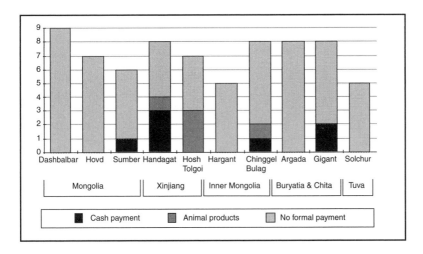

FIGURE 4.3. Payments given by interviewed 'herd placers' to herding families

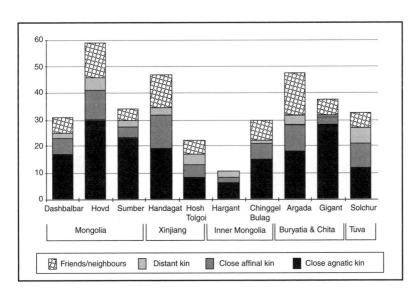

FIGURE 4.4. Categories of those most relied upon, as listed by respondents

the relative proportions of agnatic and affinal kin, distant kin[14] and unrelated friends or neighbours specified by respondents. In each case, bilateral kin of some sort predominate, and non-kin are only 0–33% of those listed. This data is suggestive rather than definitive, and should not be considered an attempt to 'measure' mutual aid, but it does give an impression of the importance of kinship in rural networks.[15]

There appears to be a significant bias towards agnatic rather than affinal kin in most of the case-study surveys.[16] This is not surprising; indeed seven of the ten studies were carried out in communities that continue to recognise, to a greater or lesser extent, membership of patrilineal exogamous clans (see chapter 1).[17] Taken as a whole, the responses suggest that the most important relationships for help and assistance are close bilateral kin, with a bias towards agnates, and that friends and neighbours are usually more important than distant kin in this respect.

How much did households spend on presents for others? An analysis of the average percentage of the previous year's annual income (1992)[18] that interviewed households estimated they had spent on gifts provided the data shown in figure 4.5. In each case this is a small but significant item of expenditure. Given the low sample size the absolute accuracy of these figures

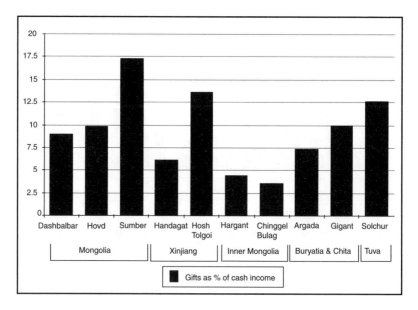

FIGURE 4.5. Gifts given as a percentage of household cash income (1992)

cannot be very high, and error is inevitable when researchers are relying on the memory, and often on the guesswork of informants, to put precise figures on their expenditures and incomes. However, the figures give some indication of the importance of this form of material transfers between households. When one also notes that in general a large percentage of income is spent on food, gifts clearly represent an important aspect of the domestic economy. Favourite gifts include alcohol, cloth, tea, sweets, other foodstuffs and money.

These figures are not the whole story, for they are based upon the cash income of the household concerned, and tend to underestimate the numbers of domestic livestock that are given to family and friends. The author notes that the herding family he lived and worked with in Sumber *sum*, Mongolia, gave no fewer than five sheep and goats to family and friends over the six months. When the formal interviews were carried out, however, the household counted only the three animals given to the more distant relatives as gifts; the other two were given to close kin but considered to be the home consumption of the family.

PATTERNS OF KINSHIP AND RESIDENCE

The following sections describe the situations in the case-study sites, and include graphs showing the kinship relations found among the residential groups included in the case-studies. The graphs with even numbers (figures 4.6 to 4.24) show the way in which each RESIDENTIAL GROUP has been classified, so that (for example) if a residential group consisted of a conjugal couple living with a dependent child in one *ger,* with their married son and his family living alongside in a second *ger,* then the residential group would be classified as a stem family. The HOUSEHOLD classification graphs (figures 4.7 to 4.25) show how each household (hearth group) has been classified, so the residential family group mentioned above would be classified as two 'component nuclear families' (that of the older conjugal couple, and that of their son and daughter-in-law).

The residential information contained in the graphs cannot be taken as highly representative statistically, because of the relatively low sample size. (The number of households for which data in each case-study was collected averaged around 26, but the number of residential groups was only 18 in each location.) However, family residential forms are not random but are culturally patterned, and the data collected does provide a picture of typical forms in the studied localities.

It must be emphasised that in the case of mobile pastoral households, the residential groups described are *by no means permanent* or unchanging formations. They often join other households, especially in the summer pastures, to form larger residential groups for a while. The residential groups, as such, are in many ways much less important than the underlying network (principally of kinship relations) that produces these flexible residential formations. For each region I include some background information in order to provide the necessary context for discussing the forms of kinship and residence found there, although this may overlap to some extent with information found in other chapters.

Buryatia, Chita and Tuva

The Siberian and Tuvan study sites are subject to the turmoil of the Russian attempts at privatisation. These reforms, described in chapter 2, created widespread economic disruption.

The collectives and state farms, and their successor institutions, continue to be the most important agricultural organisations, and the power and influence of their leadership remains very significant. In some cases the officials chose which households were to become private farmer-herders, and in general those who have set up independent family farms are usually those with the best relationships with local leaders and those with exemplary work records. These households received special support, loans and provisions to try to make their small-scale enterprises viable. The future of this small private farming sector remains uncertain, and there are some indications that it has been unable to perform even as well as the ailing collectives (see chapter 3). Agricultural production has fallen over the last few years, and rural producers, collective as well as private, have increasingly turned to their own resources to supply themselves and their relatives with necessary provisions.

In this uncertain economic climate kin relations have become increasingly important, especially in rural districts. Not only does kinship provide a mutual aid network in the face of shortages, but it is the basis for the new property-owning corporations that have become possible. All the recently established private farms were based on groups of relatives, and in an atmosphere of mistrust and uncertainty many informants felt that because they could only really trust their kin, they were unlikely to go into business with non-relatives.

Buryatian rural residence forms reflect the relatively settled nature of the population, and the fact that most families live in static buildings means that residential groups are generally constant and composed of some part of the ritual family. In Buryatia a relatively large proportion of the rural population live in settlements, and in the Argada site, for example, only about 100 to 120 of the 500 households of the district can be considered 'pastoral' households.[19] Many of the features observed in the Buryat studies are, however, common to all the study sites. The nuclear family is the most common household form. Often families are accommodated in semi-detached houses, which one might call a residential unit, but such a unit is in some important respects less significant than the ritual family. Thus families sharing a building may have been settled there by the authorities and are often not kin.

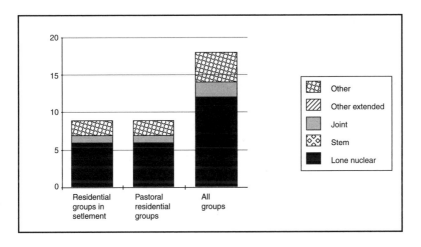

FIGURE 4.6. Classification of residential groups, Argada, Buryatia

Lone nuclear family indicates a residential group consisting of a single nuclear family; (i.e. one or both parents and their dependent children). *Stem* family is a residential group made up of a nuclear family with one or both of the parents of one of the spouses. *Joint* family is a residential group consisting of married brothers or sisters living together. *Other extended* family is used for some other form of extended family (a domestic group of two or more nuclear families linked through parent–child links or through siblings). *Other* is a category for those residential groups which do not fall into any of the categories described above. If any non-kin or more distant kin are included in the residential group then they are placed in this category, along with single people and 'grandparental' residential groups.

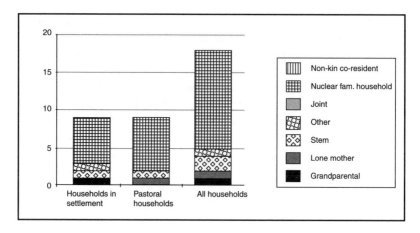

FIGURE 4.7. Classification of households, Argada, Buryatia

The units of analysis are the households (hearth groups) that make up the residential group. The *nuclear family household* is a nuclear family that exclusively occupies one dwelling, whether part of a larger family residential group or not. The *grandparental* household is where one or more grandparents live with one or more grandchildren but no other kin. The *lone mother* household is a mother and her children but no other household members. The *stem* family household indicates a stem family sharing the same dwelling, and the *joint* family household is a whole joint family living in the same dwelling. *Non-kin, co-resident* indicates households that are unrelated to the (nominal) 'first household' of each residential group. *Other* is for households that do not fall into the types outlined above.

Figures 4.6–4.11 show that the most common household form in the Russian area of the project is the nuclear or stem family, sometimes as a component part of a larger residential group. The Gigant data suggests a higher incidence of stem families forming residential groups and households than the Argada sample, where lone nuclear families are better represented.

The exact composition and permanence of the residential group depends, to a large degree, on the housing available, and the opportunities that the family has to use or gain property. Extended families usually have more than one house. If a family group has a chance to gain a house then it will usually find a subsection – such as a 'component nuclear family' to move into it. By contrast, several of the family farms formed in the early nineties, rather than splitting up to get extra housing, included a large number of kin in one officially-registered family unit so as to qualify for a large allocation of former collective property, such as a tractor or some other important capital asset.

In Argada the economic reforms led to the dissolution of the collective in the early nineties. Twenty-seven small private farms were formed, each usually containing between three and five families, who were virtually always close kin. There were three larger private farming associations, one with 80 families and two with 30, and these too were largely composed of kin. Neighbourhood networks do not generally organise much joint economic activity beyond the level of the ritual family or private farm, although sometimes two or three small private farms would get together to carry out haymaking jointly. However, far-flung networks with the cities are very important to gain access to a wide range of goods and services.

The large associations in Argada made use of the wider kin network to gain machinery and, in effect, sections of the old collective, while small private farms were based upon close kin. In the face of economic restructuring, kinship provided a ready basis for an adaptive response in social organisation. As it was difficult for administrative, service and teaching staff, who also received land and animals, to get fodder and other agricultural requirements, they generally joined up with rural relatives so as to be able to make use of their assets. Most families in the settlement have around ten cows, for milk and supplementary meat. Some they keep in the pastures around the settlement so that they can milk them regularly. The other cattle they usually sent off to be herded by relatives in the more distant pastures. As a result of this tendency, locals say, the pasture around the settlement has deteriorated badly out to a radius of a kilometre or so, and people try to avoid keeping many animals on it.

In Gigant the collective did not disappear and its assets have not been divided between new private farms, but houses have become privately owned and a number of private family farms were created by officials. As a result of the shortages and high prices of many goods which have increased the need for subsistence production and self-provisioning, kin have become more important. In 1993, when there was still the prospect of further privatisation, people were talking of the importance of families as potential property-owning corporations in the future. Since then, with only remote chances of obtaining loans to start up, few pastoral families envisage setting up as private herder-farmers.

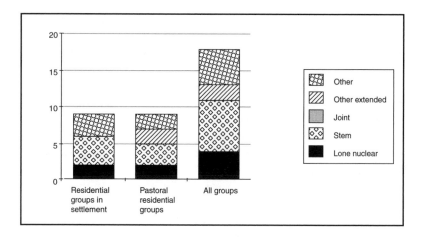

FIGURE 4.8. Classification of residential groups, Gigant, Buryatia

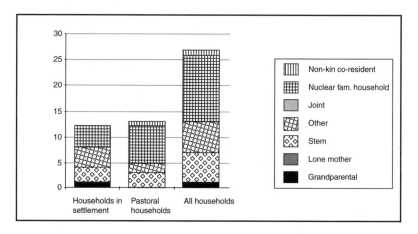

FIGURE 4.9. Classification of households, Gigant, Buryatia

The pastoral households are often based around the elder couple of an extended family who live at the *otara* (the allocated pastoral area at a distance from the settlement), and carry out herding. The married children of this couple often live in the settlement, although one couple may stay with the parental couple and form a stem family residential group. Family members often stay at each other's homes, so that the residential family could be said to have a core residential membership, and peripheral membership that includes the members of the other residential groups. The (usually elder) section of this core residential family stays most of the year round at the distant *otara* house, but may frequently visit the homes of the younger section in the settlement.

Most of the ritual family usually comes together to carry out the heaviest pastoral tasks – haymaking, and shearing. They also share goods, such as fuel, even when this is a violation of regulations. Those in the *otara* area will herd livestock belonging to other sections of the family. Pre-school-age children often stay in the *otara* during the summer with their grandparents, so there is also some sharing of childcare. The whole ritual family usually comes together for New Year and some other celebrations. The pastoral section of the family provides meat and animal products, and the (generally younger) kin living in the settlement often have networks in the settlement and elsewhere through which they can sell animal produce from the parental herds so as to get a good price.

One of the reasons that the elder sections of the families tend to stay in the *otara* collective herding stations is that they wish to make sure they keep a claim to these buildings and animals in case of further privatisation.

Most people who live in the city have relatives who live in the rural areas. The kin networks between urban and rural households may be quite extended. A young city couple, for example, may have good relations with their parents, who in turn enjoy good relations with country relatives. This indirect relationship with rural producers allows them access to important goods such as meat.

Self-provisioning has had to increase as a result of the economic difficulties of recent years. A 49 year-old male builder Erdene Budaev explained: 'In the past it was good. There are about 5 shops in our village; it was possible to buy everything. Now it is expensive and there are few food products. We don't die of hunger but often we can't buy apples, and we are short of bread.'

This has lead to an increase in the amount of domestic work, which mainly falls to women, and children also generally do more work than they used to, because they often help with a wide range of self-provisioning activity, including herding. A 31 year-old female herder, Handama noted a rise in the amount of work she carried out: 'I think the number of household tasks I have to do has increased because we are short of so many things. Goods are very expensive in the shops, so now we produce a lot of our own food, but we still generally buy clothes from the shops or from salesmen.'

In the Tuvan case-study site of Solchur, fieldwork also suggests that although the state farm still exists and regulates pastoralism in the region, work-based brigades are losing ground to kin-based groupings which are increasingly important for subsistence provisioning. Several informants echoed the sentiment expressed by a 54 year-old male herder Bujan Dongak: 'We really do not rely on anyone except members of our own family. In situations when we need help from somebody we prefer to rely on each other.'

All the interviewees agreed that close kin were the most important people with respect to mutual aid and assistance, especially in serious and important matters. None of the 23 households included in the study formed residential groups with non-kin families. The importance of such kin groups for economic activity is illustrated by the case explained by 36 year-old male herder Vadislav Solchak:

> If we need help of some sort we rely upon my two brothers, Mergen and Dayan-Chogbo, my youngest sister, Elbek, and upon the two sons and daughter of my sister – Nima, Seden, and Alla. All these people are not only the people we can rely on, they are also our informal helpers. For example, Mergen helps to graze sheep, Doyan-Chogbo drives the tractor, Nima also grazes sheep, Alla helps to milk cows etc. We have no special system of payment. We are relatives and usually a system of payment doesn't exist among relatives. To help each other is our duty and the old tradition of our ancestors. All our co-operation is based upon the principle of mutual aid.

Most of the Inner Asian case-study sites had the same pattern as the Tuvan one. The residential group is usually made up of related nuclear families. Each nuclear family usually lives in its own house and yurt.[20] These are grouped together in a small agnatic cluster of one or more of a couple's married sons. There is a slightly greater tendency for this residential family group to be composed of the extended family, rather than the stem family which is more common in the other sites (in other words, the Tuvan family groups tend to be larger). Hardly any of the pastoralists live in lone nuclear families, though this form is quite common in the village (and even these seemingly isolated families [figure 4.11] are in fact in close touch with more distant relatives). Although in Inner Asia as a whole virilocal residence after marriage is the ideal norm, the Tuva data shows that the norm is not always followed. Indeed, only a few of our sample followed this pattern, and an almost equal number lived with the wife's kin.

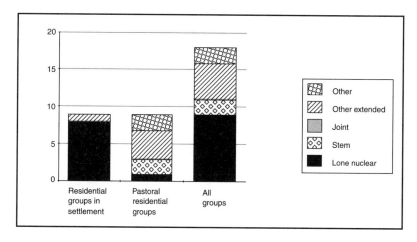

FIGURE 4.10. Classification of residential groups, Solchur, Tuva

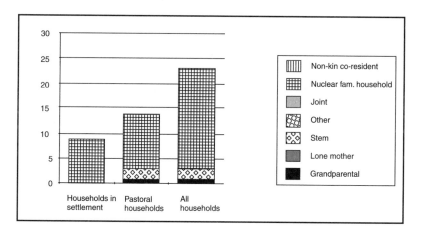

FIGURE 4.11. Classification of households, Solchur, Tuva

Static housing is widely used by families in this region, often alongside mobile yurts. All but two of the studied families had one or more houses, and all the pastoral families had one or more yurts. Tuvan family groupings tend to be large and they do not link up with neighbours and distant kin in residential units like the large Central Mongolian *ail* often found in the summer. Typically the family has a building and a yurt, and the yurt is rarely placed alongside those of other families. Families tend to flexibly use both types of dwelling, often favouring the building in winter and the yurt in summer. After moving to the summer pastures kin sometimes camp together in clusters of three to five yurts. They occasionally move so as to be with other relatives for some joint work, but not frequently.

The increased need for economic self-sufficiency has made it important for kin groups to maintain a pastoral as well as a salaried urban membership. As in the past, most rural Tuvan families want to place one or more children in higher education so as to get a good occupation in the city. But they also want to keep some children at home to help with the herding, and in the long run to take up pastoralism. The senior kin of rural families have become more important in decision-making, as they now have greater managerial responsibility. Housing is now mostly privatised, but there have been no marked changes in the forms of residential groups as yet. Although more goods are now made at home, the pastoral division of labour within the household has not noticeably changed. As described at the beginning of this chapter, women remain primarily responsible for tasks associated with the home, and men are primarily responsible for working with livestock and other tasks done far from the home.

At shearing and haymaking time close relatives will usually gather to help, generally two or three households of the wider family. In addition to this in the summer months, and sometimes during weekends, close kin often come out from the centre and help with the pastoral tasks considered appropriate to their gender.

The links between the country and the town are important; if a family has close kin living in the pastoral regions they are likely to exchange rural for urban produce. Close kin retain bonds of mutual obligation, and wider clan links are also used on occasion. Rural kin typically give meat, cheese, and other food; and urban families are often looked upon to help provide educational and job opportunities for the children of their country kin.

Mongolia

In Mongolia, privatisation of the *negdel* collectives has gone much further than in Russia and most of the livestock, and other agricultural resources, have become the private property of the members of the collectives through the issue of vouchers. By 1992 the *negdel*s had become companies, and the distribution of formerly collective assets had been completed. In some cases, such as that of the Tuyaa Company of Dalanjargalan *sum* in 1993, the company purchased animal products, or the animals themselves, from the rural producer at a price established by the company. The company also decided upon the prices of the products that the families received from it – the most important being winter hay and fodder. The balance of what the family was paid, minus what it was charged by the company, was then available to the family members to buy consumer goods in the company shop, or to withdraw as cash from the company's financial department. Since 1993 some areas have dissolved such companies; in other districts they remain only as marketing organisations, having privatised most or all of the formally collective livestock. Where State Farms have become companies, they continue to hold quite large numbers of animals. These are herded by households under 'lease' arrangements that are similar to the old 'norm' by which the collective members were given production plans.[21]

In areas that have divided formally collective assets, some enterprises termed 'co-operatives' (*horshoo* or *horshoolol*) have been formed, often it appears around some section of the old *negdel*. For instance, in the *sum* centre the small factories or plants that the collective had set up became co-operatives. Where pastoral co-operatives have been formed it appears that networks are fundamental to their membership. An example of this is the Bayan Tsagaan *horshoolol* in Bayantümen *sum*, Dornod *aimag*, mentioned in the previous chapter. Founded in April 1993, it was composed of ten families, all of whom were kin, and was formed around certain resources that used to belong to the old collective, notably some vehicles, a large winter animals enclosure, haymaking and potato fields. The membership of the co-operative was based upon the kin network of the man who was central to its formation, and not upon a residential or neighbourhood group. Several members had come from some distance to join the co-operative that their kinsman had founded. Although all ten member households helped make hay together in the summer, most of them lived in several different places for the rest of the year. During the labour-intensive haymaking season kin networks were once again in evidence as other relatives of the member households came to help, and not people from neighbouring encampments. The co-operative was described as a temporary and experimental formation, which might be disbanded if it was not seen to be working well.

The nature of the social obligations involved in the Bayan Tsagaan *horshoolol* is well demonstrated by the way that members said that they would on no account employ paid workers to help with seasonal labour, and that poor kin were included in the co-operative. The formation of this co-operative should not be seen however as typical of the changes underway in the whole of the country. In the two *sums* in Dornogov' *aimag* where I worked, for instance, there were no initiatives of this kind, and 1996 most of the *horshoolols* in Hövsgöl and Ar-Hangai *aimags* had gone bankrupt or become inactive. Throughout rural Mongolia it is mostly the case that families are left to fend for themselves.

One of the ways families manage is to make use of their far-flung networks. Produce is obtained not only by household subsistence production but also through contacts of one sort or another. Of course, this is by no means a new phenomenon. In the commandist period this practice was widespread, and as authorisation was necessary for a wide range of goods and services, links with those in positions of authority were of prime importance. During the collective period, networks tended to reflect the formal structures of power. Although there have been changes to this official structure, the networks remain, having grown around and along the lines of power of the old organisations. Today the control such officials have over the economy and society may have lessened officially, but the economic dislocation of reform (particularly the problems of distribution) has led to shortages, high inflation and general economic instability. In this situation many officials retain effective control of much of the distribution process, because they remain part of old networks that have access to goods and resources.

The response of many Mongols is to rely to an even greater degree on family and friends – these people are the resources that you can count upon. Through such networks they hope to gain access to the wide range of goods and services that are not freely available, but may be gained from those in the right position, not necessarily a senior one. (Drivers, for instance, still generally manage to supply their family and friends with transportation, although this has become much more difficult due to petrol shortages.) The increased reliance on individually produced and procured goods, and upon personalised relations for their distribution, means that the economy seems to have become more, not less, socially 'embedded' in the opening years of the 'age of the market' (as the Mongolians call the post-collective era).

Rather than selling and buying, the commercial option, the shortages in Mongolia, as in the Russian regions, have led rural households to increase the amount of self-provisioning production (see also chapter 5). Much of this work is done by women. It is particularly prevalent in distant regions where traders cannot cover the costs of transport. In the distant Hovd *sum* 52 year-old male herder Pürev commented:

There is a shortage of some goods which we were able to buy a few years ago, so we have to make some of them ourselves now. For example – we spin wool by hand and we knit our own clothes, such as socks, blouses, shirts etc. We also make Mongolian boots and make our own flour. These tasks, which were done in the past, are now being restored as a result of the economic changes.

The case-studies show the importance of networks in rural life, and that these networks cross the boundaries between the mobile and the settled sectors of Mongolian rural life (as discussed in chapter 5). The rural community includes both settled and mobile sections, and these two life-styles are inextricably interconnected. Products and personnel (particularly children) move between the settlements and the mobile pastoral encampments; meat and animal products come into the district centre, and a variety of manufactured products flow in the opposite direction, the most important of which are generally flour, tea, salt, cloth, candles, tobacco, alcohol and sugar. Most of the people in the district centre have close kin (siblings, children or parents) engaged in mobile pastoralism, whom they meet regularly. This creates a social matrix that includes both mobile and settled life, and most of the village residents are involved in pastoralism in some way. As Tsagaanhüü, the 45 year-old head of Dashbalbar *sum*, noted: 'The majority of the people of the *sum* centre help the herdsmen with seasonal labour.'

In the Hovd *sum* case-study site the dominant family residential group in our sample was the stem family, with a fairly strong tendency towards virilocality so that it is usually a married son with whom the parental couple live. Indeed, of the eighteen residential groups included in the study only one was uxorilocal and six followed the virilocal residence norm.

Pastoral residential groupings (*ail* or *hot-ail*) do not usually become very large, even in the summer pastures. Usually there are two *gers* in an *ail*, sometimes three. An analysis of the nine pastoral residential groups included in the case-study shows that all but one were composed either of stem or nuclear families. Six of the nine were stem families living in two *gers*, each dwelling containing a component nuclear family. One was a nuclear family in which none of the sons had married, and another was an older nuclear family with two remaining unmarried children. The last family was effectively a stem family with an attached affine, which we could classify as an affinally expanded family. At the times of study, September 1992 and July 1993, one of the *ails* studied had 3 *gers*, 75% of the households were in *ails* comprising of 2 *gers*, and only 2 of the 16 were single *gers*. It should be noted, however, that *ail*-formation is an ongoing process, so at various times of the year households may come together to form larger residential groups.[22]

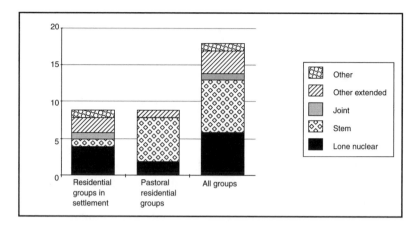

FIGURE 4.12. Classification of residential groups, Hovd *sum*, Mongolia

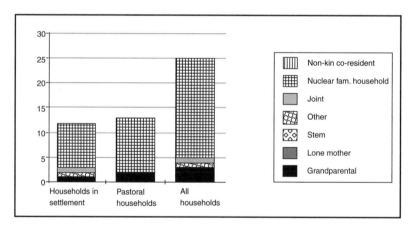

FIGURE 4.13. Classification of households, Hovd *sum*, Mongolia

Recently, informants said, the *ails* have tended to become larger, as a result of privatisation and the increased number of people in pastoral areas. Some of those who had lost their jobs in the *sum* centre moved out to live with kin and herd animals – often pooling their livestock with kin who have an established herd.

In Hovd *sum*, proximity was the basis for some co-operative activity between households, but rather little. Informants described services provided for, and received from, other households and their frequency. This showed that kith and kin provided services between two and twenty times more often than those of households which were only neighbours, described as *saahalt ail* (or *hoshoo ail* in local Uvs parlance). The sorts of activity that such neighbours co-operated with were: shearing sheep, combing cashmere and making felt. Relations and friends also helped with all these tasks, but were also relied upon for help in seasonal migration, getting fuel and herding.

In Sumber, pastoral residence followed the well documented *gov'* (Gobi) tendency of small *ails*, (described in the pre-collective period by Simukov 1935: 100–104) usually composed of a single *ger*, and sometimes two. Of the nine pastoral *ails* that were studied, four were composed of single *gers*.[23] The Sumber graphs show a high proportion of residential groups classified as 'other' – principally because of the higher numbers of non-kin living side-by-side. Interestingly, of the four *ails* that included separate *gers* of non-kin, three were considered to be 'rich' herding families, and the other was probably the next richest *ail*. Indeed, all but one of the middle and poor households included in the study were without other households in their residential group. This supports the fieldworker's impression that richer herding households can attract poorer families, both kin and non-kin, and usually herd jointly. In some cases the poorer attached households are pensioners who have no children living with them, and so would have difficulty supporting themselves independently.[24]

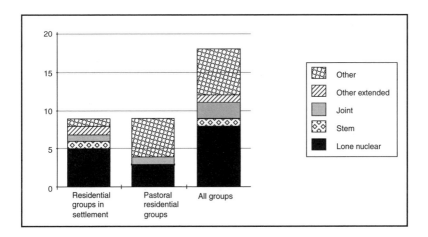

FIGURE 4.14. Classification of residential groups, Sumber, Mongolia

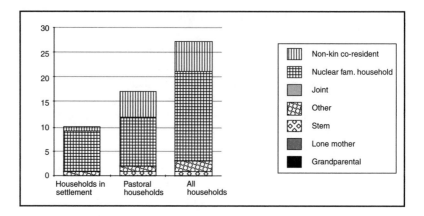

FIGURE 4.15. Classification of households, Sumber, Mongolia

Generally the importance of kinship in the *ail* formation was weak, relative to other study sites,[25] although as a vital network for both production and consumption it appears to be as important as in other regions. Evidence of virilocality is also relatively weak, because although there was only one uxorilocal residence group in the eighteen, there was also only one truly virilocal group. In this rather atomised residential pattern it is the networks that are important, the invisible social 'fields' rather than visible residential units. Kinship relations remain central to such networks, as 53 year-old female herder Altangerel explained:

> Because we are close to Choir, where our son lives, we have good access to help and resources at all times. We are also able to move to other pastures easily because we have many friends who are drivers. Our daughter-in-law is a vet, which is useful for getting the livestock treated. Also our two nephews, Sechin and Bataa, and our niece Batchimeg, help in the summer holidays – herding animals (mostly sheep), milking sheep and cows, breaking in 2 year-old horses, collecting dung, cleaning the house, and helping in general everyday work.

In Dashbalbar in north-eastern Mongolia, of the 25 households that were included in the study 18 were nuclear families, and all but one household were kin of the others in their residential groups. All but two of the eighteen family residential groups lived in wooden houses and the nine pastoral families also had one or more *gers*.

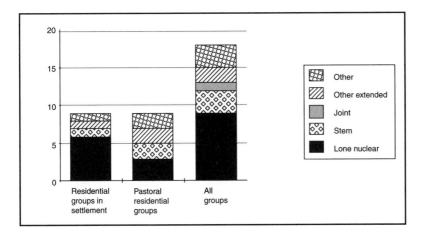

FIGURE 4.16. Classification of residential groups, Dashbalbar, Mongolia

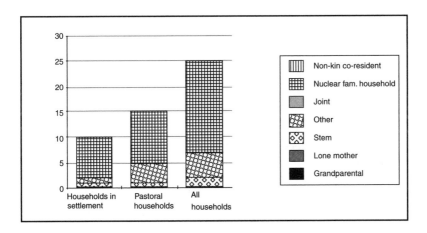

FIGURE 4.17. Classification of households, Dashbalbar, Mongolia

The most common residential pattern for pastoral households is to have a wooden house built at the winter and spring pastures, which is used most of the year around, and then a *ger* that can be used in the winter and moved to the summer and autumn sites. Some families have another building in the summer pastures. The winter buildings of neighbouring families are often within sight of each other but these households may well move to summer sites in different areas. They may meet up with others there, but these associations are very flexible and vary year-to-year. About half the households have some sort of arrangement with other households to take a part of their herds with them to pasture in some other area.

The pastoral and settled households form a single community. The relationship between 42 year-old male tractor driver Shagdarsüren, living in the *sum* centre, and his son-in-law is an example of the services accessed through the kin network, and the way in which such relations of social obligation connect pastoral and settled families:

> Because I have a tractor I help my son-in-law's family to cut hay, help with their seasonal movements, and sometimes I take wood out to them. My seven year-old son stays with their family and helps them with herding livestock – he doesn't go to school so it is better for him to stay in the countryside and learn how to herd animals. Because my son-in-law also herds our own livestock, and I help him with the tractor, he supplies us with milk and milk products.

Inner Mongolia and Xinjiang

China has not seen the drastic economic changes in the last few years that have been experienced by the other parts of the region. Although there remain a few state farms where the livestock is owned by the state, in general livestock has been privately owned since the distribution of commune property in the mid-1980s. There were, however, a number of different ways in which this was done, and a variety of official duties and obligations that herders now have, as discussed in chapter 3.

The state also continues to regulate the reproduction of pastoral households. The family planning policy that started in the 1970s at first had little effect upon the Mongolian rural regions of China, but in the nineties it has become stricter and better enforced. Now the maximum number of children for rural Mongolian families is two, or three if the first two are girls (Zhang 1996: 73). Younger families seem to be influenced by this rule and many are having two, three or four children, fewer than in the past. In the *sum* centres and towns the number of children tends to be lower – only two or so, as many of these residents have some sort of state employment and are under great pressure to abide by the laws.[26] For comparison of family sizes in Inner Mongolia and Xinjiang, see Zhang (1996).

In Inner Mongolia it appears that after the introduction of the responsibility system and the allocation of the pastures to individual families, there has been an increase in the importance of kinship as a principle for the organisation of residence, work and property-ownership.

In Chinggel Bulag the authorities instituted a formal group of households, the *hot*. These *hots* were usually composed of close kin.[27] Each constituent household was allocated grazing land in the different seasonal pastures, but as far as possible alongside that of other households of the *hot* so as to form a larger joint area of pasture.[28] Where this was impossible informal arrangements were often made so that kin could live relatively close to each other.[29]

According to local government statistics, at the beginning of 1993 there were 273 herding households in Chinggel Bulag *sum*, and of these 93 (34%) had static dwellings. They were grouped into 40 settled *hots* including a total of 449 people, and 37 mobile *hots* living in *gers*. The mobile *hots* had more households than those with buildings, but although there were more settled *hots* than mobile, they only accounted for 40% of the *sum*'s total pastoral population of 1,129.[30] In other words, the mobile households had fewer members than the settled ones, but there were more households in each residential cluster. Despite the apparent institutionalisation of the *hot* residence group, pastoral families still display a somewhat flexible residence pattern, so that residential groupings vary in the different seasonal pastures. Many households, however, stay most or all of the year in one place (usually on the 'spring' pastures where some also have a building).

Those families with static buildings are generally relatively wealthy and usually also have one or more *gers* with which part of the family residential group (usually a component nuclear family) may move to other seasonal pastures with the livestock.[31]

The allocation of pasture land, the introduction of institutionalised *hots*, and the increasing number of buildings appears to be having an important impact upon residential organisation. The official *hot* with static dwellings does seem to have significantly more members than those living in *gers* for much of the year. The average static *hot* includes 18.4 people, for example, while the average mobile *hot* has only 11.2.[32] The other important feature is the much higher incidence of joint families in the Chinggel Bulag sample than in any of the other ethnically Mongolian sites, because siblings have often been allocated buildings in the same *hot* (often different parts of a single, long, one-storey house).

In general the Chinggel Bulag site had large residential groups at the time of study, although as in other parts of the region the precise form of them at a given time is a variable expression of social relationships. In our sample

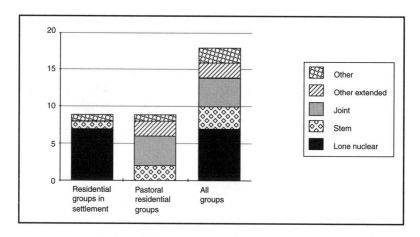

FIGURE 4.18. Classification of residential groups, Chinggel Bulag, Inner
Mongolia

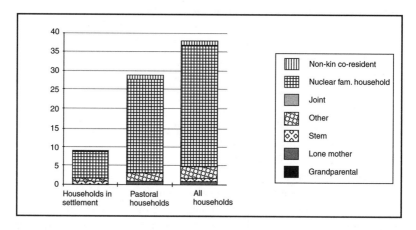

FIGURE 4.19. Classification of households, Chinggel Bulag, Inner Mongolia

the average number of households in the most permanent of the residential
groups (at the 'spring' pastures, where many families spend most or all of the
year now) is 2.9, which is the highest of any of the case-study sites.[33]
Virilocality is a marked tendency, but far from universal; of the eighteen
residential groups studied, one was uxorilocal and six were virilocal.

The member households of the *hot* generally herd their livestock jointly, often in rotation and with different members of the group specialising in an animal species. At lambing and shearing time the family members will generally look after their own animals, and not those of the other families in the *hot*. As mentioned in the previous chapter, there is virtually no active formal social group larger than the *hot*, although there is a network. At a child's hair-cutting ceremony, for instance, immediate family and friends attend, and other relatives, such as cousins, might also come, depending on the circumstances.[34] As in other case-study sites, relatives from the *sum* centre often come out to help pastoralists, especially those whose livestock is being herded for them by relatives or friends.

Rich people may ask poorer friends or relatives to herd animals for them, often in the poorer families pastures because the rich do not have enough pasture of their own to support all their livestock. Significantly, they often pay them money for keeping their animals, at the rate of around 150 yuan per month. These cash arrangements exist alongside the more traditional part-produce payment systems, whereby the herder takes the wool or some other portion of the animal's produce as payment.[35]

In general there appears to be a small but significant trend toward hiring labour in the pastoral sector, often as part of the bonds of kinship and friendship. This trend also seems to be followed by Han Chinese who have migrated into the area and taken up pastoralism. One of the two Han herders interviewed in Chinggel Bulag, 57 year old Li Wu, explained: 'My brother-in-law, who is from Hebei, helps with herding; we pay him 1000 yuan each year, plus accommodation.'

Monetary payments are playing an increasingly important role in other aspects of the pastoral economy too. The use of land that has been allocated to others, both haymaking and pasture land, has become an important asset for which the richer herding families will sometimes pay cash, as 41 year-old male Mongolian herder Bold explained: 'Rich herders are best placed to obtain important pastoral resources because they have money to buy mowers for making hay, or to buy hay. They can also afford to build nice sheds for their animals. Haymaking pasture is allocated to herders but some herders make use of other people's pasture by paying money, or giving something, or providing a service in return'.

The Hargant case-study in northern Inner Mongolia, shows a different pattern from Chinggel Bulag, with a relatively high number of stem families composing residential groups, which makes it more comparable with the results from the studies in Dashbalbar in Mongolia and Gigant in Chita.

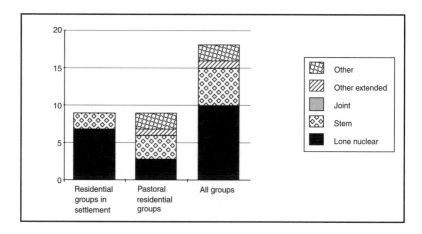

FIGURE 4.20. Classification of residential groups, Hargant, Inner Mongolia

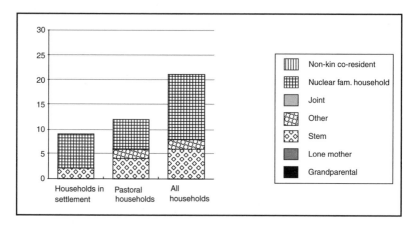

FIGURE 4.21. Classification of households, Hargant, Inner Mongolia

These areas are geographically and ethnically rather close, all of them largely inhabited by the related Barga and Buryat Mongol peoples.

Most pastoral families have a static dwelling in this region. Of the nine herding family residential groups, seven had buildings, and all of them had one or more *gers*. Virilocality appears to be relatively strong; the Hargant sample included one uxorilocal and four virilocal residential groups.

Of those mentioned as providing help by the interviewed households, no friends or neighbours were mentioned. Informants noted an increased emphasis on self-interested and exclusive close kinship relations in recent years, as 54 year-old male herdsman Choijilsüren explained:

> After privatisation relationships with kin became closer and stronger, and people's circles of friends became smaller. People help their close kin and friends more, but make a distinction with other people and are not so helpful and friendly with others as they were in the collective period. Each household is more individualistic, and has more freedom. They do not respect the officials as much as they did.

Large differences in wealth between rich and poor have emerged in Hargant over the last ten years, and many rich herd-owners now hire herders to pasture their large numbers of animals, not always to their satisfaction, as Chuluunbaatar, a rich 56 year-old herdsman explained: 'Usually, we hire regular helpers to look after the herds, but we just can't find any good ones! We pay 150 yuan per month for a labourer, and 10-15 yuan per day for a temporary employee.'

Moving now to Xinjiang in Far Western China, the case studies suggest that Mongolian rural social organisation there follows similar principles to those found in the other case-study sites, with strong kinship bonds and flexible residence. In Hosh Tolgoi the pastoral residential group *ail* is generally small, often a single *ger*. This is usually the stem or nuclear family, see figures 4.22, 4.23.

Most pastoral families have access to a permanent dwelling, sometimes more than one. Of the nine pastoral family residential groups interviewed, all had both *gers* and permanent dwellings. Two of the households had three houses and two had two. None of them, however, had more than one *ger*. This is another example of the flexibility of the residential group, fitting into different forms of accommodation at different times. Among the mobile pastoral part of the community the most common residential formations are of three types: firstly the stem family living in an *ail*; secondly the nuclear family alone; and thirdly the stem or nuclear family with some poor relative living in a residential group. The residential family group is fairly constant, and is usually together all year round. In autumn other families often come out to help with haymaking.

Chapter 4

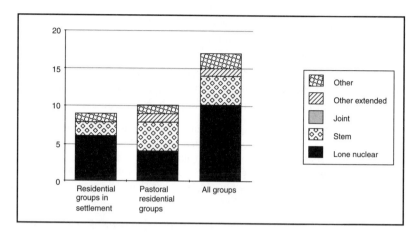

FIGURE 4.22. Classification of residential groups, Hosh Tolgoi, Xinjiang

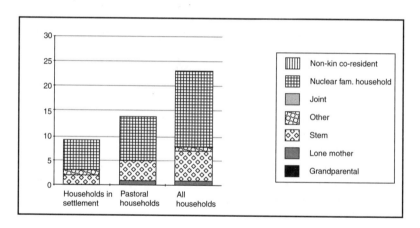

FIGURE 4.23. Classification of households, Hosh Tolgoi, Xinjiang

     Hosh Tolgoi is one of the case-study sites in which clans appear to be of increasing importance. Conceptually, the *arabat* ('clans') are the second most important kin category after the ritual family.[36] During the commune period the significance of clan identity declined, but it appears to be of increasing importance recently, and clans have revived something of their old ceremonial role at annual *oboo* ceremonies (see chapter 1). Now that most livestock is privately owned and inherited, it seems that some other aspects of pre-collective social organisation are also reviving. For example, the traditional ceremony to mark the separation of property after a man has married, *ömch salgana*, whereby a newly married couple receives a share of the herd from the husband's father, is reappearing in this region.

In autumn, family residential groups sometimes form temporary groupings of *ails* which help each other with large tasks such as haymaking. These families are often related, but in many cases these groups are formed with whoever is nearby. In the pre-collective period pastoralists used to make use of *sahalt ail* arrangements[37] (whereby the lambs would be exchanged between neighbouring *ails* so that the ewes could be better milked) but this arrangement is not widely practised now.

The Handagat case-study, carried out in a predominantly Kazakh region, has noticeably different residential forms from most of the other sites. The high number of joint (expanded) families is in contrast with most of the other sites. The family residential groups are composed, in roughly equal proportions, of agnatic and affinal kin. All the interviewed families have built dwellings, including the pastoral families, who also have one or more yurts.

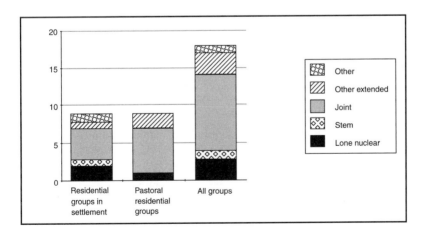

FIGURE 4.24. Classification of residential groups, Handagat, Xinjiang

Chapter 4

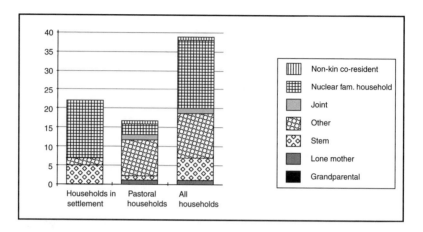

FIGURE 4.25. Classification of households, Handagat, Xinjiang

Since privatisation there has been a more central role for kinship in production relations. In 1993 there was local discussion that in the future clusters of kin should try to organise production formally, possibly in the form of co-operatives. However, property relations are extremely important and here it is not just kin who are involved: those with hay-cutting machinery, for example, tend to attract friends as well as relatives who need the use of it.

Both the Xinjiang case-studies indicated that as in the rest of China, labour was increasingly a purchasable commodity. In the settlement of Handagat, for example, domestic servants are occasionally employed to look after young children, and the hire of those with haymaking machinery is becoming commonplace. However, unlike the Inner Mongolian case-study sites there was little or no regular hiring of labour among the pastoral families, who generally appeared to retain a strong norm of mutual aid, as 38 year-old male herder Dodan explained: 'We do not hire anyone to work for us. Sometimes relatives and neighbours come and help from time to time. This is a very common thing. Of course we don't pay for this. To do so would be shameful!'

Comparing patterns of kinship and residence

The case-studies provide some points of comparison as to the way in which kinship and residence forms resemble each other across the region, and the factors that influence them. In general the Mongolian and Tuvan data suggests a predominance of lone nuclear and stem families, and very few joint families. The Kazakhs of the Handagat case-study are in marked contrast in that they have many more joint families, and relatively few lone nuclear and stem families, even among those families living in the settlement. Interestingly, the only other study site that seems to have had a significant number of joint family residential groups was Chinggel Bulag, where it seems likely that it is associated with the allocation of housing and pasture to the *hot*, which made it advantageous for close kin to form joint residential groups. Another general trend in the Mongolian, Inner Mongolian and Tuvan regions is that lone nuclear families are generally much more common among the families in the settlements than among the pastoral ones. This is to be expected as in the settlement housing is often allocated in such a way as to reduce the ability of kin to live in close proximity. Mobile pastoral households are generally better able to be flexible in the way they form residential groups.

There are some interesting similarities between several of the case-study site graphs. The highest numbers of pastoral stem families are found in the Hovd *sum* and Hosh Tolgoi, which are the most westerly study sites. It is interesting to note that apart from the Kazakh study site in Handagat, these are also the areas that appear to practice the most mobile form of pastoralism. Mongolian tradition favours the stem family, as the youngest son was customarily supposed to remain with his parents after marriage. It may be that such norms are more easily reflected in practice in the relatively mobile western case-study sites.

The single Kazakh case-study site (Handagat) stands out as having a very different residence pattern, with a much higher incidence of joint households. The Tuvan language is also Turkic, but the Solchur study site has a residential pattern that more closely resembles Buryat and Mongolian areas such as Dashbalbar and Gigant, although there are more extended families than in any of the other studies. Both Buryat studies show little difference between the pastoral residential groups and those living in the settlement, and this can be seen to reflect the relatively settled nature of the rural population.

It is interesting to note the similarities between the Dashbalbar and Hargant patterns, and this suggests that despite different administrative and economic contexts, the rural residence patterns of north-east Mongolia and Inner Mongolia bear close comparison.

PRE-COLLECTIVE MONGOLIAN PASTORAL RESIDENTIAL PATTERNS: THE HOT-AIL OR HOT

It is informative to place the current residential forms in context by examining what is known of pre-collective pastoral residential groups. Some of the best information we have for Mongolia is the work of A.D. Simukov, a Russian ethnographer who worked throughout Mongolia in the early 1930s, before collectivisation. His work includes a wealth of valuable observational material.

Simukov made a particularly detailed study (1933) of pastoral residential groups – *hotons* (*hot-ails*)[38] in one sub-district (*bag*) in Arhangai *aimag*. In this region, he notes, the *hot-ails* tended to be the largest in Mongolia, and this is still noticeable today. He found the average size to be around 4–5 households and points out that they were largest in the summer. He wrote 'each separate *hoton* is not a constant organisation. Existing today, it may disappear tomorrow [...] the number of *hotons* in one *sum* (district) is constantly changing.' He studied 100 *hotons* and classifies them thus: '*hotons* with constant composition 45 percent, *hotons* of mixed character 25 percent, *hotons* with inconstant composition 30 percent.' He notes that those households who camp together as one *hoton* continuously are those with the highest number of kinship links between the member households.

Simukov avoids describing the *hoton* as a group, instead he talks of 'the *process* of joining-up in *hotons*' (my emphasis). Simukov found that kinship was the most important feature of this process. 'There is a clear tendency to join up in *hotons* according to kinship lines in this *bag* (sub-district)', he writes, noting that agnatic kinship between household heads was most important, accounting for 41% of the *hot-ails*. Those camping with their sons-in-law came second with 21% of the studied encampments, and other relatives accounted for 35%. I propose that this social process of *hot-ail* formation involved the manifestation of social relations in a residential form. Rather than rigid and stable, these relations were a fluid and flexible network, based largely on kinship, but also on patron-client relations and friendship.

The co-operative activity Simukov describes as undertaken by members of *hot-ails* is herding animals and felt-making. Joint activities by members of neighbouring encampments, he noted, were almost entirely absent. 'Sometimes', he explains, 'two *hot-ails* will come close enough together to exchange lambs. It is the only form of co-operation between *hotons* that we managed to observe' he wrote. It is clear, then, that within the *bag* administrative unit there was little or no collaboration between *hot-ails* along the lines of common residence or the use of a given water source.

Simukov also notes that the rich tended to join up with poor households to make use of their labour, and the poor were only too willing to herd for the rich as they had great difficulty living independently. Simukov describes the senior figure who could usually be seen as the head of each *hot-ail*, characterised not only by generally being an older male, but also by being rich. Those households who camped together usually recognised this senior and referred to him using the term '*ah*' (a term used to mean elder brother, elder male relative or a senior close friend), but this person had no formal administrative position. These relations seem highly comparable with what I describe below as 'patron-client' relations in the Inner Mongolian case study sites.[39]

The pre-collective *hot-ail* that Simukov describes is not itself an institution, whilst the process of forming *hot-ails* is! This suggests that in China the local government may have forced a permanence upon what would in the past have been a semi-permanent grouping. The advantages for an administration is evident: in order to allocate rights over land it is necessary to define clearly the group to which they can be allocated. It remains to be seen, however, how successful the *hot* unit is as a holder of individuated rights to pasture land.

CONCLUSION

Mobile pastoral societies, as Lefebure notes (1979: 4), tend to be characterised by 'the mobility of domestic units of production and the fluidity of their consequent aggregates'. In the case of Inner Asia, at least, it should be pointed out that this flexibility extends to the *composition* of domestic units of production among mobile pastoralists, indeed these 'units' are often versatile residential groups within a wider network of kin.

The importance of understanding that residence forms are only manifestations of the social network is underlined by the fact that most rural families have alternative forms of accommodation. Most of the pastoral households interviewed as part of the ten case studies had access to both a static dwelling and a mobile yurt. This means that residence units can and must be reconstituted when family members make use of the various forms of accommodation. Another reflection of this underlying characteristic is the widespread inclusion of other relatives – particularly children – at certain times of the year such as summer.

The other important aspect of this underlying form is that in many cases, where circumstances permit, families may have both settled and mobile sections. Older family members, and children of school-going age for example, are likely to remain in the settlement (especially in Tuva), while the more active adult population may be carrying out mobile pastoralism.

The material gathered by the case-studies also suggests another general point: that social organisation, and indeed residence, reflects the changing forms of property relations.[40] This is illustrated by the tendency in Inner Mongolia for residential family groups to be relatively large, because the pastoral resources have been allocated to *hot* groupings.[41] It is interesting to note the way in which the local government in Inner Mongolia chose to see the *hot* as an institutional unit, and in the allocation and division of pasture, created powerful pressures for the concretising of this grouping.

The studies have also suggested that specific ethnic traditions play an important role in some aspects of the organisation of residential formations and family structure. Some of the most dramatic differences in the form of family residential groups (particularly the importance of joint family residential groups)[42] were not found to be between sites in different states, but between the only case-study site with a significant Kazakh presence and the rest. This suggests that certain aspects of social organisation are more deeply influenced by cultural traditions than the political and economic administration.

The importance of the economic aspects of social networks is another finding to have emerged from the studies. Social relations of obligation remain very important in all the case-study sites, particularly in the formerly Soviet and Mongolian regions where, as has been noted above, they have increased in significance in response to recent shortages and inflation. However, in the Inner Mongolian case-study sites there were indications that the increased wealth differences between rich and poor, greater commoditisation of the economy, and more individualised rights to resources have contributed to more monetary-based, commercial relationships than were found in the other studies areas.

In Inner Mongolia there appears to be a marked change in the nature of rural networks, though not necessarily in their importance. The social networks around individuals seem increasingly to reflect the differences of wealth between pastoral families. While obligation may form the essence of social relations between family and friends, the norm of reciprocity means that these links are most stable where obligations can be seen to be mutual and reciprocal. In this sense, extreme inequality between actors linked in this way may undermine their relations. I suggest, then, that where individuals amass extreme wealth, relative to their relations and friends, there are likely to be strains on these 'relations of obligation'. One would expect that either the circle of those included in this category would be restricted, as mentioned in the Hargant case study site, or that the assistance offered to other members of the network would be increasingly conditional.

Conditional commercial relations between pastoralists are a growing possibility throughout Inner Asia. But apart from China, where they have been developing since the mid-1980s, the other regions have seen only limited emergence of extreme differentiation in wealth in rural areas. The people still in, or only recently having left, the collectives expect other households to be approximately their equals. They retain an expectation of household self-reliance and resent becoming dependent on richer families. For this reason, networks still retain the value of mutual obligations.

In Inner Mongolia, on the other hand, the increased use of hired pastoral labour indicates an important change in the nature of rural social organisation. However, the people hired are often distant relatives and friends (i.e. members of the wealthy people's networks). Accounts of these personalised arrangements suggest that these relations are not yet those of an impersonal labour market. However, they also appear much less egalitarian than those generally found in the Buryat and Mongolian rural networks. These *asymmetrical* social relations of obligation, between the wealthy and those they hire, can be described as more like patron-client relations than those of purely commercial employment. Social obligations remain important in the choice and treatment of hired helpers; but whereas the relationship between close kin tends to be relatively unconditional, those between 'patrons' and 'clients' are generally conditional on the work being done to the patron's satisfaction. It may be, therefore, that in Inner Mongolia we are not simply observing the emergence of an ideal-typical market economy of the Western type. This analysis suggests that the large differences in wealth between rich and poor are reshaping the social relations of obligation. As in the Russian and Mongolian cases, socialist organisation produced a certain form of commoditisation and hierarchy, but whereas in the former two countries these qualities have declined and not yet been replaced, in Inner Mongolia they never entirely disappeared, and have been transformed into specific types of relations that hover between the commercial and the personal.

The networks described in this chapter create a social matrix that includes both mobile and settled life. As has been noted above, goods and persons move continually between the settlements and the mobile encampments; and most pastoral families have members living in the central settlement. In many respects it would be inappropriate to consider the mobile sector as distinct from the settled, centred communities around which they orbit. The picture of pastoral Inner Asia would be incomplete, therefore, without an examination of the processes of settlement in this vast region.

Chapter 5

SETTLEMENT AND URBANISM

Caroline Humphrey[1]

INTRODUCTION

The last chapter showed how a variety of personal strategies are realised in a complex and flexible variety of household, family and residential group-ings within the institutional frameworks described in chapter 3. This chapter describes how both institutions and more individual strategies take material form in equally complex processes of dwelling and settlement.

It is not always realised that even in the distant steppe areas of Inner Asia a large proportion of the population lives settled in townships. Little is published about the size, distribution and composition of these settlements. The present chapter analyses the systems of settlement in rural Inner Asia, their interaction with the cultures of land-use, and their relation to the environment. It attempts to reach some conclusions about the relation between movement, sedentarisation and urbanisation. In sum, I deal here with wide social processes of settlement and movement of people, while the next chapter analyses movement as part of pastoral techniques. Over the two chapters it will be argued that, contrary to stereotypes of pastoralists, mobility encourages advanced and specialised knowledge (chapter 6) and is not a bar to acquisition of urban culture, while sedentarisation of herders may lead to isolation and 'de-urbanism' of culture.

The topic of settlement has three facets, which are closely inter-connected:

1) the relation between the character of settlements and the systems of pastoral land-use;

2) the organisation of economic relations and the process of 'sedentarisation'; and

3) the impact of systems of settlement on the environment.

The term 'settlement pattern' as used here includes urban and rural, seasonal and mobile settlements. Such patterns constitute a synchronic current picture of the longer-term dynamic processes involved in 'systems of settlement'.

Systems of settlement over time involve two processes that can be separated analytically, although they may be connected in practice. The first process concerns 'SEDENTARISATION' and its converse, increased mobility. This is the relation of static to mobile ways of life as this has been changing through time. The second process is one of 'URBANISATION', or alternatively 'de-urbanisation', which indicates the dynamics of change in the extent to which communities live in, and are subject to the socio-economic influences of, towns and cities.

Urbanisation is accompanied by a greater number of people living in urban centres and an increase in the proportion of the total population living in urban centres. This is often associated with administrative centralisation and the development of infrastructures such as roads or railways allowing communication between rural and urban centres. Cities have variable economic and cultural influence (here called 'urbanism') on surrounding regions. Figure 5.1 provides an approximate picture of the possible spheres of influence of the large cities and major railways in Inner Asia as indicated by their size and importance. This shows that case-study sites 4 (Hargant), 7 (Hosh Tolgoi, Hoboksair) and 8 (Handagat, Altai) are all relatively close to large cities, and case-study sites 4 (Hargant) and 6 (Sumber) are on major railways. According to these criteria Hargant is the most urbanised of our case-study sites. However, as will be shown later, simple proximity to a city is not necessarily a good indicator of urban influence when this is understood in a more nuanced way. This leads me to develop a distinction between URBANISATION (broadly, population living in 'urban' centres) and URBANISM (the integration of people with city activities and culture).

Urbanisation is often accompanied by a tendency for more static types of dwelling and decreased seasonal mobility. However, it is an important argument of this chapter that this association does not always apply. There are people who live in mobile dwellings within cities and towns, such as the yurt-dwellers in the outskirts of Ulaanbaatar. On the other hand, there are rural areas, such as Gigant (site 2, Russia), where even the herders live an almost completely settled life in houses although they are distant from any urban centre.

An important argument of this chapter will be that *processes of urbanisation and urbanism in rural economies do not necessarily have a negative impact on the environment*. However, increased sedentarisation

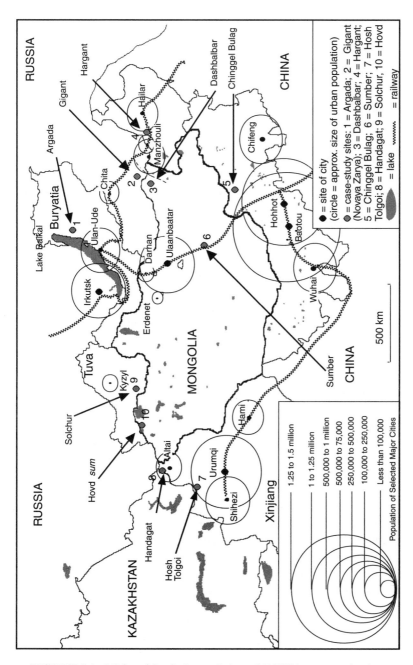

FIGURE 5.1. Major cities in Inner Asia and ECCIA case-study sites

('staticisation') of the population is having negative effects in certain locales and under certain economic conditions.

SOME NEW TOOLS OF ANALYSIS

Let me first explain the terms which will be used in this chapter. The existing terminology used to describe settlement patterns and types of household is limited to three categories: 'nomadic', 'sedentary' and 'semi-nomadic' (and the last of these is taken as a synonym for the term 'semi-sedentary'). It is generally understood that these terms relate to types of land-use. So 'nomadic' forms of settlement are associated with livestock herding, sedentary types are related to agriculture, and 'semi-nomadic' forms are related to mixed herding-agricultural land-use. However, this terminology is misleading and does not adequately represent either the settlement patterns or the character of land-use in Inner Asia. Our field-studies show that the above terms are unable to reflect the complexity of the dwelling types (stationary and mobile), the number of dwellings per household and the seasonal movements of Inner Asian rural people.

Furthermore, the terms 'nomadic' and 'sedentary' have acquired an ideological character in the writings of Inner Asian sociologists, particularly in Russia and China. In effect they have come to be associated with the ideas of 'backwardness' and 'development' respectively, and there is understood to be an evolutionary distinction between them. But B. Zhimbiev (1989) has shown that the ideological views put forward in Russia about so-called 'nomadic peoples' require re-thinking in relation to Buryatia.

The Buryats have been described as a traditionally 'nomadic' people, but sedentary forms of dwelling and agriculture have been present among them from early times.[2] Zhimbiev's analysis of the materials of the Kulomzin Commission at the end of the 19th century shows that the terms 'nomadic' and 'sedentary' to describe types of dwelling cannot be correlated with particular types of economy. At that time around half of Buryat households obtained their basic income from plough agriculture and the other half were dependent on livestock herding. However the forms of dwelling present a quite different pattern: around 80% of Buryat households used only stationary houses (and 18% of these used only one house and did not migrate, while 61.4% had several houses located at seasonally used sites). Only 6% of households used felt tents exclusively, while 14.6% had both stationary and mobile dwellings.[3] Thus, analysis of the relation between land-use and types of dwelling among Buryats shows that along with 'nomadic herders' and 'sedentary farmers' there were many households which are exceptions to these stereotypes: there were 'nomadic agriculturalists' and 'sedentary herders'. It is necessary to create new terminological and methodological principles that can express more accurately the systems of settlement and complexes of dwellings found in Inner Asia. This is particularly important for the local settlement patterns within districts, which remain virtually unstudied. To this end, we outline below some new categories for analysis at two levels of households and rural communities.

Households

At the household level we suggest that analysis be carried out on the basis of seven 'types of household living complex' (THLC), in each of which there are different associations of various kinds of dwelling (figure 5.2). The important point to note is that *pastoral households in Inner Asia, however poor, very frequently have more than one dwelling and/or more than one place of settlement.*

1) STATIC: households with only stationary dwellings and which do not move (Stat 1)

2) STATIC: households which have stationary dwellings in seasonal sites (e.g. summer and winter sites) (Stat 2)

3) COMBINED STATIC-MOBILE: households using stationary dwellings at winter and summer sites combined with a mobile dwelling (Comb 3)

4) COMBINED STATIC-MOBILE: households with stationary dwellings at the winter site only, and which otherwise use mobile dwellings (Comb 4)

5) COMBINED STATIC-MOBILE: households with a stationary dwelling only at the summer site, and otherwise using mobile dwellings (Comb 5)

6) MOBILE: households only using mobile dwellings in winter and summer camps (Mob 6)

7) MOBILE: households with mobile dwellings in more than two sites (Mob 7)

This typology allows us to distinguish household dwelling types into a series of categories, ranging from the entirely 'static' to the entirely 'mobile', and including a number of combinations in between. These combinations are in fact the most common forms of pastoral dwelling types in Inner Asia.

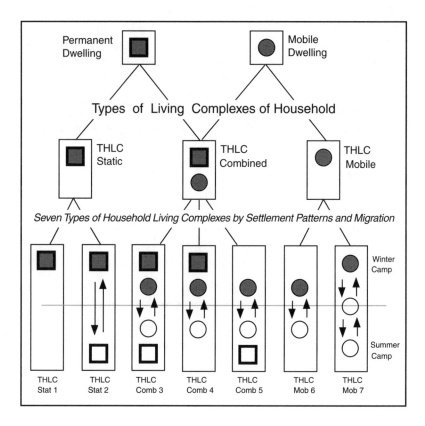

FIGURE 5.2. Seven types of household living complexes by settlement patterns and migration

As pointed out in the last chapter the household in Inner Asia is socially a flexible entity. The 'household' shares a hearth, has a common economy, a commonly-owned set of dwellings, and members normally eat together. This group can vary in size during the year and it uses various family types, as well as patron-client and other social ties, as its basis for recruitment. In much of Inner Asia the household uses a complex of living quarters, both stationary and mobile, together with sheds, pens, stores, bath-houses and other facilities (figure 5.4). The household frequently lives adjacently to other households in a single residential group (the *ail* in Mongolian), or it may at certain times of year reside on its own. The household may also send some of its members some distance away on short-term or seasonal herding trips (*otor*). This is why it is not possible to define the household only by the criterion of those people who eat together. The household changes not only over the course of an annual cycle but also over the generational cycle of the family which is its base. Thus over the years a given household might change from using one type of living complex to another (see previous chapter).

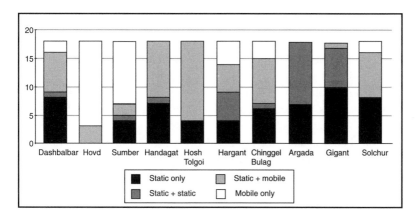

FIGURE 5.3. Patterns of dwelling at case-study sites (studied households)

Although it was not possible to enumerate all the dwellings of all the households in the ten case-study sites, we collected information on the dwellings of the 18 studied households in each place. This information is given in summarised form in figure 5.3, which for ease of reading divides dwelling complexes into four types: one static house only (Stat 1), more than one static house (Stat 2), a static house plus a mobile dwelling (Comb 3–5), and one or more mobile dwellings (Mob 6 and 7). The table shows that Hovd and Sumber in Mongolia have the most mobile types of dwelling complex, while Argada and Gigant in Buryatia, Russia have the most static.

If we look only at the nine herder households out of the total of 18 in each site, some interesting differences emerge between the three countries. In Mongolia two-thirds of all herders have mobile dwellings only, while the remaining third have permanent plus mobile dwellings. In China, the great majority of all herders have permanent plus seasonal mobile dwellings and only seven out of 36 households have mobile dwellings only. In Russia, around half the herders live in static dwellings that are used all year round, while most of the others have at least two houses. Tuva is the only site in Russia in our study that retains felt tents. In Russia and Mongolia differences of wealth of the herders are not clearly reflected in such different living complexes. However, in China it is only among the 'poor' herders that one finds households with mobile dwellings only.

Rural communities

Moving on to look at local communities, comprised of camps, settlements or townships internal to the district, we use the terms SEDENTARY and SEASONAL. We distinguish sedentary from seasonal settlements mainly by the presence in the former of a majority of year-round inhabitants. The above types of living complex are also useful in describing the various kinds of community settlement. Thus, for example, the inhabitants of a sedentary settlement will normally be households of types 1–4 in figure 5.2, while seasonal settlements will contain households of types 2–7. In other words, sedentary settlements may contain not only the houses of people who live there permanently and do not move (Stat 1), but also some dwellings that are only used seasonally (e.g. 'winter houses') although the houses themselves are permanently sited (Stat 2). However, it is worth noting that the physical nature of the dwelling is not always an indication of how it is used. In Mongolia mobile dwellings, felt tents (*ger*), are frequently placed permanently in sedentary settlements. But at the same time one finds the converse: occasionally even the district administrative centre township can be a seasonal settlement, e.g. in Hovd *sum*. The centre moves twice a year from its summer to its winter site. In each place there are some stationary houses, offices, etc. but the bulk of the population lives in movable felt tents. Table 5.1 gives additional information on each case-study site.

It will be appreciated that settlements in Inner Asia are highly complex, as they are agglomerations of dwelling-types which range from the most static to the most mobile. Each living complex type might be represented by anything from one to numerous households. Apart from the settled only and mobile only settlements, there are 26 theoretically possible combinations of living types in settlements.

In practice, settlements do not combine all the theoretically possible types at once. For example, a common type of settlement found in Mongolia,

	District 'C' population	District households	Useful land area, sq.m.	Population per sq.m.	Population in settlement	Households in settlement	Rural population	Rural households	Rural population density
Argada	2643	649	233	11.3	2220	555	423	99	1.82
Gigant	1459	388	360	4.05	1308	348	151	40	0.42
Dashbalbar	3184		7163	0.4	1292		1892	?222	0.26
Hargant	1412		990	1.4	612		800	160	0.81
Chinggel Bulag	1354	339	1933	0.7	263	66	1091	2773	0.56
Sumber	5907	1441	3846	1.56	4031		1976	482	0.51
Hosh Tolgoi	5158	848	800	6.4	4138	688	840	160	1.05
Handagat	4133		1720	3.24	2500		1633	311	1.29
Solchur	1482	382	800	1.8	1138		350	90	0.44
Hovd sum	2775	669	2900	0.96	1197	292	1578	377	0.54

TABLE 5.1. Population in case-study districts

Blank cells indicate information not available.
'Settlement' refers to district centre township.
Source: local statistics.

at the *sum* centre, is a mixture of people who live year round in static houses (type Stat 1) together with some who are very mobile (types Mob 6 and 7) and come into the settlement for irregular periods of the year with their *gers*. Some theoretically possible combinations are rarely found, if ever. This is because people in a given settlement tend to have similar living patterns. So it would be unlikely that one would find people who have winter houses and use tents for summer living in the same settlement as people who have summer houses and use tents for winter. Having said this, living patterns in Inner Asia are extraordinarily flexible, and some individuals may make their own choices whatever the prevailing cultural norm around them.

SEDENTARISATION

The historical dynamics of sedentarisation[4]

Studies carried out among the Buryats from the end of the 19th century onwards show that the percentages of households using the various types of dwelling complex were not fixed over time, especially over long periods. In fact, over a hundred year period the Buryat population experienced a change to almost complete sedentarisation. For example (in the early 1990s) 60% of the Buryat population lives in towns and cities rather than in rural areas. Of the rural population 95% use a single stationary dwelling only (Stat 1) and the remaining 5% have further seasonal stationary houses as well as the main dwelling (Stat 2). Only a tiny number of households of shepherds have recently started to use mobile dwellings. These are felt tents, or wagons on wheels, or on wooden runners, which are used for pasturing collectively-owned livestock on so-called 'summer pastures'. It is important to mention this, because half of the 18 sample households of the case-studies were herders (figure 5.3) and this is not representative of the generality of the Buryat rural population. In comparison with other regions of Inner Asia not only do relatively few Buryats have the occupation of 'herder', but even those who are herders sometimes live fully sedentary lives.

There is a widely-held view that before the Buryats became subjects of the Tsarist state at the end of the 17th century they were 'nomads' using only mobile dwellings and then gradually became sedentarised, with stationary dwellings appearing only under Russian influence.[5] However, documentary evidence shows that in the 17th century the Buryats of Trans-Baikal had *all* of the types of living complex (1-7), although in very different proportions to those found at the end of the 19th century, let alone today. The types of living complex in the 17th century were more 'mobile'. The processes of sedentarisation and urbanisation of households and settlements in the Russian state were closely connected with their inclusion in the commodity and fiscal economy of the neighbouring Russian population. These processes were intensified by compulsion during the period of 'total collectivisation' and 'mass transformation to sedentarisation of the nomadic population' in the 1920s and 1930s. Only with recent privatisation are a very small number of Buryat herders beginning to experiment again with more mobile forms.

The character of settlements is changeable in other areas of Inner Asia too. Without going into the history of each case site, we can note some characteristic dynamic processes. *Over the past 15 years in the whole of Inner*

Asia there has been a change towards more sedentary household living complexes and increase in population of the administrative centre settlement of the district.

Let us look briefly at four examples. In eastern Mongolia (Dornod *aimag*, Bayantümen *sum*) a sedentarisation process can be seen in the tendency since the 1940s–50s to use wagons or small houses on wheels, instead of – or as well as – the 'traditional' felt tent on the pastures. Such wagons require powerful traction in order to be moved and cannot cross rough terrain. In fact, it was clear from field observation that many of these dwellings were virtually immovable, with tiny wheels already rusted up. 'Mobility' here was symbolic rather than real. The wagons were in year-round use by a few families, especially the old people. At the same time, the administrative centre of Bayantümen district has increased in size over the past twenty years, because of its location close to the city of Choibalsan. In some ways it functions as a suburb, with workers travelling to the city by bus each day. At the same time, city-dwellers' relatives live in Bayantümen, where they pasture numerous livestock for them. This has resulted in severe degradation of pastures close to the district centre.

In south-central Mongolia (Gov'sumber Aimag, Sumber *sum*, case-study 6) the central village of Sumber has increased greatly in size since the 1960s. The reason for this is that Sumber is the district surrounding the town of Choir, located on the railway-line between Ulaanbaatar and Beijing, which became a base for a Soviet army division. Though the army has now left, Choir still contains Mongolian workers connected with various services: a railway workshop, a power sub-station, and a now defunct central-heating facility. Sumber is also home to mineworkers who work at a nearby coalmine. Over half the population of Sumber (not including the municipality of Choir) lives in felt tents, but these are treated as though they were permanent static dwellings; they have wooden floors and are surrounded by store sheds and fences. The village population decreases in summer, when children and old people leave to join their relatives on the pastures. On the pastures too there has been a decline in mobility. Winter camps are now inhabited for longer (around 5 months) than previously, and winter sites also now contain livestock sheds built of wood (*hashaa*).[6] This means that herders have to return to exactly the same sites year after year.

In eastern Inner Mongolia (Hargant Sum, Hulun Buir prefecture, case-study 4) recently intensified processes of sedentarisation have meant that only a few herders live exclusively in mobile dwellings. The principal 'winter-spring' pastures are now allocated to each household by the *sum* administration and these are now turning into all-year pastures for many people. Most herders have 'winter-spring' houses, built of clay or brick, and either spend the whole of the year in them, or move short distances to other houses for summer and winter *otor* pasturing.[7] Some herders have started to plant potato crops near their houses. The pre-1949 distant summer pastures are now out of bounds (located in a different administrative territory) and even the closer ones within the *sum* are used mainly by the richer herders. There is a tendency for poorer herders to build their houses close to the *sum* administrative centre, because this makes it easier to market milk. The over-use of these close pastures has caused severe degradation.

Finally, Chinggel Bulag in Inner Mongolia (case-study 5) has become more sedentarised since the economic reforms of the early 1980s. The pastures were divided into sub-districts (*gachaa*) on the basis of the previous production brigades, and then virtually all pastures were further subdivided into household pastures at the various seasonally-used areas within the *gachaa*. The richer herders all now have houses at winter-spring sites. Many herders live in one place all year round (though their herds may be taken some kilometres away) and those who do move tend not to go very far.

Estimating sedentarisation at present

Sedentarisation is a process in time, but we also need to be able to characterise it as a 'pattern' at the moment of our studies, 1992–3. There are four types of evidence we bring forward to determine how sedentary a living complex is: 1) the number of herders who simply do not move during the year; 2) the average length of annual migrations in the case of herders who do move; 3) the number of fixed structures, such as pens and storage sheds used by a household; and 4) the character of local 'ways of life' and activities. It is not enough to know that people move or do not move, or that they move, say, between two houses twice a year (though this is of course essential information). We also need to understand *how* people live in their settlements and camps. A sedentary lifestyle can be perceived in the degree of use of fixed structures, such as winter sheds, fenced pastures or wells, or the presence of static activities, such as tending pigs, chickens and vegetable gardens. It is particularly significant when herders, as opposed to the people living in district centres, engage in these activities. In our view all three factors should be taken together to give an indication of the degree of sedentarisation of a given community.

The case-study sites with the highest number of 'immobile' herders, in terms of the use of dwellings, are Argada and Gigant in Russia and

Chinggel Bulag in China. These are also places with serious pasture degradation. Hovd *sum* (Mongolia), on the other hand, is the most 'mobile' district among our case-studies (as noted earlier, even the district centre settlement is moved twice a year).

Figure 6.13 in the next chapter shows the average length of annual migrations of those herders who do move. It can be seen that the three case-studies in the mountainous west, Hovd, Hosh Tolgoi and Handagat (Altai), show the longest annual migrations. The Handagat migration is particularly lengthy, with an average total of 380km travelled by herder households each year. However, the length of the Handagat migrations may give a misleading impression of non-intensive use of pastures. In fact, Handagat district is shaped like a long corridor and the amount of pasture is limited. Short migrations, on the other hand, *are* a good indication of intensive use of pasture, particularly when accompanied by a high stocking rate. The districts with the shortest migrations are Gigant (Chita, Russia) and Chinggel Bulag (Inner Mongolia), followed by Dashbalbar (eastern Mongolia) and Argada (Buryatia). All of these places are in the eastern lowland steppes.

Figure 5.4 shows the presence of built structures alongside the main dwelling at the site used by herder households for the longest period of the year (usually the 'winter settlement'). This shows that Argada and Gigant (Russia) have large numbers of such structures, notably including bathhouses, while Hosh Tolgoi (Hoboksair, Xinjiang) and Sumber (Mongolia) have the fewest. The most interesting case is Handagat in Xinjiang, where barns, stores, extra clay houses, chicken coops and livestock sheds abound. The people of Handagat have separate sheds built for each type of animal, and

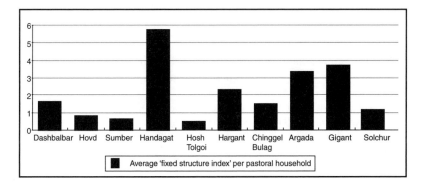

FIGURE 5.4. Fixed structures at the main sites of herders in case-study sites

in some cases also special sheds for delivery of the lambs. This again is evidence of a relatively sedentarised culture in Handagat, despite the fact that herders here make a long migration each year. There is no evidence that this reflects the relative proximity of Altai city (see figure 5.1); rather, it seems characteristic of longstanding traditions among the Turkic peoples of this region (see Mongush 1996).

Figure 5.5 gives an indication of the sedentary productive activities in district settlements and among herders, as indicated by the presence of pigs, chickens and vegetable gardens. Pigs and chickens require constant attention and cannot be taken on migrations; their presence implies either non-movement or that someone is left at the main site to look after these animals. Keeping a vegetable plot is compatible with migration, as the plot cannot be cultivated during the winter. Nevertheless, having a vegetable plot requires the household to return to exactly the same place each year. Clearing and fencing a plot implies a kind of particularised attachment to land that is

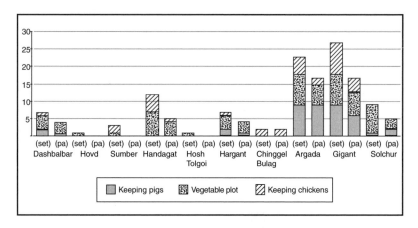

FIGURE 5.5. Sedentary activities of households in district centre (set) and on pastures (pa)

'Set' = households living in district centre (9 in each site); 'pa' = pastoral households living on the grasslands (9 in each site).The chart represents the numbers of households engaging in the three activities of keeping pigs, cultivating vegetables, and keeping chickens. A total of eighteen households were studied in each site. Numbers over 9 in any given column indicate that some households engaged in more than one of these activities.

different from the more general sense of belonging to a homeland (*nutag*) of pastoralists. As might be expected, sedentary activities are more common in the district settlements than on the pastures in all our case-studies. However, herders and villagers in the same community are still relatively similar to one another. The database shows that Argada and Gigant in Russia have the highest incidence of sedentary activities, followed by Handagat in Xinjiang. Hosh Tolgoi (Xinjiang) and Hovd (Mongolia) have virtually no such activities.

There is very little plough agriculture in our case-study districts, and only Argada and Gigant in Russia have a sizeable acreage. The presence of agriculture clearly is a factor in the overall level of sedentarisation in a district, but it does not directly affect the pastoral households, because there are no people who simultaneously work as agriculturalists and herders. In Argada and Gigant much of the agricultural work is done by Russians. It is highly mechanised and has nothing in common with the indigenous agriculture, long since discontinued, which was practised in certain parts of the Buryat and Tuvan regions from early times (Vainshtein 1980; Humphrey 1983).

State policies and indigenous cultures

Many external political and economic factors have influenced processes of sedentarisation, notably the Soviet 'agro-pastoralism' policies of the collectivised period and the centralisation of rural economies in China under the communes. In both countries, but especially in Russia, small far-flung settlements were abandoned and state-managed services were concentrated at a single village for each district. In both countries, also, the assumption has been that sedentarisation implies social development towards 'civilisation'. Such assumptions had a less strong influence on Mongolian policies, because the government retained a certain independence from Russia and traditions of mobility were in any case more widespread in Mongolia than in Buryatia. In the whole of Inner Asia, however, sedentarisation has to be seen in the context of administrative-economic planning. During the socialist period the plans designated which people (by occupation) would live where, and whether they should live a settled or a migratory life. In the case of herders, it was also designated where and when they should move. Particular policies on the technologies of livestock production influenced this, e.g. those connected with the introduction of new breeds. Overall such planning had the paradoxical effect that some people, let us say 'milkers' in a brigade tending state-owned cows, might be limited to a more static life than they wanted, whereas others, such as horse-herders, would be forced to keep on the move when they might have preferred a less exhausting working life. 'Forced sedentarisation' was thus accompanied by 'forced seasonal migration'. Although local control of this kind now has much less power in Russia and has been more or less abandoned in Mongolia, its residue remains an important factor in patterns of sedentarisation.

At the same time it is important to acknowledge that state planning encountered indigenous traditions and practices of livestock herding which differed from place to place. This raises the question of the role of cultural values in relation to sedentary lifestyles. Despite its relative cultural homogeneity in many ways (see Introduction), Inner Asia has distinctive cultural economic traditions. These traditions are not territorially bounded, but overlap in respect of this or that customary activity. Nevertheless, within certain broad zones economic practices, customs of land-use, concepts of territory, skills in herding, building and artisanry, etc. – all of which may be called 'economic culture' for short – are active principles used by people in creating more (or less) sedentarised lives for themselves. One important such distinction is between a culture which tends to operate in terms of two seasons and one which conceptualises the year in terms of four seasons.

The two-season (summer and winter) variant can be identified with the Buryats. Long before the revolution Buryats, especially western Buryats, were basically transhumant, moving from a scattered winter settlement along a river and close to fertilised and irrigated hayfields (*utug*) to a summer settlement at higher altitude. Short-term pasturing forays (*hutor*) were made by young men from both of these bases, but the rest of the community lived a settled life in two places during the year. Eastern Khori Buryats went on longer seasonal migrations, but they too had a tendency to operate with a two-season system.

Among our case-studies the communities of Argada, Gigant and Dashbalbar are all mainly Buryat, though the first two districts are in Russia while Dashbalbar is in Mongolia. Culturally all three have much in common: people retain clan traditions, go on short migrations, prefer to live in wooden houses, cut large amounts of hay for their animals, grow and eat vegetables, and construct wooden fences and sheds for their livestock. Unlike Argada, Dashbalbar is located to the south of the forest belt and wood is sparse in the district. Yet when they moved into the open steppe the Dashbalbar Buryats went on building wooden houses, presumably at some cost and difficulty. Although the *utug* system was abandoned after collectivisation, the traditionally rather sedentary living complexes of these three communities remain closely related to wood craftsmanship and to a strategy of reliance on hay.[8]

Yet the Argada–Gigant–Dashbalbar trio does not indicate that there is a separate Buryat 'cultural system' totally distinct from other Inner Asian communities. The people of Hargant in Inner Mongolia have certain cultural features in common with the Eastern Buryats, such as clan names and shamanic traditions, though they are called by a different ethnonym, 'Barga'. But there are some differences in pastoral techniques. Before the Communist period some Barga herders of Hargant migrated for very long distances to reach summer pastures and they also seem to have had different pastures for the four seasons. In general the people used felt yurts only. However, despite these apparent differences from the Buryats, it is possible that the community as a whole was not so different. In other words, it is probable that only some herders went on these very long migrations, and then not always with the whole household, and that a substantial section of the community stayed at two sites, summer and winter. Certainly at present the Hargant people have one main house at the winter-spring pastures (where some people stay all year round), with perhaps another at a summer site, and the herders use tents to reach other seasonal pastures. The present tendency to crowd houses near the *sum* centre in Hargant (see p. 66) is to a great extent a matter of the effect of government marketisation policies, since it is easier to realise products if one is closer to the buying organisations.

These systems can be contrasted with central Mongolia and the western mountain belt, including Tuva and Xinjiang. In both of these regions four-season pasturing is practised and the entire household accompanies the herds (in other words the herding practices directly affect settlement patterns). In both regions dwellings are traditionally mobile felt tents, and hay was used relatively little until recently. A high value is placed on strategies of energetic and frequent migration. In Tuva a prize-winning shepherd moves ten or more times a year. In pre-collectivisation times it seems to have been the more wealthy and powerful herders, pursuing a strategy of 'maximisation', who went the longest distances (see chapter 6). In general it is in the western zone that there are cultural traditions of greatest mobility, and these are linked to the 'ecological rationality' of making use of the disparate landscapes of mountains, their altitude, variable vegetation, rainfall, etc. State policies have had to adapt to some extent to these traditions, and it is probably not an accident that some of the fiercest opposition to the initial drive for collectivisation in Mongolia in the 1930s was in the west of the country.

Although they have in common a high value placed on mobility, the cultures of the western zone are otherwise differentiated by ethnicity and religion. The people of Hosh Tolgoi and Hovd are Western Mongols and Buddhists, while Handagat is populated by Muslim Kazakhs and Solchur by Tuvinians with traditions of both Buddhism and shamanism. These differences are not irrelevant to the question of sedentarisation, since they bear on habits, activities and values. So, for example, the Muslim Kazakhs of Handagat obviously do not keep pigs and the Torgud Mongols of Hosh Tolgoi, who live in close neighbourhood with Kazakhs, do not keep them either. The Hovd and Sumber Mongolians have the 'purest' Mongol traditions, highly valuing herd products and despising many of the products of more sedentary activities (pig-keeping, vegetable-gardening, and raising chickens). Clearly not all products of a sedentary life are despised: the Mongols have been trading for silk, tea, tobacco, etc. for centuries. But it is because certain particular activities are traditionally held in low esteem, and earlier were hardly practised among the steppe people, that they are good indices of sedentarisation processes today.[9]

Although the long-term trend through the twentieth century has been towards greater sedentarisation of the population as a whole in Inner Asia, it is important to point out that *for herders* this is not irreversible. *'De-sedentarisation' is a possibility even today.* In the last few years in Mongolia town-dwellers have taken to the herding life to benefit from the livestock distributed in privatisation (Erdenebaatar 1996). In Gigant in Russia some herders are beginning to experiment with mobile dwellings (wagons on wheels) now that the strict ideological disapproval of 'nomadism' has been lifted.

We have created figure 5.6 to show in summary form a 'sedentarisation index' for each case-study site as it was in 1992–3. It comprises an amalgam of the several different indices of 'sedentarisation' discussed above. Clearly such a chart cannot be more than a crude approximation of much more complex processes and, as with all the index-type graphs in this chapter, the weighting between the different elements has been evaluated by us on the basis of our knowledge of the region. However, the figure has an analytical purpose, since it will enable us to demonstrate the differences between sedentarisation and urbanisation processes in Inner Asia.

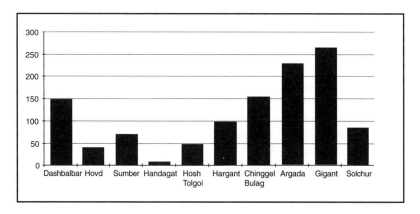

FIGURE 5.6. Sedentarisation index, case-study sites, 1992–3

This index is a composite of five elements represented numerically and weighted by the authors:
1) numbers of immobile and two-move only households;
2) presence of fixed structures such as cattle-sheds in herder living complexes;
3) sedentary activites of herders;
4) percentage of district land under ploughed agriculture;
5) [minus] average total length of seasonal migrations.

URBANISATION

Administrative hierarchies and administrative distance

The processes of urbanisation in the steppe zone during the 20th century have been closely tied to the execution of the economic policies of the states of the region. The administrative hierarchy defines the territorial divisions of the region and provides the governmental structure. In most parts of the region government is still quite intrusive, to the extent that it makes sense to say that the population requires permission to carry out most of their activities. The administration also performs many tasks of economic management and provides important transport, communications and social services for the population. The administration structure thus has an extraordinary importance.

The district (*sum, selsoviet, xiang*) has fundamental social and administrative functions in all three countries (see also chapter 3). It is the place of registration of households, the holder of many types of communal property, the distribution point for state allocations to the population, and the primary unit to which people feel they belong. The district government is where the political structure of the state meets a *social* community. The district leaders are known personally to all members of districts, whereas leaders above this level are in general not known personally. In Inner Asia it makes sense to talk of a 'member' of a district in a way that would not be appropriate in many other parts of the world.

We looked at each district and calculated its geographical distance from higher levels of administration, i.e. what we have called the 'administrative distance', the distance in kilometres by road between the district and higher levels such as the county, prefecture and republic centre. Because of the importance of governmental functions, our assumption is that 'administrative distance' is a factor in urbanisation processes. In general, the smaller the distance between administrative centres, the greater the density of governmental structures and services in a given locality, and presumably the greater the density of urban settlements. For example, the district of Hargant (case-study site 4) in Inner Mongolia is very close both to its county town and its prefectural city. Hargant in fact appears according to this criterion the district most closely surrounded by a network of other higher level towns.[10]

If we compare the distance between nodes in the administrative hierarchy in all three countries (see figure 5.1) it can be seen that Inner Mongolia is geographically the most densely integrated from the administrative point of view, followed in descending order by Chita Oblast, Tuva, Buryatia and Xinjiang. Mongolia is the least dense of the regions covered by the project. All three case-study sites in Mongolia show large distances between local districts and high-level centres. The most distant of all is Hovd *sum* in western Mongolia (case-study site 10). It is not only far from its own administrative capital, Ulaanbaatar city, but it is also relatively distant from any large urban settlement. 'Administrative distance' is to some extent notional, since it does not reflect all of the actual practicalities of communications between settlements (see below). But it does reflect a set of political relations which are important; for example, Hovd *sum* is physically closer to Altai city in China than to any large Mongolian town, but the international border effectively precludes significant interaction with Altai.[11] Though cross-border links are becoming more important, it is still the case that an administratively distant district like Hovd has only attenuated links with any city.

In this context it is important to underline the centripetal nature of administrative relations in Inner Asia. Each district is commonly divided into sub-districts (*gachaa, bag, brigada,* etc.). These maintain links with the centre, but not with each other. Likewise, the herder households within a sub-district are linked to its administrative centre. Although some new forms of 'lateral' co-operation are beginning to emerge (see chapters 3 and 4), centripetal organisation is still predominant – a legacy of the socialist period when administration and economic management were inextricably tied together into a single hierarchical structure (Humphrey 1983: 127–8). At each 'level' roads, transport, telephone lines, and distribution of services flow from the administrative centre. This is why 'administrative distance' is important.

Urbanisation and urbanism

Figure 5.7 is an index of a conventional notion of urbanisation as it applies to the ten case-study districts. Of course we are not talking about 'urban' in the sense of New York here, but of a process affecting rural dwellers.

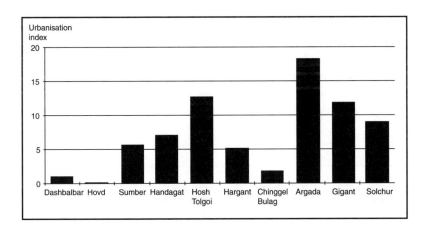

FIGURE 5.7. Urbanisation in case-study districts of Inner Asia, 1992-3

The urbanisation index is a composite made up of three elements:
   1) the percentage of population living in the district centre rather than on the pastures;
   2) the population density in the district;
   3) [minus] the 'administrative distance'.
Source: Local statistics and maps

Population geographers use various definitions of urbanisation (Clarke 1972: 49). Since there is no general agreement on the use of the term, we have adopted our own synthetic criteria for the category. 'Urbanisation' in our usage is a composite, made up of: 1) the percentage of the total population living in the central settlement of the district rather than on the pastures; 2) the overall population density in the district per sq. km. of useful land; and 3) minus the 'administrative distance' between the district and the relevant towns at higher administrative levels. Figure 5.7 shows the Buryat case studies to be the most urbanised, followed by Xinjiang, Tuva, and Inner Mongolia, with Mongolia as the least urbanised.

Note, however, that the district-level indices illustrated in figure 5.7 do not reflect country-wide statistics based only on the percentage of the total population living in urban centres.[12] I give these statistics below but do not make further use of them in this chapter, because it is not clear what criteria are used for 'urban centre' in the different countries, and because the majority of the population in China and Russia is not involved in the pastoral economy.

In my view figure 5.7 needs to be supplemented with another analysis reflecting the reality of urbanisation as it is practically experienced and as it is expressed by people in their own activities. For example, 'administrative distance' simply measured on a map does not take account of the range of difficulties hindering communications between rural areas and towns. Nor does showing the number of people living in a district settlement tell us *how* they live there – whether in a more, or a less, urban style. I have therefore made some further analyses of the data collected in order to develop a more subtle notion which can show changes in *the real degree of integration between rural districts and metropolitan cities*. I call this process URBANISM.

	Urban				Rural			
Inner Mongolia	1947	12.2%	1990	36.1%	1947	87.8%	1990	63.9%
Xinjiang			1990	28.3%			1990	71.7%
Mongolia	1956	22.6%	1989	57.1%	1956	78.4%	1989	42.9%
Tuva	1945	6.2%	1991	47.5%	1945	93.8%	1991	52.5%
Buryatia	1939	30.7%	1991	60.2%	1939	69.3%	1991	39.8%

TABLE 5.2. Urban and rural populations in Inner Asia

Source: national statistics

To begin with we need to take into account not only distance between district and city but also whether vehicles are available, the types of transport, and whether the roads are always passable. Most of the case-study sites do not have asphalted roads from county to district centres (Solchur is the exception) and several are cut off by road either in summer because of rains and/or rivers (Hovd, Dashbalbar, Argada) or in winter because of snowfalls (Hovd, Altai and Hosh Tolgoi). Cars are rare throughout the region and in rural area are used mostly by district officials. Generally, only in Argada, Gigant, and Solchur are there privately-owned cars, though motor-bikes are more widespread, notably in Argada, Gigant, Solchur, Chinggel Bulag and Hargant. Some districts (Argada, Solchur, Altai, Hosh Tolgoi) are much better supplied with communal transport such as buses and lorries than others (Hovd and Chinggel Bulag). None of the district centres, except for Handagat, has a regular air link, though most have strips where a small plane could put down in an emergency.[13] Buses are particularly important in China, and used to be so in other parts of Inner Asia until high prices made them increasingly unaffordable. Railways provide the most reliable transport to cities, and Sumber and Hargant are the only case-study districts to have this facility.[14]

However, we also need to consider the social horizons of the people, which may extend far beyond the distance that is easily travellable. Dashbalbar *sum* (case-study 3) is a case in point. The district is rather inaccessible, as it is not only distant from any city but its mud-prone roads are difficult at all seasons of the year and the single bus is often full or does not travel for one reason or another. However, the people of Dashbalbar want to maintain their economic contacts with Ulaanbaatar city. They have established a co-operative, with members in both the rural district and the city, specifically to maintain links, find buyers and sell their products.

This leads us to another important aspect of urbanism, the degree to which people make their own goods, or alternatively buy city-provided ones, i.e. the degree of economic integration with metropolitan centres through consumption. We looked at production and consumption of the following six items in each case-study area: clothing, food, footwear, alcohol, leather goods and felt. The results are interesting, as they show some changes from established practices in recent years. As might be expected, the people of distant Hovd (case-study 10) have the greatest amount of home-produced goods, including all of the items mentioned above as well as herding equipment, food utensils, and some religious and medical items. Sumber and Dashbalbar people also make a good proportion of the listed goods (much of their clothing, food, leather goods and alcohol, though no longer footwear or

FIGURE 5.8. Making felt by hand, Hovd *sum*, Uvs, Mongolia, 1993
(photo: Telenged)

felt). The production/consumption patterns of these districts has not changed much in recent years, though there is a tendency to make more and buy less because of the high prices or unavailability of many manufactured goods.

However, more dramatic recent changes are apparent in China and Russia, with diametrically opposite effects. In Russia during the collective period home production was greatly reduced and people became accustomed to buying most of their food (apart from meat and milk), clothing, footwear, etc. Even in Tuva local felt-making and production of leather goods (e.g. bridles, ropes) all but ceased. In Buryatia and Chita such goods had not been home-made for decades. In the past five years however, the economic crisis, lack of money and the unavailability of goods, has forced people to produce more at home, especially clothing and alcohol. There is unrelieved grumbling about this. In Mongolia, on the other hand, people tend to take a pride in the quality of their home-made goods, while also feeling the lack of access to manufactures. In China, by contrast with Russia, there has been an opposite process over the past ten years. The respondents in Handagat, Hargant and Hosh Tolgoi-Hoboksair all reported that they now regularly buy goods that were made at home ten years ago. One woman in Handagat replied:

> Not 10 years ago, maybe 20 years ago, at that time we made all our clothes and boots. But now my children do not like the clothes I make for them. So we buy much more than before. Even if we do not buy ready-made clothes we buy cloth and go to the tailors. The things we don't buy even now are saddles, leather ropes, etc.

And a woman from Hosh Tolgoi said:

> Yes. Nowadays we buy a lot from shops in town, most of our clothes. We also buy foods that we used to make at home, like fried dough pieces and soups. I prefer the quality of home-made goods, but buying is easier.

In Handagat almost no Kazakh clothes are to be seen, though indigenous felt-making, carpet-making, and weaving still continue. In this seemingly utterly remote corner of Asia the walls of herders' houses and tents are covered with posters and photographs of exotic scenes, from portraits of Marx to tulips in Hyde Park. Chinggel Bulag, on the other hand, is the most 'non-urbanised' of our sites in China as far as home-production goes (and it also has the worst transport to a sizeable town). Here most people still wear the home-sewn Mongolian *deel* (robe), have felt tents if they are herders, produce the majority of their own food and alcohol, and women still make elaborate embroidery. In Hargant, by contrast, only a small number of elderly people wear Mongolian clothing; and traditions of embroidery, felt and leather work have all but ceased. Romantic photographs are less in evidence here than in Handagat. However, there is an evident taste for technology in Hargant (e.g. small tractors instead of horses). In every house or yurt a large stereo or cassette-player or TV is prominently displayed. If rural Russian consumers are experiencing 'de-urbanism' these days, China is moving fast in the opposite direction.

It is clear that most of our respondents in Russia do not want this kind of de-urbanism. This raises the matter of communications with metropolitan centres and the creation of urban tastes through radio, TV, cinema, newspapers and magazines. Let us investigate further the case of the Russian rural districts. There are good grounds for arguing that the Buryat areas of Inner Asia are the most urbanised in a general sense. Although in both Buryat case-study sites, Argada and Gigant, the distance between district and county level towns is quite large (between 200 and 300km) it is important that a great deal of the land is not used, i.e. it is 'economically passive' (Gomboev 1996). The land used consists of relatively limited valleys and steppes interspersed among large tracts of mountainous forest. In these 'economically active' patches there is intensive settlement and there are dense lines of infrastructure and communications (roads, railways, electricity lines, radio and telephone). All houses in central and brigade settlements have electricity (i.e. virtually all dwellings). Every single household in our survey in Buryatia and Chita has a radio, and all but one household in Argada and Gigant has television. In Argada several surveyed households have 2–3 TVs, many have washing-machines and fridges, and in the district as a whole some 14% also have private telephones. Buryatia and Chita remain the most urbanised of our case-study sites with regard to communications, but the situation is changing. In Gigant (Chita) in 1993 not only was the only telephone in the district broken (it was in the district leader's office) but the phone in the county (*raion*) office was not working either. People could not use their radios because the supply of batteries had dried up. To communicate between the district and the county it was necessary to make a trip by car on unmade-up roads, but petrol was in very short supply. As one respondent said; 'Our only way to communicate with the outside world is to sit and watch the television!'

The situation in Buryatia nevertheless contrasts with Mongolia and parts of Inner Mongolia (e.g. Chinggel Bulag) where the central electricity supply in district settlements is intermittent.[15] In any case most rural households are not linked to any electricity supply. In the Mongolian case-study sites while virtually all households have radios less than half have television sets, and many of these are unconnected or do not work.

The radio is the probably most important means of communication for herders throughout the region. People listen to the radio in the early morning to hear the weather forecast; if bad weather is predicted they will rush out to bring in the herds. Otherwise, the radio is frequently on in the background during the day, and in the evening people, especially men, will sit and listen to it seriously. Some of our respondents mentioned 'listening to the radio' as a type of work activity for men.

Cinema used to be an important entertainment and propaganda outlet, but in Mongolia and rural parts of Russia cinemas are falling into disuse, while in Inner Mongolia and Xinjiang they seem never to have reached the district level. Similarly, all through the region written media (newspapers and magazines) are in principle widely distributed, but many distant settlements receive them only with much delay. People in Gigant in Russia and Chinggel Bulag in Inner Mongolia mentioned these problems and said that in winter the post sometimes does not arrive for weeks on end when roads are blocked by snow. In Mongolia transport problems are combined with a very limited range of available newspapers, despite the fact that numerous and varied papers appear in Ulaanbaatar. Often only the government-sponsored *Unen* reaches down to the district level. A respondent from Dashbalbar commented that people had lost interest in these out-of-date official government papers and hardly bothered to look at them. In Solchur (Tuva) on the other hand, with its good road and proximity to the county town, people were eager readers of newspapers and magazines.

Finally, we should survey in a more general way the extent to which people in the case-study communities integrate with cities. In some districts there are people who hardly participate at all in urban political-cultural life. These people have no radio, TV or telephone, do not receive newspapers and in a few cases do not have any transport, such as a motor-bike, to get to the district centre quickly. Interestingly, the greatest number of these households are found in Solchur (Tuva), Hosh Tolgoi (Xinjiang) and Handagat (Xinjiang), although these districts are otherwise relatively highly urbanised. In Argada on the other hand it is hardly possible to shut oneself off entirely from urban influences, since all houses in settlements and brigades are fitted with on-line radio (a relic of the days of stirring propaganda). Here the problem is that the long bus journey to Barguzin (the county town) has become very expensive, while that to the capital Ulan-Ude is prohibitive. The flow of people and goods is intermittent. In such places, where there has been a recent decline in communications between rural areas and cities, the frustration is intense. People know about city life and are interested in it and they are angry and despairing that communications are breaking down, that they cannot sell their goods, nor buy manufactures. The case-studies in Russia show that urbanism is not a permanent state, but may go into reverse. The people of Argada and Gigant are in effect fighting a battle against de-urbanism.

On the basis of analysis of the above types of information we have created another graph, figure 5.9, which is an index of rural-urban integration (urbanism). Note that although figure 5.9 has been created from quite different sets of information from figure 5.7, a more conventional index of urbanisation, the two charts in the end delineate very similar patterns of differences between the case-study communities. This is reassuring, as it suggests that there is an overall consistency in our materials. However, there are some significant differences between the two charts, notably the high degree of rural-urban integration in Hargant (Xinjiang, China) and Solchur (Tuva, Russia), which contrasts with their low level of urbanisation according to conventional numerical criteria. Also, figure 5.9 shows, in our view correctly, that Hovd *sum* in western Mongolia is far less integrated with any

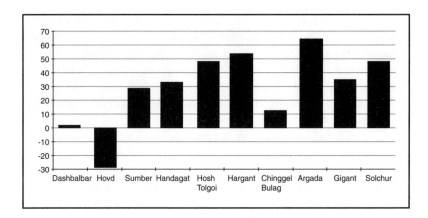

FIGURE 5.9. Index of rural-urban integration in districts, 1992-3

The index of rural-urban integration ('urbanism') is a complex made up of:
  1) active use of TV and radio and number of programmes received;
  2) physical closeness to towns and availability of transport;
  3) availability of up-to-date newspapers;
  4) numbers of private telephones;
  5) [minus] amount of home production of consumer goods;
  6) [minus] 'administrative distance'.

features of urbanism than is suggested by the 'urbanisation' graph. Indeed, with its difficulty of access (often reachable only on horse) and its high level of home production, Hovd *sum* is off the chart as far as urbanism goes. Thus it can be seen that urbanism and urbanisation are different processes in rural Inner Asia, a point which will be taken up again in the conclusion to this chapter.

Socio-economic complexity in district townships

One characteristic of an urbanised settlement is that it comprises many different socio-economic functions. Even a relatively populous township if it has only one primary function, like mining, will be dependent on other centres and may vanish when the mine closes (there are many disused mines and associated ghost-towns in Mongolia). District centre settlements, on the other hand, are 'urbanised' in this sense of involving social complexity. They provide diverse types of employment, and trade, educational, medical, cultural, entertainment, and sporting facilities. In turn, cultural complexity (in lifestyles, wealth, cultural preferences, etc.) is a feature of urbanised life. We now briefly discuss three features which influence urbanising trends: schools, gangs and shops. All three cases create their own social complexity, since they serve to divide the community as well as unite it.

One of the most noticeable differences between Russian and Chinese district settlements is in the siting and prominence given to the school. In Russia the school is invariably centrally placed and it is a large, imposing and normally well-kept building. In China schools tend to be on side streets.[16] The Russian school is associated with its own boarding-house (*internat*) and the herder children from outlying parts live there at least during the weekdays and sometimes for much longer periods. Here 'urban' ideals can be intensively absorbed (from good manners to clothes fashions or support for far-distant football teams). This is particularly important in Tuva, where herding camps are bereft of children during the working week. In China, on the other hand, the children tend to live with relatives in town. In Mongolia, though there was an attempt to emulate the Soviet model, boarding-houses are now virtually defunct, and one consequence of this is that some children do not go to school. The decline of school budgets all through Inner Asia is encouraging the emergence of private and home tuition. Many of our respondents observe how this is creating differentiation between the rich and poor, despite the fact that, especially in China, the aspiration for one's children to leave rural life is a rather general one.

Gangs of youths hanging round the district centre are particularly prevalent in Mongolia and Tuva, and only slightly less so in Buryatia.[17] Though gangs might not be indicative of urbanism in principle, we feel that in Inner Asia they are related to town life, if only because this is where they appear.[18] Gangs draw in young men from outlying camps (usually they are aggressively mounted and mobile, on horse if not on motorbike) and furthermore the excitements they seek are of an urban kind. The gangs sometimes threaten travellers, especially foreigners, demanding rock cassettes, posters, batteries, T-shirts, money and alcohol. It is as if they are trying to create a microcosmic city life of their own, though they are so distant from real cities. Peaceable middle-aged citizens object to the gangs (e.g. in letters to newspapers) but to little avail.

District centre shops are meeting-places and to some extent they function as channels for manufactured goods to reach the population. However, for Russia and Mongolia this observation is not as simple as it sounds. Formerly, state shops supplied a range of basic goods according to plan, and everyone used them, if only because there was no alternative. The range was sometimes eccentric (elegant underwear, etc.), but the main goods necessary were usually available. Now, however, state shops are in decline, or absent, and numbers of small private shops have appeared.[19] Even the state shops cannot always supply the basic goods, such as flour, oil, tea, salt, matches, vodka, or candles, and the private shops tend to market small ranges of international manufactured goods such as cheap clothing, soft drinks, cigarettes, lipstick or soap. The state shops now operate for profit and tend to be expensive. While the private shops tend to be cheaper, their goods are unreliable and the shops are only open sporadically, as if on the whim of the owners. In Russia, many of these private shops have failed. As a result, purchasers often have to have recourse to private channels or, in Mongolia, dubious wholesale suppliers. This is most serious for basic food supplies such as flour. Poorer rural dwellers cannot afford the high prices in shops and tend to use them only when there is no alternative. The rich people can easily pay the high prices, but often tend to travel to 'higher' (county and republic-level) towns to make their purchases. In China, the retail situation is, of course, much more prosperous. Even here, however, shops in the district centre settlement divide into dusty, gloomy state outlets and private shops with a rapacious atmosphere to them. For high quality goods the people who can afford it make their purchases in county or prefecture-level towns.

Thus, if schools and shops were once universal channels for state provision, they are now in many places actively creating social divisions, while gangs are a phenomenon of a society that is already divided. Only ten years ago the major social divisions of today were absent: the children without education, the wealthy entrepreneur, the unemployed. Of course, Inner Asian societies were always divided, by age, rank, gender, and occupation, but the point is that these new social divisions are related to opportunities and aspirations for integration with the city.

Urban culture and mobile herding

Pastoralists of Inner Asia have not forgotten that it was the aristocrats and high lamas who used to have the largest herds and most specialised technologies of production (see next chapter). The large herding enterprises supported establishments of scribes, doctors, personal lamas, accountants, etc. at the camp of a prince. The monastic herds maintained even more elaborate cultural facilities, not just religious institutions, but artisan workshops, schools, libraries, art studios, translation and publishing houses, and so forth. Furthermore, the aristocrats and high lamas were often more mobile even than their herds, since they constantly went on journeys to the capital to attend to administrative and ritual matters. Thus, the historical memory is that mobility and urban culture go together.

In the socialist period, likewise, it was the large collectives which could maintain long-distance migrations for certain types of livestock. It was the collectives which were the bearers of urban culture in the steppe: it was here one could see films, buy manufactured goods, hear news, make a phone call to the city, meet visitors and tourists from the capital.

Though the picture I have painted of district townships at present might seem dispiriting, it is not necessarily the case that the herders see it this way. In any case, the cities are another matter: it should be remembered that all the major cities in our region were designed as capital cities, i.e. the centres of republics or autonomous regions. They all have a full panoply of government, art, theatre, publishing, etc. and people are interested in, proud of, and attracted to these towns. This explains why mobile herders, even today, do not consider themselves to be cut off from urban culture, especially if they really do have transport they can use to travel to towns frequently. Hosh Tolgoi in Xinjiang and Solchur in Tuva are good examples of this. In general, we have found that all Inner Asian people like travelling and do it frequently when they can afford it, because this is the way to find out what is going on and maintain relationships. It is immobility – increased these days with high petrol costs – that is associated with deprivation.

URBANISATION AND SEDENTARISATION

Earlier discussion has shown that the pattern of rural-urban integration (urbanism) closely follows that of urbanisation, and so for brevity's sake we shall use the term 'urbanisation' in these concluding sections to describe both processes. It seems clear, however, that urbanisation and sedentarisation are two different (though not entirely unconnected) phenomena in our region. To see this in summarised form, compare figures 5.6, 5.7 and 5.9. Considering the reasons for the divergences between the two processes will enable us to challenge some widely-held views.

Dashbalbar is very highly sedentarised and has been so for thirty years or so. But it is relatively non-urbanised and lacks much integration with city life. Gigant with its failing transport and phones looks as though it will become increasingly similar to Dashbalbar. These places are distant from great cities, cut off by poor communications, and yet rather settled in lifestyle. The same is true of Chinggel Bulag, though here the sedentarisation is more a matter of local government pasture-allocation policy than of local traditions. But in either case, *these examples disprove the common assumption that sedentarisation goes hand in hand with urbanisation.*

Solchur, Hosh Tolgoi and Hargant, on the other hand, are districts which are relatively highly integrated with urban lifestyles, though they are not very sedentarised. In these places numerous and lengthy migrations coexist with features of urbanisation (such as high population density, large numbers living in the district centre, etc.) and with intensive cultural and economic links with cities. *These examples contradict the commonly-held view that a migration-based economy is incompatible with urbanisation.* Indeed, some of our case-studies indicate that a relatively populous district centre combined with a small number of highly mobile herders can both provide a good structure for a sustainable pastoral economy and supply adequate urban-type services. Solchur in Tuva is a particularly good example of this pattern (see table 5.1).[20]

THE RELATION BETWEEN SETTLEMENT PATTERNS AND THE ENVIRONMENT

In this section we do not attempt to explain the numerous and complex causes of pasture degradation, damage to pastures, etc. Rather, our aim is to look at the relation between settlement patterns and perceived pasture degradation, and thereby disprove certain theories held both inside and outside Inner Asia.

We begin by looking in more detail at the balance of sedentary and mobile populations in each district. Figure 5.10, which is based on table 5.1,

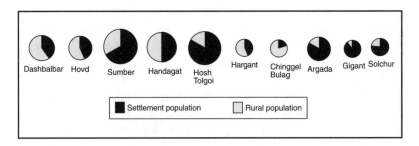

FIGURE 5.10. Population in district settlements and rural population, case-study districts, 1992-3

The size of the pie-charts indicates absolute numbers of population (see table 3.4). Source: Local statistics.

shows the proportion of the total district population living in the central
settlement and those living outside in the countryside. The size of the pie-
charts indicates the absolute numbers of the population living in each district.
In all three Russian sites, Gigant, Argada and Solchur, a relatively large
proportion of the population (over three-quarters) lives in the district centre,
while small numbers of people live rurally. In China the picture is more
variable: in Hosh Tolgoi (Xinjiang) and to a lesser extent Handagat (Xinjiang)
district centre populations are swollen by the presence of numerous Chinese
miners and agricultural workers. However, the two sites in Inner Mongolia
have a much smaller permanent Chinese population. Over half (Hargant) and
up to two-thirds (Chinggel Bulag) of the population live on the pastures.[21]
The settlement-countryside balance in Mongolia is also variable. Dashbalbar
and Hovd are characteristic of the majority of Mongolian districts, which
have high rural populations. Sumber, on the other hand, is joined to Choir,
one of the relatively few large district towns of Mongolia. It is sited on a main
railway line and the town population is swollen by workers in the various
industries and services associated with the railway.

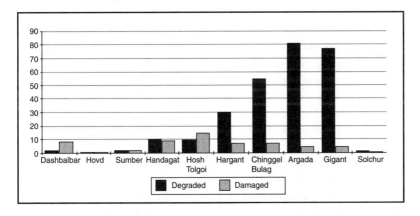

FIGURE 5.11. Percentage degraded and damaged pasture in case-study sites
(estimates)

The chart indicates information received in 1992–3 from local residents and officials.
The information from Argada, Gigant and Dashbalbar was given in sq. km, but from
the other districts was more approximate. 'Damaged pasture' refers to various types
of long and short-term damage: trampling of grasses by livestock in Argada, Gigant
and Hargant; wildfires in Dashbalbar; military and mining operations in Sumber;
digging for 'hair-grass' in Chinggel Bulag; rodent damage, locusts, road building
and mining in Hosh Tolgoi; road building and neighbours' livestock droves in
Handagat.

How do such population patterns relate to environmental conditions? If we carry out a correlation between the settlement-countryside index (figure 5.10) and the perceived degree of pasture degradation (figure 5.11; see chapter 2 for discussion) it can be seen that the relation is not strong. Solchur, Hosh Tolgoi, and Sumber all have a high percentage of inhabitants living in the district centre while they have almost no degradation of their grasslands. Nor is there a strong correlation between the absolute size of the district centre population and pasture degradation. For example, the populous town of Sumber is surrounded by a district with virtually undamaged pasture. The inference to be drawn from this is that *the creation, or emergence, of large central villages containing a majority of the population does not necessarily result in grassland problems in pastoral areas.*

It is useful next to consider the *rural* population density in the case-study sites (table 5.1). Here again there is an absence of correlation with pasture degradation. For example, Gigant has very bad grassland degradation but it has a low rural population density. The Gigant collective farm does not have a large area of land, but the great majority of the people live in the central village. More pertinent is the case of *high rural population density.* It is true that Argada has the highest rural population density and also the worst degradation, but Hosh Tolgoi and Handagat are both cases where high countryside populations are not associated with pasture degradation.

If high rural population density is not necessarily associated with pasture degradation, perhaps a sedentarised population is? Figure 5.12 shows that there is indeed a certain correlation between sedentarisation and degradation of pastures. The association can be seen in Argada and Gigant in Russia, and in Hargant and Chinggel Bulag in Inner Mongolia. When herders do not move far and the stocking rate is high the pasture is likely to be overgrazed and areas near settlements and wells will suffer in particular (see next chapter). However, sedentarisation per se does not necessarily imply pasture problems; it is the movement of the herds in relation to available pasture that matters. In Dashbalbar people have a relatively sedentary way of life, and furthermore this applies to the large number of herders as well as to *sum* centre-dwellers, but the total area of pasture is so vast that degradation is very slight and occurs only in a few spots near fixed structures.[22] While having houses in the centre and making relatively small seasonal moves, it is significant that Dashbalbar herders do make use of long-distance grazing forays (*otor,* see next chapter). The conclusion, looking at all the case-studies, is that *sedentarisation, especially of the herders, is one factor associated with pasture degradation because it is usually linked to overall reduction in herd mobility.*

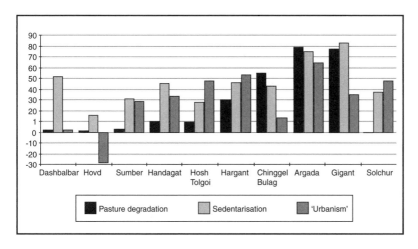

FIGURE 5.12. Pasture degradation, sedentarisation and 'urbanism' in case-
study sites

See figures 5.6, 5.9 and 5.11.

FIGURE 5.13. Milking cows in overgrazed pasture, Chinggel Bulag,
Inner Mongolia, 1993 (photo: Qi, Xiao-Hong)

Finally, let us consider urbanisation, especially that aspect which we call rural-urban integration or 'urbanism' (also shown in figure 5.12). Here the association with pasture degradation is not strong. Argada (and to a lesser extent Hargant) is the only case-study site where high levels of urbanisation occur together with significant pasture degradation. Solchur and Hosh Tolgoi, on the other hand, are significant cases in which the association does not hold. They disprove the common assumption that if people are 'urbanised' (buy most of their goods from shops, watch a lot of TV, wear non-traditional clothes, etc.) they will also disregard the environment. In fact, Solchur (Tuva) and Hosh Tolgoi (Hoboksair, Xinjiang, China) are the two communities where people expressed the strongest feelings about 'preserving nature'. Of course, it is conceivable that this reaction might itself be a result of education and the influence of urban intellectuals like teachers. However, we do not think that this is the case. In both Solchur and Hosh Tolgoi the remarks about care for plants and wild animals came from all sections of the community, including the oldest people who were relatively untouched by urban influences. In both places the concern for nature was associated with religious beliefs and rituals. In Hosh Tolgoi, though young people were more careless about such matters, prohibitions on harming the ecology were directly attached to cosmological beliefs. The researcher, Tseren, asked an old man, aged over 70, about why Mongols did not fell trees. He said that the first man and woman lived in a hole in a huge tree. For this reason cutting down a tree was like destroying your *ger* (yurt). Another old person said that when people die their souls stay for a while at the top of trees while waiting for reincarnation in a new body. For this reason trees should not be cut down. Tseren (1996: 150) further noted what people said about a gold-mine in Hoboksair mountain that was newly opened by the government in 1992, causing many new roads to be cut in the district. In July and August there were very heavy rains that washed away all the new roads. The old people said that the most important reason for this was that the mine had polluted the water-sources of the mountain, and this is well known to anger the *luus* (the spirit-owners of the place). As a result the *luus* sent the torrential rain to destroy the roads.

In Solchur, on the other hand, the concern for the environment was not just conceptual but also practical, e.g. maintaining herds well below theoretical ceilings, keeping local not foreign breeds, planting trees, strong local censure of polluting water sources or hunting out of season, etc. (see Humphrey, Mongush and Telenged, 1993). However, school teaching on environmental matters was combined with revival of religious rituals. Kara Ondar (female), aged 50, is the head teacher of the school. Her husband works for the school as an odd-job man and they have four children. Kara Ondar told Marina Mongush, the Tuvinian researcher, in her characteristically teacherly fashion:

> We constantly conduct special ecology months. All the pupils take part in this. The ecology month means special classes conducted by biologists, geographers and form teachers. Sometimes specialists from the county Ecological Committee are invited. They read lectures and show the children *The Red Book*, a listing of endangered species. All these classes are conducted within the separate age groups and after that we conduct seminars, lectures and other classes for all the pupils of our school together.
>
> Our programme of ecological conservation includes excursions to the beautiful and picturesque places of our region. For example every year the pupils of our school visit *arjaans*,[23] the mineral springs in our homeland of Ovyur. As you know, we have three main springs: 'Angaraktyg', 'Taldyk-Chardyk', 'Ulaataj'. We constantly visit them.
>
> Two years ago we began practising 'folk pedagogy'. This refers to traditional methods of raising children. We want our children to follow the traditions of their ancestors, to promote the revival of the national traditional holidays (Shagaa, the traditional New Year, Naadym, the summer festival of the herders). The children also take part in rituals honouring natural objects, such as mountains, rivers, *ovaa*[24] etc. In Tuvan culture, nature played the main role, and we are trying to return to all the traditions and customs connected with honouring nature (*ovaa dagyyr, sug bajy dagyyr*, etc).
>
> Ecological education was systematised after we had begun practising 'folk pedagogy'. In the past we had no system at all. We tried to teach our children to take care of nature but we had no programme. During the last two years we created a system in the teaching of this subject and we'll try to develop it in the future. It is easy for our children to learn the elements of ecological education, because of the influence of their parents and grandparents. All the children know that they must take care of the rivers, woods, and animals. They've heard this since their birth. At school we must consolidate these skills. This is our purpose.

Solchur, as noted earlier in this chapter, is one of the more highly urbanised of our case-study sites. Here we see that urbanism has not led to a rejection of indigenous culture, but is encouraging a reformulation of it in the younger generation. When taken together with the state farm director's insistence on retaining indigenous herding practices, it is clear that *urbanisation and strong rural-urban integration does not necessarily lead to disregard for the environment.*

CONCLUSIONS

This chapter has shown that there is a need for new tools of analysis of settlement patterns, which arises from the fact that households in Inner Asia very frequently have more than one dwelling and/or more than one place of residence. Communal settlements comprised of many households are correspondingly complex.

Historically over the past 50 years in the whole of Inner Asia there has been a change towards more sedentary forms of household life and an increase in population of the administrative centre settlement of the district.

Despite the fact that the three national governments have promoted 'sedentarisation of the nomads' and encouraged urbanisation in different ways, we found that *these two processes are not directly correlated.* Furthermore, sedentarisation and urbanisation do not simply follow country-specific patterns ordered by given state regimes. The government policies have encountered different indigenous cultural practices in specific physical environments. Whatever the policies, our studies showed close similarities in ways of life between adjacent districts in different countries. The two processes have different trajectories: urbanism in rural areas is to a great extent a function of economic opportunities in district centres, distance from the city, and the roads, railways and other communications that happen to link a given district with a metropolis. But sedentarisation draws upon local practices, traditions and landscapes. Here we observe relatively distinct cultural practices in the more sedentarised plains in the north-east of our region (Argada, Gigant, Dashbalbar, and to some extent Hargant) as distinct from the mountainous far west (Hosh Tolgoi, Handagat, Hovd and Solchur). These cultural zones cross-cut international frontiers.

Although there has been an overall increase in both sedentarisation and urbanisation these processes are separate, and have different causes and effects. Furthermore, they are not irreversible. This can be can be seen from the cases of Argada, Gigant, and Solchur, which have all experienced a recent decline in urbanisation, and Sumber and Bayantümen, where previously town-based workers have recently become mobile herders. The studies of Gigant collective farm (Chita, Russia) and Chinggel Bulag (Inner Mongolia) disprove the common assumption that sedentarisation inevitably leads to urbanisation. Decrepit infrastructures, isolation and poverty is presently reversing processes of urbanisation in certain sedentarised areas. Conversely, the cases of Solchur (Tuva) and Hosh Tolgoi (Xinjiang) contradict the commonly-held view that a migratory lifestyle is incompatible with urban cultural influences and rural-urban integration.

FIGURE 5.14. A family outside their home in the settlement, Tuva, 1991

Sedentarisation of lifestyles of the herders certainly seems to be one factor associated with pasture degradation. Furthermore, it may be associated with loss of herding skills.[25] However, the creation, or emergence, of large central villages containing a majority of the population does not necessarily result in grassland degradation in pastoral areas. The implication here is that large central villages can be combined with mobile herds and consequently a mobile lifestyle for the herder part of the population. Furthermore, in such districts urbanisation and strong rural-urban integration need not necessarily lead to lack of concern for the environment. Solchur in Tuva, for example, is relatively highly urbanised, but it is non-sedentary and its people are active both in practical and religious ways in 'preserving nature'.

This chapter has discussed the relation between settlement forms and mobility. The next chapter goes on to discuss the ways in which one might describe the different systems of movement; it describes some historical strategies of mobile pastoralism in Inner Asia to make the case that there are important differences in the nature of large and small-scale pastoral enterprise; and it suggests that co-ordinated pastoral mobility over relatively large districts is economically and environmentally advantageous.

Chapter 6

Spatial Mobility and Inner Asian Pastoralism

David Sneath

Introduction

Pastoral systems vary in Inner Asia. In different geographical regions pastoralism has taken various forms, and in some areas it has long been associated with crop cultivation.[1] This chapter concentrates on the dominant forms of pastoral movement systems in Mongolia and Inner Mongolia, and on the current systems found in the case-study sites. It does not, however, describe another important technique of pastoral intensification used in Buryatia and parts of Tuva, based on *utug* which are irrigated and fertilised hayfields (see chapter 2 and Gomboev 1996).

I suggest that pre-collective Inner Asian pastoralism cannot be seen as constituting a single productive mode or described using a single set of formal rules in which all pastoralists can be considered to have the same economic orientation. In the case of Mongolian pastoralism, the pre-collective rural economy can be seen to contain a spectrum of economic activity that can be described using a model of dual productive modes. By 'productive mode' I mean a combination of techniques, organisation and objectives. These two modes represent ideal-typical extremes in productive orientation. I have termed them the 'yield-focused' or 'specialist' mode on the one hand, and the 'subsistence' or 'domestic' mode on the other. While some pastoral units might orient themselves to one or other of these modes, it is significant that in practice it was common for a household to engage in both. For example, a herder might herd animals belonging to a yield-focused organisation ('feudal' lord, monastery, collective farm) while at the same time operating his own household economy along subsistence principles. This approach implies that we need not attempt to classify pre-collective Mongolian pastoralism as either a subsistence or a proto-commercial rural economy.

It appears to have been both. The socialist collective institutions as well as the current reforms are also analysed using this model, and I conclude that in the case of Mongolia recent economic change has led to an increase in the importance of the subsistence mode.

The chapter also attempts to review the environmental constraints on contemporary and historical pastoral movement systems, and to evaluate the importance of mobility as a response to environmental variability, particularly precipitation. The implication of recent research on 'non-equilibrial' grazing systems is that spatial flexibility is an important method for making optimum use of the available pastoral resources over much of the Inner Asian steppe. This provides further grounds for the case we have been making in this book for the importance of co-ordination of pastoral movements at a relatively wide geographical level.

MANAGEMENT OF PASTURE IN THE MANCHU AND PRE-COLLECTIVE PERIOD

The concept of 'traditional' Mongolian pastoralism is important for any discussion of the changes in pastoral management this century. However, there is no such thing as an ahistorical timeless 'tradition' in Inner Asian society. From the late seventeenth century until the twentieth, both Inner Mongolia and Mongolia were ruled by the Manchu Qing dynasty, which collapsed in 1911. Communist power was established in 1921 in Mongolia, and in 1949 in Inner Mongolia; and collectivisation was carried out in both regions in the 1950s and '60s. If we wish to describe 'traditions' of pastoralism we must refer to the pastoral practice of a particular time.

There can be little disputing the many ways in which Mongolian society of the Manchu and pre-revolutionary periods resembled ones we consider 'feudal'. Mongolian historians such as Natsagdorj (1967) and Sanjdorj (1980), drawing on the wealth of materials available to them, are able to argue convincingly that in the Manchu period, if not before, Mongolia's society was essentially feudal.[2] The land was considered to belong ultimately to the Manchu emperor, and was administered on his behalf by his officials.[3] The principal administrative district was the *hoshuu* ('banner') administered by the Zasag – the aristocratic prince of a secular *hoshuu*, or the *Hubilgan* (reincarnate senior lama) of an ecclesiastic one (Bawden 1968: 8). In everyday life the right to use pasture land was at the discretion of the secular or religious head of the *hoshuu*, and their officials.[4] It seems clear that it was the banner (which has been retained to the present day in Inner

Mongolia), rather than the smaller divisions within it, such as the *sum* or the generally smaller *bag*, that was the most important unit of pastoral land management. As an official letter dated 1877 stated 'the grass and water of a territory may be managed and assigned only by the ruler and Zasag [the ruler of a *hoshuu*] of the said land.[5]

Within the *hoshuu* , the herdsmen were assigned to sub-units (*sum*), and to the smaller *bag* or *otog*[6] – the smallest administrative division. The herdsmen were required to stay within the banner,[7] and usually had to stay within the pastures allocated to their *bag* or *otog*, certainly in winter and spring. Within these administrative sub-units there seems to have been some flexibility in rights to land-use.[8]

The early twentieth century pastoral economy, as far as we can reconstruct it, was characterised by large numbers of animals in the ownership of nobles and monastic institutions. The actual herding of animals seems to have been done by individual households the poorer of which might work for richer 'patron' families (who might be nobility or commoners) and by sections of these families themselves. Although most households owned a range of livestock breeds, there were also specialists who would look after large herds of certain breeds (particularly horses) for their noble or monastic masters.

This pattern of land management and livestock ownership continued to exist well into the twentieth century.[9] In Mongolia, although the nobility and Church were stripped of their power and much of their wealth in the twenties and thirties, pastureland continued to be controlled by officials. After the revolution and up until collectivisation, rich herd-owners still tended to act as patrons for a number of poorer 'client' families, often having their animals herded by others under lease-type arrangements.[10] These rich herders were later put under increasing pressure to reduce their holdings, and to join the collectives, by various means[11] which effectively acted as a progressive property tax.

MODELS OF PRE-COLLECTIVE PASTORALISM

The first major classificatory scheme for Mongolian pastoral movement was devised by A. D. Simukov, the Russian ethnographer. He carried out his research in the early 1930s, well before collectivisation. He developed a classification of six types of movement system based upon geographical location, and he gave each of the six types of movement system the name of the region where it was found (Simukov 1934).

Simukov's 'WESTERN TYPE' of movement,[12] was characterised by summer camps high in the mountains, these pastures being impossible to use in any other season. In autumn the pastoralists generally descended to the feet of the mountains, to hollows or plains. For the winter they climbed to the lower slopes of the mountains to gain protection from the wind, and spent spring near to these winter camps. Simukov describes this cycle of annual movement, which was often linear, as having a large diameter – about 100 kilometres. It is interesting to note that this system seems to be a relatively close match to the present-day movement that is practised in this region and which was studied in the Hovd *sum* case-study site.

A variation of the 'western type' was classed as the 'ÖVÖRHANGAI TYPE'. In this system the summer was spent at the upper reaches of rivers in the Hangai range, and the winter pastures were far to the south, in the Gov'- Altai area. In autumn and spring pastoralists made very long movements, with a lot of transitional, short-lived camps. The diameter of the migration was particularly large, 150–200km.

A third system of movement was described by Simukov as the 'HANGAI TYPE', again with the main camps being at the summer and winter pastures. Simukov also noted the link between the high variation in pasture yields in some regions and the need for higher mobility in pastoral systems. He explains that in the Hangai region the productivity of pastures was constant, year to year, and quite high. As a result there was no need to make long movements in response to drought. The diameter of the annual move- ment cycle was small, not more than 7–8km. In some cases the summer camp was as little as 2 or 3km from the winter pastures. Summer camps were usually in open low valleys, and winter camps on relatively high ground. Pastoralists preferred summer pastures near their winter sites, which should be on slopes sheltered from the wind and warmed by sun.

The 'STEPPE TYPE' that Simukov describes was characterised by summer pastures in open places, preferably near water, and winter camps on the southern slopes of mountains or in hollows to provide shelter from the wind, if at all possible. The livestock ate snow to gain water in the winter, but required other water sources at the summer pastures. Autumn camps were usually chosen for their proximity to sources of natural salt or soda. The diameter of annual movement was 30–50km, or more in some cases, with relatively frequent changes of camp and pasture.

The fifth of Simukov's categories is the 'EASTERN TYPE', being found on the eastern Mongolian steppe. The summer pastures generally were to the north, (often by the river Herlen). Part of the population moved south to make use of winter pastures in sheltered hollows with desert steppe vegetation. This system was similar to the 'Övörhangai type' in that it was characterised by long north-south movement in spring and autumn, with numerous, transitional camps. The diameter of the annual movement was about 100km.

Lastly there was Simukov's 'GOBI TYPE' in which pastoralists generally attempted to move only a short distance in a year, except when forced to go further by drought. In this case they undertook very long movements of 150–200km from their usual camps. In summer they usually stayed in flat open areas, in winter they moved to mountains or hills – with the exception of camel herders who also wintered on the plain. Some pastoralists, termed 'mountain-Gobi households' by Simukov, did not move to the plains, but habitually stayed in the mountains. Some rich herd-owners, Simukov notes, separated their herds and their work force, so as to pasture camels on the plains, and the sheep, goats and horses in the mountains. Though annual movement varied greatly in Simukov's 'Gobi type' the average diameter of movement in a non-drought year appears to have been a moderate 30–40km or so.

Simukov's classificatory scheme appears to be a general one in which, at first glance, it seems that pastoralists of a given region follow the same movement system. As he describes these various types, however, it becomes clearer that in some regions at least there were a variety of movement systems practised in the same locality. Simukov's more detailed analysis of the movement in an Övörhangai banner illuminates this in more depth, but even his general description includes the mention of different strategies of movement employed by 'some part' of the population, or, as in the 'Gobi type,' the note that those who specialised in herding certain species of livestock had different movement systems.

Simukov's 1935 study of Bayanzürh Uulyn Hoshuu[13] is a useful example, which provides an excellent picture of the contemporary pastoral system of the 1930s and of the previous pattern in use just earlier when the area was administered by a monastery. He estimates that before the 1921 revolution around 70% of the population of the *hoshuu* had herded livestock for the monastery, and were divided into groups specialising in herding particular species of livestock for their lama masters. These specialist herders were administered by officials appointed by the monastery, who organised movements and allocated pastures and duties. They were also responsible for collecting a quota of animal products that was supplied to the monastery every year, and the herding households were allowed to keep for themselves the surplus produce once the quota had been fulfilled. Poor households,

Simukov (1936: 50) notes, often attached themselves to the rich and to those who were herding livestock for the monastery. They provided labour in return for a share of the animal produce. The very rich did not usually herd monastery livestock, having so many of their own, but they also made use of the labour of the poor.[14]

The most mobile of these specialist herders were those who kept horses, sheep and camels for the monastery; they used summer pastures in the mountainous Hangai region and wintered far to the south in the Gobi. It was only really these groups that carried out the long north-south annual movement that Simukov described as the 'Övörhangai type', with its large movement radius of 150–200km. The other groups, those herding the cattle of the monastery, and those keeping only their own livestock, moved less. The cattle-herders, for example, tended to move within the Hangai range and not to leave it, and the private herders of the rest of the banner did not move as far as the Hangai in the north. Simukov (1936: 49–55) notes that in the south of the banner rich Gobi households had a relatively large radius of nomadic movement, but the poor did not.[15]

Figure 6.1 shows my reconstruction of the movement system organised by the monastery, based upon Simukov's description. The specialist horse and sheep herders moved from winter and spring pastures in the Bogd mountain range to summer in the Hangai zone near the monastery, returning via autumn pastures to the north of Lake Orog. The specialist camel herders also made a very long movement, from winter and spring pastures in the Gobi region on the slopes of the Altan mountain range to summer pastures near the monastery. Specialist cattle herders never moved very far, some confining their movements to the Hangai region, and others moving all year in or very near the Bogd range. The groups known as 'Gobi herders' moved south of the Bogd range all year, reaching the Altan mountain area where they shared winter and spring camps with the camel herders.[16] This group had some monastery goats and camels as well as their own livestock. Seasonal pastures were often shared by different groups moving with different systems, and the large movements coexisted with smaller ones made by households without significant numbers of monastery livestock. The group known as the 'middle well' herders, for example, moved all year with their own private animals in the Hangai foothills near the monastery.

The monastery had been abolished in 1929, and Simukov considered the long movements that were still practised at the time of his study (1935) to be a 'feudal survival'. He concluded that the abolition of feudal relations tended to lead to a reduction of the radius of movement. Many pastoralists

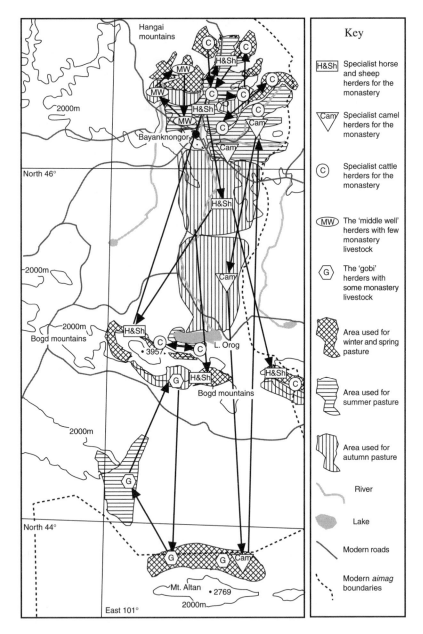

FIGURE 6.1. Reconstruction of the pastoral movement system of the subjects of the Lamyn Gegen monastery (Bayanzürh Uulyn Hoshuu)

Source: Simukov 1936: 49–56

had taken to spending all year in one area, such as around Lake Orog, and making only short distance moves. Simukov noted the paradox that he found neighbours, temporarily sharing a pasture, one of whom moved 20km a year, and the other moved 200km. Strangely, both sets of pastoralists considered their system of movement to be the best. He writes:

'Furthermore, it is interesting to note that the group 'nudeg' [the specialist horse and sheep herders][17] does not move in a specific area which is such that it necessitates a long move of 200 kilometres. Rather, this group moves to the same areas and pastures that other nomadic households use almost all year round, but who do not, however, feel the need to move long distances' (Simukov 1936: 54).

How are we to explain different pastoral movement strategies coexisting in the same region? The situation in Bayanzürh Uulyn Hoshuu was not exceptional, indeed Simukov mentions that the pastoralists of neighbouring banners had very similar practices.

DUAL PRODUCTIVE MODES

To better model the pre-collective pastoral economy so as to accommodate the variety of productive strategies, I represent pastoral households as operating within a range of productive activity bounded by two ideal-typical poles, the 'yield-focused' or 'specialist' mode at one end of the spectrum and the 'subsistence' mode at the other extreme. These two systems were interrelated, and indeed the 'specialist' mode relied upon domestic-subsistence activity to support the work-force.

The 'yield-focused' or 'specialist' mode was based upon the ownership of large numbers of animals by a single agency – usually a noble family, ecclesiastical institution, local government office, or a rich commoner. It was characterised by the specialised herding of large herds, often of a single species. It also often made use of a relatively large amount of movement, particularly of horses, camels and sheep, in terms both of length of migrations and frequency of moves.[18] Production was oriented towards gaining the maximum return on the herd-wealth that was kept in this way, the subordinate herders having contractual obligations to supply a certain quota of produce and retaining only the surplus for themselves. This mode made use of certain economies of scale, in that large herds could be herded with little more labour than small ones.

By the 19th century most of the Mongolian elite was in debt to Chinese merchant firms. In the pre-revolutionary period much of the produce of the districts ruled by the princes and senior lamas was expended on servicing this debt (Sandorj 1980: 80).[19] Such princes and lamas wore silk clothes, ate from porcelain bowls, smoked Chinese tobacco, and drank Chinese tea. The orientation of such herd-owners was towards the Chinese market, mediated by their debts to merchants, and rich herd-owners had every reason to extract the maximum surplus from the livestock economy. Their large herds meant a different strategy of production and pattern of land-use from that employed by subsistence producers.[20] The monastery was indeed, in this sense, an economic institution, in that it sought to maximise the yield on its investment of livestock. As it sought a surplus, and was able to provide the opportunity for extensive land-use, it supported the long movements of certain specialist herders.[21]

The 'subsistence' mode, by contrast, was oriented towards satisfying domestic requirements, and as such was characterised by each pastoral family owning and herding relatively small numbers of several species of domestic livestock. The various species provided different necessities for the pastoralist: sheep and goats for meat and winter clothing, cattle for milk, horses for riding and camels for transportation. As these were privately owned livestock, not herded for others under contractual obligation, the produce went directly to the working household.

All pastoral households engaged to some extent in domestic subsistence production, particularly of milk products, but those who were primarily oriented towards this mode were those who did not participate in the large-scale herding activities. These households would tend to limit their mobility to unavoidable movement, i.e. that dictated by their smaller herds grazing off all available vegetation. Pastoralists who undertook specialised herding for large herd-owners, such as monasteries, not only gained managerial control of large numbers of animals and a share of their produce, but probably also benefited from the other specialist productive activities. For example, in the case described by Simukov (1936: 55-6) the monastery also organised the cultivation of wheat. Again, much of the actual labour was carried out by poor people attached to the more prosperous pastoralists who were allocated this agricultural duty as their feudal obligation to the monastery.

This idea of two pastoral economic orientations offers an explanation of Simukov's paradox of the temporary neighbours with completely different movement systems. Those herders who moved their animals on the long migration were either those responsible and skilled enough to be chosen by the monastery to herd their animals, or those who had large herds of the more mobile livestock themselves. They thought their method was the best and considered those making smaller movements to be lazy. Those who were poorer or had few *tavisan* ('placed') animals of the rich,[22] were not bound to use the long migration methods if they did not want to. They tended to move within a relatively small locality. These households, whose orientation was primarily domestic subsistence, were able to fulfil their economic goals with small movements. For them, their less mobile and less laborious lifestyle was superior.[23]

The period following the abolition of the 'feudal' order and before collectivisation saw a decline in the specialist production organised by the feudal and ecclesiastical elite, and an increase in the subsistence mode, although the rich continued to make use of greater movement and the labour of poor households.[24]

A comparable situation in Inner Mongolia is described by Hell and Quéré in their study (1993: 254) of Ujumchin: '[After] the liberation of Inner Mongolia by Communist troops in 1947 [...] we can observe the establishment of a regime of mixed types of movement. The poorer owners who had two thirds of the total livestock stayed all year round in one region and had a very limited migratory cycle, while the large owners and their employees moved from one to two hundred kilometres to the south, as far as the pastures around the town of Shilinhot.' Vreeland (1954: 145) notes that in the 1930s, in Chahar 'it was usually the wealthier families, with sizeable horse herds, which were the ones to rely most on the use of *otor*.'

The differences in the economic orientation of rich and poor pastoralists have been noted in a number of studies. Telal Asad (1979: 424–5) described two modes of production among the Bakhtyari, (which he identified as the 'free nomad' on the one hand, and the 'landlord-chief' on the other).[25] Comparable trends can be identified in some African pastoral societies, such as Botswana (Mazonde 1987: 182–7).[26] In both cases indigenous pastoral elites had very different economic behaviour from the subsistence pastoralists, and adopted strategies designed to maximise their benefits from herd-wealth. It should not be assumed, however, that subsistence and yield-focused herd-owners necessarily had conflicting interests in the Mongolian case. The existence of specialist herding seems to have allowed smaller producers to place some of their stock with these larger herds, so benefiting from the 'economy of scale'.

When one considers what a system of wide pastoral movement in Inner Asia requires, it is clearly not the subsistence activity that is in some way 'natural' to the area. Mobility requires political organisation that allows access to large areas of land, and the movement itself requires transportation

– carts, draught animals and movable supplies. Paradoxically, one can see *extensive* land-use as an *intensification* of production in the following sense. In a given culture, long-distance herding strategies require increased labour, greater technical knowledge, more transport animals and more complex equipment than low-mobility herding of the same-sized flock. Depending on the type of herd and the given ecology, herders using these strategies will move herds long distances and also relatively frequently within a given seasonal pasture. The benefits, according to Mongolian herders, are fatter, stronger animals, with a better survival rate. It would be difficult to argue that the highly mobile form is more labour-intensive per unit of product, but it is more labour-intensive (arduous) in terms of the life-style of a herder. Furthermore, it also requires more co-ordination, investment and wider political authority over land.

No less than in other parts of Asia, the importance of economic corporations has a long history on the steppe. With the ownership of large numbers of animals, and the control of labour, steppe elites have long been able to generate extensive, mobile, specialist herding systems, making use of the economies of scale from the management of large herds.[27]

Let us look more closely at the high-mobility, extensive land-use practices of the pre-collective era; perhaps there is another explanation for its prevalence? Without careful examination, it cannot be assumed that this was a particularly sustainable or productive system.

In fact, in much of the relatively well-watered Hangai and Hentii areas pastoralism does not seem to have involved very long movements for anyone, before or after collectivisation.[28] It was mainly in the steppe and Gobi zones that the 'feudal' elite organised very long annual movements for their large herds. In these regions are such long movements really more productive, and if not, how can we explain why they were undertaken by the elite? One alternative explanation, implied by Simukov, would be that large movement was not to do with productivity, but reflected the requirement of those in command of the district that products be brought to them. In the case of ecclesiastical banners there were usually only a few centres of monastic life, the districts were large and the subjects of the monasteries had to move long distances to bring the products. This approach would suggest that as the number of centres and settlements increased in socialist times, movements naturally became shorter and came to be based upon local environmental rather than social and political conditions. This argument might imply that the wider migration of the past was not particularly efficient or environmentally sustainable (although it would not preclude this possibility). In view of the larger size of the southern districts, this sort of approach would imply that district magnitude reflected the viable size of a political unit. To be viable, the districts had to be larger in southern steppe and Gobi areas, with dry pastures and lower population densities of both people and livestock. With the increase of livestock numbers and productivity, this line of reasoning suggests, the territorial size of viable administrative units diminished.

This is not an entirely convincing explanation, however. The pre-revolutionary elite could, and did, establish new administrative centres, particularly monasteries. It seems unlikely that they found no utility in their large administrative districts. Secondly, much of the feudal elite was itself mobile, and even in the case of a static monastic overlord, there was nothing to prevent the authorities from arranging for produce to be collected at sub-centres and brought to them (which one might expect if there was no intrinsic utility to the long movement of their entire herds).

Furthermore, the shapes of the 'feudal' administrative divisions are far from random. They are not simply large enough to support a given number of people or animals. Figure 6.8 also shows the long north-south scope typical of many of the pre-revolutionary administrative districts of these lords and lamas. Many *hoshuu* stretched down to include drier Gobi regions to the south. It seems certain that this was to enable pastoralists to move to these regions in winter, (indeed, many informants in the case-study sites mentioned the value of Gobi vegetation for winter pasture, and of carrying out *otor* in this season).

A simpler and more convincing explanation is that the wealthy herd-owning agencies found that a highly mobile pastoral system, and the use of a range of pasture types, provided them with the best return in terms of livestock and products – fatter animals and more of them. This was because (as some recent African arid rangeland research also suggests) the way to support the maximum numbers of animals in a given region is by movement of the livestock, so as to exploit optimal periods in the natural resource cycles of the different ecological zones of that area (Behnke and Scoones 1993: 12–15). This explanation would correspond with the views of many interviewed herders who stressed the positive value of movement.[29]

It remains an open question, however, as to whether the extensive, large-movement system can be considered more efficient in an absolute sense (obtaining maximum returns from given resources) or was most efficient in a relative sense (better for extracting a surplus from one's subjects). A powerful herd-owning institution that is able to move its animals across the pasture in effect takes a sort of 'vegetation tithe', because the large, quickly-moving herd creams off the grass which would otherwise be used by small domestic producers. And of course, another incentive for people in a privileged position is that their herds may move far, but they themselves do not have to do all the hard work, whether they go on the migration themselves or not. A great deal more work is involved in long migrations because the animals are not used to the terrain and are likely wander away rather than returning habitually to a known encampment.

Furthermore, the elite, by making use of the economies of scale of specialised herds, had to concentrate large numbers of animals in one place, rather than distribute their herd-wealth in small numbers to all their subjects to herd in the domestic-subsistence mode. It would follow that the larger the concentration of livestock the larger the movement needs to be. The richer the household, and the more animals the owner wishes to keep under his or her personal supervision, the more they would have to move. This is by no means incompatible with the supposition that specialist, long-distance, pastoralism also gave better returns for herd-owners. This specialised move-ment seems particularly beneficial in herding horses and camels, so that in many cases they continued to be pooled and moved long distances in the collective period. With the demise of collectives this practice has declined because, as Erdenejav in Hosh Tolgoi explained (below), no single private household can easily organise a herd large enough to make this worthwhile.

In some respects the change from a 'feudal' to collective organisa-tional form was a less radical change than the one currently underway as the government attempts the transition to a market economy. In both 'feudal' and collective periods there were centralised, commandist politico-economic units that regulated residence, the use of pasture, and extracted a surplus through rights to livestock. Indeed in many cases these centres were in the same physical locations in the two periods.[30] Common subjects had legal duties to their leaders in both systems. In the Manchu period this consisted of providing livestock and produce (tax), and might include acting as servants, or performing military service. In the collectives the duty of members was to provide produce and labour in line with norms and instructions of the farm.

Like the feudal lords and the monasteries before them, the collectives organised movement, single-species herds, and allocated pasture. It is significant that the everyday term used for collective or state animals was, and still is, *alban mal* – 'official' or 'duty animals', and the root of this term is *alba* – the feudal obligation owed by pre-revolutionary subjects to their lord. Indeed the term for a common citizen or serf was *albat* – meaning 'one with duty'.

It was as if in the collectives the yield-focused specialist mode, with its official/duty animals, had expanded to include all of the pastoralists and most of the livestock. The small remaining sector dominated by domestic production was represented by the small numbers of private animals that herders were allowed to keep. The collective organised, and enforced, the movement of its members, and in this respect seems to have increased the mobility of certain herders (Humphrey 1978: 157).

One of the most noticeable changes in the Mongolian pastoral economy after the abolition of the 'feudal' social order in the 1920s was a marked increase in the numbers of all species of livestock (figure 6.2), particularly sheep. The pre-revolutionary elite had extracted a considerable

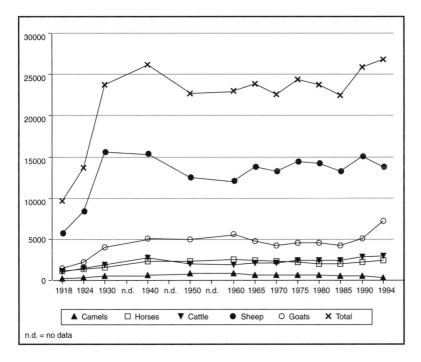

FIGURE 6.2. Livestock population of Mongolia 1918–1994 (in thousands)

Sources: Mongolian SSO 1981: 178; Sheehy 1996: 46.

surplus of livestock, and it seems that this declined during the 1920s as the livestock was redistributed among herding households. This could be said to have increased the domestic-subsistence orientation of the pastoral economy so that pastoralists tended to increase the size of their herds by reducing the high annual offtake that the old system had necessitated.

At the end of the 19th century Outer Mongolia was exporting huge numbers of domestic animals to China, probably at least one million sheep units of livestock each year.[31] In 1917 the total herd wealth of Outer Mongolia was just over 20 million sheep units, so this (conservative) estimate of export would represent about 5% of that total. This was export on a very large scale, by any standards. Livestock numbers increased after the end of the 'feudal' period but declined in the 1940s and 50s,[32] as state procurement increased and collective farms were introduced. The Mongolian state was able to procure and export large numbers of animals in the collective era. State procurement in 1985, for example, was almost 207,000 tons (live weight) of meat and livestock, and 87,400 head of horses. Of this 63,100 horses and 61,500 tons of livestock and meat were exported.[33] I estimate the total exports as equivalent to 2.1 million sheep units out of a total national herd of 45 million sheep units. This represents an annual export of 4.7% of the national herd, comparable to the estimated pre-revolutionary figure given above. Exports of meat and livestock fell rapidly with the dissolution of the collectives – in 1992 the total had sunk to one fifth of the 1985 figure (Mongolian SSO 1993: 83).

The recent shift away from large-scale collective pastoralism and towards domestic-subsistence is in some ways comparable to the time after the end of the 'feudal' period. Figure 6.2 shows a slight increase in livestock numbers since the dissolution of most of the collectives in 1992. It seems unlikely that this increase will be sustained for very long, however, considering the seriousness of the problems faced by pastoral households, such as the increasing difficulty in obtaining hay and winter fodder, which is likely to limit herd sizes. In the short-term at least, however, it does seem likely that the new pastoral economy will tend to export less meat and livestock than in the collective era. In the early nineties the export of all categories of livestock products fell, except for wool and cashmere. (This is a significant exception, as these are raw materials that can be sold by a pastoral household without reducing the numbers of their livestock). The export of finished woollen and cashmere goods also fell, however, and so the increased export of wool probably reflects the decline of Mongolian textile manufacturing (Mongolian SSO 1993).

MOVEMENT SYSTEMS IN THE COLLECTIVE PERIOD

In a way that is reminiscent of Simukov, the leading Mongolian specialists use a classification scheme for movement systems that is also based upon geographical zones. It is interesting briefly to consider these indigenous models. Bazargür, Chinbat and Shiirev-Ad'yaa (1989), for instance, give a description of the movement systems practised in each *aimag* of Mongolia, noting the variations that may be found in this or that *sum*.[34] Their descriptions are more comprehensive than earlier work, but in the *Ündesnii Atlas* these geographers, among others, created a scheme that, like Simukov's, includes six general types of pastoral movement system: The Hentii, Ar-Hangai, Gov'-Altai, Hovd, central Halh (Suhebaatar *aimag*) and Dornogov' types.[35]

These models are also largely based on altitude, so that movement is seen as a strategy by which the pastoralist uses the natural relief of the landscape to exert some control over the natural conditions affecting the family's livestock. A crude sketch of some of the principles involved, for example, illustrates the very different requirements of pastures in the warmest and coldest periods. Summer pastures should have good access to water, should be cool and with some wind to reduce the discomfort from flying insects, whereas winter pastures should be as warm as possible, preferably sheltered from the cold northerly winds, although sometimes it is helpful to have access to hilly areas where the wind blows off winter snow if it gets too deep.[36]

If we compare Simukov's model and that of modern Mongolian geographers the principles are broadly similar, and if we take each type in turn we see that many features have been retained since the 1930s, particularly the seasonal use of altitude and relief. Simukov did extensive fieldwork and the Mongolian geographers are well-acquainted with their own land, so the similarity of their models suggests a degree of continuity in practice between pre-revolutionary and collective pastoral systems.[37]

Simukov's 'western type' corresponds closely with the modern Hovd movement system.[38] This is characterised by high summer pastures, above 2500 metres; autumn is spent in the lowest pastures – between 1000m and 1500m; winter pastures are higher, around 2000m; and spring is spent on the lower slopes between 1000m and 2000m.[39] This seems to have changed very little since Simukov's day, except that he reported an annual diameter of movement of about 100 kilometres, and in many cases the recent movement seems to be a little less, from 60 to 90km. The system practised in Bayan-

Ölgii *aimag* is also similar, with high summer pastures, generally above 3000m, and autumn camps much lower in the river valleys and plains, around 1700m. Winter is spent in mountain passes and valleys between 1900m and 2700m, and the spring pastures are lower, generally less than 2000m, situated by lakes if possible (Bazargür, Chinbat and Shiirev-Ad'yaa 1989: 46–8).[40]

Pastoral movement in Gov'-Altai *aimag* is also described by the geographers as following the same principles; summer is spent in the mountains between 2400m and 3000m, autumn down in the Gobi regions at 1200–1400m. The winter pastures are located on the slopes of the Altai, or other mountain ranges, at an altitude of 1800–2400m, and for spring the pastoralists move down to passes or the foothills of the mountains at around 1400–1800m (Bazargür, Chinbat and Shiirev-Ad'yaa 1989: 55). The amount of movement appears to be much less than that of Simukov's model, being only 15–30km in some cases.[41]

The Ar-Hangai movement system seems to resemble Simukov's Hangai type, although in this case it seems as if during the collective period the diameter of annual movement had become greater, in some cases, than the 7–8km mentioned by Simukov in his model, ranging up to 35km or more. There are still two main pasture areas, as in Simukov's description, summer and autumn pastures in river valleys, and winter and spring is usually spent at higher altitude on the southern slopes of mountains, around 1700–2100m (Bazargür, Chinbat and Shiirev-Ad'yaa 1989: 43–6).[42] I studied 30 *ails* in Ih Tamir *sum*, Ar-Hangai, in late summer 1996. This was the exact location in which Simukov had worked more than 60 years before, as I found from speaking to some of the older herders, who still remembered him.[43] Among this sample the total average annual movement was 18km (with an 'average diameter' of annual movement, as Simukov would have termed it, of 8km), with some households moving as far as 20km from winter to summer pastures. This seems virtually unchanged from Simukov's time (Simukov 1934: 40–1). Furthermore, over 80% of the households interviewed in 1996 regularly carried out *otor*, moving their livestock even further afield to fatten them for the winter, and over 70% of them moved their encampments four or more times per year to change pastures. This confirms the general picture that in this region pastoralists seem to be about as mobile as they were in Simukov's day. Although they may not move far, they continue to move fairly frequently, and the recent decline in motor transport has reduced mobility less in this region than in those areas where the previous movement pattern involved much longer journeys.

The Hentii movement system, like the Ar-Hangai type, is described as having winter pastures at relatively high altitude, and summer camps are generally below 1200m, in river valleys.[44] As such this system appears to follow similar principles to Simukov's Hangai type, although, once again, it often involves higher mobility, the annual diameter of movement in one case ranging from 7 to around 50km.[45]

The central Halh type is characterised as having summer pastures in the northern part of the administrative districts, and winter camps in the south, often, as in much of Suhebaatar *aimag* with winter pastures on knolls and hillocks around 1000–1100m, and summers being spent in slightly lower valleys and plains, around 900–1000m in altitude. The annual diameter of movement is not generally very high, being around 15–30km, but Bazargür, Chinbat and Shiirev-Ad'yaa (1989: 72–4) note that the variable precipitation found in this region means that sometimes livestock have to be moved a long way to find adequate pasture. This bears some resemblance to Simukov's 'eastern' type, in that it retains a tendency towards northern summer and southern winter pastures, but the usual amount of annual movement appears to be much lower in the modern type.

The Dornogov' system is described as having summer camps in open areas near water sources, often on northern plains. Winter and spring pastures are typically situated in sheltered hollows, or hillocks, often above 1000m. Autumn tends to be spent on plains near water resources, sometimes near salt marshes (Bazargür, Chinbat and Shiirev-Ad'yaa 1989: 58–9). The amount of movement is not described as very high, except in drought conditions, annual diameter of movement often between 7 and 20km.[46]

I conclude that the movement systems described by Simukov and those of the collective period are based on principles that have remained broadly the same. However, there were also some important differences. In the pre-revolutionary period there seems to have been considerably more north-south movement, which was reflected in the shape of the *hoshuu* – which often took the form of a giant strip including both southerly arid land and better-watered northern pastures, (see figure 6.16). The territories were this shape and size not necessarily because all of the pastoralists made the long annual north-south migrations, but because it was to the benefit of the feudal rulers and other large herd-owners to make use of such a range of pastures in the long movements of their herds. Indeed the amount of pastoral movement that Simukov describes for the most mobile section of the pre-collective herding community is generally greater than that organised by the collectives for their mobile sectors. I was first forced to think about this in

Mongolia when elderly herders insisted that before the collectives they used to make long journeys to distant pastures. Nevertheless, it appears that the principles governing pastoral movement systems were adapted during the collective era, and not changed out of all recognition.

PASTORAL MOVEMENT SYSTEMS IN THE CASE-STUDY SITES

The studies carried out of the case-study sites provide examples of the variety of pastoral movement systems now practised in Inner Asia, and some indication of the perceived environmental problems associated with them. In the following section I also discuss the use of dry fodder and stocking levels in the different pastoral systems. Decollectivisation in Mongolia has generally led to a decrease in use of hay as a result of the reduction in mechanised hay-cutting; it seems that this is detrimental to livestock nutrition, as it is not being compensated for by longer or more frequent moves.

Hay fodder is most crucial in late winter and early spring. In previous systems the technique had been to fatten up the animals during late-summer and autumn by taking them on *otor* (short, frequent pasturing moves) so that they should have sufficient fat reserves to last until late spring. It seems that even in Manchu times a certain amount of hay was given in spring, but this was greatly increased during the collective period. As a result there was less use of autumn *otor* pasturing in the collective period, and now use of *otor* depends on individual initiative and some weaker households do not make the effort.

Hovd sum, *Uvs* aimag, *Mongolia*[47]

The general pattern of pastoral movement is shown in figures 6.3A and 6.3B. Summer pastures are high in the mountains (generally above 2400m), and in autumn pastoral households move down to the lakes, at around 1600m. Winter is spent higher on the mountain slopes, at around 2200m, and the spring pastures are slightly lower, at 2000m.

This conforms very closely with Simukov's 'western type', and it seems that in terms of the grounds for the selection of pastures the pre-collective movement system closely resembled that of the collective period, and that this is largely unchanged today. However, the amount of annual movement seems to have declined recently, particularly since reduced motor transport has made it difficult for some families to be as mobile as they were. As Mönhöö, a wealthy 67 year-old herder recounted:

6.3A. Map showing pastoral land-use

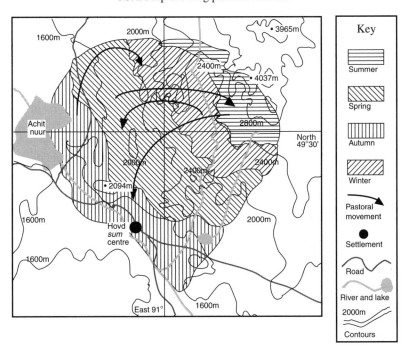

6.3B. Cross-section showing pastoral movement

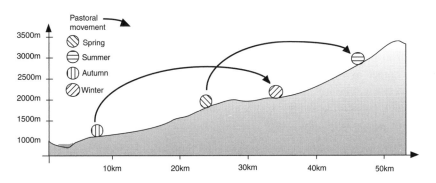

FIGURE 6.3. Hovd *sum*

Location: Uvs *aimag*, Mongolia.
Total land area: 297,200 hectares.
Researcher: B. Telenged.

In the past [before collectivisation] I moved much more. For instance in autumn I used to cross the Hovd river to get to the autumn camp and then I moved again, far away, into the present Bayan-Ölgii *aimag*'s Altantsögt *sum*'s land to get to the winter camp. After February I used to move back, [...] or sometimes go through the present Böhmörön *sum*'s territory to cross the river; then I moved down here during the springtime. I would stay in this *sum*'s land [summer camp] only during the summer months.

There seems to be little, if any, perceived problems of grassland degradation, in this region, and informants generally felt the quality of their pastures has remained good. However, as was the case in most of the case-study sites, elderly informants were emphatic that the large amount of movement practised before collectivisation resulted in the good condition of their livestock,[48] as Mönhöö explained:

Our animals were only as good as they were because of these movements. Before collectivisation there were about 20 moves per winter and spring season and rather fewer in the summer and autumn seasons.

One of the important aspects of the long migration system was that it had a low reliance on hay. However, the large-scale collective was an organisation able to produce and distribute large amounts of hay, thereby enabling the authorities to reduce pastoral movement while retaining large numbers of livestock. Therefore it is important to examine the amount of hay used in current pastoral systems.

In much of Mongolia the collective period saw an increase in the amount of hay used for livestock, (particularly in winter and spring). In Hovd *sum*, however, the amount of fodder used seems to be relatively low and to have declined recently. In 1992 the total amount of hay used in the *sum* was 1,700 tonnes, and when divided among the livestock of the district this gives a higher average of 12 kilograms per sheep unit. The amount used by interviewed households in 1993 was less than 5kg per sheep unit (see figure 6.14). These are both relatively low figures, and some pastoralists do not use any hay, as Jambaldorj, a 69 year-old male herder, explained:

We don't make hay, because our pasture is very good all the time. However, in autumn we gather just a small amount of mountain grass which is of good quality. This we use as hay in spring for the weaker animals such as lambs, kids and calves. We don't use fodder or concentrates.

More than 97% of the *sum* is classified as pasture, and a tiny 20 hectares or so is used for agriculture. The *sum* supported almost 140,000 sheep units of livestock in 1992,[49] and stocking levels were around 0.48 sheep units per hectare.[50] This rate is low, but still comparable with those of nearby Tuvan and Xinjiang pastoral regions.

Hosh Tolgoi, Hoboksair county, Xinjiang, China[51]

Hoboksair, in Xinjiang, is another mountainous region. As shown in figures 6.4A and 6.4B, the current movement system entails wintering in the relatively low hills at around 1500m, then moving north, across the Hoboksair valley and climbing to the spring pastures at around 2000m. The summer camps are situated in the highest pastures, around 2500–3000m. Then the herders move down to spend autumn in the Hoboksair river valley, between 1000 and 1500m. The average amount of annual movement is an estimated 120km, (giving a diameter of 60km).[52] It should also be noted that the southern part of the district was used for winter *otor* movement for the more mobile livestock species – horses and camels. This follows the same principles as Simukov's pre-collective 'western' type, and the current system used in the Mongolian case-study site in Hovd *sum*, Uvs. However, rather than wintering on the same range of mountains where the other seasonal pastures are located, the pastoralists cross the Hoboksair valley to winter, again at reasonably high altitude, in more southerly hills.

The pattern of seasonal movement does not appear to have changed dramatically with collectivisation, and among the case-study sites it is generally the more mountainous regions that seem to have changed least with respect to seasonal movement patterns. However, various factors have led to a decrease in the mobility of at least some of the herding families. One of these was the introduction of the Merino sheep which was carried out as part of the collectivisation process that began in 1957. The resulting cross-breed was poorly adapted to the local conditions of the region and, as the deputy head of the district, 42 year-old Erdenejav notes:

> In 1957 we began to cross-breed Mongolian sheep with the imported Merino. This cross-breeding has continued until the present day. The result of the cross-breeding effort has been to produce a sheep that is prone to loosing its fleece, and dying from gut diseases (diarrhoea) because it gets very cold. Many of them have died. When there is a lot of snow the Merinos do not dig through the snow to get to grass, and in the hot summers they tend to stay together in one herd, do not move, and do not eat grass. They are much slower at moving than the Mongol sheep, and so they cannot go to the more distant pastures for good grass. For the above reasons, and because the Merino needs special enclosures and sheds, after the privatisation of 1983 the numbers of Merinos have been declining, relative to the Mongol sheep.

6.4A. Map showing pastoral land-use

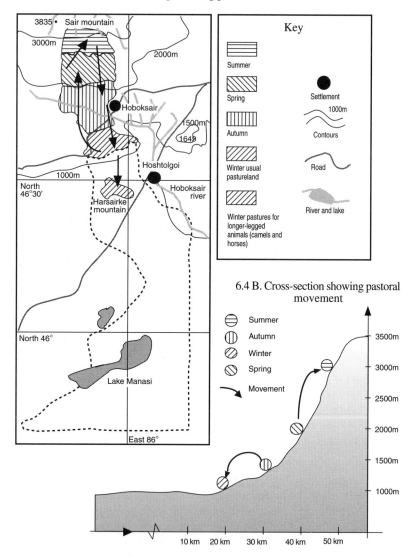

FIGURE 6.4. Hosh Tolgoi *xiang*

Location: Hoboksair *xian*, Xinjiang-Uighur Autonomous Region, People's Republic of China. 'Long-legged animals' are still sometimes grazed on an area of high ground to the south-west of Hosh Tolgoi. These herds are usually composed of camels and horses.
Researcher: Tseren, B. P.

Those households that were assigned the new cross-breed were restricted in their movement, and tended to remain in the Hoboksair valley – customarily used for autumn pasture. Being more sensitive to cold the Merino also required winter sheds, as the elderly herdsman Damdinsüren explained:

> Traditionally [...] herdsmen used sheltered, warm areas (hollows and valleys) for the winter pastures, and so for this reason there was no need for enclosures and sheds. Since they introduced the Merino many enclosures and sheds have had to be built.

The case-study data suggest that the diameter of movement of most pastoral households varies between about 25 and 50km. There were also, however, more distant movements made by specialist herders with some animals. As Erdenejav explained:

> In the past [in the collective period] all the local *sums* would organise *otor* for the 'long-legged livestock' [i.e. the horses and camels], and took them about 100 kilometres south to the northern edge of the Kurban Tungus desert, for winter pasture. Since 1983 this has not been possible, because no one private household has enough large animals to organise a big enough herd to make this worthwhile.

In the Hosh Tolgoi case-study site the development of settlements, agriculture, coal mines and oil fields, has meant that there has been a certain decrease in the amount of pasture since 1949. Locals perceived a series of environmental problems that had contributed to the loss of pasture land. The loss of pasture to agriculture and other forms of land use, such as mineral extraction, was mentioned by several informants as having restricted pastoral movement. Erdenejav singled out mining as a particularly serious problem.

> Much pasture has been destroyed because so many coal mines have been opened. In Hoboksair as a whole there are 24 mining areas, each mining area has damaged and polluted the pasture to a different extent. Some of these mines claim and control more and more land. Also, the waste coal and dust is spread over large areas of pasture, damaging it. A grassland station reported this problem to the Xinjiang government, and in January 1994 the local government began a survey to find out the extent of the problem.[53] There are other problems, where there are many mines a great number of trucks, large and small, and other machines, drive across the pastures of the region. As a result a total of 67,500 *mu* [4,500 hectares] has been damaged in this way. The recent Rangeland Law [1989] that has been issued by the government was designed to protect pasture, and a detailed law was issued by the Xinjiang government regarding the use of roads.[54] This policy seems to have improved

the situation a great deal. The Karamai oil field to the south of Hoboksair was also allocated 15,000 *mu* of pasture for oil pumps and so on, and the pasture of this oil field has been badly damaged.

The number of livestock in Hosh Tolgoi has decreased since the early 1960s (when numbers peaked at 37,000), and in 1993 there were 22,300 domestic livestock in the district, representing an estimated 37,500 standard stocking (sheep) units.[55] However, there appears to have been some decrease in the amount of available pasture so that the pressure on pastures has not lessened proportionally. Local specialists at the Hoboksair County Pasture Management Station have estimated that Hosh Tolgoi contains 576,954 *mu* of winter pasture, 261,439 *mu* of spring and autumn pasture[56] and 168,409 *mu* of summer pasture. Using their theoretical stocking rate the Pasture Management Station calculate that the winter pasture should support 56,132 sheep units, the spring and autumn pasture 35,469 sheep units, and the summer pastures 60,444 sheep units.[57] The current numbers of livestock appear to be within the limits that the government's stocking norms seek to impose, which is about 0.56 sheep units per hectare, (taking all the seasonal pasture into account and averaging the seasonal stocking rates). However, the '60s livestock totals seem to have significantly exceeded them. Local herders did not report dramatic grassland degradation, indeed one suggested that the pasture could support the high numbers of livestock seen in the sixties. According to local specialists, Hoboksair county as a whole has seen a widespread degradation of pastures, with almost all winter and spring/autumn pastures degraded, which they ascribe to overstocking (Longworth and Williamson 1993: 286–7). This raises the question as to what extent the perceptions of officials and experts of environmental damage and its causes diverge from those of local herdsmen in this region.[58]

Handagat, Altai county, Xinjiang, China[59]

The most mobile of the movement systems examined in any of the case-study sites is that of Handagat, another mountainous region, as shown in figures 6.5A and 6.5B. There is more than one movement system in this region; specialist camel herders, for example, have a different set of seasonal pastures. Horses are still gathered together from individual families and taken on special winter movement to more distant pastures.[60] In general, however, most of the pastoralists move to summer pastures that are high up in the mountain valleys, between 1700m and 2000m. They move down to autumn pastures that are considerably lower, at the feet of the mountains, around 1000m, and then make a long move to the winter camps by the Irtysh

6.5A. Map showing pastoral land-use

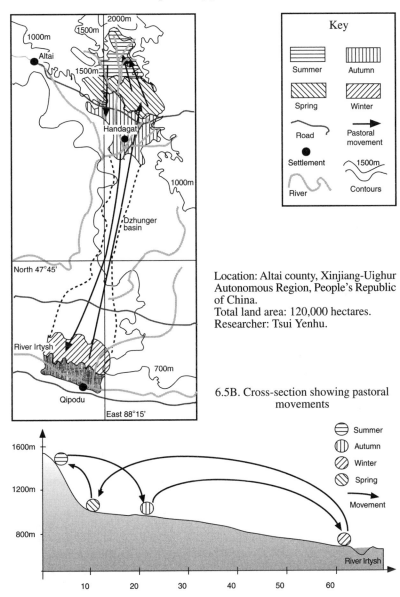

Location: Altai county, Xinjiang-Uighur Autonomous Region, People's Republic of China.
Total land area: 120,000 hectares.
Researcher: Tsui Yenhu.

6.5B. Cross-section showing pastoral movements

FIGURE 6.5. Handagat *sum*

river which are around 800m. The spring pastures are a little higher than the autumn ones, around 1100m and above. The length of this north-south movement gives rise to the very high annual average reported by informants of over 350km, indicating a diameter of movement of over 175km.

This does not correspond closely with any of Simukov's pre-revolutionary Mongolian pastoral movement types, but it does follow some similar principles to the model of the Gov'-Altai system described in the *Ündesnii Atlas* (MAS 1990: 112). Summer pastures are similarly high in the mountains, and autumn and spring pastures at lower altitude. The principal difference seems to be that in Handagat the winter camps are apparently lower yet, in the river valley, and not on the mountain slopes as in the Gov'-Altai model. The movement system has not been altered radically by collectivisation or since, but there has been an increase in the amount of land used for agriculture, as Qorqa, a 66-year-old female herder explained:

> As I remember about 50 years ago people started farming (in our district). In the beginning they used the land near the river banks and then the area around the *xiang* [district] centre. Before this all these lands were pastures and used as haymaking lands (especially the land near the river banks). Now most of the land near the river banks and around the *xiang* centre is farmland. There is no doubt that the area of pasture has been reduced a lot.

The amount of hay used for livestock appears to be moderate relative to other case-study sites, at around 18kg per sheep unit (see figure 6.14). There is some perceived pasture degradation, but most of this is localised or attributed to agriculture rather than the overstocking of pastures, as Madar, the district head, explained:

> As I see it the degradation of our pastures is a slow process which can not be seen very clearly in a short period of time. If you are talking about pasture that has become so bad that animals can not graze on it, well, we do have this kind of damage as well. In the area of our *xiang* there is a migration route for herds (not only ours but also those from other counties). This route is about 30 kilometres long and about 5 metres wide, in the past it was one of the best pastures we had, but now you do not see any grass on it. Isn't this a case of pasture damage? Another example I could give you is that recently some pastures have been used as farmland and this process continues now. The third example, of course, is the farmland you have seen around the *xiang* centre, which was excellent pasture 70 years ago but now is not pasture at all. And you see the vehicle routes made by our drivers and the drivers from other areas; they are also damaging the pasture.

Solchur, Ovyur raion, *Tuva*[61]

In Solchur the summer pastures are generally at relatively high altitude; even the high *taiga* (forest) regions are sometimes used, and summer camps may be as high as 1800m. In other areas the summer camps are often at around 1600m, and associated winter camps generally lower, around 1300m. Although the region is relatively mountainous, it does not approach the high altitude of the Uvs and Hoboksair case-study sites, and the movement system does not seem to resemble theirs. Indeed it does not resemble any of Simukov's types very closely, but this does not mean it no longer resembles the pre-collective movement system. Several informants said that the pastures that they used had been used by their families since before the collective period, as 54 year-old male herder Huresh Irgit explained:

> Every shepherd had, and still has, his seasonal pastures, which belong to him.[62] In most cases these pastures are inherited, and in the past the ancestors of the shepherd herded the animals on those same pastures. The State Farm only assigns this land to the shepherd.

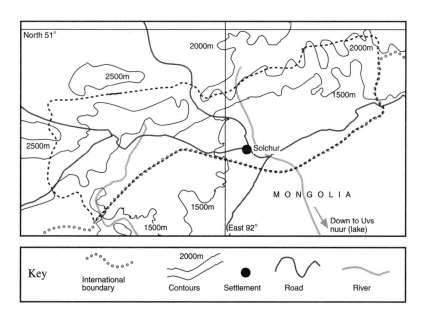

FIGURE 6.6. Solchur *selsoviet*

Location: Ovyur *raion*, Republic of Tuva, The Russian Federation.
Total land area: 63,800 hectares.
Researcher: Marina Mongush.

Indeed, the 'traditional' high value placed on diligent movement of the herds lasted throughout the collective period. It was enshrined in the notion of the model herder, who moved around ten times a year with the collective's flocks of sheep.[63] The amount of annual movement is moderately high (1992–3), with interviewed households moving between 50 and 100 km a year (annual diameter of movement being 25–50km, see figure 6.13). Most of this movement is accomplished with the use of motor transport provided by the State Farm, which also supplies water during the winter months, as many winter camps are far from water sources. The amount of hay used also appears to be moderately high, being over 40kg per sheep unit,[64] and is also supplied by the State Farm. Since 1993 the State Farm has probably had to discontinue such services. However, we argue that mechanised support (for transport, water and hay distribution) is of central importance as a theoretical avenue for pastoral development, and it will be discussed further in the concluding chapter.

There was virtually no perception of pasture degradation in Solchur, and local leaders attributed this to their keeping the number of livestock below the maximum stocking levels that have been calculated for their pasture land,[65] which amounts to an equivalent of 36,000 sheep equivalent standard stocking units. This stocking rate of 0.65 sheep units per hectare is a little higher than the stocking rate calculated by the Xinjiang specialists for Hosh Tolgoi.[66] Locals also noted, with some pride, that they kept the local breeds of livestock and not any of the introduced breeds. These native breeds were easier to care for and keep mobile, requiring less shelter and prepared fodder.

Dashbalbar sum, *Dornod* aimag, *Mongolia*[67]

The pastoral movement of Dashbalbar *sum* is shown in figures 6.7A and 6.7B, and not being a mountainous region the selection of pastures is less clearly influenced by altitude. The average amount of movement is relatively low, being little more than 25km (see figure 6.13), with a few pastoral households staying in one location all year round. It is quite common in this district for pastoralists with small herds of livestock to have other herders take some of their animals with them when they move to more distant winter pastures.[68]

There are six *bag* sub-districts in the *sum*, and several different sets of seasonal pastures used by different sections of the pastoral population. In general they spend winter and spring in relatively low areas in river or stream valleys, with autumn and summer pastures often a little higher in altitude.

6.7A. Map showing pastoral land-use

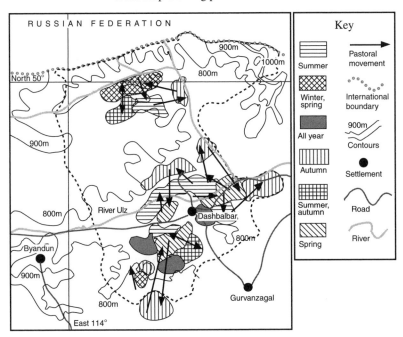

6.7B. Cross-section showing pastoral movement

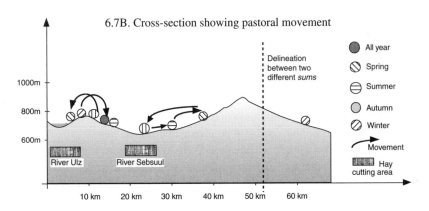

FIGURE 6.7. Dashbalbar *sum*

Researcher: Batbuyan, B.
Location: Dornod *aimag*, Mongolia.

The system corresponds fairly well with the description of the movement system of Dornod *aimag* given by Bazargür, Chinbat and Shiirev-Ad'yaa (1989: 56–7).[69] In addition to the seasonal pastures marked on figure 6.7A, some pastoralists carry out *otor*[70] beyond the southern border of the *sum*, where the vegetation is closer to the Gobi type and is considered good winter pasture. Informants reported that this is less common than it was, and the herdsmen of the neighbouring *sum* are less tolerant of this practice than they used to be. It appears that the distances moved, certainly by some pastoral families, have decreased over the last few decades.

One of the reasons for the decrease in mobility during the collective period was the introduction of new breeds of livestock. In the early 1970s a new breed of fine haired sheep was introduced, and in the early 1980s a high productivity breed of cattle was also introduced. The numbers of these special breeds rose to 500 cattle and 20,000 fine-haired sheep. Winter sheds and other special facilities were built for these introduced breeds, which were moved rather little, particularly the cattle. They required special care and large amounts of hay and fodder.[71] Privatisation led to dissolution of the fine-haired sheep facility, the livestock were privatised and divided between households that could not easily care for them; this resulted in a rapid decline in the numbers of this breed. There was also a reorganisation and reduction of the special cattle-breeding.

Hay used to be supplied by a specialist unit of the collective farm, which used to cut 13,000 tonnes of hay per year, 70% of this being cut by machine. This hay was supplied to the herding families by truck. Since privatisation this service has disappeared and herding families have to cut hay for themselves. Most of this is done by hand or by using old horse-drawn machines, because the privatised tractors often lack petrol and spare parts. The limited amount of private haymaking equipment has become private property and the family and friends of those who own it tend to help them with the use of such machines, so as to receive a share of the hay.

Dashbalbar appears to have relatively low hay consumption among the case-studies, although higher than the other Mongolian sites. The average from the interviewed households was around 12kg of hay per sheep unit, but the actual value may well be higher than this.[72] It certainly appears, however, that the amount of hay used has declined since the dissolution of the collective, as the 13,000 tonnes of hay that used to be produced represents approximately 80kg per sheep unit, although much of this was earmarked for the special breeds and some may have been exported from the *sum*.

The prospect of increasingly unequal access to hay is an important issue, and we shall have occasion to discuss it later in connection with Inner Mongolia.

The use of winter *otor* is a traditional strategy in the face of a late frost in this area. There is the retention of the older strategies of high winter mobility, as well as the use of hay. As Bat, a 47 year-old male herdsman commented:

> I use only hay for my livestock [no other fodder]. Last year I cut about 20 tonnes of hay [200 haystacks], using my neighbour's machine. I use this hay only as fodder for weak livestock, but I take other livestock to *otor* in the Gobi pasture [to the south].

There is very little perception of pasture degradation in the district, although large grass fires are very frequent in the dry summer months, and some indications suggest that pasture was degraded in some limited areas where herders kept livestock all year.[73] In general, however, there appears to be no widespread degradation of pastures.

The numbers of livestock have fallen recently, largely as a result of the disruption of the economic reforms and the reduction in veterinary services. In 1993 there were around 161,000 sheep units in the *sum*, and at their peak level in 1975, there were nearly 225,000. Dashbalbar has a large territory, however, and almost all of it is pasture.[74] Stocking levels were very low even in 1975, around 0.32 sheep units per hectare, and in 1993 this has fallen to about 0.22, the lowest of any of the study sites.

Dashbalbar is a particularly interesting district, in that it has approximately the same size and location as 'Bishrelt Wangiin Hoshuu'.[75] A comparison of the contemporary and 1918 population[76] and livestock totals shows that these numbers have not changed out of all recognition, and this suggests that stocking levels today are something like one third higher than in pre-revolutionary times.

The numbers of sheep and cattle have increased markedly; and although there has also been an even larger increase in the number of camels, their total number remains relatively low. Looking at the livestock density maps in chapter 2, we can see that this region, like most of the easternmost portion of Mongolia, has a very low density of livestock. The differential between the densely populated central regions and the peripheral areas is not a new phenomenon in Mongolia; the same was true of the pre-revolutionary situation. (It also appears that the number of livestock herded per pastoral household is much greater now than in the pre-revolutionary period, when it is likely that much of the population of the banner kept animals.)

	Vishrelt Vangiin Hoshuu 1918	Dashbalbar *sum* 1975	1993	% increase 1918–1993
Total human population	3,816		3,184	-17%
Number of households	1,069		720	-33%
Average household size	3.6		4.4	+22%
Number of horses	8,531	8,387	8,262	-3%
Number of camels	766	2,258	1,105	+89%
Number of cattle	5,998	10,138	8,102	+50%
Number of sheep & goats	59,008	08,936	64,358	+50%
Total SSUs (sheep units)	145,556	224,958	161,367	+33%

TABLE 6.1.

There has been an increase in the amount of land used for agriculture, although such land represents only a tiny fraction of the total area of pasture.[77] The recent economic changes have also led to a decline in agricultural production, Tsagaanhüü the head of the *sum* explained:

> Until 1950 we used the land around the river Döch for agriculture and after 1950 we started to use land near the river Ulz. The new agricultural area was much larger and during the collective period it increased to 2,000 hectares. At the moment we use only 500 hectares of this because of poor supplies of petrol, spare parts and the shortage of money. This is not just the situation in our district, but is typical of the whole region. The development of agriculture in 1950s helped increase the living standards and the material security of our community. In our *sum* we now have a special company that undertakes agriculture. They have 1,500 hectares of which only 500 hectares are used for wheat and five for potatoes. They only use fertiliser on about 100 hectares of this land and use animal manure for this. They plant vegetables in the field every other year, so that the land lies fallow every second year.

This new agricultural company is based upon the former agricultural brigade of the collective, and appears to be going slowly bankrupt as a result of the difficulty of obtaining supplies.

Hargant sum, *Hulun Buir* aimag, *Inner Mongolia, China*[78]

The pastoral movement system of Hargant *sum* is described in figures 6.8A and 6.8B, with a moderate amount of annual movement reported by our informants – around 60km,[79] (see figure 6.13).

6.8A. Map showing pastoral land-use

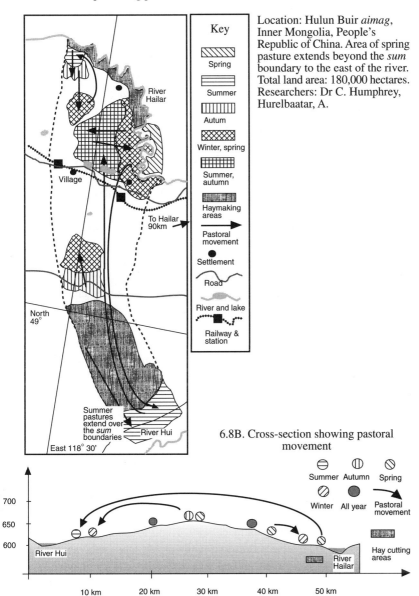

Key

Spring

River
Hailar

Summer

Autum

Winter, spring

Summer,
autumn

Haymaking
areas

Pastoral
movement

Settlement

Road

River and lake

Railway &
station

Location: Hulun Buir *aimag*,
Inner Mongolia, People's
Republic of China. Area of spring
pasture extends beyond the *sum*
boundary to the east of the river.
Total land area: 180,000 hectares.
Researchers: Dr C. Humphrey,
Hurelbaatar, A.

Village

To Hailar
90km

North
49°

Summer
pastures
extend over
the *sum*
boundaries

River Hui

East 118° 30'

6.8B. Cross-section showing pastoral
movement

Summer   Autumn   Spring

Winter   All year   Pastoral
movement

Hay cutting
areas

River Hui

River
Hailar

700

650

600

10 km   20 km   30 km   40 km   50 km

FIGURE 6.8. Hargant *sum*

The area of the *sum* is divided into four *gachaa* sub-districts, each one with around 50 households. The territory of each sub-district is divided between the seasonal pastures, with the exception of the summer pastures (*zuslan*) which are further away and are used in common, (see figure 6.8A). Movement to the summer pastures has greatly declined, however, since the dissolution of the People's Commune, for reasons that are discussed below.

Inside the winter/autumn/spring territory of the *gachaa* each pastoral household has been allocated its own share of the land, and there is now a given area that is reserved for haymaking. Informants reported that before the dissolution of the People's Commune in 1984 the haymaking fields were not fixed. There were several possible sites where the grass could grow high enough for hay, usually around the small, salty lakes that are common to this district. Before 1984 the local pastoralists and the *sum* authorities decided which places to use for haymaking, and this meant that in a dry year when some lakes were dry and the grass poor, other areas would be used instead.[80] The use of these sites was alternated, locals explained, so that each year different places tended to be used for haymaking, and if the soil in one place was exhausted it would be left to recover. After 1984 huge haymaking areas were established, totalling 586 square kilometres (36% of the entire *sum*). These are now are used each year, the hay being cut with tractors, rather than the earlier horse-drawn machinery. Local officials were worried about the large amount of hay that is being made and sold for profit by outsiders who often export it from the *sum*,[81] and several of those interviewed perceived a rapid deterioration of the haymaking pastures, as 54 year-old Choijilsüren explained:

> The grass in the haymaking pasture is lower each year, and more sparse. This is because every year people cut hay in the same places [...]. If you want to solve this problem you should periodically change the haymaking fields. It is also very clear that the pasture is badly degraded around water sources and settled houses.

There are many poor families without tractors and hay-cutting machines. Differential access to hay is another factor in the growth of inequality between households. Even with machinery, access to the hayfields may be difficult, as the *sum* officials reserve land for hay and make their own contracts to sell large amounts of hay outside the district (see chapter 3).

In the past herders moved much further than they do today. In the 1930s pre-communist herders of Hargant *sum* wintered in the low-lying area (around 700m) in the central area of the modern *sum*. They used these pastures from November to March. They then moved about 100km north-east to the banks of the Mergel river, this journey taking two months or so. The summer pastures were on slightly higher ground, around 800m, and were occupied from June until August. Then they would move 60km or so west to autumn pastures just north of the Hailar river, on land around 700m. These pastures were used from September to November. Then the animals could cross the frozen river to return to the winter pastures, a journey of around 40km.

One of the interesting features of this past system of movement is that it corresponds, in a general way, with the altitude-based model of Bazargür, Chinbat and Shiirev-Ad'yaa, and the movement system described by Simukov as 'eastern steppe type', with summer pastures in the north, by rivers, and winter pastures in the more Gobi-like southern regions, and an annual diameter of movement around 100km.

In Hargant *sum* today very little is left of the older pattern of land-use, by which herds were moved as far as the Mergel river for summer, and within the *sum* the herding households moved between winter, spring and autumn pastures. After the foundation of the People's Communes in 1958–9, the movement of the herdsmen (now members of the new Production Brigades of the Commune) was somewhat restricted, so that the people of Hargant *sum* could no longer spend autumn north of the Hailar river, but they could still move their animals to the Mergel in the summer.

This pattern was first markedly changed in the early 1980s when access to the summer pastures by the Mergel was blocked. By the 1990s the rural reforms had produced a new pattern of land-use. Many households now remain in one location all year round with their livestock.

This marked reduction in the mobility of pastoralists was mentioned by many informants as the principal reason for pasture degradation in the district, as Lubsandorj, the 41 year-old head of the local branch of the Party explained:

> There are many reasons for the damage done to the pastures. Firstly, there is a concentration of livestock around the centre of the *sum*, due to the fact that many herdsmen no longer go to any of their seasonal pastures, nor do they practice *otor*. The pasture is suffering because of the increased year-round pressure on certain areas. Herding families are less inclined to move so far from the *sum* centre (because of the need for schooling, selling milk etc.) and so the pasture around these settlements has been badly affected. Also, many herders do not go to the summer pastures any more because those families without large numbers of animals do not feel it is worth while. Nowadays,

herdsman generally use motor transport when they move, and many of them are beginning to dislike any movement, even some of the richer families. When moving one must drive ones animals across the pasture habitually used by other herding families, who generally resent this extra grazing on their allocation [...]. Pasture has also been damaged by rodents who ate the roots of the grasses [...] by fires [...] and the increased use of tractors, especially around the *sum* centre.

The head of the *sum* did not attribute any of the pasture degradation to general overstocking of the district. He said that the total number of livestock in the *sum* amounted to 56,000 sheep units, while the theoretical carrying capacity for the *sum* has been officially set at 91,153. (This gives an official theoretical stocking rate, averaged for the whole year and all pasture types, at around 0.56 sheep units per hectare, very similar to that calculated for Hosh Tolgoi, Xinjiang). The *sum* head, however, felt that this stocking limit was too low. He said: 'In my opinion our pasture could support 100,000 sheep units if we made good use of seasonal pastures.' It seems that the actual number of livestock in the *sum* was a little more than the *sum* head reported, around 58,750 sheep units[82] and this gives an actual stocking rate of approximately 0.36 sheep units per hectare, which is relatively low.

The richer herders are generally more mobile than poorer ones. They have the carts and motor transport to move their livestock to the summer and winter pastures. The poorer herders cannot do this, and having smaller herds, have less incentive to do so. Their more meagre flocks can survive on the pastures around their usually fixed dwellings. These herders will sometimes make a few moves, with a *ger*, to take their animals to different pastures near their dwellings.

The effect of the privatisation carried out in the 1980s was to atomise pastoral production and reduce the mobility and flexibility of pastoralism in this district still further, as Choijilsüren commented:

During the collective period we could organise flexible herding, make use of the pastures flexibly, and herd composition and size were also flexible. We could order herdsmen to pasture a varying number of animals in the places we chose in response to different natural conditions. In the collective period there was also a motor pool of several tractors, and these could be used to fulfil the needs of the Commune. Now there is no longer this sort of efficient concentration, no economy of scale. Many households have their own small, private tractors which they need for maybe only a few weeks each year [...]. One more thing; we used to make good use of the excellent *zuslan* [summer pastures] at the river Mergel, and the government helped by providing access to this area.[83]

Flexible and opportunistic herding has not entirely disappeared, however, despite recent trends, as 42-year-old male herder Tömörbaatar mentioned:

> We share our pastures between three brothers and this seems to be enough pasture for our livestock. If there is a bad summer then the pasture is not enough and we move to the Angirt lake area where the pasture is greener. We keep the horses and cattle round our settled area and after the snows we graze them in the winter pasture. In summer we graze our milk cows close to the *sum* centre, in this way we save the pastures round the settled area.

Gigant, Chita Oblast, Russia[84]

Of all the case-study sites, Gigant has the highest number of livestock per herder (figure 2.14), the least pastoral movement (figures 6.9A; 6.9B; 6.13), and the highest fodder inputs (figure 6.14). The interviewed pastoral households used a yearly average of over 60kg of cultivated fodder and 30kg of hay per sheep unit. Most of the pastoral households spend the whole year in the same location, only a few move their animals to distant pastures. Gigant also is the case-study site that has the highest degree of mechanisation, fencing, fodder production and other intensive 'European' farming techniques. It also has a very high degree of perceived pasture degradation. Zorig Dorjiev, the 57-year-old local government head, explained:

> Unfortunately, the area of pasture land in Gigant collective farm has been reduced in recent years and this process continues. Lots of pasture land has been converted into fields. There is a big problem of soil erosion. Recently the quality of grass on the pastures also changed [for the worse] [...]. This degradation is related to the pressure of animals [on the land]. For example, in 1940 the grass was of very good quality. In this period the number of animals in the collective farm was only about 4,000 sheep [...]. But in 1991 the amount of pasture land in Gigant collective farm was 27,737 hectares and 21,339 hectares of that was damaged by erosion [76.9 %].

There are different estimates of the amount of land actually used for pasture in Gigant, but the stocking rate does indeed seem to be comparatively high, and can be estimated as between 1 and 1.5 sheep units per hectare,[85] which is something like twice as high as most of the other sites. A very large amount of land is used for hay and fodder production, around 7,000ha in Gigant itself, and until recently 2,400ha in neighbouring districts of Mongolia. This amounts to almost a quarter of the total amount of land used by the Gigant collective.[86]

6.9A. Map showing pastoral land-use

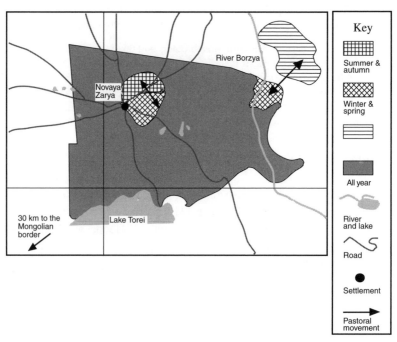

6.9B. Cross-section showing pastoral movement

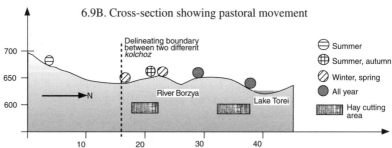

FIGURE 6.9. Gigant – Novaya Zarya *selsoviet*

Location: Borzya *raion*, Chita Oblast, The Russian Federation. Area of summer pasture to the north extends over the *selsoviet* boundary.
Total land area: 41,000 hectares.
Researcher: Balzhan Zhimbiev.

The pre-collective pastoral system appears to have been much more mobile, comparable to those of neighbouring Mongolian regions, with some pastoralists moving as much as 200km a year (Gomboev 1996: 36).

Argada, Buryatia, Russia[87]

The Argada pastoral movement system is a basic transhumance back and forth between summer and winter pastures, see figures 6.10A and 6.10B. Like Gigant, it is a highly mechanised, low-mobility, livestock raising system. It also has a relatively high level of hay fodder use; the average used by interviewed households was around 45kg per sheep unit (see figure 6.14), and the actual figures are likely to be considerably higher than this.[88]

Local officials also reported the highest amount of degraded pasture of any of the case-study sites, almost 80%. The stocking rate also appears to be by far the highest of the sites, the 30,700 sheep units[89] were apparently kept on 11,228ha of pasture, giving an average of 2.7 sheep units per hectare.[90] Local administrators were very conscious of this high stocking rate, and attributed soil erosion to overgrazing and the practice of agriculture, as Jargal Ochirov the 51 year-old male district head explained:

> From the mid 1950s the total number of sheep increased very quickly and by 1980 there were about 25,000 sheep [in our district]. Cattle and horses reached maximum numbers of 4,500–5,000 and 550–600 respectively. At the same time the area of land used for agriculture also increased to more than 8,000 hectares. The large amount of pressure on these areas caused erosion of the arable land and of the pastures as well […]. During the last few years the number of livestock in our State Farm decreased […]. The reduction of pasture land and the increase of livestock numbers caused great pressure on the pastures. Consequently there has been soil erosion and an increase in the amount of sandy areas. Besides this, the increase of arable land causes erosion of the fields because of the thin stratum of soil.

The pre-collective pastoral system does not appear to have been a highly mobile one, as in the case of Gigant. Mobility, as such, has not been radically reduced, but the pattern of land-use has certainly changed markedly over the last few decades. Bair Gomboev (1996) argues that the more dispersed distribution of herding households in the pre-collective period avoided the concentration of livestock in certain areas that is now found.[91]

Chapter 6

6.10A. Map showing pastoral land-use

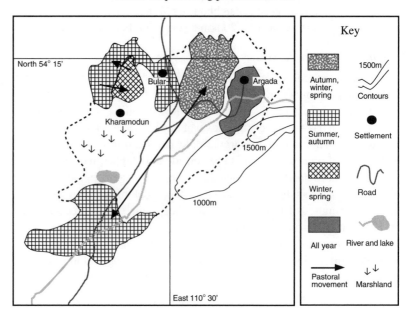

6.10B. Cross-section showing pastoral land-use

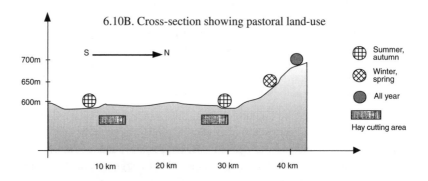

FIGURE 6.10. Argada *selsoviet*

Location: Barguzin *raion*, Republic of Buryatia, the Russian Federation.
Total land area: 34,754 hectares.
Researcher: Bair Gomboev.

Chinggel Bulag sum, *Shilingol* aimag, *Inner Mongolia, China*[92]

Chinggel Bulag is divided into four *gachaas* (sub-districts), each of which have areas for seasonal pastures. Within the *gachaa* there are allocated pastures for each household, and usually these are grouped together to form a larger area of land for each *hot* (group of households). These pastures are generally divided into three seasonal allocations: a summer and autumn site, a winter site, and a spring site, see figure 6.11.

*Gachaa*s 3 and 4 have parallel territories, north of the *sum* centre, and have a similar division of pastures. The summer pastures are around 1250m, near the *sum* centre. The winter pastures are on the higher ground in the north of the district, mostly above 1400m, and spring pastures are slightly lower than this, around 1350–1400m. Not all pastoralists move to these seasonal areas, however. Many households spend all year in one location, usually in the spring pastures, or those nearest to the *sum* centre. Poor households are particularly likely to do this.

Gachaa 1 has a winter area in the far south of the *sum*, under 1,100m. The summer pastures are on higher ground around 1200m. Many pastoralists, however, spend all year in the intermediate area between 1100m and 1200m. *Gachaa* 2 has land around the *sum* centre, and immediately south of it. Winter pastures are to the south, around 1200m, the summer pastures rather higher, around the *sum* centre, and the spring pastures are between. Here too, however, people are spending an increasing amount of time in the spring area.

More than a third of pastoral households now have a house at one of their sites, usually the spring one,[93] and rich households may have houses in more than one location. Some *hot*s divide their livestock and leave sections of the family at the different seasonal allocated pastures, herding small numbers of animals at each spot.

There is a perception among both officials and herders that there has been a certain amount of pasture degradation. As 35 year-old male administrator, Batbayar, explained:

> The pasture in our *sum* is not as good as it was before; even in the 1960s the grasses were tall, but now the grasses are shorter and the coverage is much less than before. The reason is drought and too many animals. Also the road construction damaged some pasture too [...]. The condition of the grassland varies a little within the *sum*; there is obvious degradation of the grassland in some places, especially where the strong winds hit a hillside which has been heavily grazed [topsoil is lost, leaving a very sandy surface with a high proportion of small stones].

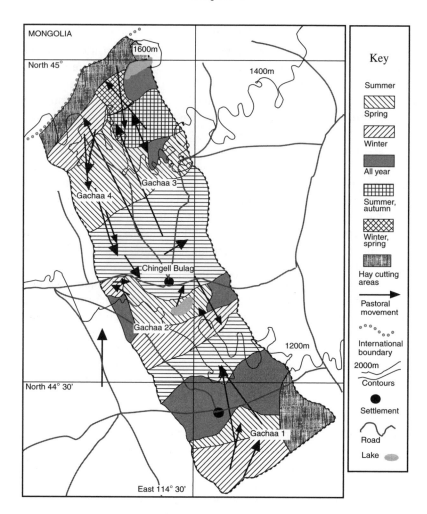

FIGURE 6.11. Chinggel Bulag *sum*

Location: Abag *hoshuu*, Shilingol *aimag*, Inner Mongolia, People's Republic of China. Chinggel Bulag *sum* is itself divided into 4 *gachaa*, or sub-districts, each of which use their own grazing areas. The best areas of pasture in the *sum* are located at the far north and south. The central areas around Chinggel Bulag have problems with degraded pastures.
Total land area: 214,000 hectares.
Researcher: Qi Xiao-Hong

The pasture problems are most acute around the *sum* centre, where there is a concentration of livestock. Many households move further than their allocated pasture would permit so as to get closer to the *sum* centre. If one of the perceived advantages of the allocation of pastures to individual households was that it would prevent the concentration of animals around pressure points, such as the district centres, it does not seem to have been very effective. In some cases pastoralists appear to be either ignoring their allocation or overusing the existing ones.

Close to the Mongolian border, this part of Shilingol would probably have fallen, theoretically, into Simukov's 'steppe type' of pre-collective movement system, and by the typology of Bazargür, Chinbat and Shiirev-Ad'yaa would come somewhere between Dornogov' and Dundgov' types of movement. We can hypothesise that pre-collective movement patterns are likely to have been of moderate mobility for the time, but still with much greater movement than at present. Households would tend to summer near water sources, and winter on the southern slopes of hills or in other sheltered spots.

Informants confirmed that the pre-revolutionary herding patterns were much more mobile than during the collective period, although they also noted that there were fewer animals. Bold, a 41 year-old herdsman, described the situation in the '50s – before the establishment of the People's Communes:

> People moved around a lot and were truly nomadic. The condition of the grasslands was good in those days so people could move if there was not enough rainfall in their area; so drought was not such a big problem. But in 1966 there was a big drought for which we were not adequately prepared and [this was serious] because there were too many animals and people could not avoid the worst drought areas; even though they could move around, they could not move far enough because other places also had a lot of animals by that time.

In the collective period movement was confined within four production brigades, which have now become the current *gachaa*. Interviewed herders attributed grassland degradation to the lower mobility that pastoralists now have, as well as larger numbers of livestock. Bold explained:

> The main cause of desertification is overgrazing, in that too many animals stay in the same place for a long time; they eat all the grass and sometimes even the roots of the grass. Also, sheep and goats tend to scratch up the roots of grasses [with their feet] when they graze. When roots are eaten or destroyed

the soil cannot be held in place, and when you have a strong wind desertification occurs.

The total number of livestock in the *sum* was about 108,000 sheep units[94] in January 1993, and this broadly corresponds with the official stocking norms. The average stocking norm for all the pasture of the *sum* was set at 28*mu* per sheep unit, which is 0.54 sheep units per hectare.[95] The *sum* official, Batbayar, felt that the limit should be increased to 120,000 sheep units, and this suggests that locals feel that an increase in livestock numbers is possible if the pasture is better utilised.[96]

The average amount of hay used by the interviewed pastoral households is relatively high and amounts to around 48kg per sheep unit, and this figure coincides with district statistics. The total amount of hay produced in the *sum* in 1993 was 5,500 tonnes, and dividing this by the total number of livestock in the district the average works out at just over 50kg per sheep unit. As elsewhere in Inner Mongolia, access to machinery was an important factor in getting supplies of hay.

Sumber sum, Dornogov' aimag, Mongolia[97]

The pastoral movement system is described in figure 6.12, showing the annual movement of each of the three *ferms* – the sub-units of the State Farm. In each case the most important camps are at the winter and summer pastures. The first sub-unit has winter pastures on relatively high ground, between around 1300m and 1500m, and summer pastures are lower, around 1150–1250m, by the Herlen river to the north of the *sum*. The second *ferm* uses winter pastures that are relatively low, around 1150m, gaining some shelter from the high ground to the north, and moves to slightly higher ground for summer, around 1250m. The third sub-unit winters on the slopes of Mount Sansar, around 1400–1600m, and moves north to lower ground for winter, around 1200–1400m. The spring and autumn camps tend to be transitional, located between summer and winter sites. The amount of movement appears to have declined a little in recent years, as a result of the difficulties of transportation affecting Mongolia as a whole.

In general the movement is broadly north/south, and corresponds reasonably well with the model of the Dornogov' variety of the 'central Halh' pastoral movement type described by Bazargür, Chinbat and Shiirev-Ad'yaa.[98] By Simukov's typology the movement pattern of this region would approximate to the eastern steppe type. Before collectivisation the summer pastures were in the northerly part of the districts, apparently, by the river Herlen. In winter at least part of the population moved south to hollows with desert steppe vegetation. The diameter of the movement was described by Simukov as about 100km. During the collective period the annual diameter of movement shortened to something around 25km,[99] but the selection of seasonal pastures can be seen to have utilised the same principal of favouring areas with more marked relief as shelter for the winter camps, and spending summer by rivers or streams.

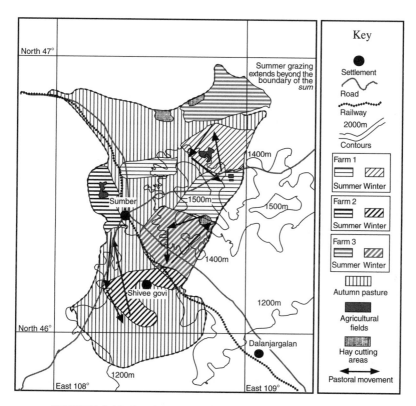

FIGURE 6.12. Sumber *sum*. Map showing pastoral land-use

Location: Dornogov' *aimag*, Mongolia. There are three seperate sub-units (*ferms* or farms) used by the *sum* to organise livestock grazing. Each of the farms has its own areas for grazing. Land between the main summer and winter pastures is also used for grazing in the spring and autumn. Some of the agricultural and haymaking fields may no longer be in use.
Total land area: 540,000 hectares

In pre-revolutionary times the territory of Sumber was part of Borjigin Tsetsen Vangiin Hoshuu, which also included the areas of two other modern *sums*.[100] The administrative sub-units of the *hoshuu* were the *otog* (this term was used for ecclesiastical districts). The *otog* were units of people and their animals, and although they had territory assigned to them, this was not necessarily contiguous. Elderly respondents in Sumber and the neighbouring *sum* of Dalanjargalan agreed that pre-collective pastoral practice in this region included much more seasonal movement than today, with a much shorter stays in any given place. Davaasambuu, a 69 year-old herder, said:

> Before collectivisation [...] people stayed in their winter camps for just three months, from November to February, and then they moved to the Spring pastures. We used stone or *hörzön* [packed, dried dung] to build the animal enclosures in those days, and there were no roofs on them. The wooden winter cattle-sheds are a mistake, because they accustom the livestock to warmth so that they die if they are caught out in the cold.

Officials, and most of the herders, considered the amount of pasture degradation to be negligible; however, several elderly informants said that the pastures were better in their youth. Davaasambuu commented: 'The pasture was much better, and there were many more animals at that time.'

In the case of Sumber it would be easy to dismiss these elderly herders' perceptions of a decline in the amount of vegetation as nostalgia, if it were not for evidence such as that presented by Erdenebaatar (1996), that there has indeed been a measurable reduction in the yield of certain grasslands even in Mongolia, where problems of grassland degradation appear to be relatively slight. One informant, 47 year-old male herder Pürevsüren, considered there to have been a decline in both mobility and pasture quality since the 1970s.

> In the 1970s all the *ails* used to go to *otor*, and the *ails* were all spread out. But now most of the *ails* do not move from their winter pastures during the winter and autumn, and the animals eat all the vegetation, so there has been a reduction in the amount of vegetation.

In 1993 there were just over 165,000 sheep units in the district,[101] giving Sumber a low stocking level of about 0.36 sheep units per hectare. Almost all (98%) of the 462,498 ha of useful land is pasture, and there is very little land used for crop cultivation.[102]

Comparing Inner Asian pastoral systems

Reviewing the change in pastoral land-use in the 20th century it seems that the overall trend throughout Inner Asia has been a reduction in the size of the migratory cycle and in the frequency of moves, although in the mountainous western regions the reduction appears to have been minimal. The decline in movement was most marked in Chita and Inner Mongolia, and it is in these areas that some of the most severe problems of pasture degradation are reported, as shown in figures 6.13–6.15, which compare selected aspects of the pastoral systems of the different localities.

The Buryat case, Argada, is the notable exception, having the greatest amount of perceived pasture degradation, while at the same time the herds are moved a significant distance. However, the important point is that these moves are very infrequent (only twice a year). Argada never had a highly mobile pre-collective pastoral regime. Bair Gomboev (1996: 28–33) argues, moreover, that collective organisation increased the pressure on pastures by centralising settlement patterns which had the effect of concentrating large numbers of collective livestock in certain areas. Argada has also seen a dramatic reduction in the amount of available pasture, and a great increase in the level of mechanised agriculture and fodder production.

In general we can characterise the pastoral systems of Inner Asia along regional lines. The Buryatian and Chitan study sites have a high level of mechanisation, little or no mobility, a pattern of land-use that is markedly different from the pre-collective system, very high numbers of livestock on the available pastures, and high fodder inputs (see figure 6.14). Pasture is still generally allocated by a central authority and is not private. They also have very serious perceived problems of pasture degradation.

Mongolia has a pastoral system that has retained many of the features of pre-collective land-use, mobility remains relatively high (although it has been reduced in many cases), hay and fodder inputs in the study sites are relatively low, and pasture is still to some extent flexibly allocated by the district authorities. There are moderate numbers of domestic animals, and pasture degradation is in general very slight.

Inner Mongolia's pastoral system has undergone considerable change since the end of collectivisation, has relatively high hay and fodder inputs, low mobility, and the exclusive use of most of the pasture is now allocated to individual households. Stocking levels appear to be quite high in the study sites but theoretically subject to government limits. There are serious problems of perceived pasture degradation.

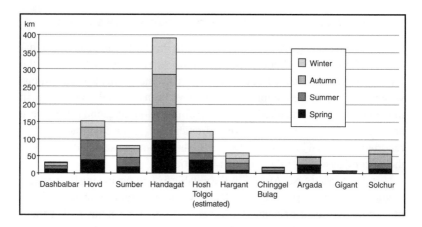

FIGURE 6.13. Average seasonal movement (in kilometres) of interviewed households in case-study sites

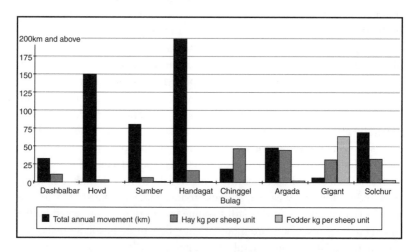

FIGURE 6.14. Comparison of mobility and fodder inputs in case-study sites

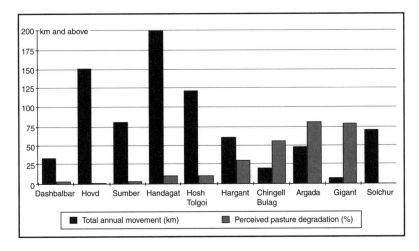

FIGURE 6.15. Comparison of mobility and perceived pasture degradation
in case-study sites

Xinjiang has retained relatively high mobility in the mountainous
pastoral areas, resembling pre-collective systems of movement. Pastoralists
seem to make use of a moderate amount of hay and fodder, and like Inner
Mongolia there are quite high stocking levels which appear to be controlled
by government limits. The case-study sites seem to have a low to medium
level of perceived pasture degradation.

Tuva has a pastoral system that appears to have retained some
traditional aspects, with quite lengthy and (more important in this case)
frequent movement at the case-study site. At the time of our study in 1993 this
movement was strongly supported by mechanised transportation. Stocking
levels and the use of hay seem to be moderate to high, (although not
approaching the levels of the Buryat and Chitan study sites). Pasture is still
flexibly allocated by the district authorities, and there appears to be little or
no perceived pasture degradation.

MOBILITY AND SUSTAINABLE PASTORALISM

Having summarised the broad picture, I should point out that issues of mobility and sustainable pastoralism involve a number of interesting and dynamic tensions.

In several of the case-study sites elderly informants considered some or all of the current problems of pastoralism to be associated with a decline in the amount of movement, and the frequency of changing pastures. In Hovd the quality of livestock was considered lower as a result of reduced mobility; in Hargant, Sumber, Chinggel Bulag (and to a small extent Dashbalbar) the pasture was said to have suffered to a greater or lesser degree. Simukov's description of pastoralism in the 1930s supports the general picture that there was greater movement in the pre-collective period. Not all pastoral households, however, moved further at that time, indeed some appear to have moved rather little. The legacy of that time left to the collectives was to accord highest value to the 'yield-focused' or 'specialist' pastoral strategy. This involved high mobility, and was seen as a 'professional' and diligent herding technique, associated with high positions of trust and prestige. The 'model herder' of the collectives inherited these values, and strove to get yields over the norm set in the plan. The collectives supported the long moves basically because they produced an excellent return of livestock products. This explains the emphasis placed upon movement by informants, particularly the elderly.[103] Many pastoral informants from all over Inner Asia also placed a positive value on the practice of *otor* and the frequent moving of animals so as to rotate the use of pasture.

As pointed out in chapter 3, socialist ideology encouraged 'the settlement of nomads' (partly for greater control and partly for access to 'civilising' institutions), but as this chapter shows the work ethic of the herders emphasised high mobility. In Mongolia and Tuva this tension was managed by reorganising herding so that it retained mobility, but in Buryatia and Chita the herders were definitively settled early on.

Movement is generally considered to be a great deal of work and is not undertaken lightly. However, this experience of arduous work exists in tension with a complementary cultural attitude, according to which the migration is ritualised and festive, and there is a certain excitement in setting off and travelling. This reflects, we think, the pride taken by expert herders in managing migrations, in their love of rich pastures, and the pleasure taken in the whole pastoral lifestyle. Nevertheless, in many regions herding households have become understandably reliant upon motor transport for the longer movements. In Mongolia itself the decline in the amount of transportation available has meant that many recognise the need for more draft animals, and a return to animal transport – such as the camel-cart. (This has led to a campaign to promote the number of camels in the country.) In Inner Mongolia the reduction in annual movement has been especially acute among poorer households who do not have the vehicles, draft animals, carts, or indeed the herds that would justify the movement.

Several informants in the Sumber case-study site saw laziness as a key factor in a herder's willingness to move. Telenged, who carried out the case-study in Hovd *sum*, mentioned that there were some households who spent all year in one smallish area, and therefore when there was a white *zud* [104] almost all their animals were killed. However, in this kind of well-watered mountain environment, if herders made the moves it was felt that they could always feed their animals. The households considered most rich and responsible tended to move furthest.[105] Gantömör, the 49 year-old male head of one of the *bag* sub-districts, explained that:

> ...the amount of pasture used depends upon the number and distance of the moves undertaken. If you move enough you can get enough pasture.

In the relatively uncrowded regions of Uvs *aimag*, the limit on the amount of nutrition gained by the livestock is related to the amount of work put in to move the herds. This pattern is environmentally sustainable, given hard work and plentiful available land. However, in crowded regions with high stocking rates and limited movement, the total amount of vegetation will put a ceiling on herd nutrition. In such a case, degradation of pasture may continue despite hard work on the part of the herders.

NON-EQUILIBRIAL GRAZING SYSTEMS AND THE ALLOCATION OF PASTURE LAND

The principal theoretical justification for Inner Mongolia's introduction of individuated rights to fixed areas of pasture is something akin to Hardin's (1968) 'tragedy of the commons'. Briefly stated, this theory proposed that where many actors graze their livestock on communally-owned land, it is in each individual's interest to keep adding to the number of his or her animals, even if the land is facing overgrazing and degradation. His model was based upon a number of assumptions, particularly the applicability of the concept of carrying capacity. Hardin and others suggested that the way out of this destructive cycle was to have the land owned by the same person(s) who owned the livestock. They would then have an interest in maintaining the potential of the land. This model has been widely rejected by many pastoral specialists (Sandford 1983: 118–27; McCabe 1990), but it appears to be one of the primary justifications for the pastoral reforms in China. Ma Rong and Li Ou, Beijing-based experts, provide an example of this thinking when they write (1993): 'Because pastures are also under the management of individual households, herdsmen then have a long-run plan to utilise their pastures'. However, as pointed out in chapter 3, Inner Asian land-use, as in pastoral societies elsewhere, is not based on exclusive individual rights but has long been based on institutions which regulate usage. Furthermore, exclusive private ownership of land often does not lead to its conservation: individual small-scale owners may overgraze their land because of financial impera-tives generated by market conditions.

The limitation on stocking levels found in the Chinese parts of the region, is also based upon the notion that pasture land has a carrying capacity – i.e. that a certain amount of land is capable of supporting a maximum number of animals, and to exceed this level will lead to overgrazing. This previously widely-accepted approach suggests a natural equilibrium be-tween animals and land.[106] One of the difficulties faced by this conceptual framework is the new research that has emerged in recent years, which suggest that in areas with low and highly variable rainfall the concept of 'carrying capacity' is of questionable utility.

The work of Ellis, Coughenour and Swift (among others) suggests that in some rangeland environments the performance of the grazing system can not be said to vary about an equilibrial norm. Instead there is high variation in rainfall and hence also of vegetation from one year to the next, causing volatile changes in livestock numbers. They termed these 'non-equilibrial' grazing systems.[107] Indeed this 'non-equilibrium' model sup-ports the view that flexible access to large areas of land, and the spatial mobility of pastoralists, are likely to be more effective than the allocation of limited areas of pasture to individual households (Behnke and Scoones 1993: 28–30).

This new research suggests that where the coefficient of variation of annual rainfall exceeds about 0.3 (30%) it is better to characterise the performance of such grazing systems in terms of non-equilibrium than by measures of average (mean) vegetation yields (Ellis, Coughenour and Swift 1993: 33–9). This applies to much of Inner Asia. Figure 6.16 shows an estimate of the coefficient of inter-annual rainfall variation, calculated from yearly precipitation figures from more than 280 meteorological stations all

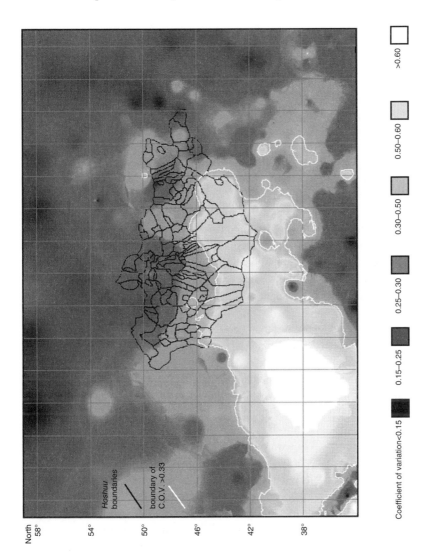

FIGURE 6.16. Distribution of inter-annual variation in precipitation and
the Bogd Khan *aimags* of Mongolia, 1918

Source: MacArthur Project GIS. Political boundaries digitised by M. J. Chopping
(Onon map). Climate data was kindly supplied by Dr. Mike Hume, Climate Research
Unit, University of East Anglia.
Note: coefficient calculated as standard deviation/mean. Based on almost 14,000
records interpolated using a 6-point distance-weighted model.

over Inner Asia.[108] The white line marks out those areas where the coefficient of variation exceeds 0.33 (33%).

The map also shows the pre-revolutionary administrative boundaries of the Bogd Khan autonomous period, and it is significant that in general the largest administrative districts (*hoshuu*) appear to be those where the variability is highest. This finding is a powerful support for the argument that mobility is related to the amount and variability of rainfall, that pastoral movement tended, in some years at least, to be greater in regions with a higher variability of rainfall, and that pre-revolutionary pastoralism required administrative regions large enough for pastoralists to contain most of their movement within them.[109]

Figure 6.16 suggests that much of central and northern Mongolia, eastern Inner Mongolia, Xinjiang, Tuva, Chita and Buryatia, are likely to exhibit equilibrial characteristics; and consequently in these parts the notions of stocking level and carrying capacity of land are appropriate. In southern parts of Mongolia and the western part of Inner Mongolia, on the other hand, pastoralism may well be better described in terms of non-equilibrial grazing systems.

This model implies that, because of a high level of spatial variability in rainfall, there is an advantage to having flexible access to land so that the pastoralist can move livestock at will to where the best vegetation is. However, the reality is that herdsmen are fairly regular with their movements and their camps are fairly localised, even in the areas of highly variable rainfall. In most years we do not see the opportunistic use of pasture land that might be expected from the non-equilibrial model, and the historical evidence suggests that this was also true of the pre-collective period. Instead it seems that in most years vegetation condition is predictable enough to permit the habitual use of certain areas of land. It is possible that although the variation in precipitation at a particular location is high, the amount of variation in available moisture is not so high if rainfall is measured throughout a moderate-sized area of pasture. This would mean that one could be reasonably confident of finding sufficient vegetation within a few kilometres of one's habitual camping place.[110] Migration and seasonal land-use could be relatively stable, year to year, but entirely static strategies would be less viable.

Much of the evidence would suggest that the importance of flexible access to pasture is greatest in the regions with the greatest variability of precipitation (also the areas with the least rainfall). As mentioned earlier, although the usual annual movement in the Gobi regions was not very great (either in the pre-collective or collective periods) pastoralists did, and still do, occasionally have to move long distances in case of drought, or some other adverse natural condition.

Hardin's model would have predicted that overgrazing would result from individual private livestock ownership without individuated rights to land. However, the degradation of the Inner Mongolian grasslands began in the communal period when both land and livestock effectively belonged to the same institution; it did not suddenly emerge as a result of the private ownership of livestock on communal land. Throughout the communal period the Chinese government policies reduced the mobility of the Inner Mongolian pastoralist, whilst changing the balance of animals herded. It may be that this reduction in mobility is a major cause for the pasture damage that has occurred, and if this is so then individuated rights to pasture are only likely to make this worse. If a large part of Inner Mongolia is indeed 'non-equilibrial' then the authorities may have to re-think both their assessment of overgrazing as a problem, and their policy of individually allocated pastures with stocking limits as a solution.

Indeed, in Inner Mongolia there almost appears to be a paradox. Problems of high grazing pressure on pastures near the *sum* centre were reported by informants in Chinggel Bulag and Hargant, despite the pasture being allocated to individual households. If this is a widespread problem it would be an example of the opposite scenario to Hardin's classic 'tragedy of the commons'. Individually-assigned (if not owned) land appears to be being damaged by its exclusive users (see Williams 1996a). It may be that the long-term conservation of pasture is not necessarily more important to individuals than to land-allocating institutions. Some individuals may well over-use their natural resources in an effort to make enough money to escape rural poverty in the short-term. This is an area in which people's hopes and aspirations become of central importance, and in Inner Mongolia our studies showed that many parents in pastoral areas hope that their children will be able to leave animal husbandry and gain salaried positions in urban centres.[111]

MONGOLIAN PASTORALISM AND THE MARKET

The effect of privatisation has been to dissolve the large institutions which organised specialist 'yield-oriented' production. As described in chapter 3, in Mongolia, privatisation of the *negdel* collectives is officially complete. The aim of the privatisation of the rural economy was to effect the transition to a market economy; however, this does not seem to be what is happening

FIGURE 6.17. Shepherd with a prize ram, Hovd *sum*, Uvs, Mongolia,
1993 (photo: Telenged)

in the short-term. In practice, special breeds of livestock, bred for marketable high-quality produce, have declined throughout Mongolia since privatisation.[112] In Dashbalbar, for example, the numbers of fine-haired sheep had fallen, and in Sumber the numbers of Karakul sheep have declined since the State Farm was split into smaller companies in 1995.

Shombodon (n.d.) points out that privatisation has led to most rural families owning a small number of livestock, and as a result the market for these products has declined. Worse conditions for herders have been created, and most rural households are short of consumer goods, and have had to increase the amount of self-provisioning. Comments made by interviewed herders indicate that for many pastoral households the consumption and sale of private livestock is primarily aimed at meeting the households' subsistence needs. A typical comment was made by Dorjsüren, a 40 year-old, middle-income herder in Sumber, Dornogov' *aimag*, who mentioned the link between livestock sales and the number of mouths he had to feed in his household.

We have many family members, and therefore it is necessary for us to sell some livestock. The price of everything has increased a great deal, so sometimes there is a need to sell. If livestock must be sold, they should be of an animal species that you have many of. If you do not increase the numbers of the livestock that you sell, soon you will have none left. For this reason you should increase your animal numbers.

All the pastoral households in the case-studies were asked what they would do in response to rises in the prices of livestock and livestock products. More than half the respondents in both the Chinese and Mongolian surveys said they would make no appreciable changes at all.[113] Around 20% of the respondents in both countries thought they might increase wool production if prices rose dramatically, but only between 10% and 15% said they would sell more livestock in response to higher prices. The aim of most pastoral households in all sites appeared to be to increase the number of their animals by consuming or selling as few as possible.[114] Shombodon (n.d.) suggests that only around 15% of herding households can produce consumer goods for the market, something like 45% can be self-sufficient, and 40% need extra resources to make a living.[115]

The two strategies described in this chapter would suggest that subsistence-domestic production tends towards self-sufficiency, which is the primary aim of this mode. In instances where this mode is dominant; only surplus products are usually marketed, and this is likely to reduce the commercial circulation of goods.[116] The contrasting alternative, specialist production, tends to be more often undertaken by rich herders or by the clients of some large herd-owning institution. It seems that the organisation of such large-scale pastoral activity (including the long movement of certain species, or the keeping of special breeds) is difficult for a 'community' (however that might be constituted) to do spontaneously. Some form of institution seems to be necessary. In almost every historical case this strategy was organised by some section of the authorities, and was then of wider benefit since it could be used to support the pastoralism of individual households.[117] In Inner Asian history political legitimation has deep roots in concepts of the relation between the land of a locality and those authorised to interact with it on behalf of the people living there. The *oboo* ceremony (see chapter 3) can be seen as a ritual expression of this relationship. The role of the public authorities in regulating land use remains central. In theory, private companies could take up specialist herding techniques and extract a surplus to be marketed to the cities.[118] However, to do this successfully they would have to have the support of the *darga*s of the local government in relation to land use.

CONCLUSION

It seems that in Mongolia the privatisation process, which gave the livestock to the herding households, is leading to an increase in the domestic-subsistence orientation, and (in the short-term at least) a decline in the economies of scale of collectives and other specialist-yield-focused agencies. This appears to have happened in Inner Mongolia in the 1980s, where it contributed to the decline of pastoral movement, particularly among the poor. Similar changes seem to have contributed to some reduction in pastoral movement in Mongolia.[119] This model suggests that we are not witnessing the rapid emergence of ideal-typical 'modern' market economy, but observing another shift in the relationship between these two strategies of production.

Inner Asian pastoralism, historically or currently, is not an entirely opportunistic grazing system of the sort suggested by the strong version of the 'non-equilibrial' grazing system hypothesis. In most of the region it is generally 'equilibrial' in that it involves broadly predictable vegetation yields in most years and usually entails the regular use of established seasonal pastures. However, it contains the contingency of an opportunistic strategy in the face of adverse natural conditions. This can be seen in the plans and arrangements between *sum* authorities for the movement of animals into the territories of other districts in the face of overwhelming need (usually very harsh winters). Secondly, in the Gobi regions long movements were used to avoid drought in pre-revolutionary times (as described by Simukov); and the variability of precipitation and natural conditions in such areas[120] still leads, on occasion, to contemporary pastoralists moving long distances beyond the normal annual circuit. The third way that this flexibility is manifest is in the practice of *otor* – which as a relatively opportunistic local strategy entails high mobility so as to make use of the best grazing that might be found in the particular season, and involves a more flexible selection of pasture than the regular seasonal movements. The large areas of Inner Asia that appear to be subject to non-equilibrial pastoral dynamics, and the traditional wisdom of Mongolian herders themselves, must make us take seriously the importance of flexible access to large areas of land for pastoralism in this region.

It appears that high levels of perceived pasture degradation are found in regions that have low-mobility, and in the Russian case, highly mechanised, systems of animal husbandry. Given that all the case-study sites were located in nominally arid areas (all with levels of mean annual precipitation between 200mm and 350mm per year over most of their territories),[121] at first glance it might be expected that overgrazing, as a result of overstocking, was a more accurate guide to the level of reported pasture degradation. However, this relationship only appears strong at the extremes. Those sites with the very highest stocking levels, in Chita and Buryatia, also had the worst perceived problems of pasture degradation, (and these areas also had little or no pastoral mobility). However, the next highest stocking rate was at the Solchur site, in Tuva, which reported virtually no pasture degradation at all, and interestingly, has retained a relatively mobile pastoral system, supported by mechanised transportation and moderately high hay inputs. By contrast one of the lowest stocking rates was found in Hargant, where informants reported serious pasture degradation in localities where the livestock were kept all year. The Hosh Tolgoi site in Xinjiang had a slightly higher stocking level than that of Chinggel Bulag, but appeared to have much less perceived pasture degradation. The stocking rate in the highly mobile Hovd *sum*, Uvs, was higher than that in relatively static Hargant, (and only around 10% lower than in Chinggel Bulag), but there was no reported pasture degradation at all.[122]

Some, such as Ma Rong and Li Ou (1993), paint a positive picture of the prospects for sustainable pastoral development in Inner Mongolia now that pasture has been allocated to individual households. The results of this policy will become clearer as time passes, but it appears that this approach contradicts both the historically dominant Mongolian pastoral philosophy, and some of the latest research as to the value of mobility in the face of low and variable precipitation. As the Tushetu Khan Tsetsendorj of Khalkha wrote in 1717, 'a large territory is the means of life [...] for the increase of the herds it is necessary to expand the territory for ample migration and grazing the stock' (Natsagdorj 1967: 26). There are still many areas of Inner Asia where pasture is seldom used. Perhaps, today, the lessons to be learned from the venerable Khan are that if you still have an extensive pastoral movement system over a large area you should preserve it, and if you have a region limited to small year-round pastures it may be worth expanding your horizons, pooling your herds, and liasing with your neighbours to co-ordinate wider pastoral movements.

Chapter 7

A Family and its Networks

In this chapter we illustrate some of the changes taking place in the life of herders using the example of a Mongolian family. This example will also enable us to describe some typical networks, the skeins of informal and sometimes ephemeral ties which link people across the region. We should say at the outset that we decided, for reasons of confidentiality, not to use a real family as an illustration. The family described is therefore a composite, but all the elements discussed are based on actual cases known to us from fieldwork.

Dorj and his wife Chimid are former members of the Gerelt Tuya *negdel* (collective) and they live in the wide, flat steppes of north-eastern Mongolia. Dorj has been a *malchin* (literally 'livestock-person') all his life. Indeed, he was a model herder in times past. He is much attached to his *nutag*, his 'homeland', and he knows it like the back of his hand: the rich pasture where wild onion grows, the marshes, and the barren waterless areas roamed by wolves. When the collective was voted out of existence in 1992, Dorj had a fair-sized herd of some 100 head, but he was only too pleased to take on some new *huviin mal* (private animals) by handing in his vouchers. Dorj and Chimid are in their fifties and they have a fairly large family, three sons and two daughters. When all stages of privatisation were over they received some former collective animals of each type (cattle, sheep, horses and goats). By summer 1996 the family counted themselves lucky: between them they had a total of 46 cattle, 285 sheep, 19 horses and 64 goats, and furthermore, their son Enhbold, who had been a driver for the *negdel*, had wangled his way into obtaining a truck from the privatisation.

Dorj and Chimid live in a beautiful new white *ger* (yurt) with their youngest son Badamjav. Enhbold and the younger daughter Otgonchimeg live there too, but both are often away, Enhbold driving his truck and Otgonchimeg at school in the district (*sum*) centre. Nearby is a small, brown *ger*, roughly covered with old felts and without a canvas facing. This is the *iluu ger*, the 'extra tent', used as a kitchen and as a sleeping-place for old Pagma, Dorj's mother. Pagma and her daughter-in-law Chimid did not get on so well to begin with, but they have long since got used to one another, and now Pagma has become somewhat aloof from family life. She has shaven her head, taken to wearing a reddish coloured gown, and spends much of her time telling her prayer-beads and gazing off into space. In other words, she has become a *chavgants*, a female lay Buddhist devotee. She helps Chimid with the milking, especially of the more fiddly small stock when the family decides to make ewe's cheese. Otherwise, Pagma enjoys languidly keeping an eye on her great-grandchildren. Sometimes she stirs herself to take them off gathering *argal*, dried cow-pats, which the family uses for fuel in the stove. In fine autumn weather, it is a pleasure to roam about near the camp, prising the dung from the clinging grasses with a wooden claw, and tossing the lumps into a basket.

Chimid's staunchest female helper in the camp is her older daughter Enhtuyaa, a young woman in her twenties who lives in her own *ger* alongside that of her parents. Enhtuyaa has not married, but she has three children and presently she lives with Boldbaatar, the father of her latest. Enhtuyaa and Boldbaatar have a few cattle and sheep of their own, but they are herded together with the rest of those of the family. Enhtuyaa has a careworn look, which is not surprising as she is busy from morn till night. Boldbaatar is a

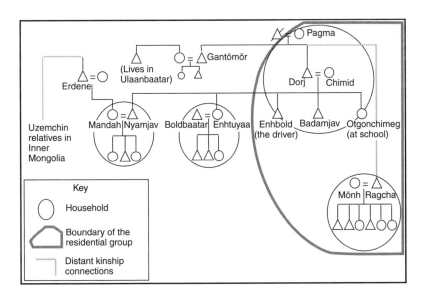

FIGURE 7.1.

worry to her too. He likes drinking, and he goes off hunting when he feels like it, disregarding the rules about closed seasons. So in Enhtuyaa's *ger* there are hidden things, pelts and meat of marmots hunted (and even trapped) out of season, and Boldbaatar's gun, a .22 rifle. Boldbaatar is a lazy fellow and his favourite hunting method is to get a lift with a friend who drives an old Russian jeep, drive close to a marmot hole, and not even getting out of the car, pot at the marmots as they emerge. This is also a highly effective method, as marmots recognise humans as a threat but seem strangely unpanicked by vehicles. Enhtuyaa is devoted to her man and would be quite prepared to distil milk-based liquor for him, but Boldbaatar turns up his nose at the home-made stuff and spends his money from selling marmot furs on the cheapest of the strong local vodkas. When he is desperate, Boldbaatar even has recourse to Chinese spirits, though he wrinkles his puffy face in disgust at himself for drinking 'poisoned stuff'.

Dorj and Chimid's middle son Enhbold is an important member of the family. With his truck and the lucrative opportunities it offers he is potentially rich. So far he has put his money into livestock, some 80 sheep, 16 goats, 15 cattle and 12 horses. All of these are kept at home with Dorj. Enhbold is a dashing figure who wears shiny leather boots, dark glasses, and an expensive watch. He has a TV, but the family has not so far been able to watch it, as there is no electricity at any of their camping places. Affable and full of jokes, Enhbold is welcome whenever he comes home. He comes back loaded with gifts, T-shirts for the children, scarves for his sisters, biscuits, sweets and other treats, and also a bottle of *arhi* (vodka) for Dorj to share out round the stove that evening.

Pagma's favourite grandson is Badamjav, a shy lad of seventeen. He is strong, good with horses and hopeless at school. Dorj and Chimid long ago chose him to be heir of their household. The others might leave the herding life, they decided, but Badamjav must stay and carry on the family tradition. In accordance with his role, Badamjav is silent and submissive at home. But he becomes a more assertive figure outside. He has no hesitation in wrestling young horses to the ground, and he knows how to slaughter cattle by plunging a long knife between the vertebrae of the neck and wrenching it from side to side to sever the spinal cord. He is at his most confident as a budding wrestler. He did well at last year's *naadam* festival at the local *oboo*, and he expects to do still better at the more amateurish wrestling planned for his aunt's wedding.

The three *gers* of Dorj, Pagma and Enhtuyaa make up a residential family group (see chapter 4) and this summer they have been joined by a distant kinsman of Dorj's, Ragchaa. Ragchaa used to be an accountant in the *negdel*, but lost his job when the collective was dissolved. In 1992–3 he got some animals in the privatisation, but sold half of them in order to buy an old car which soon broke down and now cannot be repaired. The rusting shell now lies behind his wooden house in the *sum* centre. Ragchaa spends most of the year hanging round the *sum* centre doing a bit of repair work, and doing odd jobs for other families. In the summer he comes out to join Dorj, together with his wife, six children and their own separate *ger*. He has placed his remaining sheep, cattle and goats with his brother elsewhere for safe keeping, but he brings his eight beloved horses with him to Dorj's camp where they are pooled with Dorj's larger herd. The herd consists mainly of untrained mares and Ragchaa comes out personally to help in the milking in order to make his favourite drink, *airag* (fermented mare's milk).

Including Ragchaa, the camp makes up a 'residential group' of four *gers*. There are three 'hearth groups' here: Dorj and Chimid eat together with granny Pagma and Badamjav, and Otgonchimeg and Enhbold when they are at home. Enhtuyaa and Boldbaatar and their children have their own hearth, and Ragchaa also eats separately with his wife Mönh and their family.

Dorj's close 'ritual family' includes his eldest son Nyamjav, who separated off from the household when he married his wife Gerel and received a share of the family livestock. Gerel comes from the Uzemchin Mongols, a group mainly living over the border in Inner Mongolia. Gerel's grandparents had fled to eastern Mongolia when the Chinese Communists gained power in the late 1940s. Nyamjav and Gerel now live in the *sum* centre, close to Gerel's father, the former *sum* 'broker'.

A year or two ago, Dorj had enthusiastically joined a marketing association (see chapter 3), the Jargal *horshoo*. He even contributed some money to the association fund. Ragchaa had been its accountant, but he was faced with the impossible task of paying the spiralling costs of trucks and fuel to collect the wool, cashmere and hair from the 40 scattered members to sell in the *aimag* (province) centre. Prices were disastrously low and the members even suspected Ragchaa of not passing on the full price. In short, the association collapsed and now exists only in name. Ragchaa still hopes to revive it, but Dorj is adamant that he will never again provide any resources on trust for such a venture.

Now, Dorj and Chimid live off their own household economy, but for the time being they also have some income from the 100 sheep they keep for a coal mine nearby. The mine owns around a thousand sheep in order to provide meat for its workers. These animals are farmed out in small flocks to herdsmen considered reliable by the manager. The mine gets some wool every year, which it sells, and access to meat whenever it is needed. Dorj's side of the bargain is that he gets around half the wool, hay from the mine's mechanised haymaking team, and the price of the sheep when the mine needs meat. Last winter, the mine sent a truck to collect 40 of their sheep, and Dorj and Badamjav spent a couple of hours rounding up the sheep into the pen, selecting the ones belonging to the mine, and wrestling them onto the lorry in the freezing cold. It would not be true of all herdsmen, but Dorj, having been a model herder in socialist times, prides himself on giving as much attention to the mine's sheep as he does to his own.

The lorry-load of hay that Dorj gets from the mine is used for his own livestock during the hard months of January to March. This surviving help from a large institution is but a shadow of the support Dorj fondly remembers from *negdel* days. Then, he used to get three times as much hay, enough to feed all his own private livestock as well as the 500 sheep he kept for the collective. Furthermore, the *negdel* had paid salaries to both Dorj and Chimid, collected their meat and wool for them, sent out helpers at lambing and shearing times, and provided trucks for their long migrations. Regretfully as he now looks back on those days, Dorj realises they will never come back. Now, he and Chimid have to manage on their own.

In June and July, Chimid and Enhtuyaa have to struggle with the 46 cows. Around 20 of these are lactating this summer, and it takes the two women two hours in the morning and two hours in the evening to do the milking. With their stiff fingers and aching backs, they feel a distinct sense of resentment against granny Pagma for not helping out more. They are relieved that young Otgonchimeg has come back from school to help out. Meanwhile, Dorj and the reliable Badamjav water all the animals at the well for an hour or two each day, hauling up the buckets by hand. Then they drive the cattle in one direction, the sheep and goats in another, and the horses in a third. The horses don't come back for watering every day, and so Dorj has to ride out to find them and round them up and bring them back for milking every day or two. Milking the total of 17 lactating mares is another time-consuming task for hard-working Chimid and Enhtuyaa. Ragchaa, the languid former accountant, deigns to hold the foals near their mothers, but it is a woman's job to do the actual milking. Ragchaa's wife Mönh lends a hand, as does the eldest of her daughters, but neither of them are much good; they are slow and inefficient at extracting the milk. While granny Pagma twirls hers beads and Boldbaatar snores in a drunken haze, nearly everyone else is busy. Even the children take turns churning the *airag*, or taking the lambs and kids to close pastures; though to tell the truth, Ragchaa's crew of six is rather harum-scarum – tormenting frogs is their favourite pastime.

Summer is a good time for food, as there is so much milk. But Chimid still worries about adequate sustenance (*hüns*) for the family. Her chief concern is getting enough flour. She reckons she needs a 25-kilo sack per month at least, and prices have risen to almost 400 *tugrik*s a kilo. The main problem is that there is no flour in the *sum* shops. Chimid was recently scandalised to hear that Chinese traders are demanding a whole sheep for a sack of flour. At that rate, what with the 15 or so sheep killed for meat a year, even her family's relatively numerous flocks will gradually be depleted. She cannot rely on Enhbold's 80 sheep, because he recently said he wants to sell most of them to buy a new clutch for his truck. Dorj and Chimid question every visitor: where to get flour? (not to speak of rice, pasta, or sugar). Chimid's worries are even affecting the hospitality she was brought up to cherish. Last year as usual she put out her *boortsog* (fried dough pieces) on the low table in her *ger* for visitors to enjoy, and Ragchaa's children were merely brushed away when they tried to eat too many. This year, despite the hungry faces of the neighbours' kids peering round the door, she has hidden away her *boortsog* in the cupboard. One of granny Pagma's good points, in Chimid's view, is that she has a excellent memory of places to look for gathered food, wild onions, garlic, berries, nuts or mushrooms. All of these things have come to seem more valuable recently and it is a pleasure of the summer season to go off in search parties with a picnic.

Chimid's anxiety is beginning to affect everyone, though Dorj re-mains stolidly sure that, come what may, a Mongol herding family can always survive. Still, even Dorj listens attentively when his oldest son Nyamjav arrives one day and tells the family about an exciting scheme. Nyamjav's father-in-law, Erdeni, the former broker of the *negdel* and now a businessman, has recently found a reliable buyer for Mongolian cashmere among his Uzumchin relatives in Inner Mongolia. He plans to take two lorry loads of cashmere across the border, sell them in China, buy flour and sugar with the proceeds, and bring them back to sell them at home. This plan only has a hope of success because everyone knows that Erdeni, the father-in-law, has excellent relations with the head of the *sum*. Furthermore, it is rumoured that his network includes a good friend at the border customs post. Enhbold is hoping that his truck, re-equipped with a new clutch, might be one of the vehicles to make the trip, and even Dorj is quietly pleased that he had set aside a large sack of cashmere earlier in the summer. So many things are available in China! Enhtuyaa glances up at the calendar from China hanging over

Chimid's bed: a sinuous female in a glittering silk negligée is draped over a shiny motor-bike. Enhtuyaa begins dreaming of shampoo, face-cream and lipstick. Ragchaa is also agog to join in somehow, and Boldbaatar grandiloquently offers himself as a 'negotiator' on the offchance that he could go too. Nyamjav knows very well that his father-in-law will never take either of them, but Enhbold with his truck has a chance if one of the other trucks needs repairs.

Deep down, Dorj knows that his most reliable connections are those through his brother Gantömör, a foreman at the local mine. Not only was Gantömör useful in arranging the contract for herding the 100 sheep, but he can usually supply a truck when the time comes to move to the winter pastures. Furthermore, Gantömör's wife's brother lives in Ulaanbaatar. Whenever she can she obliges him by having his children to stay, but in any case she could count on his feeling of obligation to help her. Dorj is able to get medicines and rifle ammunition from the city via this line. He makes sure that Gantömör has meat in winter when he needs it, and sooner or later the goods from the capital city will appear.

Otgonchimeg is doing well at school, and Dorj and Chimid have aims for her to train as a vet at the a*imag* centre, or perhaps even Ulaanbaatar. Recently, however, they have begun to worry how they could afford to support her if she does get a place at college. The cost of education is one of the issues they discussed with the head of the *sum*, Amarsaihan. He arrived by jeep in late summer to canvas their support for the forthcoming local elections. Amarsaihan is a member of the old pro-Soviet Mongolian People's Revolutionary Party. On this visit he was making a special effort to drum up support for re-election, since the Democratic coalition had won control of the national government earlier that summer. Dorj and Chimid were easily persuaded to vote for him. Not only was he related to Chimid's sister's husband, but he had been the head of their brigade in the *negdel*, and Dorj had been a model herder. To make his point about the need to vote for his Party, Amarsaihan had only to turn the conversation to the sudden jump in prices caused by the new government's deregulation of the prices of fuel. When her own name and the cost of education came up, Otgonchimeg shyly hung back and soon retreated to granny's *ger* next door. Soon there was general head-shaking and complaint about the 'youngster' politicians now running the country. Ragchaa joined the discussion with some relish, wondering aloud if the old Revolutionary party had done any better. Badamjav, the son, however, soon became bored with the conversation and wandered away to look for the horses with his binoculars. When the leader left, accompanied by some colleagues and a driver, Chimid gave them some clotted cream. Suddenly Boldbaatar lurched out of his *ger*. He was tired of life in the encampment and wanted a lift to the *sum* centre. Everyone waited while he sorted out a couple of sheep skins to take with him to sell for rifle ammunition and *arhi*.

As summer drew to a close, Dorj began thinking about making his move to autumn pastures (see chapter 6). He did not really have to wonder where to go, because he generally went to the pastures where he had always gone during the collective days. He was not even concerned about anyone else using his autumn pasture, as this was a transient stopping-place. But he was concerned when a traveller told him that one of the households from the *sum* centre had an eye on his treasured winter pasture. Last year, he had been distinctly annoyed when someone had placed their encampment too close to his winter site, so their animals strayed onto the pastures he thought of as his.

Now, his main problem was transportation. Even Gantömör, his brother at the mine, who had said he would send a truck, was this time beginning to equivocate. He was now saying that Dorj would have to pay for the petrol and in any case the truck might be unavailable. Enhbold was still searching around for a clutch for his vehicle. In short, Dorj was beginning to wonder whether he shouldn't invest in a few camels. Not since his childhood had Dorj made the long journey by camel-cart. So now he was thinking about how to herd camels, which he had never done personally, and in the evening he carefully read the sections on camels in Sambuu's textbook *Advice to Herdsmen*. Still, he thought he ought to drop in on old Bayarsüren, who lived only a dozen kilometres away, and who kept a herd of some 6 camels. Dorj wanted to find out about camels, and the price Bayarsüren would ask for selling a couple.

Chimid was resigned to the change from truck to camel transport, and she was already beginning to think about the loading and packing. Essentially, she was working out 'how to manage' (*argalah*). Ragchaa would not be going to the autumn pasture, but there were still three yurts and their contents to be taken. The family's two carts, simple affairs with two wooden wheels, would not be sufficient. True, a camel could pull a much bigger weight than a horse, and if Dorj bought three camels the spare one could be loaded up too, but even so Chimid knew they would have to make two trips. And there was the crockery. Even if you put the layers of yurt felt at the bottom, wooden carts jolt terribly over the steppes. Her precious wedding bowls might get chipped, Chimid worried, and this set her off thinking about how the family's carefully accumulated marks of town culture were being abandoned one by one (chapter 5). She had never seen Enhbold's TV working, though that was only to be expected living out on the grasslands, but now batteries were difficult to obtain for the radio, and kerosene for the lamp. Last winter, with only candles, she had strained her eyes trying to do her sewing, and how could she get hold of spectacles?

One fine day, Dorj set off for Bayarsüren's on his favourite gelding. On the way, as he reached to top of a low pass, he paused to tie a horse-hair to a branch sticking out of the *oboo* (cairn), and he glanced away into the steppes before him. Far in the distance, he could see two *gers*, and wondered who had turned up to stay with Bayarsüren. As he descended the hill, he noticed a miserably small flock of sheep and goats. The camels were nowhere to be seen.

Bayarsüren's scraggy dog raced out from the camp, barking furiously. Soon the old man emerged to call the dog back. He was a dignified figure with a worn Manchu-style jacket over his gown and ancient decorated boots with turned up toes. Bayarsüren apologised as he showed Dorj into his *ger*, for it was cold and dirty, without a fire in the stove, and the ragged cloths on which the old man slept had not been tidied away. His wife had died some years ago. Still, Bayarsüren tried his best. He offered Dorj his lustrous onyx snuff-bottle with a respectful gesture. Dorj's eyes wandered over the tangled heap of bridles and halters and the framed jewel-like pictures of Buddhist gods in the *hoimor* (the respected part of the *ger*). Meanwhile, his host poured luke-warm tea from a Chinese thermos and fumbled in an ancient bag for pieces of stale, rock-hard cheese. It turned out that Bayarsüren was not particularly interested in selling his camels. He did not bother much about them and was not even sure quite where they were at the moment. And what would he do with the money anyway, since there was such inflation? '*Yaah we-e*', he said, 'What's the point?' He lit his pipe and said, 'I've got a sack of flour, I'm all right for the time being. I'll sell when I have to.' He saw the whole deal as too much trouble. '*Yarshig, yarshig*', he muttered.

'That's someone not suited to getting rich (*bayajihad taaügüi hün*)', Dorj thought. But after a time Dorj won Bayarsüren round. He more or less persuaded the old man to part with a couple of camels in exchange for two good milking cows. But Bayarsüren was not going to exert himself. The deal was that Dorj would continue to look after the cows and regularly provide the old man with milk.

The door opened and the recently arrived neighbour Nergüi entered. Nergüi was a new herder. He had been a factory-worker at the *aimag* centre, but the factory had gone bankrupt. So when the *negdel* livestock were being privatised, Nergüi had come out to join his herder father and share in the proceeds of privatisation. Just then, the father had died. Largely ignorant of herding, Nergüi, his wife Suvd, and their three young children, had decided to tag along with Bayarsüren. Nergüi felt sure that the old man could teach them the ropes, and he had been a friend of his father. Bayarsüren himself was doubtful of Nergüi's talents as a herder, but it was helpful to have Suvd in the encampment to do the milking. None of this was mentioned to Dorj.

A week or two later, Enhbold, the driver middle son, brought exciting news to Dorj's camp. He was to go on the trading trip to China. Erdeni, the organiser, was *aztai* (lucky), though who could tell if the affair would be a success?. Enhbold had been able to find a clutch and repair his truck, and tomorrow three trucks would set off, loaded with precious cashmere and also with other things the resourceful Nyamjav had found to sell. These included wool, hides, and scrap metal, including old fuel tanks and guttering appropriated from an abandoned Russian army base.

The next day, as Enhbold was leaving, granny Pagma gave him an amulet for good luck to hang around his neck, and as the lorry began to roll, Chimid flung a libation of milk in the direction of the travel. With such a propitious start the journey could only go smoothly. The little convoy reached the border, and Erdene, Nyamjav's father-in-law, had found his friend at the customs post with no trouble. The journey to Erdene's relatives in Inner Mongolia passed without a hitch.

Though he had travelled to Russia, China was new to Enhbold. He was secretly amazed to find Mongolian herders living in rows of mud-brick houses in the dusty plains. In the villages, a few of them had even taken to growing vegetables in little gardens, though their patches were more haphazard than the exquisitely neat rows of salad and greens of their Chinese neighbours. Erdeni's relatives had shrewdly acquired the flour and sugar at a low price wholesale, so nothing remained but the visit to the prefectural capital town to spend the party's extra money. Glittering buildings, with a post-modern mix of darkened glass walling and pseudo-traditional tiled roofs, were going up in the centre. Countless restaurants, not to speak of Muslim bakers, Southern Chinese cycle-repairers, stationers, tailors and so forth, lined the streets. The market was a densely-crowded area of stalls, decked high with fancy clothes and toys. Enhbold lit a cigarette and refused to be impressed. He could not help glancing at the digital watches, but he resolved to go only for what he needed and to make sure he was not cheated. He was determined to get batteries and he had some confidence about the right prices, because batteries had been the subject of long discussions with other drivers back in Mongolia. So he headed for a stall where the Chinese seller had put up a notice in Mongol, 'Buy Here!', and seemed to speak some broken Mongol. Enhbold bargained hard and tested a battery with his tongue to see how live it was. Deliberately impassive, he handed over the money and took the batteries, not bothering to respond to the chatter of the Chinese trader. But inside he was satisfied, and he then homed in on the other things he wanted: a particular brand of pair of trainers for himself and a huge heap of sweets for the children back home. He was choosy about the sweets: the kids vociferously expressed their likes and dislikes. Suddenly he remembered the shampoo and lipstick for his sister and he spent some time checking the prices before settling on some European-looking items. The last thing to get was some alcohol for home and the journey back. Several *oboo*s would have to be propitiated on the way, and of course many friends would expect presents. Enhbold tried to avoid any spirits with Chinese labels (they might be *hortoi*, poisoned) and he looked for some with foreign-looking labels, not thinking too hard about the fact that they might have been made in China too.

Enhbold was hardly aware of it, but he had created a rather bad impression on Erdeni's Inner Mongolian relatives. He had brought some gifts for the old people, particularly a prized bottle of Chinggis Khan vodka. But the trouble was that from the Uzemchin point of view, these gifts did not come up to standard: the manufactured goods they saw as shoddy, and as for vodka, their tastes had already moved towards Chinese alcohol. What really troubled the Inner Mongolians was what they saw as Enhbold's rough edges. Inner Mongolians are very careful about what they say and what political comments they make, and who knows who is loyal to whom. Enhbold, on the other hand, was a Halh Mongol, from the dominant people in an independent country. What he saw as proper behaviour, his relatives took to be improper, and even politically irresponsible (his extolling of Mongol brotherhood, his proud boast about getting rid of the Russians). Even culturally they were a little offended at his 'modernness', his Russified manner as they saw it, his casual clothes, his foreign Marxist egalitarian way of speaking, without due respect to elders and seniors. They considered respect for seniors as 'traditional' and 'Mongolian', and therefore part of customary behaviour to be protected against Chinese influences. Back in the Uzemchin pastures, Enhbold had made remarks, which were taken by his relatives to be pointed and hurtful.

'Oh, you still have a trivet (*tuulga*)!' he had said, (which was indeed unusual even in Inner Mongolia), and comparing their Chinese shoes to his sturdy Russian-style boots, he had said, 'We don't do it that way at home'

(*Manaid tegt ügui shüu dee!*). This was taken by the Inner Mongolians as annoying superiority, the presumption that they were so 'backward' as to still use a trivet (rather than choosing to use one, as they saw it), revealing the condescending assumption that the way it is done in Halh is natural and right.

On the journey home it poured with rain and a cold wind swept over the grassland. The travellers decided to call in on some of Erdeni's other relatives and turned off down a hummocky track. As darkness fell the truck lurched through a muddy village and nearly ran down an ox-cart standing stationary in the centre of the road. They asked the way to the relatives' camp: it was miles away through dunes and bogs. To cheer themselves up they had quite a few drinks of spirits and by the time they arrived in the middle of the night they were too tired to do anything but tumble into the yurt and fall asleep, all three drivers together. In the morning it was still damp and dark. Enhbold suddenly thought to inspect his flour and sugar: some of the sacks were sodden, but '*Yaah we*' ('Too bad'), he said to himself. He went back into the *ger* and said nothing. Portraits of the Panchen Lama, Chinggis Khan and film-stars were in the *hoimor*, and a wind-generator hummed outside, but the salty milk tea and boiled meat were familiar enough.

Enhbold was telling his hosts about his time in Russia. He had not much liked the Buryats. Not only were they clannish and unreliable, but they were no longer really Mongol at all. In fact, few of them seemed in the slightest interested in Mongolia and most of them seemed only to speak Russian. He recounted how he had met a Buryat school-teacher, who told him she was perfectly well-off, because she had three cows! The hosts were duly surprised, so Enhbold felt he should add for fairness sake that the school-teacher also had a vegetable plot, 2 pigs and a few chickens. Still, pretty miserable, they all thought.

'But, you know', someone said, 'The good thing about Russia is their good strong (*böh*) products.'

'No longer. Look how the quality of the Russian UAZ jeep has gone downhill. Four-year old Russian jeeps are better than new ones these days.'

The hostess peered out of the door at the misty distance. 'There's the jeep of the *hiliin chagdaa* (border police)', she observed. Enhbold and his co-drivers were not overly concerned, but the relatives hinted that it might be better if they went at this stage. Saying a friendly good-bye, but without a word of thanks, they rattled off round the other side of the hill.

When they got back home, it was to find that Erdeni had made a very astute deal to sell most of the flour and sugar to one of the *sum* officials. Most of the sacks, damp or dry, were piled into the *sum* official's newly constructed wooden store and firmly locked up. Enhbold and his mates stashed away their piles of cash. They were delighted that the official had given Nyamjav permission to raid the old Russian base again for scrap-iron for another run. Taking his share of the flour and sugar, and having stocked up with goods and kerosene, Enhbold drove cheerfully out to Dorj's camp. His truck needed a new wheel and one of the front lights was not working, but '*Yaah we*', and he even began to sing.

Dorj was now well supplied with flour, sugar and even money, and decided that the time had come to see about the camels. The designated day for the autumn move, established by the collective, was fast approaching. Even granny Pagma seemed to have migration on her mind as she scanned the landscape for omens. So Dorj and Badamjav set out to collect the camels, taking the binoculars and ropes. As they reached the pass Dorj felt generous and grateful. He made a libation of alcohol and he offered sweets and money at the *oboo* this time. He looked away into the steppes as usual, but he was surprised to see no sign of the small flock of sheep and goats. When he arrived at Bayarsüren's yurt he heard a sad story. In the month since his last visit, Nergüi had sold some of the sheep to passing traders; then the old dog had died; and finally, to both men's dismay, without a dog as guard, only a week later wolves had killed all the remaining lambs and kids. Now the camp of two *gers* had only a miserable 6 sheep and 3 goats, and no young stock at all. This was barely enough to provide meat to get through the winter. When he heard of the kids and lambs being killed, Dorj sighed '*Höörhii, höörhii*' ('poor things'), and he made a mental note to go wolf-hunting as soon as it snowed and revealed the tracks.

Bayarsüren was now prepared to barter another camel for nine sheep, to ensure enough winter meat. 'They'd have to be big ones', he said. Dorj agreed.

The old man then asked a little awkwardly, 'Do you have any flour?'

'No, not much', Dorj replied. Badamjav kept silent.

'I hear you can buy flour from the *sum* official's new store', Dorj proffered.

'Heck, where will I get the money for that?' said Bayarsüren.

As Dorj and Badamjav got up to go, Nergüi mooched close and asked, 'Do you have any paid work I could do?' Bayarsüren gave a disapproving glance, deliberately not looking at the younger man.

'Nope', said Dorj. Still, as he stepped out into the sunlight he reflected that he and his son Badamjav could well do with some help. 'But not an unknown person like that Nergüi', he thought. 'And he's a useless townee.'

Nergüi returned, dispirited, to the empty *ger,* and helped himself to a lukewarm bowl of Bayarsüren's milkless tea. Last week his wife Suvd had gone away to the *aimag* centre where her sister lived, to try to find some flour, leaving the children to stay with Nergüi's aunt in the *sum* centre. Suvd was worried about provisioning for the family, and she thought her brother-in-law, an Army officer, Bazar, could help. He made occasional trading trips across the border into Chita. Suvd had decided to join him: he was sure to be able to get some army boots to sell and she was hopeful about selling some small painted pictures of Buddhist gods which were family heirlooms. Nergüi had no idea how this venture would go. But he was not quite without ideas of his own. He had kept a little money back from selling sheep earlier. Sitting in the *ger* he planned how he might get some ammunition to buy for Bayarsüren's old rifle. Maybe he could shoot a few marmots before the season was over, and have the pelts to show Suvd when she got back.

The rain lashed down as Dorj and Badamjav set out to look for the camels. The old man came along to help them catch them, and after a few kilometres they came to a hill when Badamjav could use his beloved binoculars to scan the scene. The camels were grazing calmly near a salt-pan. As they came closer, Dorj began to select which ones he would take: the ones with upright humps would last the winter well. The camels were semi-wild by now and they slowly scattered. The three men had to struggle to get the chosen camels moving back to the camp; the remaining three gave mournful bellows.

Our story ends with three different scenes that night. Otgonchimeg had gone back to school and was staying comfortably with her uncle Nyamjav at the *sum* centre. The electricity was on that evening, and she was gazing with fascination at the elaborate romances rapidly revolving in *Maria,* her favourite Mexican soap-opera. Meanwhile, back in their distant encampment, Dorj and Chimid were sitting by their kerosene lamp. They were talking in low tones. What were they to do about Boldbaatar, their drunken 'son-in-law'? He was now saying he would not come with them on the autumn move, but seemed to expect them to take along all his animals anyway. And what would happen if Badamjav got conscripted into the army? How would they manage without him? Over the windswept pass, in the dark steppes, there was scarcely a glimmer from Bayarsüren and Nergüi's camp. The old man was sitting silent by the embers of his stove. In the next tent, Nergüi was sitting and smoking in the darkness: there was no reason even to light a candle. They would probably have to kill their last cow to get through the winter, he was thinking, but would Suvd bring back the flour?

Chapter 8

CONCLUSION

In this volume we have tried to provide a perspective that challenges a number of stereotypes or 'myths' held about Inner Asia and pastoral society, and to suggest some new avenues for investigation. In the conclusion we briefly outline our understandings in relation to several widely-held assumptions. It should be noted, however, that the stereotypes about Inner Asia do not themselves form a coherent argument, since they derive from various different sources and stances towards pastoralism and development.

MOBILITY AND LAND-USE

The case-studies suggest that pasture degradation is associated with the loss of mobility in pastoral systems. In both pre-revolutionary and collective periods it seems that pastoral movement was often facilitated by large herd-owning institutions, and one of the effects of privatising livestock has been to reduce the amount of movement undertaken by many pastoral households. The more mobile of the case-study sites were those in mountainous regions, and those (in Tuva and Mongolia) where a state or collective farm continued to organise and support pastoral movement. Very low mobility and the cultivation of fodder crops with the use of heavy machinery in the Buryatian regions is associated with severe problems of pasture degradation. Privatisation in China, also accompanied by reduction of movement, again seems to be correlated with a decline in pasture quality in many areas. These findings challenge the idea that sustainable pastoralism in Inner Asian steppe regions can be achieved without retaining mobility.

In Mongolia in the past, in both the pre-revolutionary and the socialist period long migrations were used as a strategy to increase pastoral production. This technique was used by large herd-owners and institutions to produce for non-subsistence exchange, as described in chapter 6. This argument challenges the stereotypical view that seasonal migration is merely a 'primitive survival technique', and that the only way to improve pastoral production is to reduce mobility.

There has been a general reduction in livestock mobility over the twentieth century. The effect of the move away from socialist institutions has not been to reverse this, as some observers expected, but on the contrary has been to introduce a further series of processes decreasing mobility. These processes may not be irreversible, but it is quite hard to imagine the social scenario in which ordinary herders would reintroduce difficult long seasonal migrations. However, in Mongolia it is conceivable that individuals or institutions owning large numbers of livestock might organise such systems, using hired labour. It seems unlikely, on the other hand, for livestock movement to be much extended in China, unless there is a change of pastoral policy, while in Russia it may be possible to increase the frequency of moves, but lack of pasture looks set to inhibit long distance movement.

INSTITUTIONS

Proposing optimal institutional frameworks for Inner Asia is impossible, because of the great regional differences in social, cultural and economic conditions. However, on the basis of our studies, we do think that it is possible to draw some conclusions about the relation between institutional form and certain pastoral techniques and strategies.

Large-scale institutions have had an important role in maintaining and supporting the mobility of Inner Asian pastoral communities in a number of different ways. They permitted the administration of a sufficiently large area of land to make long migrations practicable for the herders, and provided central services and facilities (such as boarding accommodation at schools) that supported the resulting lifestyle of the community. They also could provide mechanised support to the productive process, and organise the collection and marketing of products. Another important result of such large-scale productive enterprises was that they were in a position to keep specialised herds and rotate them over pasture in such a way as to retain good grazing, as is illustrated by the contrasting situations in Red Star State Farm in Barkol and Sarq'ok district described in chapter 3. In the State Farm pasture and livestock were considered by our informants to be in good condition, whereas in Sarq'ok the numerous small private herds were said to be damaging the grassland. Whereas we cannot entirely discount the possible influence of the personal interests of the informant administrators (who may have preferred the State farm model for their own reasons), similar opinions were expressed by ordinary pastoralists and others in many regions.

Our research suggests that where they still exist, large-scale organisations can have a positive role to play in the management of the livestock economy in combination with other forms of organisation. To note these positive roles, however, is certainly not to advocate collectivisation. It is clear that a wholesale return to socialist collectives of the old type is now impossible, as well as being undesirable, but these monolithic institutions are not the only forms of large-scale organisation imaginable, as noted in the section above. Certain specialist functions might be organised on a large-scale, leaving households or small associations free to manage other activities. Technical continuities in history suggest that sheep, horse and camel herding are good candidates for such wider organisation (see figure 6.1). Furthermore, a wide-scale strategy does not necessarily imply a collective institution; such a strategy could equally be employed by an individual herder were his enterprise to become large enough.

The 'privatisation' process should not be seen as simply the removal of intrusive government institutions. It has been about creating new institutional forms – principally the private household enterprise. This has no good precedent in the region as the *only* form of economic unit. Nevertheless the household was always very important in Inner Asia as a productive institution. This was true no less in the collective period than before it, and now the household has emerged, for better or worse, as the main pastoral unit almost everywhere but Russia. However, the primary focus of the pastoral household in Inner Asian conditions is subsistence for its members. It is becoming increasingly difficult for households, which generally lack security for loans, to attract investment so as to start new ventures specifically aimed at market sales. Without this, it seems that only under advantageous conditions (for example, close to towns or other markets in China) can the pastoral household function well as a miniature firm.

As part of some larger organisation, however, households are remarkably adaptable, as we have just seen in chapter 6. Some attempts have been made to establish associations of households, such as the Mongolian *horshuulal* or Buryat and Tuvan joint private farms, and in principle these could be useful for sharing machinery, access to resources, marketing and sharing herding tasks. These nascent small associations have been very diverse across the region, and the reasons for their coming into existence and organisational frameworks are also very varied. Most of them have failed in the harsh economic climate of the past few years (high inflation, low prices for pastoral products, distant markets, high fuel costs, etc.), but it looks as though some people will go on trying to establish them in Buryatia at least because the mechanised form of agriculture there encourages people to join together to share technology.

In the past the long-distance specialist herding strategy was important mostly in mountainous, steppe and sometimes Gobi regions where a variety of terrains afforded advantageous seasonal pastures for herds of given species and age. There were, however, many areas where this strategy was rarely employed, especially in the forest fringes of the north. In these regions, particularly in Buryat areas, sheep and horses were less important than cattle in pre-revolutionary times (Tulokhonov 1992). In the mid-1990s, with the massive decline in sheep numbers in these regions, it looks as though there will be a return to a mixed, cattle-based pastoral economy combined with fodder production. This is based on the household, at present usually supported by institutions deriving from the collective farm, either as direct successor or some part of the farm. These larger institutions provide me-chanical support without which it would be difficult for the smallholdings to operate (see chapter 3). Without wanting to strike out entirely on their own as 'private farmers', householders have told us that within the somewhat protected orbit of the former collective, they appreciate their new self-sufficiency, the chance to work for themselves, and to make their own decisions.

One of the most interesting and important socio-economic issues is the centrality of local leadership after the removal of overtly authoritarian regimes. The culture of leadership reaches back into history, and it has long played a central role in the organisation of the economy. For example, the late Manchu crop cultivation system in Mongolia described by Erdenebaatar (1996) was directed. This agriculture was carried out by officially recognised farming sections (*tarig*) made up of several households, each commanded by a single head (*angiin daamal*). The system of land-use was not simply a set of mutual aid customs followed by independent farming families; it was explicitly co-ordinated by the heads of the farming groups. The Buryat *utug* (cultivated hay-meadow) system was comparable. Settlement communities had joint rights in the fields, but a headman or a small number of elders made the decisions annually about land and water allocation to the families, organised irrigation-channel maintenance, etc. In Mongolia, the success of intensified specialist pastoralism was based on direction by central leader-ship, and this applied not only to tradition-minded princes and high monastic officials but also to innovative figures, like Togtoh Taij, who introduced new techniques, skills and artisan crafts in the 19th century. In present-day Mongolia, good leadership at the *sum* and *bag* level can prevent the predicted conflicts over pasture after privatisation. These local leaders maintain detailed information on where 'their' herders are moving, and they are important not only for conflict resolution but also for obtaining permits of various kinds (this varies from place to place, but can include obtaining fuel, registration of domicile, pasturing outside the *bag*, and dealing with emergencies). Our research suggests that leadership of groups is an important structuring principle in Inner Asian society and is regarded by respondents as the 'natural' way to organise affairs. It is interesting to note that where *horshoo* 'co-operatives' have been founded in Mongolia since de-collectivisation, these have been centred upon a leader able to organise the newly independent economic unit (see chapter 3). If successful means of organising production emerge, they are likely to depend on effective leadership, though it is difficult to predict what forms the institutions will otherwise take.

PASTORAL PRODUCTION, LABOUR AND MECHANISATION

Another stereotype prevalent in those who write about pastoralism is that extensive movements are low input-low output productive systems. Chapter 6, however, suggests that in Inner Asian conditions this is an over-simplistic conclusion. Well-managed, long-distance and frequent moves require high levels of certain inputs (work involving herd management, equipment, geographical knowledge, transport, etc.) with the aim of achieving high outputs of certain kinds (meat and wool). These inputs and outputs are 'high' relative to the alternative strategy pastoralists might employ with the same breeds, namely minimal movement with low labour inputs. It is in this sense that a system of wide pastoral movement can be seen as a long-standing method of pastoral 'intensification', especially of labour. That is, although the amplification of seasonal movements requires more *ex*tensive amounts of land, it is labour-*in*tensive. Throughout the region local herders reported that this is more productive and better for the land than using minimal movement, although everyone recognises that high productivity per animal could also be achieved if the technological basis were changed to provide a high level of cultivated fodder supplements for new breeds.

It is nevertheless interesting to compare the high mobility strategy with this third, more recent, strategy for economic intensification – that of agro-industrial sedentarisation. If we take feeding the livestock as one of the inputs, we can see that there are two ways that human labour can be applied so as to increase it. In a highly mobile pastoral system natural vegetation is made available to animals by frequently moving them. In the sedentary model labour is expended on growing fodder which is then harvested and fed to relatively static animals. Both require more work, foresight and organisation than grazing the animals within a range of a few kilometres all year round. It is commonly imagined that the distant migration is an archaic remnant and that technology is appropriate only for the stall-fed modern variant. But the interesting point is that in fact in both cases the necessary labour can be supported through the application of mechanisation. This might suggest the following simplified and notional model – figure 8.1, in which the points A and C do not represent the same types of labour input but simply an increase in both quality and quantity, from the herder's point of view, over the minimal-work level at B.

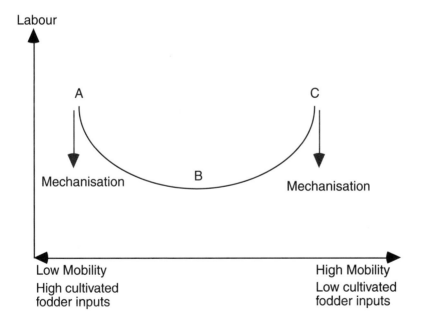

FIGURE 8.1.

FIGURE 8.2. Loading camel-carts for seasonal move to spring pastures in Sumber *sum*, Mongolia, 1993

FIGURE 8.3. Moving a pastoral encampment by truck, Tuva, 1991

In this sketch, the term 'labour' is used to refer to the effort and difficulty of a particular system, not the number of workers as such. Point C represents a highly mobile extensive system of pastoral land use with frequent movement. It requires a relatively high level of labour, not necessarily in terms of a large labour force, but a flexible and hardy one prepared to move animals, families and belongings frequently and sometimes over long distances. Some of this work can be eased by the utilisation of animal power, but it is greatly lessened by use of mechanised transport and haulage. Mechanisation also supports herders using this method with the collection of produce, the supply of water, fuel, hay, and consumer goods, and with transportable technology (diesel generators, milk separators, etc.). Point A represents the relatively high amount of labour needed to support an entirely static herding system on steppe land. Land must be ploughed, and hay and fodder cultivated, harvested and supplied to the herds. Irrigation and manuring of fields is often necessary in Inner Asian conditions. Again, animal power has been applied to this task, but mechanisation allows for a great reduction in the necessary labour.

The static mode normally generates more produce per animal, but we are making this comparison because we are interested in a larger unit of analysis, that of an entire pastoral system employed in a locality. Here, though the productivity per animal may be somewhat greater for the new breeds in the static system,[1] it is by no means so clear that this latter system is more efficient if one takes into account *all* the inputs and all the outputs, especially as the Buryat system of this kind has exhausted its pasture base.

The point here is that small producers, at point B on the diagram, are unable, without incoming investment, to provide the labour and/or mechanisation necessary to achieve either form of intensification successfully. (They also lack the organisational resources of a larger institution to facilitate access to large areas of land.) Without institutional support there is a tendency to 'fall back' to an achievable system that does not require much labour and is also relatively immobile. It is important to note that state and collective farms have been able to support both forms of intensification through mechanisation. Thus in Mongun-Taiga in Tuva in 1988, where there was a highly mobile system of pastoralism, all herders' migrations were carried out by trucks supplied by the farm, and herders often used motorcycles to get to pastures and even for certain types of herding. It is not that we would recommend the last-mentioned practice, but the point is that mechanisation (water-carrying trucks, mobile shops, livestock transport, haycutters, etc.) can be used to support the distinctive Inner Asian 'tradition' of

high pastoral productivity through mobility. In present economic circumstances this would require a definite policy decision from local authorities to
provide petrol, vehicles and repair-shops strategically and in the public
interest. In Inner Mongolia at present the herders are no strangers to the idea
that mechanisation reduces labour, and around one third of herders in the case
studies had mini-tractors used for personal transport or minor haulage. But
the high price and unavailability of petrol and repair facilities, and the uneven
distribution of tractors, mean that many pastoralists cannot afford to move to
distant pastures, and in Hargant for example, certain distant tracts are underused. The message is that district-wide organisation, possibly underpinned
by specific herding institutions, could reconstitute efficient and market-
oriented production on a mobile model – but this unlikely to happen without
a change in wider economic conditions.

RURAL-URBAN INTEGRATION, SEDENTARISATION AND LIVING STANDARDS

The herders of Inner Asia have a legitimate desire for living standards equal
to those of the rest of the population, as well as access to goods, services,
culture and information from towns and cities. But such rural-urban integration need not be achieved at the expense of degraded pasture. The Tuvan case,
among others, shows that 'urbanism' is compatible with both a highly mobile
pastoral system, and an environment that is perceived as undamaged. It is
virtually total sedentarisation of the rural population that seems problematic
from the point of view of environmental conservation. Furthermore,
sedentarisation of herders may be associated with cultural and economic
isolation, and with relatively greater dependence on subsistence production
than in more mobile areas. The existence of townships in the steppe, on the
other hand, is not incompatible with maintaining a mobile herding working
sector. In fact, there is a long history in Inner Asia of social groups which have
both 'urban' and rural sectors (for example, Buddhist monasteries with their
dependent herds); equally longstanding is the existence of towns in which the
population is only present for part of the year. More recently, demographic
urbanisation has advanced, and elements of urban culture have been taken up
even in the most distant places. This does not, however, mean that the
devotees of Mexican soap-opera are necessarily sedentarised. One month
they may be chasing yaks in the mountains, far from TV sets and electricity
supplies, and the next they may visit an aunt in the capital and sit glued to the
screen in her flat. Our research shows that urbanism (rural-urban integration)

and year-round sedentarisation are two separate processes in Inner Asia, and it challenges the stereotype that the two necessarily go hand in hand.

The effacement of the division between urban and rural was a long-standing theme of the Marxist-Leninist project of social engineering. Rather than the western modernist project of creating suburbs, garden cities and 'ruralising' the town, the attempt, especially in Russia and Mongolia, was to urbanise the countryside. The goal of social engineering has collapsed, but the dream of creating civilised urban conditions for the majority of the population (much of which still lives in the countryside) still remains. In Inner Asia there is every reason to suggest that a neat division between the urban and pastoral (the settled and the mobile) is not only analytically inappropriate as a descriptive device, but undesirable as a goal. The integration of settled and mobile lifestyles was one of the advantages of large collective structures, despite their many failings. In Buryatia mechanisation developed mainly in the direction of settled agro-pastoralism, which allowed the rural people a relatively comfortable lifestyle in villages supplied with electricity; in Tuva and Mongolia, mechanisation, although never very highly developed, supported the other, mobile trajectory. Today herders much regret the loss of previous mechanised facilities, such as mobile shops, hay and water deliveries, transport for moves, and so forth. Where these mechanised facilities, and other state provisions such as medical, veterinary and educational services are being wound down, a process of de-urbanism is under way (see chapter 5). In China, the relatively prosperous individual herders of Inner Mongolia have chosen to use their money for mechanisation, replacing draft animals with versatile mini-tractors and riding-horses with motor-bikes.[2] This is not part of a system to apply technology to large-scale production (for which other sturdier long-range vehicles would be required), but it does show that herders want to minimise manual labour and get themselves quickly to towns.

Because of the nature of mobile pastoralism, the large geographic distances involved, the difficulties of running machinery in remote regions and getting investment to pastoralists, it could be argued that there is a need for overarching public institutions that bridge the gap between pastoral and local manufacturing production, and between settled and mobile sectors of the population. If there is nothing between the city with its lights, and the isolated country shacks and *gers* with their candles, it is likely to be only by state regulation (such as residence permit schemes) that rural life will not be drained of its energy as young people slip away to the cities.

MARGINALISATION AND INDIGENOUS KNOWLEDGE

All the signs are of increasingly polarised social and economic fields in the
regions of Inner Asia. Inner Mongolia and Xinjiang are raw-material producing regions in relation to the fast-developing eastern seaboard of China. With
the growing economic influence of China throughout the region, Mongolia,
and even more northerly parts of Inner Asia, may begin to act as an economic
periphery to powerful Chinese urban markets. The industries and infrastructures formerly dependent on Russian expertise, fuel and spare parts are in
drastic decline. Of course, if one produces raw materials there is every reason
(in the short term) to export them. However, without investment in local
infrastructures and local manufacturing, Inner Asian economies cannot
prosper. This applies as much to Inner Asian parts of Russia and China as it
does to Mongolia. If the management of herding also continues on a path
which becomes environmentally unsustainable, the prospects for the pastoral
population of these huge regions will be bleak indeed.

In the recent past, Inner Asia was not only an economic but also a
political periphery in relation to the dominant centres of Russia and China –
the 'big brothers' of the native peoples. Therefore, in the collectivist period,
Inner Asia implemented policies originally designed to solve the problems
of Russian and Chinese society, rather than its own. The current reforms
aimed to effect a transformation into a market economy have also been
formulated with respect to Russian and Chinese society. Of course, many of
the perceived faults of the dominant societies, such as inefficiency,
bureaucratisation and lack of motivation, had taken root in Inner Asia, and
in this sense the reform efforts addressed problems that had become common
to all parts of the Chinese and Soviet empires.

Nevertheless, during the socialist period the political autonomy of
Mongolia, and to some extent Tuva, allowed for a certain amount of local
adaptation of socialist institutional models, allowing the perpetuation of
important pastoral knowledge and techniques. Indeed, Sambuu, the Chairman of the Praesidium of Mongolia published a book about herding (1956)
which was essentially a compilation of traditional wisdom. This book is still
widely consulted by herdsmen today. Unfortunately however, the example
of the Buryat regions of Russia shows that keeping such knowledge alive and
meaningful requires conscious support. Sambuu's book was republished
several times in Mongolia, but to publish a similar book in Buryatia would
have been to invite accusations of nationalist backwardness. This loss is

becoming increasingly evident to Buryat scholars, who are now seeking to reintroduce old native breeds and publish booklets about traditional pastoral methods.

We do not think, however, that a return to old methods, where they have disappeared, can possibly solve the economic problems of modern pastoralism. Our research suggests that new thinking is required related to the particular conditions of the localities of Inner Asia. On the one hand, it would be possible to strengthen those elements of the sustainable practices of the collective period which still survive and are viable locally, and on the other to use imaginatively indigenous techniques and modern technology to generate new solutions in the current economic climate. The problems may be general, but the solutions will have to be local. In the present situation, in which not only Moscow and Beijing, but also Tokyo and Washington, exert great influence on policy-makers, it is still worth pointing out that it is not always true that 'big brother' knows best.

ENVIRONMENTALISM, INTELLECTUALS AND LOCAL CULTURE

Uncertainty over the future of indigenous culture is evident. In much of the region there has been a conscious movement on the part of the educational elite to stress local and national 'traditions', emphasising and reformulating cultural elements that used to be officially denigrated. The culture of Inner Asia was closely tied to mobile pastoralism with its connotations of space and freedom of movement, and to Buddhism, associated with respect for all life-forms and the cultivation of individual and communal spirituality. Relaxation of ideological controls has allowed these ideals to form the bases for social action once again. It is remarkable that right through Inner Asia the most widespread current ritual practice is the *oboo* ceremony, which is explicitly aimed at reproducing beneficent environmental relations and has a local and folk basis. But this has occurred just as economic conditions worsen and global culture penetrates (e.g. horror videos in Buryatia, American clothing and satellite TV in Mongolia, Chinese kitsch practically everywhere). So, while some people, as in rural Tuva and Buryatia, are consciously seeking to resurrect ancient rituals in an innocent and pristine form, signifying this by wearing bits and pieces of an imagined national costume, others reject the past and are sceptical about the efficacy of traditional rites. They eagerly embrace new cults of all kinds, including fundamentalist Christianity, Bahai, etc. The situation is volatile now and many fear that the new sects in Mongolia (sometimes disguised as 'development projects') will sow the seeds of future conflicts.

The political importance of environmental issues seems likely to grow, partly because of the focus of indigenous religion on nature. We have found a high sensitivity to ecological vulnerability throughout the region. This coexists with the increasing carelessness in some sectors of the population as well as despoilation by outside interests which are often supported by the state. So the situation is one of potential social conflict.

Indigenous Inner Asian pastoral people represent their 'traditional' orientation toward surrounding nature (*baigal orchin*) as respectful and holistic. Where they constitute minorities they tend to contrast their own views to the 'exploitative' attitudes of the dominant majority ethnicity. Among herding populations environmental concerns are most deeply felt in Tuva, western Mongolia and Mongol-inhabited parts of Xinjiang (the 'western zone' of our Project), where they are associated with religious values. Elsewhere such concerns are in conflict with survival strategies, especially among young people. Old people scold them for being callous, whereas they are often just practically concerned with other matters. Nevertheless, environmental conservationism is either a nascent or an actual element in minority nationality politics in all three states. It is both a vehicle for various local interests, and an expression of aspirations. In certain areas, such as Buryatia and Ulaanbaatar, environmentalism also seems to be well understood as a potential means of linking local interests with powerful and wealthy western conservation organisations. Activism in Russia has resulted in some environmental projects being set up with neighbouring areas of Mongolia and China.[3] Public perceptions of threat to the environment have led to political protests, e.g. against the proposed Egiin Gol hydro-electric scheme in Mongolia; and there is widespread resentment of Russians and Han Chinese on whom blame for careless exploitation of the environment also tends to fall. The opposition between the Russian and Tuvan ethnic uses of natural resources is said to be one of the main causes of sporadic Tuvan uprisings in 1990-91.[4]

There is a danger that the environmental concerns of urban intellectuals, such as those who set up the projects mentioned, may not coincide with those of the pastoralists. Our research shows (Tsui 1996a) that there are certain concerns which all the studied pastoral communities hold in common in all three countries, in particular those relating to the purity of water and the reproduction of grasses and trees, while there are others which arouse more diversity of opinion and practice. This research suggests that some environmental issues are likely to strike a chord with local opinion, while others, like hunting, are more disputable. The Inner Asian beliefs can have practical effects. For example, Gomboev et al. (1996) note that the only area of non-degraded pasture in the Barguzin valley is a hill where a local spirit is worshipped and people do not take their herds to graze. Elsewhere, such as in Tuva, herding communities link strong religious beliefs with a wide range of observances (not cutting trees, regulation and avoidance of hunting, etc.). This is evidence of the close relation between indigenous cultural values and the interaction with the environment of local people. Although we do not suggest a straightforwardly causal relationship, we found that the areas where native culture is under threat (shown, for example, by a decline in the use of the indigenous language, or disappearance of native pastoralism) are also the areas where ecological problems are most severe. Examples of this are found in Chita Oblast in Russia and certain regions of Inner Mongolia.

CONCLUDING REMARKS

Finally, we return to the question of nomads. This book problematises the characterisation of 'nomads' as having an intrinsically low-technology, one-sided economy which forces them to depend on sedentary neighbours (see discussion in Khazanov 1984). It is true that historically pastoralists have often relied on neighbouring agriculturalists and cities in order to acquire goods they want, for example the eastern Mongolians' reliance on China in the 19th century. However, as Vainshtein points out (1980, see also Introduction by Humphrey), the western Mongolians and Tuvinians in the same period had quite a different and diverse economy which was largely self-reliant. Vainshtein demonstrates the existence of *indigenous* mining, metallurgy, smithing, agriculture, irrigation systems, craft technology using wood, wool and leather, as well as quite complex techniques of hunting, fishing, and reindeer-herding. We hope that our book has shown that in central steppes of Inner Asia pastoralism in itself can also be a sophisticated technology. This indicates that although the recent mechanisation mentioned in the section above does come from outside, using, developing and taking a pride in technology is not foreign to steppe culture. So to answer the question in the title: if what is imagined by 'the nomad' is the low-tech, rapacious, disorganised wanderer, then we think that this has been a rather rare character in Inner Asian history and only ever applied to a minority of the population. Maybe a few such individuals are around today. If we are talking about mobile pastoralism, on the other hand, this technique remains viable and useful in the modern age. It can be the main productive technique of a group, which would then normally engage in trade for non-pastoral products; or it can be a specialised technique in a broader repertoire. 'Nomads' of this kind are quite numerous in Inner Asia,[5] but, as our book has shown, this way of life is facing threats of many kinds.

Many pastoralists, however, have a surprisingly nonchalant ability to adapt to circumstances and live with the moment. A herder from hard-hit Argada in Buryatia said, 'I live more or less all right. I have lived like this all my life.'

When asked, 'What do you think about the reforms then?', he replied, 'What can I think? The way life turns out, that's the way you should live. We cannot change anything.' He laughed. 'A day later, everything is upside down anyway.'

Inner Asia continues to change. The history of these areas shows that the different parts of Inner Asia are not all moving in the same direction in an inexorable process of 'modernisation'. The paths followed by Chinese, Russian and Mongolian administrations have left different areas oriented towards different future social forms. There has been a return of interest in native languages and religions in Russian and to some extent Mongolian regions; a continued pressure towards linguistic and cultural assimilation in China; an economic step 'backwards' in terms of mechanisation and infrastructural provision in Mongolia and Russia; and a retention of authoritarian state socialist political control in China. Even the trends towards commercialism and the globalisation of consumption are taking different forms. However, Inner Asian peoples share a common consciousness of their intertwined history. Pastoral life is intrinsically tied to the vast grassland steppe which is common to them all, and the literature and art of the region continue to be inspired by it. Faced as they are by certain common problems and comparable experiences, we hope this study shows why these peripheral parts of larger states also constitute a separate sphere with its own concerns; in this sense, the parts can learn from each other.

Notes

Introduction

1. See Ingold 1980; Sandford 1983; Baxter and Hogg n.d.; Casimiar and Rao 1992. One anthropologist who retains the term nomadism, while discussing the myths and problems associated with the category, is Khazanov 1984.

2. Vainshtein (1980: 48) defined 'economic-cultural types' as 'economic and cultural complexes evolved through history and characteristic of peoples living under defined natural geographic conditions'. The concept is useful because the 'economic-cultural type' does not coincide with ethnic boundaries, so, for example, one might find the same type in Tuva and adjacent areas of Mongolia.

3. Small populations of Kazakhs living alongside Mongol populations in Xinjiang and Mongolia were included in the scope of the research project.

4. The Mongolian pattern, followed to varying degrees in surrounding regions, ideally employs 'the five domestic animals' (*tavan hoshuu mal*): sheep, horses, camels, cattle and goats.

5. Most grain products were acquired from neighbouring settled peoples, as were products of pottery and weaving. Indigenous artisan products included metal, leather and felt goods.

6. There were serious setbacks in this, such as during the famine in parts of China in the early 1960s.

7. The project was funded by the MacArthur Foundation (Chicago) and based at the University of Cambridge, UK.

8. We also did not include the Islamic countries of Kazakhstan and Kyrgyzstan, as our aim was to examine a geographically contiguous and relatively homogenous cultural area.

9. The ten main case-studies were supplemented by research at two secondary sites, one at Barkol in Xinjiang (China) and one at Bayantümen *sum* in Dornod *aimag*, Mongolia. For the most part the fieldwork was conducted in 1993. However, some materials from Tuva (Solchur) and Mongolia (Hovd *sum*) were collected in 1992.

10. See table 3.2 for the different state administrative hierarchies.

11. See plate 5 in Humphrey and Sneath 1996a.

12. For a discussion of Mongolian agriculture in the 1980s see Humphrey 1986.

13. For further analysis of this situation see Humphrey and Sneath 1996c.

CHAPTER 1

1. In the 17th century the wars between the Western Oirat Mongols and the central Halh forced many groups northwards into Russia, while in the early 20th century revolution and civil war impelled others to move southwards, from Russia into Mongolia and Manchuria, and later from Mongolia into Inner Mongolia.

2. Stalin's definition of nationhood included a common culture, language and territory.

3. Bulag (1998) notes the increasing 'Halh nationalism' in Mongolia which serves to distance Buryats, Oirats and especially Inner Mongols from the Halh majority in Mongolia. At the same time, movements in Buryatia and Tuva in the early 1990s, aiming to explore the possibilities of joining Mongolia, have now all but died. China, of course, has never countenanced the idea of Inner Mongolia forming close ties with other Mongol nations.

4. An eight-year initiative from 1982 to educate Xinjiang Mongols in command of the Mongol classical script had spread to 70% of cadres and urban employees and 60% of peasants and herders by the end of 1990. There were considerable difficulties in promoting the classical script, and this initiative is still continuing (Xinjiang LHCC 1991: 423).

5. Hamnigan are widely held to be long-since Mongolised or Buryatised Tungus (Evenk).

6. Confusingly, perhaps, Hovd *sum* is a district located inside Uvs *aimag*, not within the nearby *aimag* of Hovd. See table 3.2 for state administrative hierarchies.

7. It has been argued (Sneath n.d.) that a society-wide clan system was not present in the central area of present Mongolia at the time of Chinggis Khan, though there were a number of noble clans and lineages which do seem to have been eliminated by the Chinggisid state. There is no evidence that commoners had strong clan identities. It is possible that earlier states in the region had previously organised society on a patrimonial, rather than a clan, basis.

8. Religion, especially Buddhism, was tolerated to some extent by the Ulanhu regime during the 1950s and early 60s, but the Cultural Revolution (1966–72) brought a savage repression of all forms of religion.

9. We use the word shamanism for a variety of indigenous rituals and religious beliefs, dating largely from the pre-Buddhist period, and including the possibility of mediation between human and spirit worlds, carried out by a specialist medium – the shaman.

10. Budaeva, in a special report written for the project (1995), notes a similar situation in Oka. In this region in the mountainous far west of the Buryat Republic the Buryat language is strongly maintained, and religion has been revived. However, traditional culture in the form of native dress, utensils, food, jewellery, hunting rules, etc. has almost disappeared. The indigenous reindeer-herding economy, together with all the skills and techniques associated with it, has also been discontinued. Furthermore, there are virtually no people left who could revive use of such techniques. Budaeva attributes this loss to the purges, migrations of the

1920s–30s and to the Soviet suppression of native forms of economy (complex herding of yak, horses, reindeer and local breeds of cattle and sheep).

11. For example, in the use of lamas and shamans for curing disease, for rituals before long journeys, etc., and for communal festivals which mark 'Buryatness' as distinct from local Russian festivals.

12. The *oboo* is a cairn of stones where seasonal rituals are held for communal prosperity (see chapter 3).

CHAPTER 2

1. Until 1996 Sumber *sum* was part of Dornogov' *aimag*, which has since been divided to form Gov'sumber and Dornogov' *aimags*.

2. In choosing a standard for calculating stocking units, we adopted that used by local specialists in Mongolia. This gives the value of sheep as 1, goats as 0.9, cattle as 5, horses as 6, and camels as 7.

3. Not having separate figures for each species in pre-revolutionary Inner Mongolia we calculated each 'big animal' as six sheep units, and each 'small animal' as one.

4. There were 48,710 square km of cropland in 1988, which is 4.2% of the total area of Inner Mongolia, (see Longworth & Williamson, 1993, p.81). Grassland accounts for 67% of the total land area of the Inner Mongolian Autonomous Republic; however, only 75.58% of this is classed as utilisable for grazing.

5. Although Inner Mongolia has changed its boundaries several times in the intervening period, this estimate is based on a comparable area.

6. They write that of the total area of grassland (791,529 sq. km) only 75.58% is utilisable for grazing. They calculate the yearly forage yield as 91,286,657 tons. If stalks are also taken into account the total yearly forage is estimated as 107,666,000 tons. Based on this total yield they calculate a 'carrying capacity' of 70,663,000 units in sheep equivalent SSUs. In 1986 the livestock present amounted to 69,373,600 SSUs.

7. The problems include the variability of vegetation yields from year to year, the problems of not taking into account local pastoral practices (e.g. grazing behaviour of different species, succession of flocks on a given pasture), the vegetation re-growth factor, the problem of mathematical extrapolation in a highly varied landscape, the ecological characteristics of long cycles, and possible assumptions of livestock-vegetation equilibria where no such equilibria may exist.

8. In Mongolia the data were collected at the level of the *sum*; in Inner Mongolia the banner (*hoshuu*), and in Buryatia, Chita and Tuva the *raion* statistics were used. When mapping livestock density we removed areas not usable for pasture (desert, thick forest, ploughed fields, etc.), shown as white on the maps, then used the livestock numbers in small, local districts to calculate the density for each locale, so building up a map of the entire region.

9. A study of remote sensing data for 1986–88 seems to show a noticeably lower amount of vegetation in the Jirim region of Inner Mongolia than one might expect from precipitation levels. This may well reflect the intensive use of the land in

these localities. The percentage of land used for agriculture is largest in the city districts of Hohhot and Baotou, where they reach 26% and 22% respectively. Of the other leagues and prefectures the percentage of land used for agriculture is as follows: Wuhai – 2% cropland, 87% pasture; Chifeng – 9% cropland, 63% pasture; Hulun Buir – 2% cropland, 46% pasture; Hinggan – 7% cropland, 51% pasture; Jirim – 12% cropland, 76% pasture; Shilingol – 1% cropland, 96% pasture; Ulanchab – 15% cropland, 68% pasture; Ihe Jao – 2% cropland, 63% pasture; Bayannur – 5% cropland, 81% pasture; and Alashan – less than 1% cropland and 68% pasture. The Inner Mongolian Autonomous Republic total is 4% cropland and 67% pasture. See Longworth and Williamson 1993: 81.

10. Kurbatskaya's report (1993) for the MacArthur ECCIA Project gives data on pasture degradation in Tuva as a whole, indicating that our case-study site at Solchur was typical of rural regions without arable agriculture.

11. Perceived degradation in figure 2.12 is reckoned on the basis of statements by local managers.

12. An estimated 60,000 workers were unemployed in Mongolia in early 1995, in a population of 2.2 million. However, ILO (1992) estimates 108,000 actual unemployment in urban areas, and IMF estimates 135,000 in 1993 (see Odgaard 1996: 117).

13. In 1994 of the total of Mongolia's exports 27.7% went to Russia, 19% to China, 13% to Japan, and 12% to Kazakhstan (Sanders 1996: 237, quoting IMF sources).

14. The continuing use of nuclear text sites in Xinjiang has resulted in pastoralists being denied the use of considerable areas of arid pasture and the movement of local populations. This has also had an adverse effect on health in the Alashan area.

15. In Huuchin Barga County as a whole, only 30% of herders are 'nomadic' (i.e. move with the herds); all of the rest live in settled dwellings.

16. Williams (1996a: 312) discusses 'grassland policies that call upon common herders to fix moving sand dunes and check advanced wind and soil erosion processes without the benefit of investment capital or even meaningful institutional support'.

17. In Handagat (Altai) district officials said that local processing industries had lost 4.5% income in 1992 in relation to the average income of the previous five years.

18. Herders mentioned a winter stocking rate but it is not clear whether this is the county one, a local one, or some internalised picture of sustainable numbers.

CHAPTER 3

1. Banners were the main administrative units of the Manchu government in Inner Mongolia and Mongolia. They approximated in area to the present counties (banners) in Inner Mongolia. In Mongolia territories of banner size no longer exist; they were amalgamated into *aimags*, which are divided into *sum* (more numerous and mostly smaller units than the previous banners).

2. The serf households received some of the produce of the herds they tended and the arrangement could be terminated if they failed to satisfy the noble or monastic owners. So it was not that serfs were entitled to a share of the institution's property, but that, when the herds were being allocated, they would go to people of certain statuses only.

3. The 'administrative clan' (*rodovaya uprava*) in Buryat areas of Russia was in some ways similar to the banner in Mongolia. Monasteries were founded by clans, which placed their sons in them as lamas. The treasury (*jas*) of the monastery was divided into two parts, one for the institution as a whole and one to be divided among the lamas according to their religious status. Besides this, lamas had their own personal property, gifted to them by the faithful.

4. Sagja Lama (1858–1909) of the Aga Monastery is said to have owned 7,000 cows, 4,000 horses, 3,000 sheep and over 1,000 camels (Galdanova et al. 1983: 72).

5. In practice there was some conflation of the two, especially with the personal debts of Mongol princes, which were frequently paid off by payments due to the banner.

6. Leaders, however, were normally appointed from the ranks of Party members, and certain specialists were allocated to collective institutions from outside bodies such as ministries.

7. For further discussion of the household as an institution see chapter 4.

8. Soil erosion and water loss affect over 14 million hectares (or 15.7% of the total land area). Desertification continues to grow by 350,000 hectares per year. Sixty-seven of the region's total of 88 counties (banners) suffer from sandstorm damage. The human population on the grasslands of Xinjiang doubled between 1965 and 1983, while sheep carcass weights fell from an average of 19.5 kg in 1965 to 13 kg in 1983 (Wang and Bai 1991: 160).

9. Mining and industry are fast developing in some pastoral regions, e.g. in Hoboksair County, Xinjiang. However, the mining settlements, etc. are usually administratively separate from pastoral districts.

10. In Mongolia in 1996 rural companies and co-operatives (*horshoo*) owned a total of 9.7 million animals, about a third of the national herd. Erdenebaatar, private communication, 1996.

11. This city does not appear on publicly available maps. Some 2,000 Russian citizens remained in the town in 1993.

12. It was abolished by Presidential decree but was revived after protests by members. However, in the process, the Party split into around six parties of generally 'communist' leanings. The Russian Communist Party remains the strongest of these and has some support in the region of our Project, but it has never regained the governing position it had in the past.

13. In Buryatia, for example, collective and state farms were set up in such a way that they were either 'Buryat' or 'Russian', with a few members of other nationalities. This is despite the fact that in Buryatia as a whole Buryats, Russians and others live interspersed.

14. According to a private farmer in Argada, V. Dandurov, aged 57, young people used to be guaranteed 120 days work per year in the collective. Now (1993) many young people cannot find work.

15. They leave the collective from a legal point of view. Physically the private herder or farmer continues to live in the farm settlement and the privatised land consists of patches within the farm boundary.

16. *Buryatia,* no 30, 17th Feb 1994. This newspaper is the daily publication of the Supreme Soviet and the Soviet of Ministers of the Buryat Republic.

17. It is not always clear whether enterprises described as 'joint stock companies', 'co-operatives' , 'collectives' and 'unions of peasant farmers' are (in my terms) collectives or associations. Each of the Russian terms in fact covers a range of type of organisation.

18. Farmers allotted ploughing land by voucher, but unable to use that land, may get a share of the produce if the land is worked by another group. However, there is no guarantee that they will actually be paid their share of grain, as the legal situation is completely unclear.

19. For example V. Dandurov, a private farmer of Argada, Buryatia, had an association linking his farm with six others in the neighbourhood. The association is informal and operates only for particular tasks.

20. The associations and private farmers held land in a variety of ways: 'collectively', 'use for indefinite period', 'use for life', 'leased' and 'in proprietorship'. The information on Kurumkan was collected for the Project by members of Raleigh International.

21. Private traders prefer to buy more profitable goods than bulky agricultural products. Traders may travel to the countryside to buy meat, but not from private farmers, whose prices are clearly higher than those of collective workers selling 'a bit on the side'. Besides, the traders are irregular and unreliable.

22. In the Argada farm several people reported that they were made to become private farmers against their will. They had no choice in the land allocated to them.

23. The total number of workers before the change was 476. The reformed collective seems to have been relatively successful ('self-sufficient', according to its Director) in 1993. It had formed itself in more numerous, smaller and more flexible production teams than the earlier brigades.

24. B. Uskeev, Director of the Kharbatskii Joint Enterprise (*sovmestnoe khozyaistvo*), Tunka *raion,* Buryatia.

25. Though general (market) prices have been freed, prices paid by state organisations to farms are set by the Minister of Agriculture in Buryatia (summer 1994).

26. In early 1995 farms in the Hori region of Buryatia received 200 roubles per litre of milk from the regional dairy, but milk was sold for over 1000 roubles per litre in Ulan-Ude (Bazarzhapov 1995).

27. The following account is based on case-studies in three districts in Xinjiang and two in Inner Mongolia: 1) Handagat district, Altai county, Altai prefecture, Xinjiang (Kazakh, Urianghai and Han); 2) Sarq'ok district, Barkol county, Hami prefecture, Xinjiang (Kazakh, Urianghai and Han); 3) Hosh Tolgoi district, Hoboksair county, Tacheng prefecture, Xinjiang (Oirad Mongol and Han); 4)

Chinggel Bulag district, Abag county, Shilingol prefecture, Inner Mongolia (Abag Mongol); and 5) Hargant district, Huuchin Barga county, Hulun Buir prefecture, Inner Mongolia (Barga Mongol). In all of these places the institutions were of two basic types: a) state, and b) households. State institutions were departments of the district and county governments. However, the Project also collected information in neighbouring districts on 'state farms' under separate jurisdiction, and these will also be described below.

28. 'Pastoral regions' here does not include Tibet, which has had a rather different history (see for example Goldstein, Beall and Cincotta 1990).

29. In Xinjiang the work-force for these projects was mostly brought in from elsewhere in China and mostly concentrated in cities (Yuan 1990). However, in Inner Mongolia in-migration has been more diffuse, going both to cities and the countryside (Ma 1993).

30. This confirms political decisions and laws of the Party and Government.

31. This debates and ratifies decisions of the Party and Government.

32. In Hargant *sum*, Huuchin Barga banner, Inner Mongolia in 1993 there were 60 members of the Party out of a total *sum* population of 1,412.

33. Huuchin Barga banner (county) in Hulun Buir prefecture, Inner Mongolia, for example has the following sub-divisions: eight *sum* (districts), of which six are herding based and two agricultural; two towns; and three state farms. One state farm specialises in pig rearing and has 430,000 head. The other two specialise in milk production and have 180,000 head between them.

34. For example, in Otog Front banner in Yeke Juu league (prefecture) in Inner Mongolia a large amount of natural gas has been discovered. Without the knowledge of the local people and local government the central state authorities built underground pipes across their territory, transferring the gas to the neighbouring Ningxia Hui Autonomous Region where a Ministry-controlled refinery is located. The tension concerns the compensation to Otog Front banner for removal of 'its' resources, and also arises because the banner itself wants to manage the industry. This banner is one of the 100 counties designated by the state as being the poorest in China. There is considerable unemployment. The population is one third Mongol (U. E. Bulag, pers. comm.).

35. A sub-district has a centre, with administration buildings, a meeting hall, and some dwellings. However, in many places (e.g. Hargant) these facilities have closed as political controls have relaxed and the herders relate directly with the district (see Yan 1992).

36. HK News Service, 26th Nov 1994.

37. The Chinese reforms were launched in 1979, but the date at which they were effective in rural pastoralist areas varies in different regions.

38. The cost to herders was less than one third of market prices at the time (Handagat, Altai, Xinjiang), in others the distribution was free (Chinggel Bulag, Inner Mongolia).

39. About 60% of herders were able to pay half or over of the sum required straight away, while others will take years to pay back the credit.

40. 'Responsibility may be acquired or required, and however it might be allocated, assumed or imposed, appropriated or volunteered, its meanings can be variously defined as claim, obligation, duty or gift. That is, responsibility involves an exchange that may simultaneously endow, enact, enable and entitle and which is rarely equal in authority or permanent in form and content. Rather, its devolution or distribution involves agency and the exercise of power with shifting contests and alliances...' (Croll 1994: 17).

41. A proportion of the taxes is paid by the *gachaa* to the district (*sum*). In Hargant (Inner Mongolia) herders do not pay taxes on land, but only on livestock and it is paid directly to the *sum*. The money from taxes is used for a variety of purposes, including subsidies to very poor families.

42. There are 29 such state farms along the Hulun Buir border with Russia. All belong to Hailar Agricultural and Pastoral Farm Administrative Bureau. There is another such Bureau in arable areas called the Great Hinggan Mountain Agricultural Farm Administration Bureau.

43. For example, the Bureau Leader could offer a direct rail link to Beijing for his business contracts. He sent his children abroad to study, using Bureau funds. The Bureau office is the tallest and most impressive building in the border town of Manzhouli.

44. In Inner Mongolia the leaders in the Bureaux include both Han Chinese and Mongolians.

45. The Red Star State Farm was set up in 1952. It has 1,460 workers and 193,333 hectares of land, of which 1,653 is arable and the rest grassland. It has (1993) 29,000 sheep, 3,900 goats, 1,200 cattle, 2,180 horses, 850 pigs and 260 camels as public property, and the herders owned 1,560 sheep, 680 goats, 420 cattle, 228 horses, 150 pigs and 28 camels as private property. It pays an annual tax of 3–5% of profits. The other districts within the county are Sarq'ok (herding), the Red Hill State farm (farming, forestry and herding), and the Yiwu Horse Farm (owned by the army).

46. The farm came under pressure both from its members, who wanted the animals distributed to them as elsewhere, and from the central authorities. After a major newspaper in Urumqi criticised the farm for 'not carrying out the policies of the Party and government', the leaders submitted. They sold the animals on instalment credit. But after a year they discovered it would be impossible to recover the debts. Some herders (3–5%) had immediately sold the animals and spent the money, and most of the others 'refused to repay a penny'. What was worse, the herders mixed all their livestock in one herd and gave up herding methods that had produced fine quality animals in the past. So in 1986 a meeting was held in which it was decided, by a majority, that the decision of 1984 was rescinded and all the animals were recollectivised, with the exception of those that had been sold or originally belonged to individuals.

47. The bonus is 10–20% of the surplus; the fine is 5–40% of the annual wages.

48. 'Vanguard' state farms were sited on especially good quality land.

49. For details of the complex laws involved, see Longworth and Williamson (1993: 289–90). In theory, every year the land is inspected and quotas are given to each

family. If they exceed the designated numbers, they should sell or kill the excess animals, and may have to pay fines.

50. It should be noted that 'traditional' Inner Asia pastoralism is conceived of as involving access to most, if not all, of the five species of domestic livestock (camels, horses, cattle, sheep and goats). However, in the pre-collective period there was also important specialisation, with some pastoralists herding large single-species herds for the rich and for herd-owning institutions. This point is discussed further in chapter 6.

51. Handagat was wealthy compared to its neighbours. In the Altai region the average cash income of herding households in 1992 was apparently 8,256 yuan, and in the Altai County it was reported as 9,072 yuan.

52. There were 3–5% of such households in Sarq'ok.

53. In Hoboksair people without work, both Mongols and Kazakhs, had been given employment in salt mines and coal mines. They could not adapt to the life, and most soon returned to scratch a living in the villages.

54. In West Ujumchin, studied by Hell and Quéré, only 30% of households had hay-cutting machinery (1993: 267).

55. The existing pasture-holders often do not return land when old people die. Also, as mentioned earlier, the district is required to maintain positions for those who leave temporarily. Both practices cause pressure on availability of pastures for allocation.

56. U. E. Bulag, personal communication.

57. As social organisation in Mongolia is covered in some detail in chapter 4, this chapter gives only a brief account.

58. This may have been the case historically, since the large proportion of males entering Buddhist monasteries was a factor in the low rate of growth of the Mongolian population until the 1940s (Humphrey 1978: 137).

59. The district and the farm were formally distinct, with different functions, but the officials could overlap.

60. In each sub-district there are four posts paid by the district: the *bag* leader, a doctor, a vet, and a postman.

61. The total number of households in Bayantümen was 814, of which around 400 were not herders but administrators, artisans, retired, unemployed, teachers, doctors, occasional labourers, guards, etc.

62. Evidence of the malleability of such institutions in Mongolia can be seen from the Hugjil Kompan in Hovd *sum*, Uvs *aimag*. The *kompan* is based on a former *negdel*, but the old division into brigades with settled centres has gone. The brigades were permanently serviced by six or seven households of officials, but now the staff have moved off to herd their own animals. *Kompan* members only come together in the winter and otherwise are distributed in various *nutag*s (home pastures) where they form temporary neighbourhood groups (*hoshoo*).

63. In some parts of Mongolia whole districts have privatised completely and there are no companies.

64. See chapter 6 on the high prestige of horse-herding in Mongolian culture.

65. In Buryatia in 1992–3 accidents rose by 26%, killings rose by 25%, suicides rose by 35%, and deaths from alcoholism rose by 85%.

66. A despairing article by the head of district government in Onokhoi (Buryatia) recounts how he dreads the 1994–5 winter, because he does not have funds to pay for the fuel for the most essential need of all, the central heating system of the village (Nikolaev 1994: 2). The district used to be the 'child' of the local logging and wood factory. But that enterprise has virtually closed: in 1994 it had no money and paid its remaining workers in furniture ('Take it, sell it, but survive'). The factory also tried to obtain food for its workers by barter. Receiving no tax from this factory, the district head approached the Ministry of Finance of the Buryat Republic. The Ministry official replied that he had prepared the necessary documents on finance for communal housing and sent them to Moscow, but 'there was no actual money'. In September 1994 the district head was preparing to approach his Deputy to the Republic Parliament, and he warned though the newspaper that, if he was unsuccessful, in the next few days people should find or build stoves, cut firewood, and construct chimneys through their windows, because that would be the only way to save themselves from the winter cold. In December 1994 temperatures reached -40°C in Buryatia.

67. See Griffin 1994: 73–4. See also Randall 1993: 209–29.

68. A 3–5 household group was also officially instituted in Handagat, Altai. The households own livestock individually, but their allocated pastures are close and this allows them to co-operate in some herding tasks, hay-making, etc. The *hoton* is further discussed in chapter 4.

69. In 1992–3 petrol was obtainable at high market prices which few people could afford. A ration of cheaper petrol at state prices was distributed to districts, and it was eagerly awaited. In China this petrol was sold to each household on an equal share basis, but in Russia it was acquired by contacts and/or bribes. Since then the price of petrol has risen greatly in Mongolia and it is now generally possible to buy it without the intercession of officials.

70. Government officials, as opposed to the heads of enterprises, are appointed, not elected.

71. In Handagat the leading district officials on average earned around 14,800 yuan in 1992 as against 21,600 for herders; in Hosh Tolgoi, officials' income was 11,000 as against 9,600 among the herders; in Chinggel Bulag the figures were 8,200 and 20,500; and in Hargant 8,000 and 24,000. Of course leaders also had other benefits, such as use of state housing and transport.

72. Shue (1988: 152) suggests that the reforms in the interest of economic efficiency may not result in increased freedoms for the rural people but in a reconsolidation and reinvigoration of state power in new social groups. Our research, admittedly in very limited areas, does not entirely confirm this hypothesis. The present rural leaders are socially linked to the pre-reform era cadres and have not really transformed themselves into economic supremos, for all the efforts of some of them. Meanwhile herders do seem to have enhanced freedoms, since some of them are able to by-pass the district by making independent contacts with cities and higher level bureaucrats.

73. This intensive use of land may not be environmentally damaging. Gomboev et al. (1996) suggest that it results in declining productivity of the hayfields. However, earlier native technologies improved hayfields by using animal dung as fertiliser. Probably, the usefulness of this method depends on the siting of the hayfields. A moist riverine site, or irrigation, was required to make the native *utug* hayfield flourish.

74. In Kurumkan and elsewhere in the Barguzin valley private herders did say they were trying to revive the *utugs*.

75. It was difficult for the few officials to patrol such a huge area. People were effectively prevented from taking their animals to graze there. But, every kilometre or so there were squatter hay-makers living in makeshift tents, and the district leader drove from place to place to order them off (with little success).

CHAPTER 4

1. B. Gomboev, 1994, personal communication.

2. It should be noted, however, that the situation is very different in large Siberian cities, where families tend to be smaller. In some cases entrepreneurs would like to avoid employing kin in their new businesses, and prefer impersonal relationships with business partners. There are often strong family and social pressures not to do this, however.

3. This web, although with different colours and characteristics, appears to have long been a fundamental aspect of social organisation throughout Inner Asia, but it is understood much less clearly than the formal economic and political structures that have been created by the different governments of the region.

4. Three of the nine interviewed pastoral families in each case study site. All those hiring labour in this way were relatively wealthy, being classified locally as either 'rich' or of 'middle income.' They all paid about 150 yuan a month to their hired herders.

5. The terms have different connotations, the term *ail ger* approximates to the English term 'household', *am örh* is mostly used to mean the formally registered household members, the term *ger bül* is often used to mean immediate kin or 'nuclear' family.

6. The celebration of the lunar new year is known as *tsagaan sar* in Mongolian, *tsagaalgan* in Buryat Mongolian, and *shagaa* in Tuvan.

7. Radcliffe-Brown (1977[1940]: 190) described the social network as the 'set of social relations which exist in reality'. Since then those concerned with network analysis, such as Lomnitz, have linked it with reciprocity and made much use of the concept of 'the reciprocity network'. This is not a social group or institution; rather it is 'a social field defined by an intense flow of reciprocal exchange between neighbours' (Lomnitz 1977: 209). I wish to decouple the concepts of network and reciprocity, and so throughout this chapter my use of the term conforms with Radcliffe-Brown's early definition.

8. An analysis based on 'reciprocal' relations (generalised or restricted) will not, I think, accurately reflect the nature of the bonds marked by the transfers of assistance and gifts. It is the obligation implicit in the relationship that is crucial. These obligations are mutual, but the transfers that they engender are not necessarily reciprocal.

9. Aberle (1962: 17) also mentions the 'strongly nepotistic nature' of the administration.

10. In Kalgan Gillmore (1893: 168) could not buy camels for any price, but had to wait until a Mongol friend arrived who could use personal links to find some. Elsewhere (p. 89) he notes the large number of acquaintances of a lama who was travelling with him, and how the lama felt obliged to bring them all presents from his stay in Urga. He also notes (p, 168) that lamas in a distant monastery relied upon connections with certain pastoralists and were at pains to cultivate them.

11. Among the interviewed households in Chinggel Bulag and Hargant the majority of parental couples had three or more children, and families with four or five children were still not uncommon. See Zhang 1996: 72. The 1990 regulations allow Mongolian rural families two children, and a third if the first two are girls; one more child than the Han.

12. This wording comes from the Mongolian term (*süreg tavih*) for placing herds in this way.

13. The money payment in Sumber shown in figure 4.3 is explained by the presence of one *tögrög* millionaire (a scrap-metal dealer) in the *sum*, who had large herds kept for him by paid workers.

14. i.e. more distant than nephews, nieces and cousins.

15. It is interesting to note that households in the Sumber and Gigant case-studies, which show relatively high numbers of agnatic kin listed as those relied upon from outside the household, are not strongly virilocal, as one might expect. In the Gigant study data there are recorded five virilocal and five uxorilocal households, in the Sumber study only one of each. The other residential groups were neolocal or included non-kin. This suggests that where agnates do not live adjacently they nevertheless supply a great deal of help to one another.

16. It is also interesting to note that the sites with the highest proportion of close affinal kin are Handagat and Solchur, linguistically Turkic regions, which also seem to have more extended and joint family residential groups.

17. However, the sites where clans seem to be of greatest importance, Hosh Tolgoi, Hargant, Hovd *sum* and Handagat, do not seem to have significantly different responses from the other case-studies, and the areas where clans appear to be essentially absent, Sumber, Chinggel Bulag and Argada, also present no clear differences from the other sites.

18. In this case this is taken to mean cash income as gained from salaries and sales. It does not include the value of home produce that is consumed by the household. These figures are slightly different from earlier analyses, as they have been generated using more complete data on the total cash annual income of the households concerned.

19. See chapter 3, table 3.4, for a comparative overview of the local ratios of village and pastoral households.

20. Twenty of the 23 studied households were composed of a nuclear family.

21. The 'norm' specified a certain number of livestock of a specific type for each herding unit, number of live births, surviving young, weight to be achieved by a certain date, wool per sheep, milk per cow, and so forth. The exact levels of the norms varied from region to region (for the Tuvan case, see Humphrey 1989). The present leases specify similar levels, but do not specify quite so many targets.

22. Mongolia is a very diverse country, and residential patterns differ. In the Gobi part of the country, for instance, the *hot-ail* is usually smaller than in wetter regions, usually being composed of one or two *gers*. In the central and northern regions the encampment is usually larger.

23. One of these, however, included non-kin and so could not be classified as a lone nuclear family in figure 4.14.

24 The data from other case-study sites is inconclusive on this point, however, and no comparable trend is detectable in the data we have from the other studies, considering the low sample sizes.

25. Of the five *ails* composed of more than a single *ger*, there was one with affinal relations and one with agnatic. The other three were made up of unrelated families, and one with an unrelated single individual.

26. A similar trend was found in the other case-study sites in China. Both Mongol and Kazakh rural populations tend to have much larger families than urban families of either ethnicity. One of the reasons for this is that, as in Inner Mongolia, those with official jobs and those living in the town or city areas are more subject to the government regulations limiting the number of children.

27. The *hot* also has an official head – usually the senior male relative. This is an position officially registered by the *gachaa* local government.

28. In 1991 the *gachaa* issued the Grassland Certificates, stating how much land was allocated to each *hot*, and the location of it. This figure was arrived at in different ways in different *gachaas* – sometimes based on the number of privatised livestock, the number of adults, or the number of household members. In the best studied *gachaa* each *hot* was allocated 1300 *mu* (86.7 hectares) per person, including children, plus one *mu* for each of their animals.

29. One herding household, for example, that of 41 year-old Bold, was originally allocated land next to a Chinese family and shared animal sheds with them. A deal was struck so that the Chinese family moved away and now stays all-year-round in the autumn pastures that Bold had been allocated, while the Mongolian and his brothers stay together on the combined pasture at the spring site.

30. Qi Xiao-hong, 1994, personal communication.

31. Only one of the nine pastoral families interviewed had no *ger*, seven had access to both *gers* and buildings, and only one had *gers* but no house.

32. The average static household size was 4.83, while the average mobile household size was only 3.78. The number of households in a settled *hot* was just 2.33, the number in a mobile *hot* was more than twice as many – 4.86. It should be stressed,

however, that the officially registered *hot*s do not always correspond to the residential groups which, as noted above, may vary.

33. It appears that this level of concentration of the pastoral population, with relatively large clusters of kin (and others), is a relatively recent development in this region. It is certainly a contrast to the earlier patterns reported by Simukov (1935: 100–104) for the northern edges of the Gobi, where *hot-ail* sizes are traditionally small.

34. The hair-cutting ceremony, found over most of Inner Asia, is a celebration of the entry of the child into social life. The effective size of an individual's network depends, to a large extent, on their local importance. If the haircutting ceremony is for the grandchild of a local official, for example, then it is likely to be well attended.

35. This form of payment seems to have a long history in Mongolian rural society, and could be described as 'traditional'. In the Sumber case-study site where I carried out research there had been a widespread practice of herding animals for rich owners before collectivisation. The poor often relied upon such arrangements for their subsistence.

36. The *arabat* can be translated as 'clan' because all genealogical links are not recalled, but members are considered to be descended from a common ancestor. The *arabat* are nominally patrilineal and exogamous. Affines can be incorporated into the clan genealogy, but those who are considered to be related by marriage to the clan are known to be 'second-best'. The depth of most of the clans is around eight generations, this being the genealogical time since the families returned to Xinjiang from the Kalmyk regions on the Volga. It is interesting to note how similar this term is to *arban*, an administrative unit of a nominal ten families that probably dates back to the 13th century.

37. This is seen as a labour-saving practice as the ewes will not suckle the strange lambs and so milk is retained for milking while labour is saved by the unification of the lambs with the adult herd.

38. Simukov uses the term *hoton* which today is largely interchangeable with the term *hot-ail* (1933: 22–3). Simukov also mentions that the term 'khot-ail', was sometimes used, and I have included this term in brackets as it is more widely used in Mongolia today than *hot* or *hoton*.

39. Simukov (1933) suggests that the reason that poor households were dependent upon rich 'patron' families was not just their need for food, even if they could provide this for themselves; they were often reliant on richer households for the use of draft animals. In addition there were occasional needs arising for various religious and medical expenses which the poor could not pay, and would expect help in these matters from their rich relatives or patron.

40. The influence of property on residential forms is well documented. In pre-revolutionary China, for example, the poor rural households tended to be composed of stem families, while the rich tended to have extended family residential groups, with the conjugal couple living with most or all of their married sons and their families. See Fei, Hsiao-Tung and Chih-I Chang (1948).

41. There are some indications that in Inner Mongolia many young families tend to herd livestock that their parents continue to own rather than inherit livestock on marriage. This may be another reason for Inner Mongolian residential groupings being larger than in other parts of Inner Asia. However, as residence is a flexible manifestation of underlying social relations it need not directly reflect the larger size of property-owning family corporations.
42. See the graphs throughout this chapter.

CHAPTER 5

1. This chapter is based on a paper written in collaboration with Balzhan Zhimbiev. (see Humphrey and Zhimbiev 1995). Zhimbiev's collaboration is warmly acknowledged, especially in relation to the formulation of 'types of living complexes' and the conceptual model of the composition of possible settlements.
2. There is a traditional point of view according to which the Buryats and other 'nomadic peoples' learned agriculture from the Russians from the end of the 17th century onwards, after Buryatia had entered the Russian empire. Our opinion is that what was learned was a certain technology of peasant farming, but not agriculture itself. The Buryats had an earlier indigenous agriculture using irrigation (Humphrey 1983).
3. Forms of land-use by Buryats in this period were not fixed, nor identical over the whole of Buryatia, but varied according to political, economic and technological conditions, see Humphrey 1979.
4. This chapter deals only with sedentarisation of herders, not with the history of monasteries, trading towns, or fortresses.
5. Stereotypes of the Siberian Russian peasantry are also called into question by our material. It is interesting to note that the living complex of Russian peasants is widely supposed to have consisted only of the single, settled *izba* (cottage), i.e. type Stat 1, whereas in fact at the end of the 19th century around 10% of households also had, besides their house in the village, another house in the 'winter quarters' (distant settlements used for pasturing livestock and also used during winter hunts, i.e. type Stat 2).
6. In the past the people of Sumber also used pens for livestock, but these were made of dried packed dung (*hörzön*) and did not have a roof like the present sheds. The old ones were much simpler and less of an investment.
7. Felt tents, and tents covered with reeds rather than felt, are used for *otor* and also for short periods spent cutting hay (*hadlang*).
8. Many Dashbalbar herders now operate with a four-season pasturing regime, possibly under Halh Mongolian influence.
9. The people of Solchur keep a few pigs, perhaps under Russian influence and because they are the most efficient way for village-dwelling non-herders to obtain meat. However, for some reason, not a single household keeps chickens.
10. However, it is rather distant from the highest administrative level (the link to Beijing).

11. Hovd *sum* has greater trade relations with its erstwhile 'friendly socialist brother' Tuva than with China.

12. In Mongolia a recent study showed that 56.8% of the population lives in the district centre in the forest-steppe region, 40.4% in the steppe region, and 53.1% in the gobi region (Shombodon 1996: 213).

13. All republic and province level centres have airports. However planes are used infrequently by rural people because there are few regular services and they are expensive.

14. Although Gigant collective farm at Novaya Zarya and Dashbalbar in Mongolia are not far from railways as the crow flies, the nearest stations are in different administrative counties. Respondents did not mention using the railways, but frequently complained of the lack of petrol, broken machines, bad roads, marshy conditions, etc. when using cars. They said their remoteness made it difficult to sell goods and that all incoming goods were expensive. The line closest to Dashbalbar was used mostly for freight and military purposes rather than passengers.

15. Sumber had a better power supply than average for Mongolia because there was an electricity station nearby. Chinggel Bulag seems to have been worse off than many parts of Inner Mongolia, as it had only 5 hours electricity per day in winter and 3 hours in summer. Around half the herders in Chinggel had TVs, but they could only watch one station (a local Mongolian-language station) and then only if they had a generator.

16. In townships in China there may be more than one school, with differences in fees and in the quality of teaching.

17. Police presence in China effectively prevents widespread public appearance of gangs.

18. In this gangs are different from the historically earlier phenomenon of 'bandits', which tended to operate in the countryside.

19. 'State shops' in the Russian context refers to shops run by the former state retail co-operative association (*prodsoyuz*). In recent years some collective farm shops functioned almost to isolate the community, since they operated with coupons not money, and the coupons were given instead of wages to members of the farm. Since not all inhabitants of the district centre are members of the collective, this meant that the shop no longer functioned as a universal and equal source for the whole community. By 1996 collective farms no longer maintained such internal shops.

20. In Solchur 76.7% of the population lives in the district centre, yet the herding families are mobile (average 70 km migrations per year). By contrast, in relatively 'non-urbanised' Dashbalbar only 40.5% of the population lives in the centre, yet the average total migrations per household in a year is only 32.2km.

21. It is worth noting that Hargant in 1992 also had a sizeable floating population of around 1,300 temporary workers who were not registered in the district and not included in figure 5.9. Many of these were drawn in by the seasonal hay-harvest work. We were not able to include them in the 'district centre'/'rural' calculation as it is not clear where they live.

22. The biggest problem with pastures in Dashbalbar is wildfires, which local residents say are caused by carelessness and children playing. Although wildfire does not cause long-term pasture damage, the local people spoke of it as a problem.
23. *Arjaan* is the Tuvinian equivalent of *arshan* in Mongolian.
24. *vaa* is the Tuvinian equivalent of *oboo* in Mongolian.
25. As Williams (1996b: 687) writes about Inner Mongolia, 'rangelend restructuration has rendered much indigenous ecological knowledge superfluous'.

CHAPTER 6

1. Western Mongolia, for example, appears to have a long history of crop cultivation alongside mobile pastoralism, as does Tuva (see Vainshtein 1980: 146).
2. There has been much discussion as to the applicability of the term 'feudal' to describe Mongolia under the Manchus. The matter has been hotly argued in Soviet literature, and is neatly summarised by Gellner (1988) in *State and Society in Soviet Thought*. I find 'feudal' an acceptable term because I consider the key criteria of feudalism to be enfiefment, the division between commoners and nobility, and a legal system which tied commoners to land administered by the enfiefed lord; all these conditions existed in pre-revolutionary Mongolia. However, as a full evaluation of the suitability of the term would require an entire book, it seems reasonable for the purposes of this debate to accept Bawden's (1968) point that 'feudal' is a useful shorthand to describe the stratified social order.
3. Sanjdorj (1980: 1) takes a Marxist line and states that in the 16th and 17th centuries 'the land ... was the property of the feudal classes'; this may obscure the way in which the ultimate rights over land was vested in the emperor, and the *hoshuu* was administered in his name by the *Zasag noyan*.
4. Banner officials did not always have their commands obeyed without question, however. This is illustrated by an example of the difficulty with which customary grazing rights were changed by banner officials in 19th century. A noble from another banner was awarded rights to land. He was driven off and it is probable that this was because, as an outsider, he had little influence among the locals. (Bawden 1968: 90–1).
5. Cited by Natsagdorj (1967: 267) and also referred to by Bawden (1968: 89).
6. The *bag* was the usual secular sub-division, the *otog* was the sub-unit used in the ecclesiastical districts.
7. Commoners were given permission to leave their banner on occasion, e.g. for state corvee duties.
8. It also seems that there was some notion of a man's allotment of land (*ere-in gazar*) and there are records of an amount of territory described as 'land for fifteen men' being allocated to an official in 1805 (Natsagdorj 1967: 268). But it seems most likely that this allotment was entirely nominal, not that each man of a banner was allocated a standard amount of land. Indeed we do not even know if this 'land for fifteen men' refers to pasture or land for farming.

9. That the 'feudal' control of land by the banner officials continued unchanged into the period of the Bogd Khan government is evidenced by legal petitions to the Bogd that mention cases such as that which follows: 'Zandan, Damdin and Little Khaltar were punished under the pretext that they had lived in a place that the Jasag [banner prince] had forbidden' (Rasidondug and Veit 1975: 142).

10. According to informants' accounts these arrangements were largely informal and broadly similar in Mongolia and Inner Mongolia. The herding household retained a share of the animal produce, in some cases half, and supplied the owner with produce or animals upon request.

11. Such as the *Ulaan tölövlögöö* ('red [economic] plan').

12. This was typified by that found in the Ulaangom region, apparently.

13. Simukov (1936) does not use this name, but rather the term that locals continued to use – the *hoshuu* of Lamyn Gegen, which was the title of the lamaist head of the monastery that also bore this name. Brown and Onon's map of the Bogd Khan period (Shirendev et al. 1976: 880) names this as the banner of the subjects of Erdene Bandid Hutagt (Gegen is a title rather than the name of a particular Hutagt). Their map for 1925 gives the new (secular) name of the district as Bayanzürh Uulyn Hoshuu. Today the territory of the *hoshuu* is included in six *sums* of Bayanhongor *aimag*: Bayangov', Bayanlig, Bogd, Jinst, Ölziit, and Erdenetsogt.

14. In the pre-collective period the actual herding of animals seems to have been done by flexible combinations of individual households, the poorer ones tending to cluster about richer families, in a relationship that can, I think, be described using the term 'patron-client' bonds.

15. See Simukov 1936: 49–55.

16. The location of their summer pastures is a speculation on my part, but seems logical in that there are some seasonal rivers in that region and summer is both the most rainy period and the time when livestock drink most.

17. This is actually the habitual form of the Mongolian verb *nuuh* (to change pastures, or to move around) Simukov seemed to think that the term *nudeg* was the name of a group of formerly monastery herders who made long annual movements.

18. In the pre-collective period one of the characteristics of noble and rich families was their ownership of large numbers of horses. The notion of maximising and subsistence modes, suggests that this ownership pattern would be compatible with a maximising mode, because the larger animals – the horse in particular – are able to move more rapidly and can be grazed on more pasture. Cattle were less mobile, as is evidenced by the monastery's cattle-herders staying in the Hangai. For comparable practices in the collective period see Humphrey and Zhimbiev 1995.

19. Sandorj suggests that in effect Mongolia had virtually become an economic periphery of China. Huge numbers of animals were exported to China, probably much more than 2 million sheep units a year (Sanjdorj 1980: 91).

20. It could be argued that this was the product of the historically unprecedented incorporation of Mongolia into the Qing polity and economy, and that pre-Qing

Mongolian elites did not have a comparable position in the pastoral economy. It is worth noting, however, that as long ago as the Chinggisid period Mongolian aristocrats owned enormous herds, and Ibn Battuta noted the active horse trade from Mongol herdlords on the southern Russian steppes to India (Spuler 1972: 183).

21. The monasteries were very powerful economic institutions, involved with trade and usury (Sanjdorj 1980: 100).

22. 'Placed' animals were those which were given into the care of herder households under obligation to supply certain products and offspring to the owners.

23. In agrarian and less extensive land-use systems, where there has been individual private ownership of land, there has usually been the specialisation of land-use, so that a given piece of land will be used for a particular purpose. It seems that in the pre-collective pastoral economy one could typify the specialisation in terms of strategies, or systems of land-use. The same area might be used by different specialists in different ways, some through grazing small flocks and herds all year round, and some by grazing large herds for a short period.

24. This is confirmed by Vreeland's description of an ecclesiastical district near Uliastai in the 1920s. Vreeland (1954: 43, 89) mentions that wealthy families made long movements into the highlands in summer, while the poor tended to stay all year in the vicinity of the river Zavhan, and he also notes the importance of poor families who acted as informal servants of the rich.

25. Asad considers the essential characteristics of these two modes to be that one is essentially subsistence-oriented (the free nomad) while the other is more comparable to an incipient capitalist mode, with hired labour and privately owned land. The Schneiders' work on Sicilian joint farms – where the rich and groups of brothers make use of the economy of scale of pooling their herds – also seems to be an interesting parallel (Schneider and Schneider 1976: 75).

26. Isaac Mazonde argues that in Botswana, communal lands were controlled by 'chiefly authority which had regulated grazing patterns in the commons before and during the colonial era' (p. 182). The Botswanan aristocracy, the 'cattle barons' realised that their continued position rested on 'greater accumulation' of cattle. See Mazonde 1987:. 182–7.

27. In the 13th century Batu Khan's entire *ordu* (camp and mobile capital) made a huge migration up and down the Volga. One could argue that the steppe polity, modelled as it was on household-centred notions of authority, conceived of wealth as the herds of the central authority, who had servants and vassals to herd them. Having the political authority to make use of all the land of the Volga region, Batu Khan simply did so, moving up and down the river, grazing-off grass to maintain and increase his vast herds. This suggests that Batu Khan (and by implication other steppe authorities) alongside 'tax-farming' the existing (Turkic) herding population, and extracting some surplus this way, actually generated a huge entourage (a colossal extension of his household) that was mobile, extracting vegetation resources directly by grazing-off his subjects' pasture as it passed. For a description of Batu Khan's *ordu* see Fletcher 1991.

28. It could be supposed that the elite were able to makes use of particularly good areas, which had a micro-climatic variation great enough so that they could move relatively little within a small locality.

29. Shombodon (1996: 230) notes the specialisation of pastoral production employed by Mongolian emperors, kings and monasteries. He is also of the opinion that the pre-revolutionary and early pre-collective patterns of land-use was based upon the optimum use of natural conditions. He points out that after collectivisation social, educational and medical services became very important constraints on pastoral practice and land-use.

30. Collective farm (*negdel*) centres were often located at the sites of former monasteries, indeed sometimes constructed of the very same bricks.

31. Sanjdorj (1980: 91) notes that in the late 19th century Chinese traders were taking 25,000 horses, 10,000 cows, and 250,000 sheep from the area of Ih Hüree alone every year. This represents about 0.45 million sheep units. Considering that Uliastai and Hovd would have probably been engaged in comparable but smaller amounts of export trade and southerly regions are unlikely to have traded with China via Ih Hüree, I think it safe to assume that the total export was more than twice that of the Ih Hüree figure.

32. During the Second World War Mongolia exported many livestock to Russia to help the war effort.

33. See Mongolian SSO 1993: 45, 82. I estimate the total state procurement to be 6.3 million sheep units using the average live weight of each species of livestock procured by the state in 1980 (Mongolian SSO 1981: 221). Using the same average ratio between tons of meat and sheep units I estimate that exports represented 1.72 million sheep units of cattle, sheep and goats; adding the 0.38 million sheep units for the exported horses gives the 2.1 million figure.

34. In their 1989 volume *Bügd Nairamdah Mongol Ard Ulsyn Malchdyn Nuudel,* and this largely corresponds with the models of pastoral movement described in the *Ündesnii Atlas* (MAS 1990).

35. The first two movement systems were classified together as variants of the larger Hangai-Hentii type, in which high areas are used for winter pastures and low lands in summer. The third and forth types were similarly grouped together to form the Altai type, in which summer pastures are at high altitude, and winter pastures are lower. The central Halh type is characterised as having summer pastures in the northern part of the administrative districts, and winter camps in the south. The Dornogov' system involves winter pastures in sheltered hollows and summer in open areas. See *Ündesnii Atlas* (Mongolian Academy of Science, 1990: 112).

36. Some of these principles are discussed more fully by Batbuyan 1996.

37. The Mongolian geographers certainly know Simukov's work, but they have added a highly interesting focus on mountains as the centres with respect to which herders plan out their movements (Batbuyan 1996: 202–6).

38. Described in Bazargür, Chinbat and Shiirev-Ad'yaa 1989, and also as the 'Hovd type' in the *Ündesnii Atlas.*

39. The case-study site in Uvs *aimag* shows an almost identical pattern – see below.

40. Bayan Hongor *aimag* is described as having two types of movement system. The northerly *sum*s spend summer low on the steppes at the feet of the Hangai mountains, spend winter and spring in mountain valleys or passes. The more southerly *sum*s spend winter and spring on the southern slopes of Altai mountains at around 1700–2000m, summer lower on plateau plains, and in autumn follow the latest grass. Some *sum*s and State Farms organise a long migration right up to the mountain steppe in the north. This seems comparable to the Övörhangai system described by Simukov, except that the long moves organised by the northerly monastery have been replaced by (rather shorter) movements by southerly state enterprises. See Bazargür, Chinbat and Shiirev-Ad'yaa 1989: 49–50.

41. See the model of Gov'-Altai movement in the *Ündesnii Atlas* (MAS 1990: 112)

42. The two systems used to describe movement in Bulgan *aimag* also follow similar guidelines. One involves summer and autumn pastures that are usually located in river valleys (around 1200–1300m). Winter is spent on southern slopes and mountain passes, from 1500 to 1700 m., and spring pastures are in river valleys or mountain passes, around 1200–1400m. The other system, found in the south of Bulgan, involves summer in valleys near rivers, autumn by rivers or in the southern dry steppe, and spring on the southern side of hills or, again, by a river. Winter camps are generally on the plateau plains and valleys, sheltered on the southern side of hills (1200–1500m), or mountains (1400–1600m). See Bazargür, Chinbat and Shiirev-Ad'yaa 1989: 51–2. The description of the movement systems of most of the *sum*s of Övörhangai *aimag* is also broadly similar, with winter and autumn pastures on southern slopes of mountains 1500–2100m in altitude, and summer and spring at lower altitude by the Orhon and other rivers. Some other *sum*s spend winter and spring on high land, summer in mountain steppe, and autumn in lowlands. See Bazargür, Chinbat and Shiirev-Ad'yaa 1989: 66–8.

43. I adopted Simukov's methodology so as to be able to compare my results and his, and surveyed 100 *ail*s in the district, and thirty in some depth. The results of this comparison will, I hope, appear in print elsewhere.

44. The variety of movement systems of Zavhan *aimag* generally conform to a similar strategy. Summer pastures tend to be at relatively low altitude, on plains by water sources such as lakes (around 1200–1800m). Winter is spent on the southern slopes of mountains (around 2500m). Spring and autumn pastures are at the feet of mountains (1300–2000m); and the diameter of annual movement is considered quite great, ranging from 50–150km. See Bazargür, Chinbat and Shiirev-Ad'yaa 1989: 65–6.

45. The example shown in the *Ündesnii Atlas* has approximately this amount of movement.

46. Movement in Dundgov' appears to conform to the same general principles. Winter on hillocks 1200–1400m, summer on northern plain, autumn on plain with salt marshes (Bazargür pp. 63–4). The system used in Ömnögov' *aimag* appears to be a variation on the system described above, in that summer pastures are

frequently at higher altitude, on plateaus and mountain tops (1600–1800m), while winter and spring pastures are usually located on the southern slopes of hills (1400–1800m), and autumn is spent at the feet of hills (1100–1300m). Some other *sums* spend all year on the Gobi plains making only small moves, which is similar to some of the Gobi households described by Simukov.

47. The source for all data in this section is Telenged 1993.

48. There is also some evidence to suggest large movements undertaken by the nobility and the very rich in that they came a long way to spend the summer in the mountains. As 67 year-old Batbayar explained: 'In the pre-collective period one of the mountain valleys was the favourite for rich men and nobles from all over the region. Even Zorigt Khan himself is said to have spent summer here. Another valley to the north-east of this is little used now, but in the past a famous rich man would use the area to pasture his ten thousand white horses!'

49. Consisting of 1,679 camels, 6,159 horses, 6,358 cattle, 39,647 sheep and 22,001 goats.

50. Total pasture was reported as 289,471 hectares, out of a total *sum* territory of 297,175ha.

51. The source for all data in this section is Tseren 1993.

52. Unfortunately, there is rather poor interview data on the distances moved by households included in the study; however, an estimate based upon the overall movement system practised in Hosh Tolgoi gives a total annual movement of around 120km, although there is wide variation in movement.

53. The district head explained further: 'The aim is to allocate land to each mine so that it will be forbidden for mines to make use of land outside their area. The survey is also intended to decide how much compensation the mines should pay for the damage they have done to the pastures, and the amount they should pay in the future for the use of their allocated land.'

54. 'A single road was designated between each centre, and markers (signs) placed on all other roads warning that they could not be used (those who do will be fined).'

55. This is estimated by assuming that there were the same proportion of the total different species in the total livestock figures as is found in Hoboksair county as a whole in 1990 (Longworth and Williamson 1993: 287–8).

56. The autumn and spring pastures are contiguous and not clearly separated, so this figure represents the total area used in both seasons. In hectares this comes to 17,429ha for the spring and autumn pastures, 38,464ha for winter and 11,227ha of summer pasture.

57. The amount of natural pasture used for making hay is given as 73,050*mu* (4,870ha), and there is 120,225*mu* (8,015ha) of the pasture reserved for the breeding period of the Merino sheep, in November.

58. For a discussion of the importance of this issue in the case of Tibet, see Goldstein, Beall and Cincotta 1990.

59. The source for all data in this section is Tsui 1993.

60. This is identical to the Mongolian practice of *otor*.

61. The source for most of the data in this section is Mongush 1993.

62. Technically all land remains the property of the State, but this informant expressed himself in this way.

63. C. Humphrey, personal communication, based on information gathered in Mongun Taiga in 1988 at the end of the collective period.

64. These figures, based as they are upon the small sample size used in the study (18 residential groups, half of them pastoral), cannot be considered highly accurate in an absolute sense, but are helpful in generating rough estimates of movement distances and fodder inputs so as to compare case-study sites. See figure 6.14.

65. This is an estimated 55,400ha, which the local official stocking rate suggests should be able to support 22,000 sheep, 980 head of cattle, and 1500 horses.

66. This is about 0.56 sheep per hectare, taking all the seasonal pasture and averaging the seasonal stocking rates.

67. The source for all contemporary data in this section is Batbuyan 1993.

68. Batbuyan (1993) notes that in most cases the person is a relative or a good friend and it is not usual to pay him for this service; if it is a less well-known person the payment was usually something around 5 *tögrög* per sheep (in 1993).

69. Winter and spring is spent in river valleys or on the southern slopes of mountains or hills, around 1000m. Summer and autumn pastures are by the river. They also note that many families spend all year in one place. In the Hulun Buir and Bayantümen sums pastoralists generally spend winter and spring on the high steppe, at around 700 to 900m, and summer and autumn lower by rivers and streams.

70. The movement of livestock to distant pastures, usually involving rapid changes of pasture.

71. Winter animal sheds were also introduced for almost all livestock, and some consider this to have contributed to the reduction in movement.

72. In several cases there was no response from households on this question, and this reduced the average.

73. B. Batbuyan, the field-worker in this locality, noted that in this region there are some small areas of damaged pasture, due to intensive land-use caused by herdsmen not moving to seasonal pastures, and pastures used for fodder-growing. He also noted areas of land damaged by geological survey excavations.

74. 716,500 hectares, out of more than 800,000ha total territory.

75. Karamisheff (1925), following Maiskii, spells this 'Vishrelt Vangiin Hoshuu'.

76. The contemporary total includes 2,000 Russians, who are not generally integrated into the pastoral economy.

77. The total area of Dashbalbar sum is over 7,000 square kilometres, most of which is pasture. Most of the *sum* falls into the 250–300mm band for mean annual precipitation, with some land in the 300–400mm band.

78. The source for all data in this section is Hurelbaatar 1993.

79. All the interviewed households moved their livestock during the year, but there are some pastoral families in the *sum* who do not move at all, so that the actual average is likely to be lower than this value.

80. Average annual precipitation was in the 250–300mm band..

81. Locals complained that people from the towns, largely Chinese, come out and cut hay from the summer pastures for sale. The *sum* head explained that much of this activity was uncontrolled and unauthorised but continues because there is strong demand for hay. In 1988 the *sum* leader apparently sold rights to cut hay from the summer pastures, but was replaced soon after this became known. However, his replacements continue to profit from local hay by selling it directly.
82. Made up of 20,897 sheep, 4,268 goats, 5,429 cattle and 1,145 horses.
83. This informant also described the negative aspects of the collective period: 'The unsuccessful side of the People's Commune was that herders did not have the same feeling of personal responsibility for their livestock as they do now, and the standard of living was lower then... Some herders worked hard and others worked very little, but the results of their labour was shared equally.'
84. The source for all data in this section is Zhimbiev 1993.
85. The area of pasture land seems to have between 24,000 and 27,700 hectares The numbers of collective livestock were given as about 30,000 in 1991, and an additional 20% was added as an estimate of the numbers of privately-owned animals.
86. The total amount of utilised land is given as 38,409 hectares. Including the 2,400 hectares used in Mongolia the total amount of land devoted to hay and fodder production is 23% of the total.
87. The source for all data in this section is Gomboev 1993.
88. Some informants reported using as much as 3.5 tonnes of hay per sheep unit, and many of the interviewed households did not give full data on hay and fodder use.
89. This was composed of approximately 13,000 sheep, 2,700 cattle, and 700 horses.
90. It may be that some additional pasture is used. There are, apparently 300 hectares of relatively mountainous pastures in the Bauntovskii area that is used in summer time, and some 5,000 hectares of land in the district that is classified as used for other purposes or unused, some of this may be utilised as poor grazing.
91. Gomboev 1996.
92. The source for all data in this section is Qi Xiao-Hong, 1993.
93. At the beginning of 1993 there were 273 herding households, and of these 93 (34%) had static dwellings. These were officially grouped into 40 settled *hots* including a total of 449 people, and 37 mobile *hots* living in *gers*. The mobile *hots* were larger than those with buildings, so that although there were more settled *hots* than mobile, they only accounted for 40% of the *sum*'s total pastoral population of 1,129.
94. These were the figures supplied by the *sum* government. They were 31,364 sheep, 13,546 goats, 8,322 cattle, 3,728 horses and 134 camels.
95. In 1993 an official from Chinggel Bulag gave the area of pasture as 3,115,470 *mu* (207,698 hectares), and the maximum permitted number of sheep units as between 103,565 and 111,267 (the lower figure was calculated using only land classified as usable pasture, and the greater number was calculated including all possible pasture). Most of the district fell into the 200–250mm band for mean annual precipitation.

96. Locals, particularly herders, clearly have a material interest in increasing the numbers of their livestock, so such opinions cannot be accepted uncritically. However, this official did show concern with the quality of the pastures, and did not own large numbers of animals himself.

97. The source for all data in this section is Sneath 1993b.

98. Bazargür, Chinbat and Shiirev-Ad'yaa (1989: 58–9) describe the movement system of Sumber, Dalanjargalan and Airag as being similar. Winter and spring pastures are generally above 1000m. Autumn pastures are found on the plain with salt marshes, summer pastures on the plains near water sources. Mean annual precipitation is 200–300mm.

99. The Sumber State Farm breeds Karakul sheep for their lambskin, and this introduced breed, although it has been cross-bred with local sheep, requires more care and is considered to be less mobile than Mongol sheep.

100. Dalanjargalan and Darhan *sums*. It also included part of Bayanhütag *sum*.

101. The end of year 1992 livestock figures were 350 camels, 6,386 horses, 8,147 cattle, 70,730 sheep, and 14,344 goats.

102. In the late 1980s there used to be around 1600ha of ploughed land, but this had already declined by 1993.

103. This would suggest that the 'traditional' Mongolian emphasis on movement and mobility may be, in part, an attempt to overcome the lethargy that leaves subsistence households moving rather little. The wealthy elite and those with earnest upward mobility would stress this. If it is an elite strategy then this also is likely to increase its cultural importance.

104. A particularly severe winter with dangerously high levels of snow.

105. B. Telenged, 1994, personal communication.

106. This concept represents the relationship between livestock and land as a parallel with the Lotka-Volterra model of the relationship between predators and prey. It suggests that if one species feeds on another, both will exhibit an oscillation in numbers about an equilibrial ratio. Its applicability to grazing systems has been questioned for some time (see Hjort 1982).

107. Ellis, Coughenour and Swift (1993) examined the ecology of North Eastern Kenya.

108. This data was kindly supplied by Dr. Mike Hume, Climate Research Unit, University of East Anglia. For virtually all of the stations Dr. Hume had monthly data going back to 1951, and for many the data stretched as far back as the 19th century. In calculating the interannual CV we used all available annual precipitation data to calculate the value for each of the stations.

109. Occasionally, in time of crisis, there could be movements to other banners.

110. It is also interesting to speculate, (as do Ellis, Coughenour and Swift) on the differences between Inner Asian climatic conditions and those of Africa and Australia where much of the original non-equilibrial work has been done. Much of the water in the crucial spring period comes from the melting snow that has accumulated all winter, and this may also lessen variability of pasture yields.

111. The 18 households in each case-study site were asked about the aspirations of their children, and of the 26 responses in both Inner Mongolian studies only 5 wished to be herders, the rest hoped for some sort of salaried job, often in a city. These aims were often supported by parents, the response of 27 year-old male herder HUR16 was typical: 'I would like to increase my herd... and I would also like to support my brother and my future children's education so that they get good salaried jobs and live in the big city.'

112. Erdenebaatar, 1996, personal communication.

113. A typical response was that of 67 year-old Mogoltsogt from Hovd *sum*, Uvs *aimag*, Mongolia: 'I don't want to sell more sheep because I want to maintain the structure of my herds. I would like to use [money from] livestock products to obtain more animals. The doubling of the price would not encourage me to sell or slaughter more animals.' Another revealing comments was made by Dashdorj, a 63 year-old herder in Sumber, Dornogov' *aimag*, who planned his pastoral production with military precision: 'If the price of meat increased we would sell fewer [animals]. I want to keep 80% of all my livestock as breeding females. We must keep breeding males of top [superior] productivity. Male animals and sterile females I use for food. There can be 12 non-breeding animals for each person [in the household], any more than this are sold.'

114. In the three Mongolian sites 57% reported that they would make no change in the face of price increases; 20% said they would increase the amount of wool they sold, usually by increasing the number of sheep in their herds; 10% said they would try to increase their sales of livestock of prices increased; and 6% said the would sell fewer livestock as prices rose, so as to enlarge their herds faster (7% gave no response). In the Chinese studies 63% said they would make no changes; 18% said the would increase wool sales; 15% said they would increase livestock sales; and 5% made no reply at all.

115. Shombodon points out that the collectives and state farms had a number of advantages over individual producing households, including economies of scale, specialisation, and co-ordination through overall pastoral management.

116. Erdenebaatar (1996: 108) suggests that some measure of market-oriented production is emerging among private households. He describes this, however, as 'not highly commercialised' and this indicates that even where such 'market orientation' exists, it is weak.

117. Historically there seems to have been a symbiotic relationship between these two sectors. For instance, some households used to give a section of their herd to friends or relatives who were undertaking *otor* or long migration.

118. If, in a way that could be described as Chayanovian, isolated pastoral households will tend to market only their surplus products, then one approach would be to emphasise the production of consumer goods that are in demand in rural areas – as a stimulant for production. Another, possibly quicker, approach would be to retain or establish large-scale herd-owning institutions who will employ salaried or client labour to maximise pastoral products for sale to the urban population.

119. The recent decline in pastoral movement in Uvs *aimag* is also mentioned by Erdenebaatar (1996).
120. Including, for example Suhebaatar *aimag* – see Bazargür, Chinbat and Shiirev-Ad'yaa 1989: 73–4.
121. Most of the case-study sites included areas of land that fell into different bands of mean annual precipitation. The mountainous sites spanned several bands: Hovd from 100–150mm to 250–300mm; Hosh Tolgoi from 50–100mm to 300–400mm; Handagat from 150–200mm to 400–500mm. But the mid-points for these districts were all in the range 200–350mm, which was the band within which most of the other case-study sites also fell. By way of comparison, the 'non-equilibrial' grazing system of northern Kenya studied by Ellis, Coughenour and Swift had a mean annual average of 300–400mm of precipitation (Ellis, Coughenour and Swift 1993: 33).
122. It also appears significant that these sites are mountainous, with a range of climatic conditions.

CHAPTER 8

1. The stall-fed Buryat cattle achieve a live weight of 337kg per head (the average of those sold to the state in 1990, Buryat SSD 1993: 195). The average live weight had gone down to 269kg. by 1993 (Buryat SSD 1994: 73). These weights are no higher than those achieved using a mobile pastoral system in Tuva in the 1970s–1980s, which averaged between 325kg in 1985 and 342kg in 1983, (Tuva SSO 1986: 100). In Mongolia live weights of cattle sold to the state ranged between 259kg in 1985 and 245kg in 1991 (Mongolian SSO 1993: 46–7). Telenged (1996: 179) indicates that native Mongol cattle can achieve live weights of 396kg (male) and 305kg (female), while the local breed called Dornod Steppe Red can achieve a live weight as high as 620kg for a male.
2. Co-ordination of pastoral moves means that they are used for short-distance purposes, and while this facilitates travel between the camps and the *sum* centre, the effect of large numbers of vehicles moving over the crowded pasture near the settlement has been deleterious to the grass cover.
3. For example the Ubsu-Nur project linking Tuva and western Mongolia; the Baikal drainage zone project linking Buryatia with the Selenga Basin in northern Mongolia; the 'indigenous breeds' project in Buryatia, which imported native Buryat sheep breeds from Inner Mongolia to form the basis for new experimental flocks.
4. These clashes and the background to them are described in Sullivan 1995. Sullivan notes that reports of these events have been inaccurate and he argues that the ethnic aspect of the disturbances should not be overestimated.
5. A very general estimate is that 150,00 mobile herders live in Mongolia, perhaps 100,000 in Inner Mongolia, 25,000 in Tuva and at least 150,000 in Xinjiang.

BIBLIOGRAPHY

Aberle, D. F. 1962. *Chahar and Dagor Mongol Bureaucratic Administration: 1912–1945*. New Haven, Connecticut: Human Relations Area Files, Inc.

Arrow, K., Bolin, B., Costanza, R., Dasgupta, P., Folke, C., Holling, C.S., Jansson, B., Levin, S. Maler, K., Perrings, C. and Pimentel, D. 1995. Economic growth, carrying capacity, and the environment. *Science,* **268**, 520–1.

Asad, T. 1979. Equality in nomadic social systems? Notes towards the dissolution of an anthropological category. In *Pastoral Production and Society* , ed. l'Equipe écologie et anthropologie des sociétés pastorales. Cambridge: Cambridge University Press.

Batbuyan, B. 1993. Database of results from fieldwork in Dashbalbar, Dornod *aimag*. Unpublished working materials, MacArthur ECCIA, Cambridge, UK.

Batbuyan, B. 1996. Proposal for the adoption of ecologically appropriate regions for herding in Inner Asia. In *Culture and Environment in Inner Asia*, ed. C. Humphrey and D. Sneath, vol. 1, pp. 198–207. Cambridge: The White Horse Press.

Bawden, C. R. 1968. *The Modern History of Mongolia*. London: Weidenfeld and Nicolson.

Baxter P. T. W., and Hogg, R. (eds) n.d. *Property, Poverty and People: Changing Rights in Property and Problems of Pastoral Development*. Department of Social Anthropology and International Development Centre, University of Manchester, UK.

Bazargür, D. Chinbat, S. and Shiirev-Ad'yaa, S. 1989. *Bügd Nairamdah Mongol Ard Ulsyn Malchdyn Nuudel* [The Movement of Pastoralists of the MPR]. Ulaanbaatar: State Publishing House.

Bazarzhapov, B. Yu. 1995. My ne tol'ko fiksiruem fakty [We don't only fix the facts]. *Buryatiya*, 5th January, p 3.

Behnke, R.H. and Scoones, I. 1993. Rethinking range ecology: implications for rangeland management in Africa. In *Range Ecology at Disequilibrium*, ed. R.H. Behnke, I. Scoones and C. Kerven. London: ODI.

Bowles, Paul and Dong, Xiao-yuan, 1994. Current successes and future challenges in China's economic reforms. *New Left Review*, **208**: 49–77.

Bruun, O. 1996. The herding household: economy and organisation. In *Mongolia in Transition: New Patterns, New Challenges*, ed. O. Bruun and O. Odgaard. Nordic Institute of Asian Studies, Studies in Asian Topics, No. 22. Richmond, Surrey: Curzon Press.

Bruun, O. and Odgaard, O. 1996. A society and economy in transition. In *Mongolia in Transition: New Patterns, New Challenges*, ed. O. Bruun and O. Odgaard. Nordic Institute of Asian Studies, Studies in Asian Topics, No. 22. Richmond, Surrey: Curzon Press.

Budaeva, Ts. B. et al. 1992. Report on the social protection of the population. Unpublished report for the Soviet of Trade Unions of Buryatia (in Russian).

Budaeva, Ts. B. 1995. Ecological traditions and customs of a native people of the Baikal region: a sociological study. Report for the MacArthur ECCIA.

Bulag, U. E. 1998. *Nationalism and Hybridity in Mongolia.* Oxford: Clarendon Press.

Buryat SSD (Buryat ASSR Statistical Department) 1963. *Narodnoe Khozyaistvo Buryatskoi ASSR: statisticheskii sbornik* [The People's Economy of the Buryat ASSR: statistical report]. Ulan-Ude.

Buryat SSD (Buryat ASSR Statistical Department) 1986. *Narodnoe Khozyaistvo Buryatskoi ASSR: v odinnadtsatoi pyatiletke (1981–1985)* [The People's Economy of the Buryat ASSR: the eleventh five-year plan, 1981–1985]. Ulan-Ude.

Buryat SSD (Republic of Buryatia State Statistical Department) 1993. *Buryatiya 70 Lyet: Statisticheskii Sbornik* [70 years of Buryatia: statistical collection]. Ulan-Ude.

Buryat SSD (Republic of Buryatia State Statistical Department) 1994. *Sotsial'no-ekonomicheskoe razvitiye i khod realizatsiii reform v respublike buryatiya v 1993 godu* [Socio-economic development and the process of reform in the Buryat republic in 1993]. Ulan-Ude.

Campi, Alicia J. 1996. Nomadic cultural values and their influence on modernization. In *Mongolia in Transition: New Patterns, New Challenges*, ed. O. Bruun and O. Odgaard. Nordic Institute of Asian Studies, Studies in Asian Topics, no. 22. Richmond, Surrey: Curzon Press.

Casimir, M. J. and Rao, A. (eds) 1992. *Mobility and Territoriality: Social and Spatial Boundaries among Foragers, Fishers, Pastoralists and Peripatetics.* New York and Oxford: Berg.

Chang, Y. T. 1933. *The Economic Development and Prospects of Inner Mongolia.* Shanghai: The Commercial Press.

Clarke, John I. 1972. *Population Geography.* Oxford: Pergamon Press.

Croll, Elizabeth 1994. *From Heaven to Earth: Images and Experiences of Development in China.* London: Routledge.

Dahl, G. 1979. Ecology and equality: the Boran case. In *Pastoral Production and Society*, ed. l'Equipe écologie et anthropologie des sociétés pastorales. Cambridge: Cambridge University Press.

Ellis, J., Coughenour, B. and Swift, D. 1993. Climate variability, ecosystem stability, and the implications for range and livestock development. In *Range Ecology at Disequilibrium*, ed. R.H. Behnke, I. Scoones and C. Kerven. London: ODI.

Erdenebaatar, B. 1996. The socio-economic aspects of the pastoral movement patterns of Mongolian herders. In *Culture and Environment in Inner Asia*, ed. C. Humphrey and D. Sneath, vol. 1, pp. 58–110. Cambridge: The White Horse Press.

Erdenijab, E. 1996. On the future of the pastoral economy in Inner Mongolia: man, society and nature. In *Culture and Environment in Inner Asia*, ed. C. Humphrey and D. Sneath, vol. 2, pp. 102–15. Cambridge: The White Horse Press.

Fei, Hsiao-Tung and Chih-I Chang 1948. *Earth-Bound China* . London: Routledge and Kegan Paul.

Firth, R. 1951. *Elements of Social Organisation* Westport, CT: Greenwood Press.

Fletcher, R. 1991. The summer encampment of Batu Khan in AD 1253: an initial enquiry into its plan and size. *Journal of the Anglo-Mongolian Society*, **XIII**(nos. 1 and 2).

Flower, John and Leonard, Pam 1996. Community values and state cooptation: civil society in the Sichuan countryside. In *Civil Society: Challenging Western Models*, ed. Chris Hann and Elizabeth Dunn, pp. 199–221. London and New York: Routledge.

Galdanova, G. R. et al. (eds) 1983. *Lamaizm v Buryatii XVIII–nachala XX v.*, [Lamaism in Buryatia from the 18th to the beginning of the 20th century]. Moscow: Nauka.

Gell, A. 1992. Inter-tribal commodity barter and reproductive gift-exchange in old Melanesia. In *Barter, Exchange and Value: An Anthropological Approach,* ed. Humphrey & Hugh-Jones, pp. 142–69. Cambridge University Press.

Gellner, E. 1988. *State and Society in Soviet Thought*. Oxford: Basil Blackwell.

Gillmore, J. 1893. *Among the Mongols*. London: Religious Tracts Society.

Goldstein, M. C., Beall, C. M. and Cincotta, R. P. 1990. Traditional conservation on Tibet's northern plateau. *National Geographic Research*, **62**, 139–56.

Gomboev, B. 1993. Database of results from fieldwork in Argada, Buryatia. Unpublished working materials, MacArthur ECCIA, Cambridge, UK.

Gomboev, B. 1996. The structure and process of land-use in Inner Asia. In *Culture and Environment in Inner Asia*, ed. C. Humphrey and D. Sneath, vol. 1, pp. 12–57. Cambridge: The White Horse Press.

Gomboev, Bair et. al. 1996. The present condition and use of pasture in the Barguzin valley. In *Culture and Environment in Inner Asia*, ed. C. Humphrey and D. Sneath, vol. 1, pp. 124–40. Cambridge: The White Horse Press.

Griffin, K. (ed.) 1994. Poverty and the transition to a market economy in Mongolia. Report of a UNDP mission to the government of Mongolia, April.

Hann, Chris and Dunn, Elizabeth (eds) 1996. *Civil Society: Challenging Western Models*. London and New York: Routledge.

Hardin, G. 1968. The tragedy of the commons. *Science*, **16**, 1243–8.

Hell, Christian and Quéré, Philippe 1993. Le système d'élevage de la bannière Ujumchin de l'Ouest, Mongolie Interieure, Chine. *Études Mongoles et Siberiennes*, **24**, 237–90.

Hjort, A. 1982. A critique of 'Ecological' models of pastoral land use. *Nomadic Peoples*, no. 10, April 1982.

Humphrey, Caroline 1978. Pastoral nomadism in Mongolia: the role of herdsmen's cooperatives in the national economy. *Development and Change*, **9**(1): 133–60.

Humphrey, Caroline 1979. The uses of genealogy: a historical study of the nomadic and sedentarised Buryat. In *Pastoral Production and Society*, ed. l'Equipe écologie et anthropologie des sociétés pastorales. Cambridge: Cambridge University Press.

Humphrey, Caroline 1983. *Karl Marx Collective: Economy, Society and Religion in a Siberian Collective Farm*. Cambridge: Cambridge University Press.

Humphrey, Caroline 1986. Going with the grain: agriculture in Mongolia. *Inside Asia*, March: 29–31

Humphrey, Caroline 1989. *Perestroika* and the pastoralists: the example of Mongun Taiga in the Tuva ASSR. *Anthropology Today*, June: 6–10.

Humphrey, Caroline 1991a, 'Icebergs', barter and the Mafia in provincial Russia. *Anthropology Today*, **7**(2): 8–13.

Humphrey, Caroline 1991b. Buryaty: poisk natsaional' noi identichnosti, [The Buryats in search of national identity]. *Vostok–Oriens*, no. 5 (Moscow).

Humphrey, Caroline 1993. Report on fieldwork in Dornod, Summer 1993. Unpublished working paper, MacArthur ECCIA, Cambridge.

Humphrey, Caroline 1995. The Buryats. In *The Nationalities Question in the Soviet Union*, ed. Graham Smith (2nd edition). London and New York: Longman.

Humphrey, Caroline 1996 (with Urgunge Onon). *Shamans and Elders: Experience, Knowledge and Power among the Daur Mongols*. Oxford: Clarendon Press.

Humphrey, C., Mongush, M. and Telenged, B. 1993. Attitudes to nature in Mongolia and Tuva: a preliminary report. *Nomadic Peoples*, **33**, 51–62.

Humphrey, C. and Sneath, D. (eds) 1996a. *Culture and Environment in Inner Asia*, vol. 1, *The Pastoral Economy and the Environment*. Cambridge: The White Horse Press.

Humphrey, C. and Sneath, D. (eds) 1996b. *Culture and Environment in Inner Asia*, vol. 2, *Society and Culture*. Cambridge: The White Horse Press.

Humphrey, C. and Sneath, D. 1996c. Contemporary pastoralism in Inner Asia: the analysis of remotely sensed imagery and digital mapping in the light of anthropological fieldwork. Final Report for Joint Research Centre, Institute for Remote Sensing Applications, Ispra, Italy, January.

Humphrey, C. and Zhimbiev, B. 1995. Settlement, sedentarisation and urbanisation in Inner Asia. Final Report of the MacArthur ECCIA project, Cambridge, 1995.

Hurelbaatar, A. 1993. Database of results from fieldwork in Haragant, Hulun Buir *aimag*. Unpublished working materials, MacArthur ECCIA, Cambridge, UK.

Hurelbaatar, A. 1995. A Survey of Mongolians in Present day China. Unpublished paper presented at the international workshop on 'Greater Mongolia in the Twentieth Century', Princeton, 3–4 February.

Hurelbaatar, A. 1996. The transformation of the Inner Mongolian pastoral economy: the case of Hulun Buir League. In *Culture and Environment in Inner Asia*, ed. C. Humphrey and D. Sneath, vol. 2, pp. 160–75. Cambridge: The White Horse Press.

Ingold, T. 1980. *Hunters, Pastoralists and Ranchers*. Cambridge: Cambridge University Press.

Inner Mongolian TRCC (Territorial Resources Compilation Committee) 1987. *Nei Menggu Guotu Ziyuan* [Inner Mongolian Territorial Resources Survey]. Hohhot.

Inner Mongolian CML (Committee for the Mongolian Language) 1992. *Collective References*. Hohhot.

Institute of Development Studies (IDS), n.d. Options for the reform of grazing land tenure in Mongolia. Policy Alternatives for Livestock Development in Mongolia, policy options paper no. 1. Brighton, Sussex: IDS.

Jagchid, S. and Hyer, P. 1979. *Mongolia's Culture and Society.* Boulder: University of Colorado Press.

Karamisheff, W. 1925. *Mongolia and Western China; Social and Economic Study.* Tientsin.

Khazanov, A. M. 1984. *Nomads and the Outside World,* trans. Julia Crookenden. Cambridge: Cambridge University Press.

Kulomzin Commission 1898. *Vysochaishe uchrezhdennaya pod predsedatal'stvom stat'-sekretarya Kulomzina kommisiya dlya izseldovaniya zemlevladeniya i zemlepol'zovaniya v Zabaikal'skoi Oblasti* [Commission authorised under the presidency of State Secretary Kulomzin for the study of land ownership and land-use in the Trans-Baikal Oblast]. St. Petersburg.

Kurbatskaya, S. 1993. The main landscapes of Tuva and the problems of rational land-use. Unpublished report for the Mac Arthur ECCIA project.

Lampland, M. 1995. *The Object of Labour: Commodification in Socialist Hungary.* Chicago and London: University of Chicago Press

Lattimore, O. 1943. *Mongol Journeys.* London: The Travel Book Club.

Lattimore, O., 1962. *Studies in Frontier History: Collected Papers 1928–1958.* London: Oxford University Press.

Lefebure, C. 1979. Introduction. In *Pastoral Production and Society,* ed. l'Equipe écologie et anthropologie des sociétés pastorales. Cambridge: Cambridge University Press.

Li, Ou, Ma, Rong and Simpson, James R. 1993. Changes in the nomadic pattern and its impact on the Inner Mongolian grasslands ecosystem. *Nomadic Peoples,* **33**: 66–72.

Lomnitz, L.A. 1977. *Networks and Marginality: Life in a Mexican Shantytown* New York: Academic Press.

Longworth, J. and Williamson, G. 1993. *China's Pastoral Region: Sheep and Wool, Minority Nationalities, Rangeland Degradation and Sustainable Development.* Wallingford: CAB International.

Loucks, O. and Jianguo, W. 1992. *Grasslands and Grassland Sciences in Northern China..* Washington, DC: National Academy Press.

Ma, Rong 1993. Migrant and ethnic integration in the process of the socio-economic change in Inner Mongolia, China: a village study. *Nomadic Peoples,* **33**, 173–91.

Ma, Rong and Li, Ou 1993. The impact of the system reform on pasture use and environment in Inner Mongolia: a case study. Paper presented at the Wingspeed Conference Center, Racine, Wisconsin, November 4–7.

Manzanova, G. V. 1995. Women's work and conditions of employment in Buryatia. Report for the MacArthur ECCIA Project.

Mazonde, I. 1987. From communal water points to private wells and boreholes in Botswana's communal areas. In *Property, Poverty and People: Changing Rights in Property and Problems of Pastoral Development,* ed. P. T. W. Baxter and R. Hogg. University of Manchester Department of Social Anthropology and International Development Centre.

McCabe J. T. 1990. Turkana pastoralism: a case against the tragedy of the commons. *Human Ecology,* **18**(1), 81–103.

Medvedeva, T. 1996. Medical services and health issues in rural areas of Inner Asia. In *Culture and Environment in Inner Asia*, ed. C. Humphrey and D. Sneath, vol. 2, pp. 176–204. Cambridge: The White Horse Press.

Mongolian Academy of Sciences 1990. *Bügd Nairamdah Mongol Ard Uls: Ündesnii Atlas* [MPR Basic Atlas]. Ulaanbaatar.

Mongolian SSO (State Statistical Office of the MPR) 1974. *National Economy MPR 1973*. Ulaanbaatar: State Publishing House.

Mongolian SSO (State Statistical Office of the MPR) 1981. *National Economy MPR for 60 years 1921–81*. Ulaanbaatar: State Publishing House.

Mongolian SSO (State Statistical Office of Mongolia) 1991. *National Economy of the MPR for 70 years 1921–1991*. Ulaanbaatar: State Publishing House.

Mongolian SSO (State Statistical Office of Mongolia) 1993. *Mongolian Economy and Society in 1992: Statistical Yearbook*. Ulaanbaatar: State Publishing House.

Mongush, M. 1993. Database of results from fieldwork in Solchur, Ovyur raion. Unpublished working materials, MacArthur ECCIA, Cambridge, UK.

Mongush, M. 1996. The Tuvinians in China: aspects of their history, language and culture. In *Culture and Environment in Inner Asia*, ed. C. Humphrey and D. Sneath, vol. 2, pp. 116–33. Cambridge: The White Horse Press.

Nataev, P. 1994a. Otchego bolit golova u ministra [What makes the minister's head ache], *Buryatiya*, 7th September, p. 2.

Nataev, P. 1994b. Vodinochku fermeru plokho [A farmer on his own has a bad time]. *Buryatiya*, 28 December, p. 2.

Nataev, P. 1994c. Snova ne pereput'ye [Again in a mess]. *Buryatiya*, 9th December, p. 4.

Natsagdorj, S. H. 1967. The Economic Basis of Feudalism in Mongolia. *Modern Asian Studies*, **1**, 265–81.

Nikolaev, V. 1994. Onokhoiskii peredel [The Onokhoi distribution]. *Pravda Buryatii*, 9th September, p. 2.

Nolan, Peter 1995. *China's Rise, Russia's Fall: Politics, Economics and Planning in the Transition from Stalinism*. London: Macmillan.

Potaev, V. S. 1994. Fermerstvo, na moi vzglyad, – yedinstvenno vernyi put' reformy na sele [Smallholdings, in my view, are the only true path to reform the village]. *Buryatiya*, 15th December, p. 4.

Qi, Xiao-Hong, 1993. Database of results from fieldwork in Chinggel Bulag, Shilingol *aimag*. Unpublished working materials, MacArthur ECCIA, Cambridge, UK.

Radcliffe-Brown, A. R. 1977[1940]. On social structure. In *The Social Anthropology of Radcliffe-Brown*, ed. A. Kuper. London: Routledge and Kegan Paul.

Randall, Sara 1993. Issues in the demography of Mongolian nomadic pastoralism. *Nomadic Peoples*, **33**, 209–29.

Rasidondug, S. and Veit, V. (trans.) 1975. *Petitions of Grievances Submitted by the People to the Bogd Khan*. Asiatische Forschungen, no. 45. Wiesbaden: Harrassowitz.

Riskin, C. 1987. *China's Political Economy: the Quest for Development since 1949.* Oxford University Press.

Sahlins, M. D. 1961. The segmentary lineage system: an organization of predatory expansion. *American Anthropologist,* **63,** 322–45.

Sanders, Alan 1996. Foreign relations and foreign policy. In *Mongolia in Transition: New Patterns, New Challenges,* ed. O. Bruun and O. Odgaard. Nordic Institute of Asian Studies, Studies in Asian Topics, no. 22. Richmond, Surrey: Curzon Press.

Sambuu, J. 1956. *Malchidatl Oh Zovlogoo.* Ulanbaatar: State Publishing House.

Sandford, S. 1983. *Management of Pastoral Development in the Third World.* London: ODI/Chichester: John Wiley and Sons.

Sanjdorj, M. 1980. *Manchu Chinese Colonial Rule in Northern Mongolia,* trans. Urgunge Onon. London: Hurst.

Schneider, J. and Schneider P. 1976. *Culture and Political Economy in Western Sicily.* New York.

Sheehy, Dennis P. 1996. Sustainable livestock use of pastoral resources. In *Mongolia in Transition: New Patterns, New Challenges,* ed. O. Bruun and O. Odgaard. Nordic Institute of Asian Studies, Studies in Asian Topics, no. 22. Richmond, Surrey: Curzon Press.

Shirendev, B. et al. 1976. *History of the Mongolian People's Republic,* trans. William A. Brown and Urgunge Onon. Cambridge, MA: East Asian Research Center, Harvard University.

Shombodon, D. 1996. The division of labour and working conditions of herdsmen in Mongolia. In *Culture and Environment in Inner Asia,* ed. C. Humphrey and D. Sneath, vol. 1, pp. 209–37. Cambridge: The White Horse Press.

Shombodon, D. n.d. Development trends and distribution of livestock in Mongolia. *Inner Asia,* **5**(3), forthcoming. Cambridge, UK: Mongolia and Inner Asia Studies Unit.

Shue, Vivienne 1988. *The Reach of the State: Sketches of the Chinese Body Politic.* Stanford: Stanford University Press.

Simukov, A. D. 1933. Hotoni [Hotons]. *Sovrennaya Mongoliya* [Contemporary Mongolia], no. 3, 19–32.

Simukov, A. D. 1934. Mongol'skii Kochevki [Mongolian migrations]. *Sovremennaya Mongoliya* [Contemporary Mongolia], no. 4(7): 40–6 and map.

Simukov, A. D. 1935. Materialy po kochevomu byrtu naseleniya MNR [Materials about the movements of the population of Mongolia]. *Sovrennaya Mongoliya* [Contemporary Mongolia], no. 6(13), 89–104.

Simukov, A. D. 1936. Materialy po kochevomu bytu naseleniya MNR [Materials concerning the nomadic life of the population of Mongolia]. *Sovremennaya Mongoliya* [Contemporary Mongolia] no. 2(15): 49–57.

Sneath, David 1993a. Social relations, networks and social organisation in post-socialist rural Mongolia. *Nomadic Peoples,* **33,** 193–207.

Sneath, D. 1993b. Database of results from fieldwork in Sumber *sum,* Dornogov' *aimag.* Unpublished working materials, MacArthur ECCIA, Cambridge, UK.

Sneath, David n.d. *Changing Inner Mongolia: Post-Revolutionary Social and Economic Change among the Pastoral Population of Inner Mongolia* (monograph, forthcoming).

Spuler, B. 1972. *History of the Mongols, Based on Eastern and Western Accounts of the Thirteenth and Fourteenth Centuries,* trans. Helga and Stuart Drummond. London: Routledge and Kegan Paul.

Sullivan, Stefan 1995. Interethnic relations in post-Soviet Tuva. *Ethnic and Racial Studies,* **18**(1), 64–88.

Telenged, B. 1993. Database of results from fieldwork in Hovd *sum,* Uvs *aimag.* Unpublished working materials, MacArthur ECCIA, Cambridge, UK.

Telenged, B., 1996. Livestock breeding in Mongolia past and present: the advantages and disadvantages of traditional and modern animal breeding practices. In *Culture and Environment in Inner Asia,* ed. C. Humphrey and D. Sneath, vol. 1, pp. 161–88. Cambridge: The White Horse Press.

Timofeev, L. 1985. *Soviet Peasants (or: The Peasants' Art of Starving).* New York: Telos Press.

Tseren, B. 1993. Database of results from fieldwork in Hosh Tolgoi, Hoboksair county. Unpublished working materials, MacArthur ECCIA, Cambridge, UK.

Tseren, B. P. 1996. Traditional pastoral practice of the Oirat Mongols and their relationship with the environment. In *Culture and Environment in Inner Asia,* ed. C. Humphrey and D. Sneath, vol. 2, pp. 147–59.

Tsui, Yenhu 1993. Database of results from fieldwork in Handagat, Altai county. Unpublished working materials, MacArthur ECCIA, Cambridge, UK.

Tsui, Yenhu 1996a. A comparative study of the attitudes of the peoples of pastoral areas of Inner Asia towards their environments. In *Culture and Environment in Inner Asia,* ed. C. Humphrey and D. Sneath, vol. 2, pp. 1–24. Cambridge: The White Horse Press.

Tsui, Yenhu 1996b. The development of social organisations in the pastoral areas of North Xinjiang and their relationship with the environment. In *Culture and Environment in Inner Asia,* ed. C. Humphrey and D. Sneath, vol. 2, pp. 205–30. Cambridge: The White Horse Press.

Tulokhonov, A. K. 1992. The historico-geographical aspects of the connection of agriculture of the Baikal region with the environment. Unpublished research paper.

Tulokhonov, A. K. and Manzanova, G. V. 1996. Introduction of new forms of economy in the Buryat National Region. In *Culture and Environment in Inner Asia,* ed. C. Humphrey and D. Sneath, vol. 1, pp. 141–60. Cambridge: The White Horse Press.

Tuva SSO (State Statistical Office of Tuva ASSR) 1986. *Narodnoye khozyaistvo Tuvinskoi ASSR v odinnadtsatoi pyatiletke: statisticheskii sbornik.* Kyzyl.

Uskeev, B. 1994. Ne do zhiru, non ... zhivem [We won't be fat, but ... we'll survive]. *Pravda Buryatii,* 22nd July, p. 2.

Vainshtein, S. 1980. *Nomads of South Siberia: the Pastoral Economies of Tuva.* Cambridge University Press.

Vreeland, H. H. (III) 1954. *Mongol Community and Kinship Structure.* Human Relations Area Files, New Haven, Connecticut.

Wang, Xiaoqiang and Bai Nanfeng 1991. *The Poverty of Plenty.* Basingstoke: Macmillan.

Williams, Dee Mack 1996a. Grassland enclosures: catalyst of land degradation in Inner Mongolia. *Human Organization,* **55**(3), 307–13.

Williams, Dee Mack 1996b. The barbed walls of China: a contemporary grassland drama. *The Journal of Asian Studies,* **55**(3), 665–91.

World Bank 1994. Mongolia country economic memorandum: priorities in macroeconomic management. World Bank Report No. 13612-MOG, October 31. Country Operations Division, China and Mongolia Department, East Asia and Pacific Regional Office.

Xinjiang LHCC (Xinjiang-Uighur Autonomous Region Local History Compiling Committee) 1991. *Xinjiang Nian Jian 1991* [Xinjiang Year Book, 1991]. Urumqi: Xinjiang People's Publishing House.

Yan, Yunxiang 1992. The impact of rural reform on economic and social stratification in a Chinese village. *Australian Journal of Chinese Affairs,* **27**, 1–23.

Yong Shipeng and Cui Haiting, 1988. The explanation of the vegetation map (1:500,000) of Inner Mongolia Autonomous Region. In *Explanation of Series Resources Maps of Inner Mongolia Autonomous Region Science,* ed. Li Bo et al. Editorial Committee of Series Resources Maps of IMAR.

Yuan, Qing-li 1990. Population changes in the Xinjiang Uighur Autonomous Region (1949–1984), *Central Asian Survey,* **9**(1), 1–28.

Zhang, M. 1996. The effects of privatisation policies on rural women's labour and property rights in Inner Mongolia and Xinjiang. In *Culture and Environment in Inner Asia,* ed. C. Humphrey and D. Sneath, vol. 2, pp. 61–96. Cambridge: The White Horse Press.

Zhimbiev, B. 1989. Osobennost arkhitekturno-plannirovochnoi organizatsii sel'skikh naselennykh mest Vostochnoi Sibirii (na primere Buryatskoi ASSR, Irkutskoi i Chitinskoi oblastei). Précis of dissertation submitted for Kandidt degree to the Moscow Architectural Institute.

Zhimbiev, B. 1993. Database of results from fieldwork in Gigant, Chita Oblast. Unpublished working materials, MacArthur ECCIA, Cambridge, UK.

INDEX

A

administrative areas 72, 199, 219
  banner (*hoshuu*) 219, 310
    north-south scope significant 229
    property of 69–70
  district (*sum, selsoviet, xiang*) 93, 94, 98
    activities of officials 111–112
    social/administrative functions 198
  sub-district (*gachaa, bag, brigada*, etc.)
    definition 199
agriculture 2, 13, 8, 47, 86, 91, 95, 182, 193, 307, 310, 321
agro-pastoralism 44, 74–75, 193
ail (family herding group) 15, 159–164, 171
alcohol 144, 147, 159
  home production 88, 201, 203
alcoholism 8, 316
Altai 9. *See also* Handagat
anomie 8
Argada, Barguzin, Buryatia, Russia (ECCIA case-study site) 9
  built structures 191
  collectivisation 36
  family and residence 150–151
  hay and fodder use 257
  high stocking rate 257
  oboo rituals 124
  pastoral movement 257
  pasture degradation 211–212, 257
  religious activity 32
  reversal of privatisation 85
  sedentarisation 211–212
  sedentary activities 193
  short migrations of herders 191
  technological consumer goods 203
  urbanism 211–212
associations 83, 118–120, 129, 151, 294, 312
atheism 30, 127

B

baigal 2. *See also* nature
banks 94, 110
banner (*hoshuu*). *See* administrative area

Barkol

Barkol, China (ECCIA secondary study site) 9, 102
Barguzin 9. *See also* Argada
bath-houses 191
baths, public 15
Bayantümen *sum*, Dornod, Mongolia (ECCIA secondary study site) 9
  companies in 112
  economic conditions 110
  role of district officials 111
  sedentarisation 189
Bayanzürh Uulyn Hoshuu 222–224
Borjigin Tsetsen Vangiin Hoshuu 264
Buddhism. *See* religion
Buddhist church 19, 137
Buryats 5, 12, 70, 194, 308
Buryatia (Buryat Republic). *See* Russia

C

camels. *See livestock*
Campi, A. 64
carrying capacity 41, 270
case-study sites 8–9. *See also* under individual sites: Argada, Barkol, Bayantümen, Chinggel Bulag, Dashbalbar, Gigant, Handagat, Hargant, Hosh Tolgoi, Hovd, Solchur, Sumber.
  and administrative distance 198–199
  methodology 8–10
  mobility and land-use 292–293
  pasture condition and land-use 265–267
  settlement/countryside index 211
cattle. See livestock
chickens. *See* livestock
'chiefship' (*sheftsvo*) 88
children 142, 153, 156, 159, 164, 176
  large pastoral families 117, 318, 319
  parents' aspirations 273, 332
  tasks 138–139, 153
China 13, 15, 68
  pastoral regions 91–93
  conditions
  history 18–19

clans in 27–30
household economic unit 69
importance of kin 164–169
in-migration 20, 95
livestock statistics 42–52
native languages 23–24
pasture allocation 54
surviving state farms 100
dwelling types 185
Inner Mongolia 3–8, 64, 134–
136, 138, 176, 198
institutional forms 72
leadership 122
Manchuria 27–30, 308
market policy 74–78
Mongols in 34
Xinjiang 5, 6, 106, 134, 172, 198
Chinese
Han migrants 10, 20, 95, 100
merchants 39, 225
Chinggel Bulag *sum*, Shilingol *aimag*, Inner
Mongolia, China (ECCIA case-study
site) 9
clans in 27–30
communications 204
decreased mobility 261
oboo rituals 124
pastoral movement 259
pasture allocation 261
pasture degradation 211, 259
production/consumption patterns 203
reliance on hay 262
residence patterns 165
sedentarisation 209, 211
short migrations of herders 191
urbanisation 209, 211
Chinggis Khan 27, 30, 308
civil society 118
clan. *See* kinship
co-operatives (*horshoo*) 69, 113, 157–
158, 201, 296
collective farms. *See also* collectives, state
farms
in Russia
and cultural events 79
as social institution 78–80, 103
contract system 80
military 78
present role 68–69
privatisation 81
renamed collective-share enter-

prises 83
unemployment 81
welfare support 73
collectives
and environment 129
and pastoral movement 230
and residence patterns 148
and urban culture 209
as exchange organisations 88–89
centralised infrastructure 83
farm directors 86–88
in China (People's Communes) 19, 96–
97, 103, 241
in Mongolia (*negdel*) 19, 110–113, 133
in USSR 19–20, 68, 115–119, 128
mechanised support for mobility 268, 292, 299
moneyless economy 87
organisation similar to feudal 230–232
production brigades 19
social functions 103
survival 90, 128
tax from 83
collectivisation 19, 35
in China 40
in Mongolia 19, 39, 195
in Russia 36
communications 137, 197, 204
and urbanisation 180
cinema 204
newspapers 204, 205
radio 62, 109, 204, 204–206, 205
railways 180
roads 6, 83, 94, 180, 201, 201–206
telephone 83, 93, 204–206
TV 7, 62, 93, 109, 203–
206, 204, 205, 303
Communist Party
in China 6, 93, 94, 107, 121–122
in Mongolia 18, 111
in Russia 73, 78
companies (Mongolian
kompan) 69, 110, 112–113, 156–
157, 315
conservationism 304–305
consumer goods 57, 64, 137, 274, 332
consumption 202–206, 208
contracts 80
and responsibility system 96–99
base for economic relations 70–71
crime 8, 115–117, 130

Croll, E. 94, 98
culture, indigenous 17, 21, 123–127
  and environment 10
  and language 21–26
  two- and four-season 194–195
  future 303
  in western zone 26, 33, 196
  reformulation 303

D

Dashbalbar *sum*, Dornod *aimag*, Mongolia
  (ECCIA case-study site) 9–10
  communications 205
  decreased mobility 248
  hay and fodder use 248
  increase in agriculture 250
  introduced breeds 248
  oboo rituals 124
  pastoral movements 246–248
  pasture degradation 211
  patterns of residence 162–164
  production/consumption patterns 201–203
  sedentarisation 209, 211–212
  short migrations of herders 191
  stocking levels 249
  urbanisation 209, 211–212
de-sedentarisation 196
de-urbanisation 180
de-urbanism 203, 205, 301
diet 12, 13
differentiation, economic 6, 74, 92, 96,
  104, 106–107, 169, 176–178
  and education 207
  in China 61
distance
  administrative 198–199
  from roads and markets 6
district (*sum, selsoviet, xiang*). *See*
  administrative areas
Dornod *aimag* 9. *See also* Dashbalbar,
  Bayantümen
Dornogov' *aimag* 9. *See also* Sumber
dwellings
  ger (yurt) 12, 147
  in Chinggel Bulag 165
  in Dashbalbar 162–164
  in Hargant 168–169, 195
  in Handagat 172
  in Hosh Tolgoi 169

  in Mongolia 159–161
  in Sumber 161
  in Tuva 155–156
  permanently sited 186
  household types 183–186
  mobile
    and differences of wealth 186
    in Buryatia 188
    in Hargant 189–190
    in Mongolia 185–186
    in western zone 195
  otara house 152–153
  pastoral households 176
  static
    and urbanisation 180–182
    in Argada 155–156
    in Buryatia 148–149
    in Chinggel Bulag 165–166
    in Handagat 171
    in Hargant 67, 168–169
    in Hosh Tolgoi 169
    in Sumber 189
  wagons 189
  wooden houses 12
    in Buryatia 194–195
    in Dashbalbar 162–164, 194–195

E

ECCIA Project 4, 8–9,14, 72, 310
economic policies 6, 64, 54–58, 114–118
ecosystem resilience 48
education 4, 156. *See also* schools
  in Chinese pastoral areas 91, 94
  state provision 73, 78
electricity 41, 80, 83, 94
  and communications 204
Ellis, Coughenour and Swift (non-
  equilibrial grazing systems)
  270–272
environment
  and Chinese policy 14
  and political protest 304–305
  and settlement 179
  and urbanism 214
  concepts of 2
  concern for 10, 33, 132, 214, 304–305
  threats to 3, 8, 11–12, 48, 65–67
environmental education 215
environmental problems
  and Chinese revenues 130

and native culture 305
and pastoralism 127–135
environmentalism
    and western organisations 304–305
Erdenet company 62
erosion 12, 13, 257

F

family *See also* kinship, and individual
    case-study sites
    and property ownership 137, 151, 320
    component nuclear family 141, 147
    extended 150, 152, 154
    grandparental household 141
    Inner Asian 137
    joint 171
    lone mother households 141
    nuclear 149, 162, 173
    ritual 140, 149, 153, 170
    settled and mobile sections 176
    stem 139, 147, 152, 159, 167–168,
        173
family farms 148, 150
family size, Chinese limit 142, 164, 320
family team system 80
felt-making 175, 203
fences 19, 67, 190, 194
festivals 124
feudalism 219–220, 229–232, 323
fishing 88
fodder 12, 14, 74, 128. *See also* hay
    and pasture degradation 265
    and mechanisation 107, 128
    Chinese policy 74
    collectives and 128
    concentrates 86
    technologies 128
food 144, 203
    cost of 75, 110
    flour 13, 144, 208
    native 26
    non-local 57
forests 12, 130
four-season pasturing 195. *See also*
    pastoral movement systems, etc.
fuel
    dried dung 12, 138
    petrol 69, 120, 248
    provision by authorities 300
    trade in. *See* trade
    wood 12, 79

G

gangs 8, 207, 302
gifts 144–147
    between kin 143–147, 156
    household expenditure on 146–147
    in China 119
Gigant, Chita Oblast, Russia (ECCIA case-
    study site) 9–10
    built structures 191
    collective farm and *sheftsvo* 89
    communications 204
    family composition 152–153
    mechanisation 255
    oboo rituals 124
    pastoral movement 255
    pasture degradation 211–212, 255
    production/consumption patterns 202
    reliance on hay 255
    residence patterns 148–156, 151
    sedentarisation 209, 211–212
    sedentary activities 193
    short migrations of herders 191
    stocking level 255
    subsistence production 151
    technological consumer goods 203
    urbanisation 209, 211–212
goats. *See* livestock
Gomboev, B. 46, 47, 73, 128, 203,
    218, 257
grass fires 249
grass species, deterioration 48
'grassland certificates' 96, 319
grazing systems. *See also* pastoralism,
    herding, individual case-study sites
    non-equilibrial 219, 269–273, 331, 333

H

Halh Mongols 5, 308
Handagat, Altai county, Xinjiang, China
    (ECCIA case-study site) 9
    built structures 191
    communications 205
    Muslim Kazakhs in 196
    near city 180
    pastoral movement 242–244
    pasture degradation 211
    pasture loss 244
    production/consumption patterns 202–
        203
    religious activity 32

residence patterns 171–172
sedentary activities 193
sedentarisation 192, 211
tension between herders and
farmers 95
urbanism 211
Hargant *sum*, Hulun Buir *aimag*, Inner
Mongolia, China (ECCIA case-study
site) 9
decreased mobility 252–254
drop-out rate from school 23
environmental problems 131–132
haymaking and selling 252
land-use after rural reforms 253
near city and railway 180
pastoral movement 250–252
pasture degradation 253
production/consumption patterns 202–
203
residence patterns 167–169
sedentarisation 209–210
Simukov's 'eastern steppe type' 252
stocking rate 254
technological consumer goods 203
traditions 195
urbanisation 209–210
hay 12, 39, 74, 116, 128, 195, 246,
252, 262. *See also* fodder, and
individual case-study sites
Chinese policy 91
low yields 74
reliance on 19, 195, 238
trade in 64, 132, 252
unequal access to 249, 252
use on collectives 19
haymaking. *See also* machinery
and pressure on pasture 47
decrease in Mongolia 236
in exchange for cash 167
machinery 248
mechanised 117
health care 19, 56, 103. *See also* medical
services
herd-placing 143–147, 167
herders. *See also* pastoralism, etc.
and Chinese state institutions 93–94
and contract system 80
and rural development policies 104
and sedentary activities 190
annual migrations 191
economic orientation 104, 227–232

household types 185–186
in Buryatia 188
in Socialist era 193–194
living standards 40, 59–63, 300–301
property 62
ratios to village dwellers 76–78
specialist. *See* herding, specialised
herding. *See also* pastoralism, etc.
cultural values 194
mobility techniques 26, 132, 228, 268
specialised 39, 220, 222–225
and economic corporations 228
camels 39
for monastery 226
horses, sheep and camels 223, 294
in Handagat 242
on Red Star state farm 102
yield-focused production 225–226
Hoboksair county 9. *See also* Hosh Tolgoi
horses *See* livestock
Hosh Tolgoi, Hoboksair county, Xinjiang,
China (ECCIA case-study site) 9
attitude to nature 214
communications 205
mining 241
near city 180
oboo rituals 124
pastoral movement 239–242
pasture degradation 211–215
pasture loss 241
production/consumption patterns 202–
203
residence patterns 169–171
sedentarisation 209–210, 211–215
Simukov's 'western' type 239
stocking rate 242
urbanisation 209–210, 211–215
village population 76
hot (*hoton, hot-ail*) 120, 165, 174–175
household living complex types (THLC)
183–186
households 10, 139, 294
new categorisation 183–186
Hovd *sum*, Uvs *aimag*, Mongolia (ECCIA
case-study site) 9
oboo rituals 124
pastoral movement 236–238
pasture degradation 211, 238
production/consumption patterns 201
reliance on hay 238
residence pattern 159–161

sedentarisation 211
Simukov's 'Western Type' 221, 236
stocking levels 238
urbanism 211
Hulun Buir *aimag* 9. *See also* Hargant
hunting 88, 106
hydro-electric power 65

I

industries
   local 94, 310
      dairies 89, 93, 115
      meat-packing factories 89
      under-investment in 7
      wood and logging 316
   mining 65, 91, 206, 214
      and environmental damage 241
      coal 76, 241
      indigenous 305
      uranium (Mardai) 7
   oil 65, 91, 241
Inner Asia
   climate 2
   definition 2
   district capitals 209
   economic culture 10, 14–15, 16, 194
   future social forms 306
   history of cultural divergence 18
   household types 184–186
   increasing sedentarisation 188–190
   investment 64
   Mongol cultural domination 2
   pastoral systems compared 265–267
   peoples 5
   peripheral region 302–303
   population structure 58–59
   religions 30
   residence patterns 154–156
   rural institutions 67
   rural-urban integration 301
   settlement and landuse 182
   social divisions 208
   stereotypes of pastoral society 292
Inner Mongolia. *See* China
institutions
   and pastoral movement 292
   categories defined 71
   corporate, in Russia 77
   leader's role 70
   local, importance of 134–135

pre-revolutionary 69–70
socialist 70
state, in Chinese pastoral regions 93–94
Islam. *See* religion

K

Kazakhs 5, 24, 196
   joint families 173
   residence pattern 173
   residential groupings 171
   traditions 176
kin
   definitions 139
   gifts and assistance 143–147
kinship
   after decollectivisation 136
   and residence 147–174
   clan (*obog, otog*) 17, 26–30
   factor in *hot* formation 174
   historical attitudes 142
   in private farms 151

L

labour
   feudal obligation 226
   gendered division of 2, 138, 138–139, 156
   hired 96, 106, 138, 167, 169, 172, 177, 317
   of poor for rich 223, 226
land-use systems 11–12
   and pastoral movement 292–293
   pre-collective in Mongolia 228–232
languages
   native 21–24, 306
Lattimore, O. 17
leaders 120–123
   and 'charisma politics' 121
   and conflict resolution 296
   role of 121–122, 198
leadership 295–296
   compared in 3 study countries 122
livestock. *See also* pastoral movement
      systems etc
   absentee owners 143
   and subsistence production 226
   camels
      for transport 39, 226, 269
      numbers 50, 249–250

large pastoral movements 223, 225, 230, 241
cattle 37, 66, 87, 223, 226, 251
  numbers 50, 250
chickens 106, 112, 190, 192, 196
contracted 99
density 12, 14
  local government statistics 49–53
economy 75
  role of institutions 294–296
  exports from Mongolia 232, 326
foxes for fur 87
gifts of 147
goats 104, 223, 226,
  environmental problems 105
  numbers in Inner Mongolia 14, 50, 52
heated sheds 12, 14, 189, 241, 248, 264
herd composition 74
  in Chinese pastoral regions 106
herd-placing 143–147
horses 37, 50, 87, 102, 138
  large pastoral movement 220, 223, 225, 230, 241, 242
'improved' breeds 12, 14
improved by migration 228, 229, 238, 268
introduced breeds
  and decreased mobility 46, 239–241
  decline since privatisation 274
  government policies on 46
  of sheep 39, 248, 239–241
movement. *See also* mobility, etc.
  20th century decrease in 293
native breeds 12, 52, 128, 246
numbers 37, 42–44, 49, 52, 74, 231. *See also* individual case-study sites
pigs 87, 190, 192, 196
privately owned 59–62
production
  influence on mobility 193
products
  meat 4, 89, 114, 312
  milk 64, 66, 86, 226, 312
sheep 46, 89
  large pastoral movement 223, 225
  numbers 13–14, 50, 52, 128, 231
stocking rate 48–52. *See also* individual case-study sites

and pasture degradation 265, 277
  Chinese rationale 270
  in arid environment 54
  in Chinese pastoral regions 92
  in Hosh Tolgoi 242
living standards 59–63, 250, 300–301
loans 29, 84, 85, 90, 294

M

Macarthur Foundation 4, 307. *See also* ECCIA
machinery 80, 107, 151, 172, 262
Manchu period 30, 219–220
Manchu Qing dynasty 18
manufactured goods 7, 207. *See also* consumer goods
market economy 4–6, 54–58, 300, 332. *See also* trade, prices
  and pastoralism 230, 273–275
  and subsistence 57
  household strategies and 88
  in Inner Mongolia 177
  in Mongolia 58, 110, 273–275
markets
  and distance 75
  Chinese urban 302
mechanisation 74, 83
  and fodder/hay 107, 301
  and lifestyle 301
  and pasture degradation 265
  in Chinese pastoral regions 91
  in Inner Mongolia 301
  supporting pastoral mobility 297–300
medical services 4, 122. *See also* health care
  hospitals 56, 111
  in China 94
  state provision 73, 79
military developments 65
military farms 78
Ministry of Agriculture (Beijing) 100
mobility. *See also* pastoralism, etc
  and historical urban culture 209
  and land-use 292–293
  and pasture degradation 265
  and specialised knowledge 179
  and sustainability 16, 54, 268–269
  and urbanisation 180–182
  decrease in 236, 239–241
  enhanced by mechanisation 299–300
  greater in pre-collective era 268

herding technique 268
  in western study zone   195–196
  increase after collectivisation 231
  institutional support 293–296
  place in work ethic   268–269
monasteries 300
  and large pastoral movement 228
  as economic institutions 226
  as herd owners 220
  institutional role   69–70
monastery
  at Lamyn Gegen 222
  at Zuun Choir 37
Mongol Empire 17
Mongol traditions 17, 196
Mongolia 4, 12, 68–73, 134, 198
  agriculture 47
  clans in 27–30
  dwelling types 185
  economically peripheral 64
  exports 232
  foreign aid 64
  gangs 207
  history of 18
  institutional forms 72
  leadership 122
  livestock density 49–52
  livestock statistics 42–47
  debt to Chinese firms 225
  residence 138
  rural institutions 110
Mongolian languages 5, 17
  and cultural fragmentation 20–21
Mongolian script 5, 20, 24, 36, 308
  Buryat vertical 22
Mongols, definition of 18
motor transport. *See also* transport
  and pastoral movement 246
  reliance of herders on 268
motor vehicles. *See* transport
mutual aid 146–147, 172

N

nature (*baigal*) 2, 123
  religious beliefs 214
  traditional attitudes to   304
networks 15, 57, 119, 317
  after decollectivisation 136
  economic 27, 57, 88, 90, 151, 153, 176
  in collective era 142

kin   27, 85, 139,157–158,
  case studies 146–147
  in Argada 151
  in Gigant 153
  in Mongolia 158–164
  relation to residential groups   175–
    178
  livestock ownership   143–145
nomadic pastoralism 93. *See also*
    pastoralism, mobile
nomadism 196, 305–306
  cultural values and trade   64
  Buryats 182, 188
  definitions of   1
  ideological overtones   182
non-equilibrial grazing systems 269–273
  southern Mongolia and west Inner
    Mongolia 272

O

obligation, *See* social relations of obligation
oboo ritual   28, 30, 123–127, 171. *See*
    also individual case-study sites
  functions   127
  involvement of district
    government 124
  modern importance of   303
otara 152–153
otor 39, 185, 264, 276
  and reliance on fodder 236
Ovyur 9. *See also* Solchur

P

pastoral economy   68–135
  and district governments   72
  and hay-cutting 132
  and urbanisation 210
  cash 167
  divergences in 5
  in Inner Mongolia 137–138
  in Buryat areas 295
  in China 58
  in Mongolia 114, 220, 231–232
pastoral households. *See also* households
  work patterns 138–139
pastoral land-use
  20th century trends 265
pastoral mobility. *See also* mobility,
    pastoralism
  inputs/outputs 296–300

pastoral movement systems. *See also*
  individual case-study sites, Simukov,
  Ündesnii Atlas
  and delivery of produce   228
  and dual productive modes   226–227
  and environmental problems   236–264
  and specialised herding   223–225
  as 'intensification' technique   296
  as strategy   233
  classification
    Simukov   220–225
    Ündesnii Atlas   233–236
  collective era   233–236
  efficiency of large movements   229
  environmental constraints on   219
  organisation   227–232
  pre-collective   264
  rich more mobile   227–232
pastoral products. *See also* livestock
  products, trade, prices
  buying power   62
  demand for in China   75
  wool   4, 232
pastoral society
  stereotypes   292
pastoralism
  and environment   8, 14, 65
  and indigenous culture   21
  and nomadism   1
  and rural economy   8, 133–135, 303
  and technology   305–306
  compatible with urbanism   3, 300–302
  historical changes   42
  importance of flexible access   276
  institutional co-ordination   134
  mobile
    and cultural attitudes   17
    and economic development   10
    and technology   3. *See also*
    machinery, transport etc.
    techniques   1, 195–196, 276, 293–
    296, 305–306
  pre-collective   70, 218
  socio-economic aspects   77
  state planning and   4
  sustainable   3, 16, 48–53, 93, 273–276
pasture
  allocation of   8, 14, 41,
    54, 74, 91, 97–98
  and kinship   137

and non-equilibrial grazing
  systems   273
and residence pattern   165
as source of friction   107
degradation of   10, 42. *See also*
  individual case-study sites
  and agriculture   47, 49–52, 244
  and declining mobility   189, 190,
    191, 253, 265, 273, 292–293
  and fodder crops   292
  and low mobility   49–52, 53–
    54, 276
  and mechanisation   276
  and overstocking   44, 242
  and population density   212
  and sedentarisation   212
  and settlement patterns   210–217
  and static pastoralism   49
  and stocking levels   277
  and sustainability   48
  and urbanism   214
  causes of   14
  Chinese estimate of   74
  effect of herd composition   46
  Hardin's model inappropriate   273
  herders views on   46
  in Chifeng   49
  in China after privatisation   292
  in Chinese pastoral regions   130
  in Inner Mongolia   14
  in Jirim *aimag*   49
  in Sarq'ok, Xinjiang   102
  linked to haymaking   252
  none in Mongolia   75
  inherited   245
  loss of in Chinese areas   91
  loss to agriculture   241
  loss to mineral extraction   241
  machine damage   241–242, 244,
    254, 292
  management in pre-collective pe-
    riod   219–220
  planned use of in Mongolia   133
  ploughing up of   106
  rights in feudal Mongolia   219
  winter/summer requirements   233
pasturing
  four-season   194–195
  two season   194–195
patron-client relations   177, 324

pensions 88, 94, 103
  paid by collective in Russia 80
People's Communes 41, 330. *See also*
  collectives, state farms etc.
  break up of 69
population increase
  in Xinjiang and Inner Mongolia 91
poverty 81
  and over-use of land 273
  and resource distribution 65
  in Buryatia 86
prices
  basic goods 117
  food 99, 112
  fuel 110
  livestock 80
  livestock products 75, 89, 99,
    104, 110, 112, 117
  raw materials 108
private farmers 83–86, 148
private herders 84–86, 113, 116, 133
private shops 208
privatisation 35, 54, 54–58
  and *ail* size 160
  and de-sedentarisation 196
  and decline in specialist produc-
    tion 276–277
  and decreased mobility 254, 276, 292
  and differences in wealth 61
  and residence patterns 148
  anxieties about 37
  dissatisfaction with 117
  in China 56
  in Mongolia 55, 273–275
  new institutional forms 294
  of collectives 81–83, 83
  of livestock 96
  of machinery 83, 84, 96, 107
  of vehicles 54–56
  reversal of 85
production modes
  definition 218
  dual 225–232
  specialist 225–226, 275
  subsistence 226
    and the market 275
    increase after privatisation 232–233
    in Mongolia 219
productivity 299–300

R

rainfall
  and non-equilibrial systems 270, 330
  and pastoral movement 272–273
religion. *See also oboo* ritual, under
  individual case-study sites
  Buddhism 5, 17, 30–33, 303
    and shamanism 2, 31
    unifying factor 21
  folk practices 30
  indigenous, and nature 304
  indigenous cults 123
  Islam 5, 30
  new cults and sects 303
  shamanism 2, 5, 28, 30, 31
repair-shops
  provision by authorities 300
residence
  ail 159
  and kinship 147–174
  and marketisation policies 195
  and property relations 176
  and tradition 176
  case-study sites 147–174
  grandparental household 141
  household 139, 147
  hot 165, 174–175
  joint families 165
  lone mother households 141
  patterns and kinship 173–178
  patterns in pre-collective era 174–175
  residential family group 139
  residential group 139
  virilocal 154, 159, 162, 166, 169
  'responsibility' (*chen bao*) 98–99, 314
responsibility system 41, 74, 91, 96–99
  on Chinese collectives 56
  relation with contract 98–99
rural institutions
  and environmental problems 127
  categorisation of 71–72
  in China 90–109
  in Mongolia 109–114
  in Russia 78–90
  investment difficulties 115–117
Russia 12, 68
  Buryatia 3, 5, 8, 9,
    14, 18, 64, 134, 198. *See also*
    Buryats, Argada

agriculture 47
Barguzin 9, 48, 73. *See also*
Argada
clans in 27–30
collectives 81
effects of socialist policy 73
gangs 207
history of 18
language 22
livestock density 49
livestock statistics 42–47
plough agriculture 182
production and consumption
patterns 202
residence patterns 148–156
Russian settlers in 20
Chita Oblast 5, 8, 9,14, 64, 134, 198.
See also Gigant
effects of socialist policy 73
livestock density 49
funding difficulties in pastoral
regions 115
future of pastoralism 130
institutional forms 72
leadership 122
native peoples in 33
survival of collectives 54
Tuva 4, 5, 9, 18, 134, 198. *See also*
Solchur
agriculture 47
clans in 27–30
cosmology 3
cultural confrontation in 10
dwelling types 186
effects of socialist policy 73
four-season migration 195
gangs 207
history of 18
inter-ethnic relations 20
language 22
mobility 195
residence 138

S

Sambuu, author of herding manual 302
schooling
and decreased mobility 253
schools 15, 56, 101. *See also* education
boarding accommodation 293
Buryat 36

Chinese 23, 207
drop out rate 23
environmental teaching 214–215
in Bayantümen 111
in collective era 19
monastic 208
Mongolian, and language 22
role of 207
Russian 207
state provision 79
security 115–117, 127
and 'grassland certificates' 96
food 65
on collectives 88
sedentarisation 128, 179, 180, 188–196
and pasture degradation 212
and Russian economy 188
and subsistence 300
and urbanisation 209–210
built structures sign of 191–192
definition 180
environmental problems 132, 300–
301
history of 188–190
in Buryatia 188
in Chinese pastoral regions 91
index 196–197
in eastern Inner Mongolia 189–190
in eastern Mongolia 189
in south-central Mongolia 189
input/output 297
means of estimating 190
Mongolian policy 193
political and economic factors
193–197
separate process from urbanisation
216–217
separate process from urbanism 301
self-provisioning 158–159
settlement
and land-use 179
in Inner Asia 179
of nomads 268
pattern, definition of 180
seasonal 186
sedentary 186
systems of
definition 180
new terminology needed 183
socialist ideology 268
shamanism. *See* religion

Index

sheep. *See* livestock
Sheehy, D.   49, 54
shops   94, 110
    role of   207–208
Simukov, A. D.   174–175, 220–
    225, 228, 234, 239, 268, 320, 324
    classification of pastoral movement
        220–222
    compared with more recent
        233–236
social divisions   208
social relations of obligation   137, 176
    and wealth differences   177–178
    defined   141
social services   197. *See also* health care,
    etc.
    on Chinese state farms   103
Solchur, Ovyur, Tuva, Russia (ECCIA case-
    study site) 9
    attitude to nature   214
    communications   205
    family composition   154
    mutual aid   154
    oboo rituals 124
    pastoral movements   245–246
    pasture degradation   211–215, 246
    production/consumption patterns
        201–203
    reliance on hay   246
    sedentarisation   209–210, 211–215
    stocking levels   246
    urbanisation   209–210, 211–215
    urbanism 211–215
standard stocking units (SSUs)
    definition   42
state farms. *See also* collective farms,
    collectives
    in Sumber   76
    Ovyur (Tuva) positive example   128
    in China
        strategic/military type   100
        survival in pastoral regions   100–
            103, 104, 109
        'vanguard' type   100
steppe
    description   2
steppe ecology
    threats to   8, 65
    effects of national policies on   35
sub-district (*gachaa, bag, brigada,*
    etc.). *See* administrative areas

subsistence   57, 274. *See also* production
    modes
    and impoverishment   86
    and kinship   154
    economy   110
    in Mongolia   232–233
    in Tuva   58
    production   4, 57, 73, 158
Sumber *sum*, Dornogov' *aimag*, Mongolia
    (ECCIA case-study site) 9
    collectivisation in   37
    decline in pasture quality   264
    low stocking level   264
    near railway   189
    oboo ritual   124
    pastoral movement 'central Halh'
        type   262–264
    pasture degradation   211
    production/consumption patterns   201–
        203
    residence patterns   161–162
    sedentarisation 211
    Simukov's eastern steppe type   262
    urbanisation 211
    village population   76
sustainability   48–52, 268–269
    and mobility   54, 228–229, 292
    and pasture allocation   277
    pastoral ecology and 65

T

taxes   98, 111, 115
technology. *See also* machinery, mechanisa-
    tion
    sharing   295
tractors   62, 107, 151, 164, 203, 248,
    254. *See also* machinery, mechanisa-
    tion
    after privatisation   55, 56
    and wealth   107
trade   4, 65. *See also* livestock products
    and security   115
    and wealth   61
    barter   64, 88
    buying power   56, 62
        of pastoral products   59
    cashmere   104, 106, 108, 114, 232
    consumer goods   64, 114
    cross-border   7, 63–65
    cross-province   108
    export of livestock to China   232

farm-shop coupons 88
food 114
hay 89, 106, 108, 111, 114
in Chinese pastoral regions 108
meat 89, 111, 114, 312
milk 64, 66, 312
petrol 111
skins 111, 114
spare parts 64, 89, 111
terms of 74
unifying factor 21
wool 64, 104, 106, 114
'tragedy of the commons' 92, 269, 273
transport 41, 80, 144, 158, 197, 201
and pastoral movement 227–228
and production costs 86
and urban culture 209
buses 201
cars 201, 322
case-study sites compared 201–206
costs 110, 133, 158
difficulties 204–205, 262
economic importance 61
motor bikes 201, 205
support for mobility 19, 300
vehicles 157
provision by authorities 300
trees 214, 304–305
Tuva. *See* Russia

U

Uighur 5
Ündesnii Atlas 233, 244, 326, 327
unemployment 81, 310,312
in Mongolia 56
women's 81
urban culture
and collectives 209
and mobility 209
and transport 209
historical 208
urbanisation 179, 197–209
administrative structure and 197
and administrative centralisation 180
and administrative distance 198
and cultural complexity 207
and sedentarisation 209–210
contrasted with urbanism 205
definition 180, 200
economic policies and 197

urbanism
definition 200
distinct from urbanisation 180
utug (irrigated hay meadows) 47,
70, 85, 129, 194, 295, 317
Uvs *aimag*. 9. *See also* Solchur

V

vegetable growing 111, 190, 192,
194, 196
veterinary services 73, 94
Vishrelt Vangiin Hoshuu (Bishrelt Wangiin
Hoshuu) 249–250, 329

W

water pollution 65, 134, 214
ways of life
and land-use 12
indigenous 26
western zone (of study project) 33
and environmental concern 304
four-season pasturing 195
women
and *oboo* rituals 123–124
in 'Rich White Horshoolol' 113–114
in work-force of collectives 79
percentage in population 58
running private shops 108
tasks 138–139, 153–154, 158–159
unemployment 81

X

Xinjiang. *See* China

Z

Zhimbiev, B. 182–183, 321, 330